THE PROMISED SEED

IRVING D. HARRIS, M.D.

THE PROMISED SEED

A Comparative Study of Eminent First and Later Sons

The Free Press of Glencoe
Collier-Macmillan Limited, London

For Daniel and Lisa

Acknowledgments

In a book of this nature, the list of my indebtedness could easily be endless. For not only have I been influenced in the development of the several hypotheses by a considerable number of thinkers but I also have, through liberal quotation, utilized their lively prose. More specifically, I am perpetually indebted to David Riesman, who devoted one summer to a detailed critique of the first draft. Whatever uneasiness I had developed over sailing beyond psychoanalysis into the comparatively unfamiliar waters of sociology, politics, history, and economics was quite reduced by the generally supportive nature of Mr. Riesman's critique and by its challenging questions when I was in error. I am most appreciative also of the sharpening experience afforded me by the critical reactions to the first draft by Bruno Bettelheim, Roy R. Grinker, Sr., Fritz Moellenhoff, and David T. Bazelon. None of these readers, of course, should be held responsible for the opinions I express in the book.

Of crucial importance in this enterprise was the unflagging support of Noel Jenkin, Director of the Research Department of the Institute for Juvenile Research. His placing of value on a prolonged study in which the exploratory and speculative components predominated over the experimental was a very heartening morale factor. Furthermore, Dr. Jenkin, backed by Raymond E. Robertson, Superintendent of the Institute, gave unstinting help in such important areas as funds, facilities, and personnel. To this must be added the cooperation of other colleagues in the Research Department—Robert Pollack, Solomon Kobrin, Elise E.

[vii]

Lessing, Kenneth Howard, and Dorothy Nelson—who generously included birth order data in their own investigations in order for me to test my hypotheses. In the preparation of the manuscript, other members of the Research Department were exceedingly helpful: Daniel Zetland, in the executive supervision, L. P. Klems and Joan Lazarus in quotation checking and permission requesting, Ehria L. Jackson and Bettye J. Wharton in the typing.

I wish also to thank the many individuals and publishers who gave me permission to quote from their articles and books.

All through this undertaking I have been grateful to my family and friends for sharing my burdens and moods. And I am enormously indebted here to my wife whose gamut of aids included provision of hot coffee, listening to my theories and, most important, relieving me of my major domestic responsibilities.

CONTENTS

[ix]

"Though all by me is lost . . .
    By me the Promised Seed shall all restore"
        So spake our mother Eve; and Adam heard
    well pleased, but answered not.

—John Milton,
Paradise Lost

PART ONE *General Considerations*

CHAPTER I *The Hypothesis*

OBSERVERS OF HUMAN NATURE have long been in
search of general unifying laws underlying the rich variety of
psychological events. Always complicating their task is the choice
of whether to emphasize the unity and likemindedness of mankind—as in the concept "Man" or to emphasize the variety and
different-mindedness—as in the term "men." Although the first
emphasis has an attractive economy and provides general laws,
it frequently overlooks significant differences between men. Similarly, while the second emphasis appreciates these differences, it
often remains at the scientifically immature level of mere classification and does not go on to ascertain whether there is any lawfulness to human behavior. Faced with such a dilemma, some
observers have resorted to a compromise solution. They have conceived of man as being composed of different types, each of
which has its particular lawfulness. It is this kind of view that
will be offered here.

The exposition of the view begins with a summary statement
of the basic hypothesis. Although tersely stated at this point, it
will be expanded and repeated frequently. There are two fundamental psychological factors which all men possess by virtue of
their biological endowment; that, by virtue of certain early childhood experiences, one or the other of these factors tends to gain
in relative predominance; and that from these predominances
stem certain characteristic trends in the thoughts, feelings, and
actions of men.

The evidence for this general hypothesis is also quite general.
It has been gleaned from a wide span of human endeavors—

philosophy, mathematics, psychology, history, political science, literature, etc.—and from a wide range of human subjects—schoolboys as well as famous and infamous men in the past three hundred years. An important corollary to this hypothesis—and, for that matter, to any hypothesis of personality types—is that the observers of human nature themselves are not exempt from being categorized into types. The corollary requires, then, that we take into account how the personal equation of the observer influences what he perceives and thinks about human nature. Such a requirement is not necessary when the unified concept, Man, is employed. With this concept men are like-minded enough that one can be reasonably sure that little subjectivity intrudes itself into the theorizing about human nature. But with an hypothesis of types, there is no such surety. The microscope that Man trains upon man in order to understand man is not the objective instrument of the laboratories which is the same for all who observe. The microscope is Man himself. Or, to put it more squarely, the microscopes are men. Although the foregoing may give rise to a feeling of hopelessness about ever being sure about what Man is really like, the present hypothesis does suggest that, instead of a confusing multitude of different microscopes, there are two basic ones.

The following brief example may illustrate the points we have raised so far. It may indicate how a particular basic idea about Man—in this case the relative importance of the individual and social group—is shared by some but not by other thinkers; and how this sharing is independent of such external factors as the discipline in which these thinkers worked, their national characteristics, and the age in which they lived. Beginning, then, with Montesquieu and Rousseau, we find that the former emphasizes the individual, the latter the group. Durkheim, who designates these two as precursors of sociology, writes of their differences: "Montesquieu had come to conceive a society whose unity not only did not exclude the particularism of individual interests but presupposed it and followed from it. There were direct ties between individuals and the cohesion of the whole was only the result of all the individual affinities." Rousseau, on the other hand, believed that the individual will is hostile to the common will: "In a perfect act of legislation, the individual or particular will should be zero."[1] Certainly, these two sociologically preoccupied thinkers placed different emphases on the individual and the social institution. In psychoanalysis, the sharpest conflict is between Freud, who believed in freeing the individual from intrapsychic conflicts, and Adler, who stressed helping the patient to adjust to the outer social norms. In philosophy, the two American pragmatists showed similar divergencies; William James stressing the life solution which gave the individual a personal satisfaction while John Dewey was ever mindful of the social nature of the life solution.

Thus it appears that the personal equation, the subjective view of human nature, can cut across the lines that bound the formal fields of inquiry. Despite their working in different disciplines, Montesquieu, Freud, and James appear to share some commonality of viewpoint, one different from that shared by Rousseau, Adler, and Dewey. The question arises, "Are these two groupings accidental or are there some basic personality components which account for the divergence of viewpoints?" To repeat, this book is devoted to an investigation of the second alternative, to a documentation of the probability that there are two basic psychological orientations which underlie notions not only about human nature but also about reality.

The typology to be offered here needs to be viewed alongside of previous typologies. Many observers have thought in terms of two types of men. Usually, their observations have been somewhat parenthetically embedded in a large philosophical or literary work. Thus, Plato made a distinction between deep and shallow kinds of men. Heinrich Heine, among others, suggests that every man is born either a Platonist or an Aristotelian. More recently, Isaiah Berlin has discussed, in regard to Tolstoy's personality, the hedgehogs who see only one thing and the foxes who see many things. Those who have attempted a more systematic development of their proposed typologies are fewer in number. Perhaps best known is Jung's conceptualizing of the "introvert-extravert" typology. Others include William James with his two sets of dual types, "tender-minded—tough-minded," "healthy-minded—sick souls," and Riesman with his "inner-directed" and "outer-directed" characters.

The theoretical contribution to be made here will not reside particularly in the newness of the typology offered, for undoubtedly the reader will detect strong family resemblances between the types referred to above and the types to be described. Rather, it may reside in the explanation of how the types originated. Most theories about individual personality types resort to a hereditary or constitutional explanation. This trend manifests itself not only in a literary person such as Heine, when he stated that one is born either a Platonist or an Aristotelian, but also in a modern depth psychologist such as Jung, who held nature rather than nurture responsible for the introvert and extravert types. In the hypothesis offered here, however, the exclusive emphasis will be placed on the role of early nurturing experiences within the family environment in accentuating certain features of personality.

It is perhaps in the testing of the hypothesis that the reader will encounter the greatest departure from customary practice. The testing is not limited to a small number of clinical patients or experimental subjects; rather, it is principally carried out on a number of eminent men who are in the public domain. Furthermore, there are few areas left untouched in this effort to determine how generally and universally the hypothesis can be applied. The wide scope can be better appreciated if an hypothetical situation is used. If, for example, Jung had wished the broadest general base for his introvert-extravert typology, he not only would have had to describe, as he did, the different moods and interpersonal relationships of these two types, but he would also have had to explore other aspects of human behavior. He would have had to describe the type of philosophy, poetry, mathematics, political leadership, and so forth, that an introvert would produce as opposed to what an extravert would produce. It is this kind of effort that characterizes the present book. Because in such a venture the conclusions will necessarily outstrip the facts, the effort is better characterized as speculative and exploratory rather than as systematic and developmental.

The time has come to be specific about the two basic psychological factors. As indicated earlier, though they are common to all men, they frequently occur in sufficiently unequal proportions that a rough typology may be set up. The factors will be described as "connectedness" and "disconnectedness." Shortly, a fuller account will be given of these terms. But at this point it is well to emphasize that, despite the root "connect" being present in both terms, they are two different phenomena. For example, in problem-solving not only is it necessary to connect all pertinent facts for a trial solution, but it is also important that one disconnect oneself from previous errors.

The two terms are quite similar (but not identical) to Piaget's terms "syncretism" and "juxtaposition." Piaget describes syncretism (which is roughly analogous to connectedness) as a "facility in connecting everything with everything else . . ."[2]; an "immediate fusion of heterogeneous elements, and unquestioning belief in the objective inter-implication of elements condensed in this way."[3]

Juxtaposition (which is roughly analogous to disconnectedness) is described by Piaget in relation to synthetic incapacity:

For if things are perceived in the light of the moment, without order or organization, if the work of rational attention is to deal with them one by one and not in groups, then the child will naturally juxtapose things and events in his mind, without achieving their synthesis. M. Luquet has described this phenomenon under the name of synthetic incapacity in connexion with the drawings of children. The child artist will juxtapose pieces of one and the same whole, but will be unable to connect them together. He will draw, for example, an eye alongside of a head, and so on."[4]

Piaget's general conclusions are that syncretism is associated with weakness in analyzing the part and juxtaposition with weakness is synthesizing the whole. Our position is somewhat more affirmative—connectedness (possibly deriving from syncretism) is associated with strength in synthesizing the whole, whereas disconnectedness (possibly deriving from juxtaposition) is associated with strength in analyzing the part.

We have quoted Piaget at length for several reasons. First, for purposes of definition and illustration of our terms "connectedness" and "disconnectedness." Second, to show that both psychic tendencies are most likely present in all young children. Third, to indicate some differences between Piaget's viewpoint and that proposed here. The major difference is that Piaget does not subdivide children into those more prone to syncretism and those more prone to juxtaposition. Neither, of course, does he say that there are no individual predilections. That he is aware of individual differences is clearly evident from his description of marked temperamental differences between Pie and Lev, two children investigated in his first publication. For purposes of in-

[8]

vestigative focus, however, Piaget has de-emphasized the individual differences between children and has concentrated on a singular construct, the child, and has followed the maturation of his mental development. The approach here is complementary rather than contradictory to Piaget's. By de-emphasizing the effects of age and maturation, we have under focus the individual differences between persons. There is one other difference in the two approaches. Syncretism and juxtaposition are for Piaget faulty, semipathologic tendencies in thinking, the results of a breakdown of ideal rational synthesis in which whole and part are accurately evaluated. For us, connectedness and disconnectedness—though sometimes appearing in pathological degree —are, for the most part, normal psychic tendencies.

An example of the *proneness* toward connectedness or disconnectedness may be provided by the following. There are two intuitive notions which, at least up to recent times, have been held by many people. One is that if an event immediately precedes another event, the first event is likely to be the cause of the second. The other is that there is a sufficient similarity between what a person is today and what he was a year ago that one can speak of a continuous personal identity or the Self. In both notions, connectedness is prominent. One event is connected to another by a causal relationship; one temporal cross section of an individual is connected to a later cross section by a continuous core, called the Self. These intuitive notions have been so urgently self-evident to many people that they have been called an inevitable part of human nature. Yet, in the eighteenth century David Hume questioned these assumptions. It is not necessarily true, he said, that there are causal connections between events or that there is any persistent connected Self. We fool ourselves, he claimed, as to there being a real connection.

Now, the point here is not whether Hume was right or wrong. It is rather "What kind of man was Hume that he could perceive such to be the nature of the mind and of outer reality?" It cannot be just the quantity of intellectual endowment, inasmuch as equally intelligent men have thought and still think otherwise. It cannot be just the spirit of the times or the particular philosophical school, inasmuch as Locke and Berkeley, also English empiricists, did not put the matter so extremely. Hume in this skeptical, disconnected view is more like Francis Bacon,

a century earlier, and the present British school of philosophical
analysis. Thus the question remains: "What kind of man was
Hume?" And, since he was no freak of nature, "What kind of
men are men like Hume?" These men tend to see things as separate and disconnected, in contrast to men like Pascal and Einstein
who tend to see things as interconnected.

It is hoped that the foregoing examples provide some idea
of what might be included under the headings of connectedness
and disconnectedness. Later chapters will develop what is now
being sketched out. In general, however, it may be said that the
two types differ not only in thinking (as the cause-and-effect
and self-identity examples may indicate) but also in ways of
feeling and acting.

Our broad sketch needs now to take up the important question of how these differences originated; of how, for example,
Hume came to be a disconnector and Pascal a connector. Certainly the final answer to this question will take into consideration variables and complexities that are not even conceived of at
present. The very preliminary answer to be given at this point
may seem unsatisfying, if not anticlimactic. It is that the differences are somehow causally related to different early nurturing
experiences of which birth order is a rough indicator.

We shall shortly detail the implications of birth order. But
at this point it is well to emphasize that the matter goes quite
beyond the Adlerian status-power implications arising out of
whether a child is first-, second-, or third-born. Birth order may
have much more to do with the question of how the child has
been humanized. Ordinarily we are accustomed to thinking that
the parents are the principal early humanizers of the child. This
is certainly more true in small families than in large ones. An
only child would tend to have more opportunity of being humanized by his parents than would the seventh child in a family
of fifteen children. In the latter case, the child's older siblings
would have a more prominent part in his nurture.

Even if we limit ourselves to small families and consider the
parents as the principal humanizers, we still have to ask, "What
is the quality of the nurturing?" This question refers to different
phases in the same parent. The mothering of a first-born child
is usually a more tense and involved process than is the mothering of a second child. The first-born, or the first-born of the sex,

would tend to be exposed to more adult expectations and pressures than would a later-born. The first-born would tend, for better or worse, to be more *intimately connected* with the parents.

In support of this idea that humanization via parent is different from humanization via peer we can again refer to Piaget. Concerning the topic of questions and answers, Piaget believes that answers truly represent socialized language because the child has to adopt the viewpoint of his interrogators. Such socialized language is rare in young children. Thus, Piaget concludes, "answers do not belong to the spontaneous speech of the child. It would be sufficient for his neighbours to interrupt him and for adults to question him all the time, to raise the child's socialized language to a much higher percentage."[5] In regard to questions, Piaget writes: " 'whys' play an important part in all questions asked of grown-ups by children under 7. . . . Intellectual intercourse between children is still factual or descriptive, *i.e.*, little concerned with causality, which remains the subject of conversation between children and adults or of the child's own solitary reflection."[6]

It is clear from Piaget's remarks that it is one thing to be humanized or socialized principally by a parent, and another thing to be done so principally by a sibling or peer. The particular aspect Piaget was concerned with was the emergence of the concept of causality, the concept which Hume questions. In effect Piaget was saying that the greater the parent-child interaction, i.e., the more the child is exposed to an adult mind which thinks in terms of cause and effect, the sooner the child will think in terms of cause and effect, in terms of the causal connection between one thing and another. There is here more than a hint that a philosophic predilection toward the concept of causality may be based on early nurturing experiences.

We are now in a better position to restate the original hypothesis: Human beings differ as to the predominance of connectedness and disconnectedness in their personalities. The tendency toward connectedness is associated with the early nurturing experiences in which there is a more intense parent-child connection, whereas the tendency toward disconnectedness is associated with an early nurturing experience in which there is a less intense parent-child connection. Generally, there is a more intense parent-child interaction when the child is the first-born, or the first-born of his sex. Evidence supporting this hypothesis will be provided by a comparison of the thoughts, feelings, and actions of males who are first sons or only sons with those of males who are later sons. For the most part, the males are adult men who have been pre-eminent in Western civilization.

It is appropriate now to disclose that all of the foregoing has been arrived at through hindsight and in exactly the reverse order with which it has been presented. Rather than beginning with the hypothesis and using birth-order data to verify it, the investigative steps begin with certain findings in boys concerning birth order and lead inductively to the final hypothesis. The reader may well wonder why early nurturing is stressed in the hypothesis rather than birth order. To be sure, most of the tangible evidence will deal with birth order, whereas some inference is needed to support the idea about different qualities of nurturing. For those readers who take exception to inference, the whole presentation can be understood as a contribution to the subject of birth order. However, it appears to the author that the fundamental matter is what happens within the psyche as a result of early psychological and emotional environments. Although order of birth may be a leading contributor to such environments, it is not the only one—and an undue emphasis on its importance would considerably oversimplify a very complex sequence of events. Notwithstanding birth order's black or white convenience as a research instrument—a man is either a first son or he is a later son—it is still only a contributor toward and indicator of something more basic rather than being of invariable intrinsic consequence.

In order to present the broad outlines of the book, many details and complexities have necessarily been omitted. More important, little mention has been made yet of the way in which the hypothesis was reached. In other fields of science, this type of account may be desirable but not mandatory. But when a view of human nature is proposed—a proposal inevitably tinged with subjectivity—it seems highly advisable that the history of the investigation (if not the personal bias of the proposer) be revealed.

In 1949 the writer embarked on an exploratory study of normality, using as subjects 54 boys and girls and their mothers.

The children had been adjudged to be normal, at least by the school system. The purpose was to ascertain criteria of normality and to find out what kind of nurturing or mothering was associated with mental health in the child. The observation led to a principal conclusion that there was more than one kind of normal child; that one could not speak in the singular of *the normal child* but only in the plural of *normal children*. It was here that the writer's pluralistic viewpoint began to form. Beneath the variety of normality we have seen two basic psychic tendencies: that toward structure and permanence, and that toward process and change—the proper integration of the two tendencies being conducive to emotional growth. Here the emergence of a dualistic theory can be seen. In the study, notice was taken of but little theorizing was done about the effects of birth order. It was quite evident that first-borns, whether they were the children or the mothers, tended to be more tense, more driven, more driving than later-borns.

The next study, in 1957, was in regard to learning problems. The connection with the previous study lay in the interest in what promoted emotional growth—growth being considered, in part, a form of learning. Because learning problems are found predominantly in boys, the study was restricted to male subjects. One hundred boys of at least average intelligence, referred to the Institute for Juvenile Research chiefly because of school failures, were compared with one hundred boys, also of at least average intelligence, who were referred to the Institute for some emotional disturbance such as fearfulness, bedwetting, or disobedience, but who had no difficulty in school.

The results of the study indicated that there were five significant differences between the one hundred nonlearners and the one hundred learners (and between their family backgrounds) —one of the five being concerned with birth order. Specifically, a trend was found that last-born boys were more prone to have learning problems than were first-born boys, even though there was no difference in intellectual endowment. Investigation of the family background yielded the impression that the greater maturity expected by the parents of the first-borns was in part responsible for their better school performance.

With the exception of the finding on birth order, the learning study yielded results much in keeping with those reported by the great majority of other investigators—e.g., the effects on learning of socioeconomic status, of family disorganization, etc. But in regard to the repercussions of birth order, the current scientific literature revealed a sharp difference of opinion, with the majority tending to believe there was no strong evidence linking birth order with intellectual performance. This difference of opinion prompted the author to delve into the origins of the birth-order concept. In so doing, he became impressed that it has had a strange and fascinating history of attention and neglect at the hands of investigators. An historical review of the concept was included as an appendix to the learning study. Excerpts from this review are pertinent now for our purposes.[7]

"In the modern history of this idea, the first noteworthy contribution was made in 1874 by Francis Galton, an anthropologist; it was followed by the studies of Havelock Ellis in 1904, Cattell in 1917, and Terman in 1925. The first three authors investigated eminent scientists or other well-known creative individuals. Galton and Cattell found that first-borns were much more frequently found in these eminent groups than were middle- or last-borns. Ellis found a trend in favor of the first-born and last-born. Terman found a preponderance of first-borns in 1000 intellectually superior children.

"After this promising start, what happened to the interest in this topic? One cannot answer with certainly but can form some conjectures. It is not unlikely that the decline was due to the waning of Terman's interest in the matter. In his first volume of *Genetic Studies of Genius*, the above trend was mentioned. In his third volume—which consisted of a follow-up of his 1,000 gifted children, birth order is definitely mentioned as not significantly influencing *choice of profession*.

"Without Terman's leadership and authority, the topic seems to have fallen into comparative oblivion in psychological circles. Also there was no impetus from the experimental workers in learning theory who studied animals. Since most of the experiments were done with rats, there would have been no opportunity to deal with ordinal position. In a litter of rats, the first- and the last-born are not distinguished. Rather, they are observed with relation to their weight, age, heredity, whether they had ever encountered the maze before, and so on. With little or no stimulation from the experimental psychologists, then, the import of birth order dwindled. In this connection we quote from H. Jones, writing in the *Manual of Child Psychology*: 'In an earlier critique (Jones, 1933) of research in this field, evidence has been given that when . . . methodological difficulties are properly controlled . . . no birth order differences in intelligence occur in normal samples. . . . Atypical results, however, have been encountered in certain highly selected samples. . . . Studies of gifted children by Terman (1925) and of eminent men by Ellis, Cattell, and Huntington have shown a distribution of birth order differing from chance expectation and strongly favoring the first-born. . . . No satisfactory explanation of this finding has been given.'

"A similar decline in the interest in ordinal position can be seen in social psychology, the branch of psychology whose experimental subjects are mainly humans rather than animals. A promising start was supplied by Miller in the early 1930s when he studied the role of imitation in social learning. Although he did not state it explicitly, Miller used ordinal position as a factor inasmuch as he pointed out that younger children in the family imitate the older ones. However, in 1937, Murphy, Murphy, and Newcomb in *Experimental Social Psychology* reviewed about fifty studies on the topic of ordinal position. Their essential conclusion was that the results of these studies on the relationship between birth order and a number of characteristics such as intelligence, school performance, happiness, and emotional stability were inconsistent and contradictory.

"Since social psychology has been influenced by the depth psychologies, it is of interest to examine the history of this concept in psychoanalysis. Although the psychoanalysts have never been interested in the relationship of birth order to intelligence, they were once very interested in its relationship to personality. Following Freud's original interest in the influence of childhood factors upon the personality, Alfred Adler contributed many good clinical descriptions of the first-, middle-, and last-born personalities. Both before and after his split with the Freudian school in 1911, he used these descriptions to support his theory of inferiority-superiority. At present, the Adlerians are the only depth psychologists who are interested in birth order. However, probably because of the narrowness of their theory of personality and their alienation from the main rich body of Freudian theory, the Adlerians have contributed no new insights about birth order.

"There is no doubt that Adler's leaving the Freudian ranks accounts for most of the formal disinterest by psychoanalysts in the subject of birth order. But the formal neglect does not carry over to the actual work and study of psychoanalysts. In every diagnostic evaluation and in every prolonged treatment they have an opportunity to witness the effects of birth order. Furthermore, Freud himself never denied its importance. In fact, in his *Introductory Lectures*, first written five years after Adler split off, he wrote: 'Forced into second place by the birth of another child and for the first time almost entirely parted from the mother, the child finds it very hard to forgive her for this exclusion of him. . . . A child's position in the sequence of brothers and sisters is of very great significance for the course of his later life, a factor to be considered in every biography.'

"The contrast between the formal and informal attitudes is clearly seen in the writings of Ernest Jones. His adherence to formal theory is illustrated in his book *Hamlet and Oedipus*. Here he suggests that Hamlet's delay in avenging the murder of his father stems from the same conflict that afflicted Oedipus who, unknowingly, killed his father and married his mother. He further speculates that Shakespeare wrote Hamlet at this time of his life because Shakespeare's father had recently died. In other words, his father's death reactivated Shakespeare's Oedipus complex.

"Jones, in effect, accounted for the content of Shakespeare's creativity rather than for the kind of creativity itself. He does not utilize the fact that Shakespeare was his mother's oldest son. However, when Jones wrote his biography of Freud in the 1950s, his informal position on birth order becomes evident when he utilizes Freud's birth order to explain Freud's creativity:

We gather that he [Freud] appears to have been a normal sturdy child, and we can only note the few features that distinguish his circumstances from those of the average run of children. They are few, but important.

He was the eldest child, at least of his mother, and for a time therefore the center of what may be called the inner family. This is in itself a fact of significance, since an eldest child differs, for better or worse, from other children. It may give such a child a special sense of importance and responsibility.

He had a veritable passion to *understand*. [His losing his mother to his father and to subsequent siblings.] . . . His intelligence was given a task from which he never flinched till, forty years later, he found the solution in a fashion that made his name immortal.[7a]"

The impressions gained from this historical review were that there were not good and sufficient reasons for the current neglect of the birth order concept. Rather it appeared that birth order, like other scientific ideas, went into comparative oblivion because it could not explain everything, or because it was no longer advocated by investigators of authority and repute. The review went on to consider three recent rigorous studies by MacArthur, Koch, and Schacter which indicated that birth order had a significant association with certain personality characteristics. The review concluded with the statement, "The question remains, however, of what is the direct relationship of birth order to learning and creativity. The only clue supplied by the personality studies was that first-born children are inclined to be more studious than are the later-born. Though the question must be left unanswered at this time, investigation of atypical samples by the author suggests that birth order is related to the quality of creativity rather than to the quantity."[8]

It was this "investigation of atypical samples" that provided most of the data for the present book. It began rather unsystematically with a casual noting of the birth orders of the eminent or creative men the author had become acquainted with in his reading and earlier education. Very soon a difficulty was encountered. Biographical sketches infrequently mentioned all the brothers and sisters, or the exact position the eminent men had in the sequence of siblings. Much more regularly available was the information as to whether the eminent man was the first son or a later son. Accordingly, the investigation turned from that of exact birth order to one of first- and later-born sons. First sons were defined as first surviving sons of the mother. They would include only children, only sons, and the elder or eldest of more than one son. In the case of only sons, sometimes the eminent man would be the last-born child with an older sister, e.g., Mozart and Lincoln. "Surviving" was defined as living to the age of five. Beethoven had an older brother, also named Ludwig, who lived for only a week after birth. Accordingly, Beethoven is considered a first son. Lenin, whose older brother was killed in Lenin's adolescence, would not be a first son. A man such as Martin Van Buren may be the first son of his father but a later son of his mother—accordingly, he is designated a later son. Later sons were defined as those who have by the same mother an elder brother who survived past the age of five. These broad criteria sufficed in most cases to establish two groups: first sons and later sons. The biographical material was gathered from usually reliable sources, such as the British National Biography, the *Encyclopaedia Britannica*, and authoritative biographies. By the end of the investigation roughly 1000 eminent men were studied—they being about evenly divided between first and later sons.

Two principal reactions were forthcoming from viewing the entire collection of eminent men. The first was that birth order had no observable relationship to quantity of genius. Besides the obvious impossibility of measuring the amount of genius, one would be hard put even to guess whether such first sons as Newton, Kant, and Shakespeare had greater or lesser genius than such later sons as Descartes, Hume, and Dostoevski.

The second reaction came from noting the fields in which these men were eminent. There was a preponderance of first sons among poets, philosophers, and historians, and a preponderance of later sons among explorers and military and naval men. (No striking difference in preponderance was noted among scientists, prose writers, or artists.) These preponderances suggested a qualitative difference issuing from birth order—the first sons drawn toward contemplation, the later sons toward action. This was in keeping with the previously described personality differences —first-borns tending to be more studious and serious than later-borns. The trends also seemed explainable by Jung's typology, i.e., the first son being the introvert, the later son the extravert.

While this rough breakdown was somewhat illuminating it was too general to be satisfying. There were many apparent exceptions. For example, Grant, a first son, would scarcely be considered a contemplative man; Darwin, a later son, is with great difficulty seen primarily as a man of action. Accordingly, the author felt there needed to be a more discriminative qualitative analysis of these eminent men and their works. The gross indicator of activity field would not suffice. Granted, for example, that first sons are more often philosophers and later sons military geniuses, there still remained the problem of what to do with the exceptions—i.e., the first-son military men and the later-son philosophers. How, among philosophers, do the first son Pascal and the later son Hume differ—among military men, the first son Grant and the later son Lee?

It was with these questions in mind that the author began the next phase of the investigation. Needless to say, this exceedingly complicated phase not only is uncompleted but also is not within the powers of the author to complete. Mainly by creating the illusion that he was living in an earlier century when the whole body of knowledge was still within reach of the intelligent layman, when the high degree of specialized expertise was not yet present, and when an investigator could still think of himself as a natural philosopher—mainly by this device could the author feel comfortable enough to proceed with the investigation. Where it was possible and comprehensible, original sources were studied (in many other cases, secondary criticism and evaluation were utilized).

The first rays of light issued from noting a typology mentioned by Pascal. He wrote: "There are then two kinds of intellect: the one able to penetrate acutely and deeply . . . the other able to comprehend a great number of premises without confusing them, . . ."[9] Pascal further stated that the deep penetrator possesses "the precise intellect" and the comprehender of many premises possesses "the mathematical intellect."[10] At first blush, the typology seemed paradoxical because one would ordinarily equate "precise" with "mathematical" instead of opposing the two. However, since Pascal was a mathematician and a first son, the possibility arose that he was understandably biased in favor of *his* type of mathematical mind. That his type was that of the wide comprehender (and integrator) of many premises seemed evident from other of his writings. Thus he wrote: "We sail within a vast sphere, ever drifting in uncertainty, . . . we burn with a desire to find . . . an ultimate sure foundation. . . ." ". . . Man is related to all he knows . . . he is in a dependent alliance with everything." ". . . I hold it equally impossible to know the parts without knowing the whole, and to know the whole without knowing the parts in detail."[11]

The undertone in Pascal's orientation appeared to be a desire to account for everything—not just for one thing at a time. The resulting wide, macroscopic, bird's-eye view would not be as precise and accurate as it would be if all that intellectual energy were penetratingly and microscopically focused on one part. It was here that the author first thought in terms of connectedness and disconnectedness. The wide comprehender entertains many premises because he is motivated or impelled to interconnect them into an integrated whole. The deep penetrator addresses himself to the disconnected part either from a motivation to disconnect or from a lesser motivation to interconnect. It was also clear that this could not be a sharp either/or dichotomy but rather a matter of preponderance. For no man of genius could penetrate deeply without considerable ability to comprehend the premises—and vice versa.

Utilizing Pascal's birth order as a first son, the hypothesis began to take shape that first sons were predisposed to wide comprehending connectedness, and later sons to deep penetrating disconnectedness. Going back to the fields of activity, it now seemed possible to account for some of the preponderances noted. Perhaps the first sons were especially motivated or equipped to study the larger interconnected unit—be that unit the philosophical synthesis, or the poetic vision, or the historical span of time. At this point, however, the unique intellectual contribution of the later sons was not clearly seen. That a penetrating focus on the disconnected part would be very advantageous to a practical and effective man of action or to an inventor was easily evident. But what especial advantage it would give a man of thought was not fully appreciated.

The author's enlightenment on this score began with reading E. T. Bell's *Men of Mathematics*. Bell's introductory statements were of especial interest because they pointed strongly to the connectedness-disconnectedness typology. He wrote:

we may state here briefly what the main guiding clue through the whole history of mathematics is.

From the earliest times two opposing tendencies, sometimes helping one another, have governed the whole involved development of mathematics. Roughly these are the *discrete* and the *continuous*.

The discrete struggles to describe all nature and all mathematics atomistically in terms of distinct . . . elements. . . . The continuous seeks to apprehend natural phenomena—the course of a planet in its orbit . . . —in the mystical formula of Heraclitus: "All things flow."[12]

It did not seem unjustifiable to equate "continuous" with "connectedness" and "discrete" with "disconnectedness."

Here, then, was an opportunity to appreciate what special intellectual contributions could be made by minds with a discrete or disconnected viewpoint. Bell was further helpful because he supplied criteria for distinguishing the continuous from the discrete approach, and in his biographical account of the mathematicians he supplied the birth orders. Although a later chapter will detail this, it can be said now that a majority of first-son mathematicians have made their contributions in the area of the connected "continuous," whereas a majority of later-son mathematicians made theirs in the area of the "disconnected," "discrete." One of these later-son mathematicians, Descartes, is, of course, also celebrated for his disconnectedness version of reality. His disconnection of the psychical from the physical, of the subject *res cogitans* from the object *res extensa*, has created a gap which later philosophy, psychology, and science have tried to bridge.

The clues supplied by Bell and Pascal—together with the hints from the field of activity survey—served then to stimulate and shape the connectedness-disconnectedness hypothesis. With this hypothesis in mind, the author not only continued his reading in the various fields but also viewed somewhat differently the psychic material forthcoming from his patients undergoing psychoanalysis. Some increased understanding was gradually gained about the varieties of acting and thinking which are two of the three major aspects of the personality. For insights into the remaining major aspect—feeling or mood—the author is grateful to William James. In his *Varieties of Religious Experience* James offers the typology of the "healthy minded, who need to be born only once, and of the sick souls, who must be twice born in order to be happy." The faculty of remaining cheerful depends on the ability to *disconnect* oneself from the knowledge of evil. James' example of sick souls and healthy-minded cluster respectively around first sons and later sons—one of James' examples of sick souls being himself, a first son. With these considerations of depression, anxiety, and guilt the author was once more back on terra firma, on his own area of special experience. It was at this point that a rereading of Freud and other psychoanalytic writers proved to be stimulating and enriching.

The purpose of the foregoing has been to give the reader some idea of how the hypothesis was reached and of the nature of the evidence. The method can be described as a rough quantitative treatment of qualitative impressions. Wherever possible, the author tried to find a recognized authority in a particular field and use his evaluations of the contributions made by the men in the field. Thus with Bell and James. However, in most fields—and especially philosophy, literature, and politics—there was considerable difficulty in selecting one evaluator who could be utilized as the recognized authority. Because of this difficulty, occasional use was made of a quasi-official source, such as the *Encyclopaedia Britannica.*

Evidence of a more rigorous, quantitative nature has not been mentioned so far. Such evidence is, of course, impossible to obtain about eminent men who have lived in the past—and exceedingly difficult to secure about those living. Because one has to gather this type of evidence mainly from experimental subjects under artificial situations, generalizations made from it are not without risk—this, despite the greater precision. There *is* some evidence of this type, and it will be described in later chapters. In general, what can be said about it is what can be said about the more impressionistic evidence gleaned from the experiments in nature. There is no one piece of evidence which crucially and unequivocally proves the hypothesis. There are many which are strongly supportive of the hypothesis, and several which are neutral. But there are no quantitative trends which go against the hypothesis. By this we mean that, although one particular later son may show more connectedness features than a particular first son, or one particular first son shows more disconnectedness features than a particular later son, yet the trends shown in *groups* of first sons and later sons were not in a reverse direction to the hypothesis.

In demonstrating the breadth of the hypothesis we have had to omit consideration of the female sex. The omission arose from the method of study which was to rely on eminent persons. Not enough women were in that category to make a comparative study of them feasible. Furthermore, the investigation of Helen Koch and Stanley Schacter indicates that birth-order repercussions on girls are somewhat different from those on boys. For these reasons, the connectedness-disconnectedness hypothesis will not be discussed in terms of the female sex. A few instances, however, of trends in eminent women will be offered when pertinent.

In retrospect, it can be seen that the investigation began

with a limited inquiry about the effects of birth order upon intellectual achievement and ended with an hypothesis that goes much beyond the original considerations. The variety of phenomena encountered did not encourage the construction of a specific, easily tested hypothesis such as, for example, the relationship between birth order and the field of adult activity. Rather, the variety dictated the position of a rather general hypothesis, couched in such open-ended terms as "early nurturing experiences" and "connectedness." In spite of this generality, there are more aspects of psychic life *not* accounted for by the hypothesis than are accounted for.

Thus, no answers will be forthcoming as to why one man is creative and another is not; or why one man predisposed to connectedness becomes an historian, while another man, similarly predisposed, becomes a poet. Also not encompassed by the hypothesis are the important effects on the personality of such weighty factors as heredity, constitution, family stability, and social institutions.

Because of the author's psychoanalytic orientation, there was a strong temptation to deal more thoroughly with the dynamics of each eminent man and with the biographical data available about him. For the most part this temptation has been strenuously resisted. The principal reason for so doing is that, if personal interpretation of the data is carried too far, the investigation cannot be replicated by others. Though the birth-order criteria given here are rigidly confining, they have the merit of being unmistakable and of being usable the same way by all investigators. Therefore, the hypothesis must stand or fall on the basis of the birth-order criteria. Perhaps, at a later time, advantage can be taken of more specific biographical data, such as the actual number of siblings, the age gap between siblings, and parental characteristics. For, a first son who is an only child will differ from a first son who is the oldest of five siblings. And a later son who is the middle of three sons cannot be equated with a youngest son who was born ten years after the preceding sibling. Similarly with the parents. The sole criterion of being the first born of the mother does not allow full use to be made of the father-son relationship. Thus, little mention will be made about such interesting relationships as those between John Stuart Mill, Mozart, Frederick the Great and their fathers—even though the connectedness features are prominent. Likewise, interpretations are omitted about specific mother-son relationships, such as the involved ambivalent relationship between Schopenhauer and his mother.

The author's particular orientation will be seen, however, in the fact that the theoretical explorations and speculations to be offered in the ensuing chapters are predominantly psychoanalytic. This apparently simple statement requires a word of explanation. Not everything ordinarily subsumed under the heading of classical psychoanalytic theory will be utilized. Comparatively little will be said about the unconscious. But much will be discussed in regard to the superego, to narcissism, to dependent needs, and to omnipotence. Concerning the whole project, the statement cannot be made that it reflects "modern" psychoanalytic thinking. Rather, it goes back to an historical period in psychoanalysis before there was a split-off from Freud. Later narrowing, doctrinaire developments—even though understandable—have, in the author's opinion, militated against producing the kind of creative intellectual ferment which results from the clash of vigorous and able minds. Such a ferment was present when Jung and Adler were still in the psychoanalytic group. This book draws upon that earlier period, inasmuch as the birth-order notion was principally advanced by Adler; and the idea that there may be not just one universal psychological type but rather two types was primarily that of Jung. These historical side comments should not obscure the main fact, i.e., that the present author's major theoretical indebtedness is clearly to Freud, the founder of psychoanalysis.

In proposing a typology hypothesis which is not an explicit part of current psychoanalytic theory (though it is not contradictory to it) the author has leaned heavily on the fact that the typology itself—apart from the causal explanation—is rather similar to typologies offered by other observers of human nature. Already we have seen that Pascal noted two similar types of intelligence, and that Piaget described two similar types of pre-rational thinking. To these may be added the observations of Bacon, Emerson, and C. P. Snow. In his *Novum Organum* Bacon writes, "There is one principal and as it were radical distinction between different minds. . . . The steady and acute mind can fix its contemplations . . . on the subtlest distinctions; the lofty and discursive mind recognizes and puts together the finest and most general resemblances."[13] Bacon's types are almost identical with Pascal's "precise" and "mathematical" intellects. Emerson's types are quite similar: "Each man is born with a predisposition to one or the other side of nature. . . . One class has the perception of difference, and is conversant with facts and surfaces, cities and persons, and the bringing certain things to pass. . . . Another class has the perception of identity and are men of faith and philosophy."[14] With Emerson we see the typology expanding—the men who see differences are more often men of action, the men who see resemblances tend to be men of philosophic contemplation.

The similar observations of C. P. Snow are found in one of his early novels, *The Search*:

These varieties [of young scientific men] seem to me to fall into two main types. Perhaps this was a shape I imposed for myself and corresponds to nothing real; but they are types observed often enough before in human affairs. . . . I should call the first the problem-solving type; minds which choose out of all the world around them a certain piece of experience and drive through it to an explanation. [These are] the probing, analytical, pragmatic minds. . . . The second type [is] the abstracting mind. . . . These minds do not drive through a portion of experience; they wait for experience to make itself into shapes in their minds, they assimilate, correlate, find resemblances in different things, differences in similar things. At their best . . . they are the great generalisers; at their worst they are infantilely fantastic and removed from all reality."[15]

It seemed clear from the foregoing that the connectedness-disconnectedness typology had considerable foundation even though it remained to be demonstrated that it was a repercussion of early nurturing experiences. It was also evident that the typology cut across fields of activity—a probing, penetrating mind viewing the disconnected part could operate in the fields of literature, politics, philosophy, and science just as could an inter-relating mind which viewed the connected whole. The two types of mind would tend to view the same subject matter in somewhat different ways. It was found, however, that these different views were infrequently accounted for in the usual classifications in a particular field. Thus, in philosophy Locke and Hume are both classified as empiricists, James and Dewey both as pragmatists, in literature Byron and Wordsworth both as romantic poets, etc. The typology appeared, then, to have some usefulness in creating subdivisions of the customary classification. The reader will find in the following chapters that, although the usual categories have been retained, descriptive terms such as "plural minded" and "single minded," "heroic" and "militant," are used to denote the subdivisions arising from basic connectedness and disconnectedness.

As can be imagined, a difficult decision was involved in the question: which of the 1000 eminent men should be used for more detailed study and evidence? A first step was to prune the list so that, for the most part, the major eminent men remained. The reduced list still being rather numerous, a decision had to be made as to whether breadth or depth should be the ruling feature of the study. It was resolved in favor of a broad panoramic survey of many men rather than a deep study of a few men. Principal reasons were: (1) The surface manifestations of basic connectedness and disconnectedness were so variegated that only the description of many men could do justice to this variety. (2) The generality of the hypothesis required its being tested in as many fields as possible. (3) The author did not possess the expertise to make a deep, precise investigation of the works of men outside his own field.

The remaining major eminent men were then studied in regard to characteristic viewpoints and modes of behavior. If the first and later sons seemed to gravitate, respectively, toward opposite ends of a polarity, this ideational or behavioral polarity (and the men involved) became the focus of more investigation. Thus, for example, first sons Montesquieu, Freud, and James appeared differently oriented than later sons Rousseau, Adler, and Dewey on the question of the individual and society. Unless the major eminent first and later sons were at easily discernible polar ends on some question, little further attention was given them. In this way, the number of eminent men to be studied and reported on was appreciably reduced. Rarely was an entire group of eminent men in a particular field studied for the presence of a polarity. One of these rare occasions was that mentioned earlier, the polarity between "continuous" first sons and "discrete" later sons among Bell's men of mathematics. The opportunity was not taken, for example, to survey all the English prime ministers, or all the Popes, or all the American Presidents for proofs of polarity. Rather, polar viewpoints were noted and then the matter of first or later sons predominance was investigated. In the case of American history, for example, the automatic comparison of all first-son presidents with all later-son presidents was rejected in favor of a very crucial comparison between first son Jefferson and later son Hamilton. Another illuminating and important comparison—to which almost a whole chapter is devoted—is that between first son Carlyle and later son Emerson, illuminating because they wrote somewhat differently about the very subject of eminent men. While, in general, the eminent men offered in evidence are those who best illustrated polarity, some dubious examples or exceptions are also discussed in order that the fact be established that the hypothesis—like any hypothesis dealing with the complexities of human nature—cannot be rigidly applied.

Another major decision arose from the question of what kind of evidence should be submitted, and to what reader or audience should it be addressed. One solution would have been to use the general information only as a background and to focus on psychoanalytic data from clinical cases. In other words, to restrict the evidence to that issuing out of psychoanalytic investigation and to address the book to a reader-audience of psychoanalysts. For several reasons, this solution was rejected. Most important, this procedure would give a false picture of the investigative sequence. The hypothesis was arrived at extrapsychoanalytically and partially confirmed introanalytically—a sequence almost opposite to the usual one.

Second, information gathered by psychoanalysts—and for that matter by psychologists—is sometimes regarded skeptically as not being universally applicable and as not being in the public domain. Psychoanalytic patients and volunteer experimental subjects, according to this view, represent atypical samples. Because the full protocols of psychoanalytic investigation remain in the private hands of the analyst, the complaint is made that raw data have been interpretatively transformed by the particular theoretical leanings of the investigator. In order to reduce this skepticism, this feeling that one has learned all about unbalanced people and about college sophomores but little about life, the author decided that most of the evidence would come as gathered from the lives and works of the eminent men—evidence clearly in the public domain.

The solution decided on required the author to go outside the scope of his expertness and to address the book to all observers of human nature. Although the language style is nontechnical, the book is not intended principally for the nonspecialist. On the contrary, a major reason for the generalized approach is to invite the critical reaction of specialists in anthropology, sociology, history, political science, literature, and philosophy. These readers—as well as the nonspecialists—should look upon the investigation as representing an exploratory study which produced a hypothesis that requires further testing. *The author's aim is to offer enough evidence (direct and circumstantial) that the burden of proof would be as much on those who contested as on those who affirmed the validity of the hypothesis. In short, the aim is to raise the hypothesis not to the level of proof but to the level of serious respectability.* If psychoanalysts were the only experts who could participate in this decision as to validity, then the book would have been directed solely to them. But since the author believes that the other disciplines have very important contributions to make in this regard, the book is addressed to the members of the various fields.

The misgivings in going outside of one's field have already been mentioned—as has also the anachronistic device of thinking of oneself as a natural philosopher writing in the eighteenth century. No matter what devices are used, the fact remains that one is trespassing. A guide to good manners in such a situation is provided by the psychoanalyst Edward Glover. After observing that, "Already the psychological anatomy of Hamlet, Lear, and other Shakespearean figures has been displayed in psychoanalytical diagrams,"[16] he goes on to say, "Depressing as the prospect may be to the student of history or literature, the psychoanalyst cannot and in any case will not be denied the right to ransack both fields for confirmation of his views regarding the main springs of human contact. All that we may require of him is that he should refrain from aping the manners and preciosities of the litterateur and that he should not pretend to an esoteric sagacity and infallibility he in no wise possesses."[17]

Qualms about trespassing are reduced by hospitable collaborative invitations such as that extended by the historian Richard Hofstadter. He writes:

At first the historian has to read Freud more or less passively; but when he sees the use that such men as Harold Lasswell or John Dollard make of Freudian concepts in a political context, or observes, say, how David Riesman employs the concept of character-type in a historical setting, or finds that social psychologists can shed light on contemporary political movements, he begins to get an inkling of the possibilities of psychology for history. . . . They [the social sciences] bring to him a fresh store of ideas with which to disturb the excessively settled routines of his thought; but they also serve a catalytic function for him; they show him how he may adapt for his own purposes certain modern insights into human behavior and character which he cannot, on his own, immediately and directly appropriate. . . . The more the historian learns from the social sciences, the more variables he is likely to take account of, the more complex his task becomes. . . . His task has not been simplified; it has been enlarged. His work has not greater certainty, but greater range and depth.[18]

The present author accepts Hofstadter's invitation to help to catalyze the historian and make more tentative some of his assumptions. In this way, the author's own catalyzed experience induced by historians and other specialists may be reciprocated.

The somewhat encyclopedic range of this book may give pause to the selective reader who is more interested in certain subjects than in others. It may help the reader to know that, despite a distinct thread of continuity, each chapter is semi-independent. Indeed, only slight violence would be done to the organization of the book if the browsing reader went immediately to the concluding chapter and decided after reading it, what intervening chapters were of particular interest to him.

The book is organized along the lines of the author's particular experience. Thus, Part One, "General Considerations," treats psychological issues with which the author—from his clinical and research experience with individuals and families—is most familiar. Although the clinical experiences are not cited as illustrations, they provide a silent background for interpreting the thoughts and actions of the eminent men. Part Two, "Special Considerations," deals principally with matters (literature, history, science) upon which the author's experience cannot as strongly bear. These chapters are, necessarily, more speculative.

The next-to-last chapter deserves some preliminary description. Especially concerned with methods by which the basic hypothesis can be tested, it offers experimental evidence from normal children and adults that bears on two major trends noted in the eminent men. These trends deal with language (first discussed in the chapter "Tendencies in Literature") and personal identity (first discussed in the chapter "Sense of Self"). This is the only chapter in which experimental evidence is given and thus the only one which suggests that the hypothesis may be general enough to include personality types as well as creative types.

The concluding chapter is given over to several considerations. Beginning with a restatement of what are and what are not the implications of the basic hypothesis, it briefly discusses the possible sources of error in the investigation. Then follows a review of the major trends, a review which uses as a departure point Tocqueville's analysis of the political-cultural characteristics of aristocracies and democracies. The political implications lead the present author then to take the liberty of freely speculating about the current world situation. In particular, speculative attention is given to the fact that at one time in the writing of this book the political leadership of the West was largely in the hands of later sons, whereas that of the East was in the hands of first sons. It is perhaps unnecessary to advise the reader that these musings about history in the making should be considered in a different, much more tentative light than what has been discussed in earlier chapters.

Despite the foregoing explanations and qualifications, the reader will undoubtedly develop resistances as he encounters the subsequent chapters. And it may be well to anticipate some of these. Perhaps resistance will emerge from the fact that the nature of the whole enterprise is not in keeping with the times. If, as Morton Zaubel White has suggested, ours is an age of analysis, the enterprise in its attempt at encompassing synthesis can be reacted to a somewhat old-fashioned. The present author acknowledges the "old-fashionedness" of the project but submits that this reflects a particular thinking style rather than an outdated viewpoint. Concerning the author's intellectual bias, it also should be pointed out that the enterprise represents an illustration of how a connectedness-prone first son may view psychological and cultural matters. The same material in the hands of a disconnectedness-prone later son may receive a somewhat different treatment.

The scientifically oriented reader may take exception to the fact that many impressionistic chapters precede the one offering experimental evidence. If so, he may find it more comfortable to begin with this next-to-last chapter. The author's reason for using the format is mainly that many experimental findings lie dormant and do not excite the attention required for further investigation. Thus, Helen Koch's finding that the first born does not easily accept defeat has been present in the scientific literature for some years. It acquires considerably more meaningfulness when we take note of first son Churchill's efforts in the Battle of Britain and the destructive, death-before-dishonor orientation of first sons, Charles XII of Sweden and Adolf Hitler. The scientist-reader may also complain that the exceptions to the main trends are not dealt with. As was said, exceptions are acknowledged to be present and this is why the author speaks in terms of tendencies and of birth order as a *rough* indicator. Further refined work may cast some light on the exceptions, but for the present purpose of generating a hypothesis, it is considered sufficient to present the main trends.

The rather relentless portrayal of human affairs as being solely influenced by connectedness-prone first sons and disconnectedness-prone later sons may strike the reader as a gross oversimplification. The highly important historical considerations have been de-emphasized only for purposes of clearer exposition. And, undoubtedly, the summary fashion with which the complexities of certain eminent men are treated—the reduction of such complexities to a seemingly neat package or pigeonhole will also bother certain readers. All that the present author can say on this point is that he is also bothered. It would have been easier for the author and the reader if only a few eminent men were considered in some depth. But this procedure would have given a false and overly neat picture of the many ramifications issuing from the basic connectedness and disconnectedness tendencies— a depth treatment of even, say, ten men would not have done justice to these various ramifications.

The great quantity of eminent men mentioned was furthermore necessary because birth order is valuable as an indicator only when applied to large groups. And on this point it is necessary to mention that there can be errors in birth order, in ascertaining even from seemingly authoritative biographies, whether an eminent man was a first or later son. (Luther and Stalin are cases in point.) The chances for such errors are reduced when a large number of eminent men is treated. Be that as it may, the readability of the chapters necessarily suffers when the reader has to keep in mind many rather than a few personalities. The author hopes that this dilution of impact and the necessarily schematic handling of complex matters will not inordinately tax the reader's patience.

The final problem in communication deals with the question of when the investigation is at the point of publication. The usual scientific considerations have already been mentioned. As an exploratory study, it is presented for the helpful critical reaction of those whose fields have been infringed on. Scientifically, this justifies communication now rather than after a few years of more definitive work. As Benjamin Franklin wrote to Collenson regarding his exploratory work on lightning rods, "But since even short hints and imperfect experiments in any new branch of science, being communicated, have oftentimes a good effect, in exciting the attention of the ingenious to the subject . . . and so become the occasion of more exact dispositions and more complete discoveries; you are at liberty to communicate this paper to whom you please."[19]

But, in addition to these considerations which are concerned with the abstract search for truth, there may be an urgent practical one. In these days of the most infernal destructive machine, unusual significance attaches to the ideas and actions of influential men. They can be drawn toward peaceful solutions or toward pushing the lethal button. Our anxious imaginations sometimes conjure up the picture of one man—usually the head of a nation—fearfully, reluctantly, or eagerly giving the order that will begin an atomic world war. Although we may not subscribe to Carlyle's theory that history is made predominantly by great men, we are nervously aware that on a short-term basis the course of history is frequently influenced by the predilections and idiosyncrasies of a small number of men. Whatever further illumination we can gain about the actions and ideas of such men may be helpful in these days. It is this current undertone which impels the author to communicate sooner rather than later.

CHAPTER II *The Moral Authority:*

Inner and Outer

THE TOPIC OF MORALITY seems most propitious for beginning the exposition. For, not only do moral considerations play a prominent role in psychological conflicts but they also have been of central concern to philosophers and political scientists. The division of the moral authority into inner and outer varieties is more often encountered in political than in clinical thinking. It is seen for example in the question of whether man has an inner, innate conscience or whether he needs outer social laws to regulate his conduct. Indeed, as we shall see in a later chapter, much of the philosophic debate between Thomas Jefferson and Alexander Hamilton regarding the future structure of the United States turned on the very question of whether the democratic masses were unruly enough to require policing by a strong central government. Although we shall touch here on some of the political considerations, the major attention will be devoted to the psychological (and sometimes clinical) repercussions of inner and outer moral authority and in particular those of melancholia and cheerfulness.

We shall find that, due to differences in parental indoctrination, the connectedness-prone first sons tend to have a sense of good and evil stimulated by an inner voice of authority whereas the later sons tend to have such a sense stimulated by an outer social voice. Because all sensing of good and evil goes on within the person, it is, of course, not strictly accurate to speak of an "outer moral authority." What is meant by this usage is that the social or external contribution to a "moral sense" is more prominent in those we refer to as being stimulated by an outer moral voice. It should be emphasized that this difference has little to do with morality and immorality, with actual goodness or badness. As we shall see, neither the connectedness-prone first sons, hearkening to the inner moral authority, nor the disconnectedness-prone later sons, hearkening to the outer moral authority, have a monopoly on virtue or on vice.

The demonstration that the above-described trends do exist is somewhat complicated. The quality of moral sense, or locus of moral authority does not lend itself easily to paper and pencil tests or to experimental procedure. This is not to discount Robert Sears' and Charles MacArthur's respective experimental findings that first borns have a deeper moral sense and greater seriousness than later borns. But in keeping with the general objective of supplying the complex nuances which have to be ignored in experimental work, we shall rely principally upon what the eminent first and later sons have had to say on this subject.

To anticipate: the general trend is that the first sons (who are responsive to an inner moral authority) speak more of an inner or innate conscience, are more cognizant of the evils in themselves and more often have a serious, pessimistic, or melancholy mood; whereas the later sons (who are responsive to an outer moral authority) speak more of a morality derived from social norms, tend to see themselves as innocent, and are more inclined to a cheerful, light mood.

The actual demonstration is best begun by examining the views of *first son* Freud. No other depth psychologist has so explicitly and systematically discussed the nature, the workings, and the historical sources of the inner moral authority. The conscience or superego is an integral part of Freud's metapsychology. In its embryonic conceptual form it was Freud's dream censor which forbade the fullest or clearest expression of unacceptable impulses. Out of fear of this inner moral authority, the unacceptable impulse had to be disguised in the many ways described by Freud. When Freud turned his attention to the problem of melancholia, the dream censor concept was extended. In its full-fledged conceptual form, it is the superego which, though now within the child, was once the demands, values, and prohibitions of the external parents. Freud theorized that the young child achieves psychosexual maturation when he identifies sufficiently with his parents' prohibitions that they become his own.

Not everyone reaches this stage of maturation. Many children are affected only by threats to their continuing pleasurable existence. Thus, in the stage *before* the consolidation of the superego, children fear loss of love or castration. The child, without basically identifying with the parental prohibitions—without making them his own—copes with existence by being realistic. He goes along with his nurturing and prohibiting parents, with these external policemen. When these policemen are not looking, he feels comparatively free to act in his own interests. In this stage, then, self-preservation is the first law. There are no binding or intensely connecting commitments requiring the child to act as dutifully when the parents are not watching as when they are watching.

In Freud's next stage—the stage of superego anxiety—the direct threat to self-preservation is less sharply felt. More keenly sensed is the equally dire but more indirect threat to the self when the policeman is now an inner part of one's self. The first law of nature is no longer simple self-preservation. It is the avoiding of the rejection and wrath of the internalized moral authority, the superego. Because the policeman is inside him, he will tend to act as conformingly when the parents are not watching him as when they are. When the child has a strong impulse which moves counter to the dictates of his superego, he may develop feelings of guilt, unworthiness, and melancholia—feelings which are the repercussion of a part of himself, hating another part of himself. The depression is not the simple one resulting from a threat to self-preservation, as for example the depression of a man who has received a death sentence. Here the man does not want to die, does not think he should die, but he is depressed at the prospect of death. In the superego melancholia, however, even without an external death sentence, the man may feel guilty and unworthy enough that he will become his own executioner. He will feel he *ought* to die or be damaged. The only peace of mind he can obtain is through submission to the dictates of the superego.

According to Freud, the superego functions also to provide a connectedness or a continuity to society and culture, inasmuch as the transmission of social and cultural values from one generation to another is accomplished via the superego. In this way, the past is highly influential if not deterministic upon the present.

Without the superego, Freud might say that each generation would have to begin with a comparatively blank slate. To be sure, the generation has still a chance to learn values from a later source, namely society. But Freud placed particular emphasis on values transmitted and internally absorbed in the nuclear family. The superego then functions as a vehicle of connectedness, as an inner transporter of social values, as an inner time-binder.

The purpose of this brief summary of Freud's concepts has been to provide a background for what will be discussed regarding inner and outer moral authority and to illustrate how a *connectedness-prone first son* may view human nature. There is no question that for first son Freud the inner moral authority was a fundamental and paramount concept. Reconciliation with the dictates of the guilt-producing superego was as necessary for psychological existence as was the self-preservative procurement of food, shelter, and power. Furthermore, the superego is, for Freud, not merely a process or a feeling—rather *it is a persistent structural part of the psyche*. Together with the id and the ego, it comprises Freud's complex tripartite structural concept of the psyche.

Not all depth psychologists place such emphasis on the inner moral authority, nor do all view human nature so complexly. It is of interest to note briefly the views of the three principal dissidents in psychoanalysis—Jung, Adler, and Rank. Of the three, later son Adler is most divergent from Freud. Guilt, the repercussion of an inner moral authority, is rarely mentioned in Adlerian psychology. Instead, inferiority feelings and shame are the paramount affects. This emphasis arises from Adler's non-complex view that human behavior can be explained by a drive for power which compensates for feelings of inferiority. Whereas in Freudian therapy an essential feature is the coming to terms with the inner moral authority, in Adlerian therapy it is the adapting to external society, to its values and its moral authority. For Adler, then, the struggle is between the unified personality, the ego, and the external world—not between the ego and the superego. We shall return to Adler later.

In passing, we may note some pertinent characteristics of Rank and Jung. Rank, a later son, is similar to later son Adler in having a simple and single-minded view of human motivation.

For Rank, all could be reduced to the trauma of having been born and the wish to return to the womb. Although he is aware of the effect of guilt, his lack of emphasis on it led him to suggest another possible explanation for Oedipus' fate—namely, that Oedipus did not blind himself out of guilt, but rather to find the darkness reminiscent of his mother's womb.

Jung, a first son, appears much closer to first son Freud in his thinking. Perhaps this accounts for the fact that Freud was prepared to entrust the leadership of the psychoanalytic movement to Jung. Jung's greater proximity to Freud is seen not so much in an emphasis on inner moral authority per se, but rather in a similar complex and historical view of the psyche. His ideas, like those of Freud, cannot be summarized in a few sentences, as was possible to do in the case of later sons Adler and Rank. In Jungian psychology, the chances for conflict between the persona and anima, between the introversion and extraversion tendencies, are almost as great as the chances obtaining with the Freudian superego, ego, and id. More noteworthy is Jung's orientation to the past. Indeed, as to possible influences of the past on the present, Jung goes even further than Freud. With his concepts of the collective racial unconscious and of archetypes, Jung reaches back to the prehistory of Man. In general, then, first-son Jung is similar to first-son Freud in his conceptualizing of inner and innate elements in the psyche which influence Man and which provide a historical connectedness.

Human nature in general and the moral authority in particular have of course preoccupied philosophers before and since the advent of modern depth psychology. In turning to them now for evidence of a first son-later son polarity (similar to the polarity between Freud and Adler) we cannot expect these thinkers to have said much about clinical features such as guilt and melancholia. But we shall find evidence of a first son-later son polarity as to the locus and strength of the moral authority and as to whether the first law of nature is self-preservation or living with one's conscience.

The most outstanding and explicit philosophical exponent of the inner moral authority is a *first son*, Immanuel Kant. The strength of this inner voice can be easily surmised from Kant's use of the term Categorical Imperative—that is, our inner obligation to do our duty. Like Freud, he sees the psyche in a complex way, as possessing two selves. He separates the ordinary, somewhat chaotic empirical self from the more real, enduring, transcendental moral self. The inner nature of the moral dictates is obvious. As Joad writes of Kant's philosophy, "When (man) obeys the moral law, he is spoken of as obeying the law that comes from himself."[1] The innate, historical nature of this morality is conveyed by Kant's use of the term "a priori," i.e., before actual experience.

In order to indicate that the moral imperative is not solely a product of Germanic metaphysical tendencies, we turn to a lesser known, but highly influential English first son, the third Earl of Shaftesbury. The *Encyclopaedia Britannica* article states, "Shaftesbury's philosophical importance is due mainly to his ethical speculations, in which his motive was primarily the refutation of Hobbes' egoistic doctrine. . . . Just as there is a faculty which apprehends beauty in the sphere of art, so there is in the sphere of ethics a faculty which apprehends the beauty or deformity of actions. This faculty he described (for the first time in English thought) as the Moral Sense or Conscience. From this principle, it follows . . . that the distinction between right and wrong is part of the constitution of human nature. . . ."[2] It is noteworthy in this connection that the three foremost champions of the individual conscience, of the *innate* ability of the individual to make moral decisions—Milton, Locke, and Mill—are all first sons.

When we search for the opposite pole, we need to skip over a great number of first and later son philosophers who have mixed views on the source of morality. Finally, however, we come to an Italian and an Englishman, Machiavelli and Hobbes, both believers in the external policeman and in self-preservation, and both *later sons*. Of the two, Machiavelli is of course more popularly known and his point of view is so characteristic that he has earned the distinction of becoming an adjective. Machiavellian amounts now to having a realistic or cynical evaluation of men, being chiefly motivated by prospect of gain or power; weakly, if at all, by internal conscience. He says in *The Prince*, "For how we live is so far from how we ought to live, that he who abandons what is done for what ought to be done will rather learn to bring about his own ruin than his preservation."[3] Again, "And yet (The Prince) must not mind incurring the scandal of those vices, without which it would be difficult to save the state, for if one considers well, it will be found that some things which seem virtues, would, if followed, lead to one's ruin, and some others which appear vices result in one's greater security and well-being."[4]

While Machiavelli deals here with the tactics necessary for a prince to rule and advance the State, Hobbes justifies in a more systematically argued way the "good ethics" of an External Police State and the "bad ethics" of an inner individual conscience. He writes in the *Leviathan*, "For the laws of nature, as justice, equity, modesty, mercy, and in sum *doing to others as we would be done to*, of themselves without the terror of some power to cause them to be observed, are contrary to our natural passions that carry us to partiality, pride, revenge, and the like. And covenants without the sword are but words and of no strength to secure a man at all."[5] In other words, without the sword and Power of the State, there will be a chaotic self-seeking civil disobedience. Hobbes recognizes the existence of inner individual morality but regards it as a weakness of the State. "In the second place, I observe the *diseases* of a commonwealth, that proceed from the poison of seditious doctrines, whereof one is, that *every private man is judge of good and evil actions*."[6] Later, "Another doctrine repugnant to civil society is that whatsoever a man does against his conscience, is sin."[7]

Again the reader is cautioned not to jump to conclusions about the comparative virtues of first and later sons. Certainly at least on paper Kant's and Shaftesbury's views are much more attractive to a liberal mind than are Machiavelli's and Hobbes'. The latter conjure up the dictators and totalitarian state concepts violently rejected by liberals. But we have not as yet taken up Nietzsche and Hitler, both of whom were first sons. Though politics and political philosophy inevitably intrude themselves in a discussion of morality, our main interest presently is on divergence of views on the sources of morality—inner and outer. So far, evidence has been presented suggesting that first sons (Freud, Kant, Shaftesbury) emphasize the inner source of moral authority and later sons (Adler, Machiavelli, and Hobbes) emphasize the outer source.

The question arises, "Why should the first son more frequently be blessed or afflicted with this strong inner voice of conscience than the later son?" Since the question is in the form of "Why more often" rather than, "Why invariably," our conjectures can begin with what usually happens in the average family. Let us take a family of four—father, mother, older son, and younger son. Before the advent of the younger son, both parents have been active in humanizing the first son, in instructing him in what is and what is not to be done, in what is right and what is wrong. He receives the full nurturing impact of both parents. If the process has gone well, he identifies so with his parents' prohibitions and values that they become in large part his own. By the inclusion of adult values in his own psyche he tends to be somewhat older, somewhat more civilized than his chronological age. Thus the majority of investigators have found the first born to be, on the average, more serious than the later born. With the advent of the younger son, the necessities of the family life further require the first born to relinquish, at least consciously, his more childlike or infantile desires. In his disputes with the younger brother, the parents not merely hope but rather expect that he "should know better" that he "should act his age," etc.; that he should become, in short, an auxiliary parent or adult. If he does not meet these expectations, the parents are more frequently annoyed than disappointed. Furthermore, since these parental expectations have become a part of himself, the first son becomes annoyed with or unloving of himself.

Thus, in the usual course of events, the first son is more likely to be intensely connected with the past, with the older generation and its values and traditions. He stands midway as a connecting link between the older generation and his own. His violations of the older tradition are handled more often punitively than indulgently by his parents and by himself. Childhood to him, therefore, is not usually the Golden Age of carefree innocence—it tends to be an age of seriousness, responsibility, if not brooding. The younger son, on the other hand, escapes much of the intensity of parental impact. He is less intensely identified with the parental precepts; he is more just himself, than himself and his internalized parents. Often violations of the parental injunctions are treated more indulgently by his parents and by himself. Childhood for him can more easily be a Golden Age of carefree innocence.

If it is granted that the foregoing represents what *tends* to happen in the average family, then we can return again to the public domain and seek evidence of a first-born–later-son polarity. Regarding the sense of evil and innocence—which will be our first concern—it is important to emphasize that by these terms we mean an individual's conscious awareness of his own personal evil or of his own personal innocence. That a person is aware that evil lurks in the hearts of his fellow men does not signify that he is fully conscious of his own predilections in that direction. Thus, later sons Machiavelli and Hobbes, although quite realistic about what goes on in other men, did not proclaim that they themselves were evil or brutish or that their writings arose from any self-seeking or evil motives. It is in first son Freud that we may see a typical example of a sense of self-seeking of evil motives. His merciless self-examination revealed to himself and to others that the capacity of jealousy, spite, revenge, etc., resided within himself.

The awareness of one's own potential for evil does lead to a certain kind of parallel awareness that such a potential may reside in others. Again, first son Freud will serve as an example. His evil version of what goes on in the child is contrasted by Lasswell with the more innocent version offered by later son Wordsworth:

The stress which Freud laid upon the sexuality of the child, and upon socialization by intimidation, broke with revolutionary violence in a culture which swaddled its infants in sentimentality. The child of the poets was like this:

> Not in entire forgetfulness,
> And not in utter nakedness,
> But trailing clouds of glory we do come
> From God, who is our home:
> Heaven lies about us in our infancy!
> —William Wordsworth

The child of the Freudians was like this:

The child, at one time or another in its life, is, in a sense, autoerotic, narcissistic, exhibitionistic, inclined to play the rôle of "Jack the Peeper," incestuous, patricidal, or matricidal, homosexual, fetichistic, masochistic and sadistic [G. V. Hamilton, *An Introduction to Objective Psychopathology*, p. 301].[8]

In further investigating the evil-innocence polarity of first and later sons, and its family sources, we shall consult the book which underlies the Judaeo-Christian moral tradition in Western

Civilization—the Old Testament. The second oldest crime in the Bible is Cain's killing of Abel. If the oldest crime depicts the disobedience of the child in seeking to share the pleasurable forbidden fruits or sexual pleasures possessed by the parents, Cain's crime depicts the evil one brother can do another. The background of the crime is, as we know, God's partiality for the offerings of the later son, Abel. No reason is given to the first son Cain for this rather arbitrary decision. He seems to be expected to accept the favoritism shown Abel in good grace, expected in short to act his age, to realize he had his turn at individual attention and now it is Abel's turn for a comparative monopoly of *parental indulgence*. Cain, however, does not see it this way— he is enraged and slays Abel. When interrogated by God as to Abel's whereabouts, he further protests against the unwelcome grownup, parent-substitute role by asking, "Am I my brother's keeper?" The answer from God is, in effect, "Yes, you are; you see, you are obliged to share parental indulgence with your little brother and to protect him. Because you did not, and in fact killed him, you are branded everlastingly as evil." Cain's crime—that of the stronger against the weaker—has indelibly imprinted itself as evil in the Judaeo-Christian morality.

Continuing in the Bible, we come to another brother conflict, that of Esau and Jacob. Here the later son gets the better of the first son but, instead of this being labeled a crime, it tends to be ignored or to be celebrated as a wily exploit. Jacob's crafty securing, with his mother's help, of Esau's birthright from the father Isaac, brings an indulgent smile to many readers—as though they were saying, "You have to give him credit." It is the same admiration as is felt for wily Ulysses battling against great odds, or for Prometheus' stealing fire from the Gods. The point of retelling the story is to demonstrate that the weaker's aggression toward the stronger (later son against first son) is either ignored or encouraged. No branding with evil occurs with it. It is of interest that a version of the Esau-Jacob story has recently been offered which further absolves Jacob from any blame by suggesting that Isaac intentionally bypassed Esau in favor of the more promising son Jacob. Thus, Jacob need not feel guilty about deceiving his father. That this version is from the pen of a later son, Thomas Mann, is of some significance.

From the parents' point of view, the ethic of protecting the weaker and younger against the stronger and older is eminently desirable. Indeed, the preservation of the species depends on the younger being allowed to grow up without danger of being killed by the older. That everybody be given a chance to prove and establish himself is thus a basic tenet not only of democracy but also of Mankind as a species. But from the point of view of the children, the principal ethical burden falls on the shoulders of the first son. Not that he necessarily does more for humanity because of this burden, but rather he is more likely to feel guilty and evil if he violates this and other parent-transmitted ethics.

It is peculiarly appropriate now to go from the Bible to William James' *Varieties of Religious Experience*. James provides us with a number of eminent men who can be used to test our hypothesis. Furthermore, in his discussion of a sense of evil, he goes beyond the usual philosophical considerations of morality and deals, as Freud did, with the clinical repercussions of oppressive inner moral authority, namely melancholia. Quite pertinent will be his typology of the cheerful healthy-minded, able to disconnect from evil, and the melancholy sick souls, not able to break the connection. We shall attempt to demonstrate that James' principal examples of pervasive melancholic attitudes are first sons, and those of cheerful attitudes are later sons.

In his second chapter, "Circumscription of the Topic," James describes some world views and moods which are rather characteristic. Thus he recognizes the *cheerful* moods in Emerson and Voltaire, both *later sons*. He uses the term "Emersonian optimism" and states regarding Emerson's philosophy:

Whatever it [the soul of the world] is, though, it is active. As much as if it were a God, we can trust it to protect all ideal interests and keep the world's balance straight.[9]

Regarding Voltaire, James begins:

There are trifling, sneering attitudes even toward the whole of life; and in some men these attitudes are final and systematic. It would strain the ordinary use of language too much to call such attitudes religious, even though, from the point of view of an unbiased critical philosophy, they might conceivably be perfectly reasonable ways of looking upon life. Voltaire, for example, writes thus to a friend, at the age of seventy-three: "As for myself," he says, "weak as I am, I carry on the war to the last moment, I get a hundred pike-thrusts, I return two hundred, and I laugh. I see near my door Geneva on fire with quarrels over nothing, and I laugh again; and, thank God, I can look upon the world as a farce even when it becomes as tragic as it sometimes does. All comes out even at the end of the day, and all comes out still more even when all the days are over."[10]

(James describes this as a "robust old gamecock spirit. . . .")[11]

James, then, addresses himself to the *depressed, bitter* views toward life:

The world appears tragic enough in some religions, but the tragedy is realized as purging, and a way of deliverance is held to exist. . . . But melancholy, according to our ordinary use of language, forfeits all title to be called religious when, in Marcus Aurelius's racy words, the sufferer simply lies kicking and screaming after the fashion of a sacrificed pig. The mood of a Schopenhauer or a Nietzsche—and in a less degree one may sometimes say the same of our own sad Carlyle —though often an ennobling sadness, is almost as often only peevishness running away with the bit between its teeth."[12]

All three James mentions here are first sons.

If Schopenhauer, Nietzsche, and Carlyle act like sacrificed pigs, they apparently do not strongly enough question the will and wisdom of the sacrificer. True, they squeal and bitterly prophesy the end of the world, but they do not effectively fight or flee as though they believed the first law of nature is self-preservation. Instead, they stand almost transfixed, paralyzed by some force from protecting their existence and well-being. We find no evidence that Cain tried to appeal the verdict of his banishment to the east of Eden, or that he vigorously tried to re-enter his homeland despite what God had ordained. And we see no protest in the first sons, Abraham and Isaac, as they climbed the mountain preparatory to the intended sacrifice of Isaac. Similarly, in modern times, the most striking account of a passive acceptance of the inevitable is seen in the writings of the first son Kafka. In *The Castle* he accepts the unpredictableness of higher authorities, in *The Trial* he accepts his own execution, and in *Metamorphosis* he accepts his self-degrading transformation into a cockroach.

We turn back now to William James' description and explanation of the healthy-minded and the sick soul. This typology derives from the observation of Francis W. Newman:

God has two families of children on this earth, . . . *the once-born and the twice-born,* and the once-born . . . see God, not as a strict

Judge, not as a Glorious Potentate; but as the animating Spirit of a beautiful harmonious world, Beneficent and Kind, Merciful as well as Pure. The same characters generally have no metaphysical tendencies; they do not look back into themselves. . . . Of human sin they know perhaps little in their own hearts and not very much in the world; and human suffering does but melt them to tenderness."[13]

After James mentions some wholesomely cheerful examples of this type, he writes:

In some individuals optimism may become quasi-pathological. The capacity for even a transient sadness or momentary humility seems cut off from them as by a kind of congenital anaesthesia.[14]

Then, as instances of this *extremely marked optimism*, James mentions the *later son* Walt Whitman, and the *later daughter* Mary Baker Eddy. He writes: "The supreme contemporary example of such an inability to feel evil is of course Walt Whitman."[15] Then, quoting from Whitman's disciple, Dr. Bucke:

Perhaps, indeed, no man who ever lived liked so many things and disliked so few as Walt Whitman. . . . When I first knew [him], I used to think that he watched himself, and would not allow his tongue to give expression to fretfulness, antipathy, complaint, . . . After long observation, however, I satisfied myself that such absence . . . was entirely real.[16]

Regarding the founder of Christian Science, James writes:

. . . the mind-curers, so far as I am acquainted with them, profess to give no speculative explanation. . . . Christian Science so-called, the sect of Mrs. Eddy, is the most radical branch of mind-cure in its dealings with evil. For it evil is simply a *lie*, and any one who mentions it is a liar.[17]

These examples constitute for James the "once-born healthy minded."

In James' discussion of what happens to the *twice-born sick souls*, he writes:

There are people for whom evil means only a mal-adjustment with *things*, a wrong correspondence of one's life with the environment. Such evil as this is curable, . . . for merely by modifying either the self or the things, or both at once, the two terms may be made to fit, and all go merry as a marriage bell again. But there are others for whom evil is no mere relation of the subject to particular outer things, but something more radical and general, a wrongness or vice in his essential nature, which no alteration of the environment, or any superficial rearrangement of the inner self, can cure, and which requires a supernatural remedy.[18]

James goes on to say:

The securest way to the rapturous sorts of happiness of which the twice-born make report has . . . been through a more radical pessimism than anything that we have yet considered. . . . For this extremity of pessimism to be reached, something more is needed than observation of life and reflection upon death. The individual must in his own person become the prey of a pathological melancholy.[19]

James then describes two types of religious melancholy as seen in Tolstoy (a later son) and Bunyan (a first son). James' aim is to show the difference between the two, Bunyan having the deeper, more radical melancholia. Beginning with Tolstoy:

At about the age of fifty, Tolstoy relates that he began to have moments of perplexity, of what he calls arrest, as if he knew not "how to live," . . . Life had been enchanting, it was now flat sober, more than sober, dead. Things were meaningless whose meaning had always been self-evident. The questions "Why?" and "What next?" began to beset him more and more frequently. . . . "I felt," says Tolstoy, "that something had broken within me on which my life had always rested, that I had nothing left to hold on to, and that morally my life had stopped. . . . I did not know what I wanted, I was afraid of life; I was driven to leave it; and in spite of that I still hoped something from it. . . . All this took place at a time when so far as all my outer circumstances went, I ought to have been completely happy."

(Tolstoy then lists loving wife and children, respect, praise, national fame.) Then he says:

"Moreover I was neither insane nor ill. On the contrary, I possessed a physical and mental strength which I have rarely met in persons of my age. I could mow as well as the peasants, I could work with my brain eight hours uninterruptedly and feel no bad effects. . . . And yet I could give no reasonable meaning to any actions of my life. . . . My state of mind was as if some wicked and stupid jest was being played upon me by some one. One can live only so long as one is intoxicated, drunk with life; but when one grows sober one cannot fail to see that it is all a stupid cheat. . . ."[20]

Tolstoy then gives, as an illustration of his state, the fable of a traveler who jumps in a well to escape a wild beast. At the bottom of the well is ". . . a dragon waiting with open mouth to devour him." While clinging to some branches growing from the side of the well he sees ". . . two mice, one white, the other black, . . ." gnawing off the branches. While thus clinging, he sees some drops of honey on the leaves of the brush ". . . and licks them off with rapture." Tolstoy then says: "Thus I hang upon the boughs of life, knowing that the inevitable dragon of death is waiting ready to tear me, and I cannot comprehend why I am thus made a martyr."[21]

Certain clinical and general features must be pointed out in the case of Tolstoy. The depressive episode comes rather late— a feature which makes one suspect what is popularly known as a "change of life" syndrome. In such a syndrome, the accumulation of gray hairs, the necessity for bifocals, the occasional sexual impotence, all point in one direction; namely, that this glorious, vibrant, enjoyable life cannot go on forever. The open-mouthed dragon is going to separate Tolstoy from all that is delicious and living. We see little or no evidence of guilt, little personal unworthiness or that Tolstoy feels he deserves to die. On the contrary, he fights desperately for life and considers his plight as being victimized, as being cruelly jested with. These features—and especially the hungry dragon—force the conclusion that Tolstoy was suffering from anxiety over castration (bodily destruction) and loss of love. We do not see evidence of superego anxiety such as guilt and passive acceptance of fate.

This protest against the eventual cutting off of a zestful and pleasurable life is seen in the *Myth of Sisyphus* by later son Albert Camus. He writes:

It happens that the stage sets collapse. Rising, streetcar, four hours in the office or the factory, meal, streetcar, four hours of work, meal, sleep, and Monday Tuesday Wednesday Thursday Friday and Saturday according to the same rhythm— . . . But one day the "why" arises. . . . A day comes when a man notices or says that he is thirty. Thus he asserts his youth. But simultaneously he situates himself in relation to time. He takes his place in it. He admits that he stands at a certain point on a curve that he acknowledges having to travel to its end. He belongs to time, and by the horror that seizes him, he recognizes his worst enemy. Tomorrow, he was longing for tomorrow, whereas everything in him ought to reject it.[22]

In later son Camus, as in later son Tolstoy, there is a protest about rather than an acceptance of death. Camus in his depiction of depression brings out no feelings of deserving to die.

The striking features of a different kind of depression, of a superego-ridden melancholia, can be seen in James' description of first son John Bunyan's travail. James writes:

We find a somewhat different type of religious melancholy enshrined in literature in John Bunyan's autobiography. Tolstoy's preoccupations were largely objective, for the purpose and meaning of life in general was what so troubled him; but poor Bunyan's troubles were over the condition of his own personal self. He was a typical case of the psychopathic temperament, sensitive of conscience to a diseased degree, . . . Added to this were a fearful melancholy self-contempt and despair.[23]

Quoting from Bunyan's diary:

Nay, thought I, now I grow worse and worse; now I am farther from conversion than ever I was before. . . . But my original and inward pollution, that was my plague and my affliction. By reason of that, I was more loathsome in my own eyes than was a toad; and I thought I was so in God's eyes too. . . . Now I blessed the condition of the dog and toad, yea, gladly would I have been in the condition of the dog or horse, for I knew they had no soul to perish under the everlasting weight of Hell or Sin, as mine was like to do. . . . How gladly would I have been anything but myself! Anything but a man! and in any condition but my own.[24]

The heavy burden of superego guilt tempts Bunyan toward the Rebirth or Metamorphosis solution of Kafka. Anything to escape the heavy, ubiquitous superego pressure which these men believe to be equated with being human! A dog, horse, or toad for Bunyan; a cockroach for Kafka. And when we read first son James' account of himself (disguised as coming from an anonymous Frenchman) we see that it is a deteriorated epileptic for William James:

Whilst in this state of philosophic pessimism and general depression of spirits about my prospects, I went one evening into a dressing-room in the twilight to procure some article that was there; when suddenly there fell upon me without any warning, just as if it came out of the darkness, a horrible fear of my own existence. Simultaneously there arose in my mind the image of an epileptic patient whom I had seen in the asylum, a blackhaired youth with greenish skin, entirely idiotic, who used to sit all day on one of the benches, . . . He sat there like a sort of sculptured Egyptian cat or Peruvian mummy, moving nothing but his black eyes and looking absolutely non-human. This image and my fear entered into a species of combination with each other. *That shape am I,* I felt, potentially. Nothing that I possess can defend me against that fate, . . . I awoke morning after morning with a horrible dread at the pit of my stomach, and with a sense of the insecurity of life that I never knew before, and that I have never felt since.[25]

At that point, James introduced a footnote: "Compare Bunyan" [as to the sudden panic of fear].

The melancholic anxiety of James, a first son, appears more like that of the first son Bunyan than like that of the milder, more objective depression of the later son Tolstoy. The inevitability of the fate is common in James and Bunyan as contrasted to the protest of Tolstoy. The allure of becoming nonhuman is common to the first sons but not seen in Tolstoy. While it is true that Bunyan actually desired the metamorphosis, there is little doubt that behind James' fear of the transformation into the epileptic nonhuman, half-dead, half-cat existence there was a strong wish for that solution to elude and placate his oppressive conscience.

Our examination of William James and his views has been designed to test the hypothesis concerning inner and outer forces of moral authority. Not only are his examples of pessimism and cheerfulness in the direction of a first-son–later-son polarity, but also his two examples of melancholia support the hypothesis. First son Bunyan was troubled with the "conditions of his own personal self"—"sensitive of conscience to a diseased degree"— "melancholy self-contempt." Later son Tolstoy's depression was less personal and less self-divisive; it was "largely objective" and concerned with "the purpose and meaning of life in general." Bunyan felt that he *ought* to be destroyed, whereas Tolstoy feared that he *would* be destroyed.

Leaving James, we turn now to a biographer, *first son* Carl Van Doren. He affords us an opportunity to see how the prevalent mood of a man of letters may influence the choice of biographical subjects. For, as will now be described in some detail, with a whole host of men from whom to choose, Van Doren in a *melancholic* mood chose *first son* Jonathan Swift and, in his *lighter* mood, the *later son* Benjamin Franklin.

In a chapter in his book *Three Worlds* entitled "Private Depression," Van Doren begins:

In the midst of the general depression each man had a depression of his own.

I did not foresee the crash of October 1929, but by April of that year I had come to feel, not understand, a deep trouble and division in my mind. . . . I felt the change begin as irritation. There were too many parties in the winter of 1928–29, too many meetings of the same people in the same places, saying the same things. Gradually, then suddenly, I was tired of them. . . . On every side a noisy sterility. The good writers were men and women still, but the little writers . . . suspected any generosity or heroism or devotion. . . . My disgust was not for particular persons. It was worse than that. It was a general soreness, as if my skin had worn away and left my nerves bare. Because I had heavy work to do, I could not irresponsibly escape. . . . Then, almost without planning it, on a day's decision, I found a penthouse and turned hermit. . . . In my penthouse I was less a philosopher than a bear licking his wounds while Nature healed them. . . .

Now was the time to empty out my mind, like cluttered pockets, and take stock of what I had. Now the time to review my learning. Now the time to understand myself and my life. Masterly processes, and all beyond me. I felt nothing clearly but a strong instinct to rid myself of tangible bondages. I resigned from clubs to which I no longer could bear to go. I gave up my class at Columbia after fourteen unbroken years.[26]

After some description of his solitary misanthropic life, Van Doren writes:

But I could not be idle. I would write the life of Swift, that great solitary. Twenty years before, a student at Columbia, I had wanted to write about him but had given it up, baffled. . . . Now Swift arose in my imagination, substantial and alive, and compelled me. For four months I stopped working only long enough to keep an eye on my office and at intervals to eat and sleep. . . . I finished the book on the day I had set for the end.

Though it was a life of Swift, it was also a tragedy which might have called its hero by some other name. Twenty years of reading about Swift taught me less than a year's experience of solitude and silence. A biographer looks in his heart as a poet does. I had no thoroughgoing misanthropy in my nerves and had to guess at Swift's. I had to guess at the fury of his hate, which was out of my reach, and his will to rule, which was alien to me. But I understood his pride, his reserve, his directness, and his solitude. His story, as I saw it, was the story of a man of genius who failed when he tried most and succeeded when he tried least. No wonder he had been misjudged. He misjudged himself. . . .

I told the story as it came and it shaped itself into a tragedy because it was one. Some other day I would write a biography which was a comedy. Franklin would be its hero: a man of genius who rightly judged himself and never failed, because he had a talent for success.[27]

Van Doren then describes some of his dreams during this period:

I had no systematic thoughts but I had recurrent dreams. One dream, rather, in several forms. . . . Suddenly I would notice, dreaming, that there was a disorder in the sky. Any second there might be a collision fatal to the earth. I stood among innumerable men and women looking up in a hideous uncertainty. I knew no astronomical mathematics while I slept. All was mad chance. Special horrors emerged in different dreams. The moon lurched toward us and we waited for the unspeakable crash. Or a planet shot by, missing us but for a dreadful time shutting out the light of the sun. . . . Or an obscene island—was I remembering Swift's Laputa?—hovered over us, with men fighting on it and falling bloodily over the edge. Sometimes the island had come out of space. Sometimes it was only part of the earth which had detached itself and whirled away defying gravitation. . . . And always it was the sign of anarchy in the heavens, which had lost their order and obedience.[28]

Van Doren's account of his depression may be instructive concerning the connectedness in an inner moral authority. The urge to disconnect a part of himself from himself, and shed his traditional skin in order to be twice-born, can be seen in his serial statements. "I had come to feel a division in my mind." "My disgust . . . was a general soreness, as if my skin had worn away. . . ." "I felt nothing clearly but a strong instinct to rid myself of tangible bondages." In his actual behavior, he sheds by giving up his clubs and his teaching.

Thus, there can be noticed in Van Doren a strong urge to settle his inner civil war by radical disconnection of a part of himself. This dominating part of himself, the psychic superstructure Freud describes as the superego, is a formidable foe. Only in Van Doren's dreams is there a victory over it: "Anarchy in the heavens, which had lost their order and obedience." But the consequences of annihilating this inner conscience are too terrifying—total victory would be Pyrrhic. So in the rebirth, the superego is still there; less tyrannical, to be sure, but still prompting Van Doren to do his duty. He had to excuse himself, had to placate the voice of duty, by writing introductions as a penance for not working on Franklin.

Also the affinity between Van Doren and Swift is demonstrated. Just as first son William James uses first son Bunyan as a footnote to his own case, first son Van Doren makes his footnote the entire biography of first son Swift. The length of time Van Doren thought about Swift is but one testament. In the Foreword to *The Indispensable Carl Van Doren,* Van Doren writes concerning his selection of his best works:

In several respects *Swift* is the best book I have written, and it is the one for which I could most easily feel an uncritical partiality if I were disposed to feel any. I am essentially and primarily a biographer. Of all the men or women whose stories I have told, Swift with his intricate character demanded most of me in the way of biographical insight. His story took the form of a driving tragedy as naturally as Franklin's was later to take that of a wide-flowing historical comedy.[29]

Whether this psychological affinity has resulted in *Swift* actually being Van Doren's best work is beyond the competence of the present author to judge. Sometimes an overidentification, especially in times of crisis, spoils a work of art, sometimes it is the *sine qua non* for art. That an affinity need not be harmful for artistic or biographical purposes may be demonstrated in the case of one of the greatest, if not the greatest of biographies, that of first son Samuel Johnson by first son James Boswell.

We have not dealt much with later son Benjamin Franklin in the discussion except to point out that he represented the lighter, less complicated polarity for Van Doren. The practical healthy-mindedness of probably once-born Franklin is well known. That he should be used by Van Doren to exemplify historical comedy of course does not mean that Franklin is a superficial clown, any more than Voltaire with his cheerful ripostes was such. For Van Doren admiringly describes Franklin ". . . in all the masterful variety of his mind and all the permanent magic of his charm."[30] The reference to comedy rather suggests the point made throughout this chapter, that lightness and cheerfulness are more often possible when there is not a strongly connected inner conscience.

Van Doren's depressive reaction to the "noisy sterility" is echoed at least intellectually by another first son, Walter Lippmann. In his *Preface to Morals* he reveals his historical connectedness by lamenting the disconnection from the traditional religion of our forefathers. He opens the book with:

Among those who no longer believe in the religion of their fathers, some are proudly defiant, and many are indifferent. But there are also a few, perhaps an increasing number, who feel that there is a vacancy in their lives. This inquiry deals with their problem.[31]

Later in the book he calls, in effect, for a new connectedness to replace the bleak modernistic age of fragmentation:

It is my thesis that because the acids of modernity have dissolved the adjustments of the ancestral order, there exists to-day on a scale never before experienced by mankind and of an urgency without a parallel, the need for that philosophy of life of which the insight of high religion is a prophecy.[32]

Lippmann is too basically serious to be enticed by hedonistic possibilities, or to have anxiety as Tolstoy had, that this enjoyable life might terminate. He writes in Chapter I:

He [modern man] has become involved in an elaborate routine of pleasures; and they do not seem to amuse him very much. . . . He begins more or less consciously to seek satisfactions, because he is no longer satisfied, and all the while he realizes that the pursuit of happiness was always a most unhappy quest.[33]

It is significant that Lippmann writes "was always" rather than, as later son Tolstoy would have said, "has now become a most unhappy quest."

It is time to draw this chapter to a close. The ramifications of its essential theme have perhaps been so extensive that the theme itself might be lost sight of. In this chapter we have selected one phenomenon, moral authority, the conscience (or what underlies the feeling of "ought"), and have suggested that the inner voice of morality is to be considered a feature of connectedness, the outer voice a feature of disconnectedness. The principal reason for this suggestion is that the inner voice is not only more connected to the self but also derived from a more or less intense connection with the previous generation. We have further suggested that certain clues could be utilized in determining whether the moral authority was inner or outer. These clues include what men say about the sources of morality, how they feel about evil and innocence, and whether they have a tendency toward melancholia or cheerfulness. If the source is inner, the men will speak of an indwelling conscience, will be more cognizant of the world evils and personal evils and will tend to be pessimistic and melancholy (in uncomplicated cases, the result might be only a more serious outlook on life). If the source is outer, then men will speak of a morality derived from social norms, will tend to see the world more innocently, and will be inclined toward cheerfulness. Using the clues in this fashion, we have introduced evidence suggesting that the first sons cluster toward the inner-voice end of the continuum, whereas later sons cluster toward the outer-voice end. The use of indefinite terms such as "cluster toward" and "continuum" is deliberate, inasmuch as birth order is but a crude indicator of connectedness and disconnectedness.

The reader is advised that the theoretical remarks contain no prescriptions for the actual treatment of an emotionally disturbed patient. Despite the clinical undertones in this particular chapter, this is not a book about neuroses. It is about general personality types or life styles. The therapy of a patient depends on much more individual factors and involves matters not considered here.

The theoretical underpinnings brought out in this chapter will undoubtedly recall to the reader hypotheses submitted by writers other than Freud. The focus here on inner and outer brings to mind Jung's introvert and extravert, and Riesman's inner-directed and outer-directed character. Understandably, the author's approach more resembles that of Jung, inasmuch as there is in common a clinical orientation toward the individual. Thus, evidence has been presented indicating that basic human behavior transcends particular epochs or social climates—men tend to react with characteristic individual differences whether they are living in Biblical or in modern times. Not, however, that this orientation should be considered as opposed to Riesman's. Rather it should be thought of as complementary. Riesman's particular experience and training allow him to see the derivation of inner- and outer-directedness from social factors. That such an origin is probably for the more external layers of the personality is well appreciated by the author. For there is much to be said, for example, about national characteristics—as witness William James' observation and Camus' protest that the northern races tend to be more inner than the southern races in their moral deterministic metaphysical moods.

Though we close the chapter, the topic discussed will crop up again in conjunction with other aspects of connectedness and disconnectedness. It—the voice of morality—is the tempering side of our natures. At times faint, at other times extremely compelling, it speaks uniquely for what we ought and ought not to do. It cannot be divorced from the impelling psychic factor of what we would like to do. Their interaction brings us to the next chapter which is concerned with what we actually do.

CHAPTER III *Thought and Action*

THE PLURAL-MINDED AND THE
SINGLE-MINDED

How to characterize the action of men? They are much less captive than the thoughts and moods which have been entrusted to writing. Our method of attacking this problem will be to examine the states of mind that precede or accompany action. These states of mind will be considered in a very general sense. Thus, we shall not be interested in particular kinds of thoughts, but rather in whether the mind is divided or unified in regard to action. Hints of this approach have already appeared in the previous chapter. There we noted that the first sons tended to have a rather complex notion of the psyche, later sons a much simpler one. Thus, with first son Freud, the ego seems to spend as much energy coping with the two other inhabitants of psyche—the id and superego—as it does in coping actively with the external environment. Similarly with first son Kant, whose plural inhabitants of the mind are the Empirical Self and the Moral Self. But with later sons Adler and Rank, the ego or self is unified and is spending most of its energy in dealing self-preservatively with the outside environment.

These are the general considerations that will underlie our examination of eminent first and later sons in this chapter. We shall speak of those with at least temporarily divided minds as plural-minded and those with rather quickly unified minds as single-minded. Illustrative evidence will be offered indicating that the connectedness-prone first sons tend to be plural-minded, the disconnectedness-prone later sons to be single-minded. These tendencies appear to hold regardless of whether the action involved is of the active kind (as in leadership of a revolution) or of the intellectual kind (as in scientific philosophy).

There is little doubt that the moral sense, the topic of the previous chapter, is perhaps the chief inhibitor and complicator of action. Par excellence, it can divide the mind into plural conflicting components. The resulting plural-mindedness can produce a virtual stalemate in action as in the case of first son Hamlet who was morally undecided whether to direct his aggression toward the king or toward himself. His subsequent attack on the king can be called a plural-minded action because before acting he had to keep his inner moral voice quiet; the long delay was necessary to change his plural-mindedness into the single-mindedness necessary for action. It is no wonder that later son Trotsky commented that Hamlet could never have led the Russian Revolution. The period of delay in arriving at a conscience-cleared, self-justified unity of mind need not be as long as in the case of Hamlet. A plural-minded personality constantly remembering wrongs done to him or constantly alert to possible new wrongs can arrive at a self-justified unity in a shorter space of time. This apparently was the psychological situation with first son Hitler who, as we shall see more fully in the next chapter, was given to noticeable periods of ruminative indecision before each of his explosive actions.

If, on the other hand, self-preservation rather than an inner moral sense is the chief determinant, an action can more quickly spring from single-mindedness. The less oppressive morality of "It is either he or I" (an attitude attributed to later son Wild Bill Hickok) does not require the conscience-clearing device of "He started it." This person would simply act, would effectively do whatever is necessary to advance the cause he is leading on himself. After the action, ethical or extenuating reasons might be claimed by the person but in keeping with the self-preservative tendency, this could be done to placate the outer moral voice which is public opinion.

A vivid illustration of these tendencies can be seen in the brothers Ulyanov—or as they are more popularly known—later son Vladimir Lenin, the principal leader of the Russian Revolution, and his older brother Alexander, who at seventeen was executed for his part in a plot against the government. First son Alexander, a serious-minded introspective student, met his death because he insisted at his trial on taking full moral and intellectual responsibility for the conspiracy. Bertram Wolfe, in his *Three Who Made a Revolution*, comments on the difference in inner moral sense between Alexander and Vladimir. He mentions a childhood incident in which young Vladimir had broken a de-canter "but at the solemn family inquest denied all knowledge of how the bottle had met its fate."[1] It was three months later that he made a voluntary confession to his mother. "But to the older boy (Alexander) lying was an utter impossibility. It was absolute truth—or silence—for him from earliest childhood."[2]

Later son Trotsky's comments on the two brothers indicate what it takes to bring off a revolution successfully. Wolfe quotes Trotsky on Alexander:

In an implacable social struggle, such a mentality leaves you politi-cally defenseless. . . . In type Alexander resembled a knight more than a politician. And that created a psychic separation between him and his younger brother, considerably stronger, considerably more opportunistic in the question of individual ethics, better armed for the struggle, but in any case no less intransigent in his attitude toward social injustice.[3]

First son Alexander's plural-mindedness arising out of moral con-siderations limited his life of activity to one fatal action; later son Vladimir's single-mindedness made it possible for him to engage in activity after activity until his cause and goal were realized. We shall return to the matter of revolutions and effective social activity later in this chapter.

Let us turn now from moral considerations to other factors which make for plural-minded and single-minded orientations. These factors pertain more to intellectual action. Recalling Pas-cal's two types of intellect, we may say that the mind that enter-tains many premises without confusing them is acting in a plural-minded way, whereas the deeply penetrating precise mind is acting in a single-minded way. The first type which tends to see interconnected resemblances between events tries to account for the entire plurality of events; the second type which tends to see disconnected differences focuses on the single event which stands out from others.

One generalization seems possible from the foregoing. If the time span within which an action has to be taken is quite short, the single-minded perceiver of differences has the advantage; if the time span is long, the plural-minded synthesizer of resemblances is better off. In other words, the issue is how much time is available for thinking before one must act. If one is inclined to see resemblances between one thing and the other, the field of action tends to be filled (if not cluttered) with a multitude of objectives or premises which demand interconnection; nothing can be left out. Time has to be taken to make either the grand synthesis or a decision as to what to handle first. But if one is inclined to see differences, the particular single objective in disconnected isolation stands out. Priority as to action is automatically established by the strong clarity of the single objective. In medicine the contrast between the two types can be seen in the diagnostician who properly takes the time to consider many symptoms and premises, and the more active surgeon, pressed for time, whose precise penetrating scalpel is aided by the procedure of draping the entire body of the patient except for the one isolated area upon which he will operate.

Let us refer to the eminent men and view an exceedingly high intellectual level of single-mindedness. The later son is Descartes, as seen in his *Discourse on Method*. What will be illustrated is the stripping away of plural considerations until only one idea is left. He writes:

I had always a most earnest desire to know how to distinguish the true from the false, in order that I might be able clearly to discriminate the right path in life, and proceed in it with confidence.[4]

Even at this point we can see Descartes reducing the number of things he has to consider. He need only apply himself to the true; he relies on his precise intellect to separate the true from the false.

Descartes shows his preference for a single unit or a single mind operating in the following:

To speak of human affairs, I believe that the past pre-eminence of Sparta was due not to the goodness of each of its laws in particular, . . . but to the circumstance that, originated by a single individual, they all tended to a single end. In the same way I thought that the sciences contained in books . . . composed as they are of the opinions of many different individuals massed together, are farther removed from truth than the simple inferences which a man of good sense using his natural and unprejudiced judgment draws respecting the matters of his experience.[5]

We now come to the famous Cartesian method of systematic doubt. All ideas or beliefs that can be doubted are placed in the "false" pile until only one belief is left to be placed in the "true" pile. This one true belief is the cornerstone upon which Descartes can confidently erect a structure. Of his four precepts, the first is the one he appeared to follow most consistently:

Never to accept anything for true which I did not clearly know to be such; that is to say . . . comprise nothing more in my judgment than what was presented to my mind so clearly and distinctly as to exclude all ground of doubt.[6]

Descartes applied this precept to the point of doubting everything until at the very precipice of total negation. He writes:

But immediately upon this I observed that, whilst I thus wished to think that all was false, it was absolutely necessary that I, who thus thought, should be somewhat; and as I observed that this truth, *I think, hence I am,* I was so certain and of such evidence, that no ground of doubt, however extravagant, could be alleged by the sceptics capable of shaking it, I concluded that I might, without scruple, accept it as the first principle of the philosophy of which I was in search.[7]

For our purposes, the method of systematic doubt can best be described in terms of its objective. It is a *reductio ad unum,* with the purpose of attaining the certain, clearly distinct single-mindedness necessary for effective action. The same stripping away of beliefs and nuances was employed by the activist philosopher Rousseau in his arriving at the unitary concept of Man in Nature. And it is implicit in later son Dewey's opinion that plural tastes should be disputed in order that a single-minded social norm (like in Sparta) be a sure foundation for confident action.

The comments of philosopher Descartes on action itself are quite pertinent. His second maxim was, "To be as firm and resolute in my actions as I was able"[8] and to adhere as strongly to a doubtful opinion (once he had adopted it) as he would to a highly certain opinion. The reason Descartes gives for staying with a doubtful opinion is to avoid losing completely one's sense of position. He gives the example of the lost travelers,

who, when they have lost their way in a forest, ought not to wander from side to side, far less remain in one place, but proceed constantly towards the same side in as straight a line as possible, . . . for in this way, if they do not exactly reach the point they desire, they will come at least in the end to some place that will probably be preferable to the middle of the forest. In the same way, since in action it frequently happens that no delay is permissible, it is very certain that, when it is not in our power to determine what is true, we ought to act according to what is most probable; . . . This principle was sufficient thenceforward to rid me of all those repentings and pangs of remorse that usually disturb the consciences of such feeble and uncertain minds as, destitute of any clear and determinate principle of choice, allow themselves one day to adopt a course of action as the best, which they abandon the next, as the opposite.[9]

Descartes' advice about what to do when lost is almost identical with Clausewitz's observations on generals who are lost in the maze of combat events. Clausewitz wrote:

War is the province of chance. . . . From this uncertainty . . . the actor in War constantly finds things different from his expectations.[10]

Even if he wants to substitute a new plan for the old one,

The necessary data are often wanting for this, because in the course of action circumstances press for immediate decision, and allow no time to look about for fresh data, often not enough for mature consideration. . . .

Now, if it is to get safely through this perpetual conflict with the unexpected, two qualities are indispensable: in the first place an intellect which, even in the midst of this intense obscurity, is not without some traces of inner light, and then the courage to follow the faint light.[11]

If we follow Clausewitz's criteria, Descartes possessed the qualifications to be a great combat general. There was another quality mentioned by Clausewitz which seems exquisitely applicable to Descartes. The general needs

a natural mental gift of a special kind . . . sense of locality. It is the power of quickly forming a correct geometrical idea of any portion of country, and consequently of being able to find one's place in it exactly at any time. This is plainly an act of the imagination.[12]

The pertinence of this to Descartes resides not only in the latter's example of the lost traveler but, most important in Descartes' major mathematical contribution, in the locating of numbers in a system of coordinates.

Quite similar to later son Descartes in single-mindedness and tactics is later son Francis Bacon. Here again is a very high level intelligence in operation—so high that some believe only Bacon could have written Shakespeare's plays. Though he has come down to us through time as a philosopher of science, when he lived he was as much known (if not more so) as an active political figure. Thus, it is appropriate that we consider him now as a man in action. In politics he pursued power as single-mindedly as he pursued it in science. His actual political life was episodically clouded by his part in the execution of his bene-factor, the Earl of Essex, and by his imprisonment for debt. Few plural considerations issuing from an inner moral voice appeared to complicate his actions. His affinity with later son Machiavelli is seen in his writing, "We are beholden to Machiavelli and writers of that kind who openly . . . declare what men do in fact and not what they ought to do. . . ."[13] Yet this single-minded focus on self-preservation must not becloud for us his abilities. Not only was he the inspirational model for the formation of the Royal Society, but he eventually rose through his ability and knowledge to the position of Lord Chancellor.

Bacon's tendencies are seen as much in his scientific philos-ophy as in his political life. Like Descartes, he went straight to the point, sweeping aside plural metaphysical subtleties. As a general in science, he set out methodically to subdue the Fortress, Nature, in order to use her secrets for the practical betterment of mankind. His goals are tangibly solid—not the stuff that dreams are made of. As Durant comments, "It [the *Instauratio Magna*] would differ from every other philosophy in aiming at practice rather than at theory, at special concrete goals rather than at speculative symmetry. Knowledge is power, not mere argument. . . ."[14] In his military campaign against nature Bacon, as a good general, pays close attention to tactics, which we can equate with methodology. And it is his contribution to Logic, to the method of philosophy, which is acknowledged as unique. How to keep the mind clear of shibboleths and superstitions so that the logical apparatus can operate vigorously and effectively is what Bacon emphasized.

To the *single-mindedness of later sons* Descartes and Bacon may be contrasted *plural-mindedness* of *first son* Einstein. The latter, like Descartes, is famed for being a man of intellectual activity rather than a man of action. But Einstein's type of intellectual activity—like that of first sons Pascal and James—shows less tendency to spill over into the field of programmatic action than does that of Descartes and Bacon and of later son thinkers such as John Dewey and Bertrand Russell.

Einstein's plural-mindedness can be seen in his views of the individual and society. Unlike Descartes' preference for the single law from a single man as in Sparta, Einstein says:

We must not only tolerate differences between individuals and between groups, but we should indeed welcome them and look upon them as an enriching of our existence.[15]

His views on morality reveal the plural-mindedness issuing from the inner moral voice. Unlike Descartes who could act resolutely without "repentings and pangs of remorse," and unlike Bacon who follows Machiavelli, Einstein's more complicated conduct guide is similar to that of first sons Kant and Bentham—that many should benefit and few should suffer. He says in *Out of My Later Years*:

All men should let their conduct be guided by the same principles; and those principles should be such, that by following them there should accrue to all as great a measure as possible of security and satisfaction, and as small a measure as possible of suffering.[16]

In science, Einstein's aim was to account for everything whereas Descartes, as we saw, was content to be certain about one thing and to build slowly upon that. This total plurality of Einstein and his connectedness-tendency can be seen in:

It is the aim of science to establish general rules which determine the reciprocal connection of objects and events in time and space. . . .
    The aim of science is, on the one hand, a comprehension, as *complete* as possible, of the connection between the sense experiences in their totality, and, on the other hand, the accomplishment of this aim *by the use of a minimum of primary concepts and relations.*[17]

Such great speculative interconnections were distrusted by later sons Descartes and Bacon. For them, the more variables one attempted to interconnect in a grand synthesis, the more chances for error. Better to be somewhat near the truth than to gamble and find oneself a long distance from the straight road of truth. Descartes writes:

Amid many opinions held in equal repute, I chose always the most moderate, as much for the reason that these are always the most convenient for practice, and probably the best (for all excess is generally vicious), as that, in the event of my falling into error, I might be at less distance from the truth than if, having chosen one of the extremes, it should turn out to be the other which I ought to have adopted.[18]

Bacon also has anxiety about unbridled imagination: "The mind itself be from the very outset not left to take its own course, but guided at every step." "There are and can be only two ways of searching into and discovering the truth. The one flies from the senses and particulars to the most general axioms . . . this way is now in fashion. The other derives axioms from the senses and particulars, rising by a gradual and unbroken ascent, so that it arrives at the most general axiom last of all. This is the true way, but as yet untried." "The human understanding is of its own nature prone to suppose the existence of more order and regularity in the world than it finds."[19]

Later sons Descartes and Bacon can be contrasted with first son Einstein in the methods of becoming reoriented when lost in a maze. Descartes, it will be recalled, relied on the certainty of what is conceived "very clearly and distinctly." The vivid sensory experience is also preferred by Bacon as a guide. "The evidence of the sense, helped and guarded by a certain process of correction, I retain. But the mental operation which follows the act of sense I, for the most part, reject and, instead, I open and lay out a new and certain path for the mind to proceed in, starting directly from the simple sensuous perception."[20] The famous Cartesian conclusion "I think, therefore I am" is, it will be noted, phrased in the vivid immediacy of the present tense. He did not rely on less vivid mental operations such as memory and say, "I thought last year, and I thought yesterday, therefore there must be an I." He could have as well pinched himself and said, "I feel, therefore I am."

Einstein, on the other hand, relied not on immediate sense experience to orient himself but rather on concepts that *interconnect* multiple sense impressions. And as we might expect from this propounder in physics of the notion of objective time, *past* sense impressions are used to build up a concept:

I believe that the first step in the setting of a "real external world" is the formation of the concept of bodily objects and of bodily objects of various kinds. Out of the multitude of our sense of experiences we take, mentally and arbitrarily, certain *repeatedly occurring complexes of sense impressions* . . . [italics mine] . . . and we attribute to them a meaning—the meaning of the bodily object. . . .

The second step is to be found in the fact that, in our thinking, . . . we attribute to this concept of the bodily object a significance, which is to a high degree independent of the sense impression which originally gives rise to it. . . . The justification . . . rests exclusively on the fact that, by means of such concepts and mental relations between them, we are able to orient ourselves in the labyrinth of sense impressions. These notions and relations, . . . appear to us stronger and more unalterable than the individual sense experience itself. . . .[21]

In terms of practical quick action, it seems evident that a thinker like Descartes and Bacon has the advantage over a thinker like Einstein. The former is anchored in the present, he equates reality with the certain clarity of his senses and immediate thought, he simplifies his procedural task by attacking one thing at a time. The latter, however, is always one step removed from current reality. Instead of one current event, there are many current events to interconnect. Instead of only current events, there are also past and future events to interrelate. Reality is not that which impinges directly on the senses—rather it is what is meaningful and comprehensible. While puzzling out through conceptual thinking the comprehensibility of plural events, the Einstein-type thinker seems lost in reverie. Einstein is, of course, a notable example of the impractical conceptualizing dreamer—slow in school in his early youth, absent-minded in his maturity, seemingly lost in thought, he was finding and orienting himself through conceptualizations.

The aim of the foregoing has been to provide a theoretical framework concerning action. We have proposed the term plural-minded for those prone to connectedness, single-minded for those prone to disconnectedness. It has been shown how a single-minded approach—devoid of plural considerations emanating from an inner morality or a sense of the past or multiple events—leads to quick, effective action and to particular kinds of intel-

lectual solutions. Also it has been indicated how plural-mindedness produces a delay in immediate action.

Though we have used first and later sons to illustrate, respectively, what is meant by plural-mindedness and single-
mindedness, we have not introduced quantitative evidence that,
in the field of active action, later sons predominate over first
sons. This we intend to do now. Three possible sources exist for
such evidence: (a) Men who instruct how action should be
carried out—what methods and tactics are best to accomplish a
current action. (b) Men who have successfully led a mass movement. (c) Highly successful military or naval commanders.
Though the last source is not particularly reliable, we shall make
some attempts in that direction.

As to instruction in method or tactics—we have already encountered Descartes with his *Discourse on Method* and Francis
Bacon with his *Novum Organum*, which established a new
methodology in the experimental investigation of nature. Other
noteworthy *later sons* who have been similarly preoccupied with
tactics are Machiavelli with his manual for obtaining power,
Henry Taylor with his famous classic *The Statesman* dealing
with the art of personal advancement, Benjamin Franklin with
his conduct guide *Poor Richard's Almanac*, Lenin with his pam-
phlet on revolutionary method *What to Do*, and in our own day
Dale Carnegie with his *How to Win Friends and Influence
People*. It can be easily seen that there is a considerable range
in the intellects who have applied themselves to the question of
method or tactics in obtaining a practical goal. The common
denominator, however, is a single-minded tendency that disconnects all superfluous considerations from the practical, timely
essence and proceeds effectively to the what-do-we-do-now
solution.

In dealing with the second source—revolutionary leaders—
it is helpful to use Eric Hoffer's scheme. He proposes that a mass
movement begins with the intellectual man of words attacking
and undermining the existing social institutions; the resulting
moral and ideological vacuum is seized upon and exploited by
the fanatic who draws the leaderless masses to him; his frenzied
fervor having served the purposes, he makes way for the practical man of action who puts the new government on a more
solid and lasting basis. Hoffer's examples are suggestive rather

than exhaustively systematic. Furthermore, he acknowledges that it is difficult to categorize an individual precisely as a man of words *or* a fanatic, etc.

Using this scheme in a general flexible way, we can view the roles played by first sons and later sons in the successful culmination of mass movements. On the whole, it appears that the first sons cluster toward the man of words or ideas role, the later sons toward the practical man of action role. The occupancy of the fanatic role is more difficult to determine, inasmuch as it calls for an assessment of the individual's mental stability.

The major example of the polarity may be seen in the Russian revolution. Hegel, Marx, and Engels—*all first sons*—are acknowledged to be the intellectual fathers of Communism. Their systematic philosophy is utilized in a partial, pragmatic way by the principal three Makers of the Russian Revolution (to use Bertram Wolfe's phrase), Lenin, Trotsky, and Stalin.* Marx and Engels were not merely sedentary philosophers; their organizational work in the Communistic movement and their institution-attacking Communist Manifest attest to their activity. On the other hand, Lenin and Trotsky were not merely vigorous men of action; their clear thinking is shown in their successful actions and in their writings. Yet, if a division of labor were to be made, most observers would say that the first sons Marx and Engels were prominent on the ideological side, and the later sons Lenin and Trotsky on the programmatic side.

Other political or mass movements, though not as neatly clear-cut in the division of labor, still show trends toward the first and later sons polarity. In giving now some illustrations of this trend, the author is mirroring the customary (though not unanimous) assessment by authorities in the field—not his own personal views. The creation, for example, of the modern nation of Italy is generally viewed as a division of labor between the ardent ideological first son Mazzini and the vigorous programmaticist later son Garibaldi. In the case of the establishment of the English Commonwealth there is no doubt that later son Cromwell was the actual maker of it, and suggestive evidence that first son John Milton was, in this matter, one of the leading,

---

* Lenin and Trotsky were later sons. The biographical data on Stalin is obscure, and it is difficult to know definitely whether his older brothers died in early childhood or survived past the age of five.

if not the leading, ideologist. In many cases, the identity of the programmatic maker of the movement is known while there is no certainty as to who was the ideologist. Thus, we see as later son movement accomplishers Sun Yat-sen in China, Bolivar in South America, Herzog and Smuts in South Africa, Weizmann and Ben-Gurion in Israel, Castro in Cuba. In other cases, where quick revolutionary seizure of power is not so marked, the ideologist's identity is discernible while that of the maker rather vague. Thus, first son John Locke is thought of as the ideologist of the Bloodless English Revolution of 1689; first sons Thomas Paine and Thomas Jefferson the men of ideas for the American Revolution. In these two revolutions it is difficult to point to a single maker. Perhaps this is so because here there were not present the marked power vacuums that existed in other revolutionary situations, power vacuums that seem especially suited to the temperament of certain later sons.

We should mention a partial exception to this trend—the identity of the ideologist of the French Revolution. Here, later son Rousseau might be accepted as the man whose ideas and philosophy stimulated the revolutionary movement. As for who made that Revolution in the sense of creating something stable, it is fairly certain that first sons Mirabeau and Robespierre did not. They are looked upon by some as men of ideas and theory caught up as a revolutionary movement and unable to give it a clear, definite structure. The strong man called in to stabilize the chaotic French nation was, of course, Napoleon, the later son. The author has not been able to find an instance which entirely reverses the described trend, that is, one in which the later son was the ideologist and the first son the principal maker of the movement.

Another kind of programmatic action involving masses of people is contained in the successful formation of a new church. Here again a preponderance of later sons is noted—Calvin, Wesley, Brigham Young. (To this last may be added a later daughter, Mary Baker Eddy.) If we include those men who have strengthened religious organizations, the list shows even more later sons— Moses, Basil the Great who stamped out Arianism, and the founders of monastic institutions, Xavier and Loyola. Of all those mentioned, perhaps Brigham Young met the most difficult challenge. He not only had to preserve the Mormon Church after the death of Joseph Smith but he also, a la later son Moses, had to lead five thousand people to a new land and to settle them. His genius as a leader and founder of a colony is almost universally recognized. This type of genius did not run to metaphysical religious speculations but rather to solid, practical accomplishments such as the Deseret University, the Mormon Temple, and the Zion Cooperative Mercantile Institution. It is likely that the founding and strengthening of a religious organization requires especial single-mindedness. Doubt of any kind in the beliefs or dogma is fatal to the cohesion of the organization. There can be only one way—plural choices lead to uncertainty.

Equally requiring of single-mindedness is the military organization. Uncertainty leads to pessimism and then to panic. When we consider a great military or naval leader we are forced, for reasons given earlier, to be only suggestive. Most lists of such men show a predominance of later sons. The first sons are few and date from a period in history when there were hereditary kings, increasing strongly the chances of a first son being the leader—the first sons being Alexander the Great, Caesar, Gustavus Adolphus, Charles XII, and Frederick the Great. The many later sons include Cromwell, Napoleon, Wellington, and Nelson in Europe—and Lee, Jackson, and Sherman in the United States. The British custom of later sons going into the army or navy does not explain the later son predominance in America. If the Bible is utilized, the greatest warriors are two later sons, David with his "tens of thousands" and Judas Maccabeus. Though World War II is too recent for sound evaluation, many European military authorities regard later son MacArthur as the foremost American General. There is also suggestive evidence that first and later sons may differ in the time span covered in their thinking about warfare. Thus, in naval warfare, there is first son Admiral Mahan, the multipremised genius of long-term naval grand strategy and later son Admiral Nelson, the single-minded genius of comparatively short-term naval combat. In aviation, there is first son General William Mitchell, whose long-termedness was so in advance of his time that he was court-martialed, and later son Rickenbacker, the victor in the immediate single duels in the air.

Our survey up to this point has mainly stressed that quick, decisive, practical action—be it physical or mental—is best accomplished by a mind free of plural considerations. Those so plagued with moral doubts as to become plural selves rather than a single self are typically incapable of rapid action. And those who tend to think of events extending connectedly over a long span of time are not accustomed to deal decisively with the shorter time span represented by the immediate present. The long-termers and the short-termers frequently differ as to what is best for mankind. The short-termers are more cognizant of the immediate needs of men and want to act now—the long-termers are content to let history take its course. Thus, later son Lenin wanted the Communist Revolution to happen soon; first son Marx, comparatively detached, was certain that History would inevitably produce the desired result. A sharp conflict may be seen in another first- and later-son polarity. First son Hegel's philosophy of history had such a long time span that it accounted for the far past as well as the far future. Change, acording to him, might be slow but due to the inevitable production of synthesis from the thesis and antithesis it would be sure. This "it will work out in time" attitude of first son Hegel was intensely distasteful to later sons Kierkegaard and Camus. For these existentialists, the actual present is what we should be addressing ourselves to and acting upon. For them, it is how to exist in the disconnected "now" which is most urgent, whereas for Hegel it is how to view the meaningful connected then, now, and when. The implications for action are obvious. The single timed objective which keeps the immediate foreseeable future clearly in mind gives much fewer complications to action than does the plural timed one which anticipates conditions fifty years from now, or one which wants to solve matters for all times.

It is often difficult to ascertain whether the plurality complications to action are attributable to the notion of time or to inner morality, or to speculations about several premises. A case in point is that of first son Nehru. The frequent description of him as the philosopher-statesman makes one think that philosophic speculation is the complicator. Yet, at times Nehru behaves as the moral conscience of the world. Lastly, he is concerned with the complex long-term India problem, not just with its birth as a nation. Whatever the source of the plurality, there is no doubt that Nehru's ideas complicate his actions and he is not known as a man of action. He may be contrasted with his compatriot, later son Gandhi, who effectively accomplished the single objective of India's liberation from England and who, despite his idealism and his "passive" resistance, is more properly called a man of single-minded action.

As we close this chapter it is hoped that the discussion and examples have provided an initial theoretical orientation to the subject of thought and action. Plural- and single-mindedness—respective attributes of connectedness-prone first sons and disconnectedness-prone later sons—are only one set of terms which can be used to categorize acting and the thinking that precedes it. In the next chapter, we shall consider other terms.

CHAPTER IV *Ambition and Action*

THE HEROIC AND THE MILITANT

OUR INVESTIGATION OF ACTION TYPES takes a new turn. We shall deal now with what positively motivates the activities of men instead of what complicates them. The answer will not be sought for in simple physiological needs such as hunger, thirst, and sexual fulfillment. Rather, we shall investigate the psychological phenomenon of ambition, of what one must accomplish to gain approval from self or from others. That ambition energizes the person to undertake persistent or bold action is a commonplace. And it is scarcely required to quote Clausewitz on this subject: "War is the province of danger and therefore courage above all things is the first quality of a warrior. . . . Courage may proceed from motives such as personal pride, patriotism, enthusiasm of any kind."[1]

It is appropriate that, with the new focus, we turn for the moment from first son Freud, the principal theorizer about internal action inhibitors, to later son Adler, the principal theorizer about the drive for status and power. Adler's psychology is based on the theme that a person is ambitiously motivated to seek power as a compensation for inferiority feelings. Position in the family and birth order are more intensively explored by him than by Freud. Rather than the rough differentiation, as in this book, of first and later sons, Adler describes the psychology of the first-born, the middle-born, and the last-born. Put in simplified terms, the inferiority of the first-born resides in the fact that he was displaced from parental affection by the next sibling, feels unworthy and envious of the younger; the inferiority of the middle-born results from his being lost in the shuffle," he wants

[7 1]

attention and envies the adequacy of the first-born and the indul-
gences given to the last-born; the last-born's inferiority stems
largely from inadequacy feelings over being treated like the
baby, a role he compares disadvantageously to the role and rank
of the older siblings. In terms of ambition and drive to power,
the first-born wishes to hold on to his old role of being first,
and thus will have a wish to dominate; the later-borns (and
especially the middle) strive in an upwardly mobile manner to
unseat the first-born from the throne, to rebel in a self-assertive
way at the first-born's dominance.

As was indicated earlier, there is much that is clinically
accurate in Adler's observations. Also his theory accounts for
some of what goes on within the psyche. True, he pays little or
no attention to the internal restrictive forces. But to dispute his
version of what frequently happens in sibling interaction would
be to fly in the face of common-sense observation. The essence
of his theory is competitive emulation (an essence quite similar
to that of later born Thorstein Veblen's) and the external battle
between the haves and the have-nots. It has little of the internal
battle between the ought and ought not.

As useful as Adler's observations are on the ambitious drive
to power, they not only neglect the internal brakes but also give
little understanding of the ambitious drive *of* power. It is to be
expected that Adler, a later son, would appreciate keenly the
power-seeking motives and techniques possessed by later sons
who are trying to dethrone the dominating first son. But just as
Adler is well equipped to interpret the power psychology of the
out-of-power have-nots, first son Freud is so in regard to the
power psychology of the in-power haves. And, whereas Adler
is interested in interpersonal power, Freud is more concerned
with feelings of omnipotence. Thus it appears that a more complete understanding of the subject of power requires an appreciation of the Freudian viewpoint.

Freud theorized that the infant begins with a dim feeling
that all pleasures are for himself and that he is also the source
of all pleasures. This state of primary narcissism is also the state
of infantile omnipotence. Due to the regularity with which his
desires are satisfied by the mother and her breast (almost as regularly as occurred when he was in the womb), he believes that
he is the powerful maker of events. It is only when, as inevitably
happens, the mother and her breast are not predictably at his

beck and call that he senses that the breast belongs to the mother
and not to him. The Garden of Eden phase of primary narcissism and infantile omnipotence is over. Because the mother is
still loving, the chances for happiness are not completely gone.
By conforming to her, by loving her, by pleasing her, the baby
can still obtain affection and interest from her. But, inevitably,
there will be a loss of sustained maternal interest—weaning occurs,
a new baby arrives, etc. Upon this disappointment, much of the
love that he invested in his mother is withdrawn from her and
is reinvested in himself. As he once loved and admired his mother,
now he does so in regard to himself. This Freud called the stage
of secondary narcissism. In this stage, the loss of the mother is
partially healed by internalizing her, by an identification with
her. Another psychoanalyst, Ferenczi, has theorized somewhat
similarly. The baby's strong cry summons the mother, thus the
baby feels he is omnipotent; the cry later becomes unheeded, the
baby senses a loss of omnipotence, he transfers this magical
quality unto the seemingly powerful adults; by becoming like
them, by identifying with them, perhaps he may regain that
lost quality.

The foregoing represents, with some risk of oversimplification, the psychoanalytic theories about omnipotence. It can be
seen that the child's method of attaining that outside power is
not just to seize it, but to identify with it, to internalize it so
it becomes a part of one's self. We have seen how this method
leads to the formation of the superego, the inner moral voice.
Also, it can be seen that the Freudian theories stress the *original*
feeling of inner omnipotence.

What are we to make of the fact that, in regard to the source
of morality and power feelings, Freud pays more attention to
what happens inside the person, whereas Adler fastens his gaze
on the outside? An easy way out is to say that Freud was a more
discerning depth-psychologist than Adler, or that he was more
complexly creative. Although there is some truth in this, perhaps
a wiser course would be to follow C. G. Jung's cue. In *Modern
Man in Search of a Soul* he writes:

. . . philosophical criticism has helped me to see that every psychology
—my own included—has the character of a subjective confession. . . .
By his avowal of what he has found in himself, Freud has assisted
at the birth of a great truth about man. He has devoted his life and
his strength to the construction of a psychology which is a formu-

lation of his own being. . . . And since other people are differently constituted, they see things differently and express themselves differently. Adler, one of Freud's earliest pupils, is a case in point. Working with the same empirical material as Freud, he approached it from a totally different standpoint. His way of looking at things is at least as convincing as Freud's, because he also represents a well-known type. I know that the followers of both schools flatly assert that I am in the wrong, but I may hope that history and all fair-minded persons will bear me out.[2]

Is there any evidence that a first son psychologist, like Freud, will perceive the power situation of early childhood differently than will a later son, like Adler? All other things being equal, there is likely to be at least an initial overestimation by parents of the first-born or the first son. Before he begins performing in a way to disillusion his parents, he usually has enjoyed a phase of being the apple of their eyes. This connectedness of parents (especially the mother) to child would bring them quickly if he cried lustily for food or for a change of diapers. If he is the very first born, anxiety about handling the precious unfamiliar baby would also prompt haste in giving him succor. If he was—like Herbert Spencer—the first surviving child after many stillbirths, he would be greatly overestimated. As a result, the first son would tend to have early feelings of omnipotence, to think that all he need do is to bellow and cry and the world would come running.

Not usually so, however, with the later sons. Anxiety with the unfamiliar first-born is replaced by comparative matter-of-factness with later-borns. The mother has been through it once and is not as easily frightened by the baby's crying. Overestimation tends to occur less often. If the first son has fulfilled his promise, the overestimated family niche will remain occupied. This apparently was the case for later son Herman Melville. As Newton Arvin indicates:

Doubtless she [Mrs. Melville] preferred the more brilliantly promising boy Gansevoort to his less taking younger brother [Herman], and we can identify her, . . . with the mother of Timophanes and Timoleon to whom Melville, in a late poem, attributes these sentiments:

> "When boys they were I helped the bent;
> I made the junior feel his place,
> Subserve the senior, love him, too;
> And sooth he does, and that's his saving grace.

"But me the meek one never can serve,
Not he, he lacks the quality keen
To make the mother through the son
An envied dame of power, a social queen."[3]

The favoritism of the father toward the later son may not be enough to offset the inferiority feelings resulting from mother's preferences for the first son. This was apparently so in the case of Alfred Adler. In her biography of Adler, Phyllis Bottome points out that Adler was his proud father's favorite, whereas the mother preferred the first son. She writes:

Alfred spoke of his childhood as definitely unhappy—though made so chiefly by his own ambition. He felt himself put in the shade by a model eldest brother, a true "first-born" who always seemed to Alfred to be soaring far beyond him in a sphere to which Alfred—for all his efforts—could never attain.

(Quoting Adler:)

"My eldest brother . . . is a good industrious fellow—he was always ahead of me—and for the matter of that, he is *still* ahead of me!"[4]

Bottome comments:

Freud was to him "an eldest brother" with the threat that this involved to his own originality.[5]

Adler's situation can be contrasted to that of Freud. Ernest Jones writes:

Another effect of the mother's pride and love for her first-born left a more intense, indeed, indelible impression on the growing boy. As he (Freud) wrote later, "A man who has been the indisputable favorite of his mother keeps for life the feeling of a conqueror, that confidence of success that often induces real success." This self-confidence which was one of Freud's prominent characteristics was only rarely impaired, and he was doubtless right in tracing it to the security of his mother's love.[6]

It should not be surprising, then, that two depth psychologists, Adler and Freud, should have different views about power. Adler clearly did not possess the "camel's hump" of confident inner power that Freud did.

It is less likely, then, that the later son will have early feelings of *inner* omnipotence. Rather, he will usually bend his efforts toward getting power from the *outside*. Such ambitious efforts for power and influence cannot be easily hidden because they have to be made in the open where power resides. The ambition thus appears naked and obvious as in Jacob, Machiavelli, Borgia, Francis Bacon, Napoleon, etc. The ambition of the first son is not as easily recognizable, even though it may be excessive, for it draws upon interior power feelings and fantasies not always open to view.

The question arises, "How will first sons react when there is a threat or challenge to this inner omnipotence which has been quite early connected to their very selves?" A frequent outcome is simply that which was indicated by Freud. They realize in time they are not quite that powerful, they bend to the will of and identify with the father or other adults, and eventually become serious, responsible adults. This sequence, however, is not always as painless as it sounds, and often enough the pain is there without the sequence ever being completed. Once intensely connected and overestimated, now nothing. Two feelings come to the fore, depression and—what is more pertinent to the topic of action—rage. That hell may have no fury like an overestimated first son scorned is suggested by the hate shown by Swift and Carlyle and by the world-destructive gloom of Nietzsche and Spengler. Some of the rage is harnessed by a solution which affords the opportunity of retaining the inner omnipotent feeling. The solution involves the proving to oneself that one is still omnipotent. By doing great deeds, by creating great things, one can demonstrate to himself that he is still invulnerable, that the stopping of external and internal admiration was just a bad dream. Thus the first son tends to ask himself, "What must I be, what must I do to win for myself a perpetual source of admiration, so that I can feel as omnipotent and overestimated as I once felt."

Thus we see that ambition—a strong springboard to distinguished activity, and certainly present in all of our eminent men —may be different for the first and later sons. Though they both may want to prove something to themselves, what they want to prove and how they will prove it may differ. The highly ambitious first son wants to prove he is still omnipotent, he will attempt outsized heroic tasks. Due to the magnitude of his effort he will still appear glorious even if he does not succeed—magnificent in failure. The later son tends to want to prove he is as adequate and effective as the next man. In the original family, he had to compete for distinction with the comparatively life-sized older brothers—in contrast to the first sons whose principal competitor for distinction was the larger than life-sized father. To prove he is equal to the next man, the later son can accomplish normal-sized tasks quite in keeping with current realities—or he can maintain the illusion of the equality by obstructing or removing the person he feels is more than his equal.

Some of the tactics of winning distinction stem from what happens between brothers in the original family arena. Let us take again a family of four—father, mother, older brother, younger brother. The brothers are three years apart and there is at least the ordinary rivalry between them for attention and distinction. The older brother is stronger physically and, due to more exposure to education, is more generally knowledgeable. As matters stand, he is more of a power threat to the younger brother than the younger brother is to him. (Koch's study of two-children families shows that the younger wants to remove the older, but not vice versa.) What can the younger brother do in the physical combat area? The tactics of a frontal attack would be doomed to failure—unless it were done as a surprise attack. The inequality of strength dictates the use of surprise and deception, as we saw at Pearl Harbor. The single militant objective is to down the stronger older brother; there is considerable distinction in this alone; no additional distinction is required from having accomplished this in a noble or Marquis of Queensberry fashion. So we see such later sons as Jacob, Hamlet's uncle, Richard III, and Cesare Borgia using the method of deceptive attack to succeed. This method requires militancy, careful planning, a cool head and heart. Any feeling other than the determined wish to succeed would only weaken and complicate the action. The younger brother with the rapier against the older brother with the battle-ax must hit and run, or hit and deny that he hit, or seem to be friendly and then suddenly hit, etc. In the intellectual area, the younger brother has at least two methods; one is to concentrate precisely on a single special facet to offset the older brother's generalized knowledge, the other is to weaken the older brother's supremacy by refusing to be impressed by him or by picking rapierlike holes in his wide intellectual fabric. We shall discuss these intellectual tactics in more detail in the next chapters.

What about the older brother? The tactics just described are usually forbidden or alien to him. The branded immorality of crushing the younger brother has already been described. Only if there is a highly grievous or continuous provocation from the younger brother will this older brother feel justified in using his battle-ax. And when he uses it, the deed will be done in rage or in grim determination, not in the cool-headed way the later son uses the rapier. In between times, his angry bellow serves to remind himself and the younger brother that the all-powerful battle-ax is available. As for the matter of distinction, the older brother cannot nourish his feelings of omnipotence by continually besting the younger brother. There is little challenge in ordinary contest. To show himself how good he is, he may have to win the hard way. Thus, in a race he may give the younger brother a head start and then beat him. In a boxing contest he may tie one arm behind his back or expose his taut abdomen and defy the younger brother to hurt him with a punch. In winning the hard way, against odds, he would prefer the exposed frontal attack. He then feels entitled to take his distinguished place with the glorious heroes of the past whom he has heard or read about.

All that we have discussed about the two psychologies of power and their tactics prepares us to view now the actions of eminent men with perhaps more understanding. It may be useful to think of a new set of terms—"heroic" for the power psychology and tactics of the first son, and "militant" for those of the later son. They are somewhat more descriptive of the first and later sons who are highly *active rather than contemplative.* The usual meanings are contained in the *American College Dictionary.* Heroic: worthy of a hero, bold, daring, brave, illustrious. Militant: aggressively active in a cause.

There are other connotations which influenced the choice of these terms. "Heroic" is meant to imply the Cult of the Hero in which the distinguished dead are honored. By means of the word "dead" a link can be made between the first son with the inner moral voice and the first son who is also heroic. For, what they have in common is a connection with the past; with one the moral past, with the other the distinguished past. On the other hand, "militant" is intended to bring to mind the energetic, programmatic effectiveness of the military mind, of the Church Militant whose foremost examples are the later sons Loyola and

Xavier. Also by "militant" we wish to imply a comparative lack of inner "heroic" motivation even though from the outside they may, as in the case of Cromwell and Lenin, be regarded as heroes.

When the heroic and the militant engage each other in active combat, the militant appear more often successful. The various reasons for this might be summed up in an overstated generalization, "The militant later son *knows how to win a victory* while the heroic first son *cannot accept defeat.*" The former, with a cool, keen perception of external strengths and weaknesses, has created a science of the methods needed to win. Though many advantages are thus on the side of the later sons, the scientific rational approach is not particularly useful when all seems lost. It is then when a blind, compulsive belief in one's omnipotence may turn the adverse tide. Defeat would intolerably cut the first son down to normal life-size. (Webster's definition of heroic in the fine arts is pertinent here: "Larger than life size, but smaller than colossal.") The consequent unrealistic appreciation of the situation boosts the inner morale. The "I am invincible" equals "It can't happen to me," "My number is not up." Frequently, of course, this misfires in a futile blaze of glory. But often enough it does turn the tide. Its effect on the more rational opponent may be similar to the consternation felt by a man who has precisely shot his foe six times through the heart and then sees him still coming on.

We are now ready to proceed with a number of illustrations of the points we have discussed. They will, in the main, be confined to the fields of politics and warfare. Almost all the men are identified by name, the exceptions being anonymous case examples gives by Lasswell in *Psychopathology and Politics.* Somewhat more space will be given to the first sons whose predictability in action is less assured. Especial attention will be paid to their susceptibility to rage, to heroism, and to nonacceptance of defeat.

Let us begin with violence in first sons—*hot* violence, not a cool head using violent means. Mythologically we can note in passing what Cain did to Abel and what Esau wanted to do to Jacob. We can also observe the violence associated with heroics in the case of Hercules who, in a homicidal fury, slew his wife and children. Somewhat less mythologically we see in

Alexander the Great a similar association. He killed his companion in a fit of rage; his need for heroic distinction is evidenced by his complaint that his father's conquests would leave him nothing to conquer, and by his disdaining a surprise attack on the foe, "I will not steal a victory."

In more recent times, there are a number of examples to choose from. If we gaze upon the American Presidents, which ones strike us as having an undercurrent of heroics and violence? There would be little disagreement that heading the list might be first son Theodore Roosevelt, the heroizer of the cowboy, the nonacceptor of his original physical frailty—the advocate of the strenuous, against the odds of life—the lover of violent war who called his battle-ax a "big stick." Who would come next? Many might vote for later son Andrew Jackson, but not Arthur M. Schlesinger, Jr., who, from his appraisal in *The Age of Jackson*, would fit Jackson more into our "militant" category than our "heroic" one. Schlesinger wrote:

Jackson did indeed bear the reputation of being intemperate, arbitrary and ambitious for power. As a general he had tended to do necessary things with great expedition and to inquire afterward into their legality. His political opponents, building ardently upon incidents of his military past, managed almost to read into the records of history a legend of his rude violence and uncontrolled irascibility. . . .

Yet, in actual fact, virtually all the direct testimony agrees in describing Jackson of these later years as a man of great urbanity and distinction of manner.

On foot, . . . or on horseback, . . . he had a natural grandeur which few could resist.[7]

Jackson's *using* his passions rather than being *consumed* by them comes out in Schlesinger's writing:

Contrary to the Jackson myth, there was small basis for the picture of uncontrolled irascibility. Jackson, who knew his reputation, never hesitated to exploit it. "He would sometimes extemporize a fit of passion in order to overwhelm an adversary, when certain of being in the right," said one observer, "but his self-command was always perfect." . . . to committees . . . he would fly into vehement denunciation of the moneyed monopoly. When they left in disgust, he would coolly light his pipe and, chuckling "They thought I was mad, . . ."[8]

If, then, we go along with Schlesinger's evaluation, we are forced to conclude that Jackson's rages were instrumental, were used to confuse the opposition and thus effectively to drive home his point. He was not blind with fury; he was open-eyed while using the device of fury. Similarly, probably, with the grandeur. Although Schlesinger does not question the naturalness of the grandeur, one might suspect that if the fury was used for effect, perhaps the grandeur was also. Collateral reasons for thinking so are that later son Francis Bacon advocated the political use of the grand manner. As Durant writes, quoting Bacon, "Manifest pride is a help to advancement; and 'ostentation is a fault in ethics rather than in politics.' "[9] Durant continues, "Here again one is reminded of Napoleon; Bacon, like the little Corsican, was a simple man enough within his walls, but outside them he affected a ceremony and display which he thought indispensable to public repute."[10] One cannot help thinking in this connection of the possibility that the mystique of grandeur is consciously employed by later sons, De Gaulle and MacArthur. Quite similar to Jackson and to the others mentioned is the description of the later son, Cardinal Armand Jean du Plessis de Richelieu, by the *Encyclopaedia Britannica*:

His own personality was his strongest ally. The king himself quailed before that stern, august presence. His pale, drawn face was set with his iron will. His frame was sickly and wasted with disease, yet when clad in his red cardinal's robes, his stately carriage and confident bearing gave him the air of a prince. His courage was mingled with a mean sort of cunning, and his ambition loved the outward trappings of power as well as its reality; yet he never swerved from his policy in order to win approbation, and the king knew that his one motive in public affairs was the welfare of the realm. . . .[11]

The foregoing description of Richelieu and Jackson together with the reference to Bacon, Napoleon, De Gaulle, and MacArthur are designed to provide a background of contrast for what follows. These *later sons* are characterized not only by an orientation toward external symbols of power but also, and more important, by a cool-headedness. They are not consumed by their emotions. Rather, they use their emotions to further their goals and, as coolly, they utilize the emotions of those around them. To be sure, the successful first sons make use of their own and other people's emotions, but the contrast lies in the degree of coolness. As the subsequent examples will indicate, the first sons are more likely to be taken in, to be consumed by their emotions, to believe what they are saying and doing. Underlying this tendency is the inwardly oriented omnipotence which cannot accept defeat and which reacts with violence to any belittlement.

To return to the American Presidents, a leading recent candidate to follow Theodore Roosevelt might be first son Harry Truman. His "give them hell, Harry" belligerency seems to be more than skin deep, more than used for effect. He appears to to be more classifiable as "heroic" than "militant." The tie to the past appears in his deep absorption in history and in his old-fashioned responses to affronts to the honor of himself and his family. The belligerent and at the same time chivalrous threat to the critic of his daughter belongs to the heroics of yesteryear. No political advantage accrued to Truman from his letter to the music critic—if anything, it was politically disadvantageous. His nonacceptance of defeat may be seen in his resiliency after going through early business failures, and in the presidential campaign of 1948.

The problem of a man's being too recent for proper evaluation does not confront us as heavily when we consider two *first sons*, Lassalle and Bakunin, who were involved in the communist movement. Edmund Wilson devotes a chapter to each in his sweeping historical account, which begins with the historian Michelet in 1824 and ends with Lenin's arrival at the Finland Station on April 16, 1917. If we accept later sons Lenin and Trotsky as the makers of the specific Russian Revolution, and first sons Marx and Engels as the historical philosophers of the general proletariat of the revolution, how are we to regard Lassalle and Bakunin? Wilson describes them as "historical actors," a description which does not immediately help us in categorizing them as heroic or militant.

The case of Ferdinand Lassalle is interesting not only because it describes in extreme what we mean by heroic but also because it shown an interaction between an invincible heroic first son and an effective, successful, militant later son, Bismarck. Lassalle's early overestimation, the resentment of slights to his honor and omnipotence, can be seen in Wilson's writing:

In his character and his relation to his family, he in some ways strikingly resembled Marx. He was an only son and, like Marx, he was gifted and adored by his father, whom he treated with passionate arrogance. Unlike Marx, he was emotional and tumultuous and vain of his person as well as of his attainments. He used to make terrible scenes with his sister, and he attempted to fight duels with his school-mates, whom he would accuse of putting indignities upon him.

The vision of Hegel had apparently taken hold of him, for when his father asked him what he wanted to study, he answered: "The greatest, the most comprehensive study in the universe, the study that is most closely associated with the most sacred interests of mankind: the study of History."

When at fifteen, . . . he heard of the persecution of Jews in Damascus, he made a furious entry in his diary: "Even the Christians wonder at the sluggishness of our blood—wonder that we do not rise in revolt, in order that we may die on the battlefield rather than in the torture chamber."[12]

The interaction of tempestuously heroic first son Lassalle with the cool-headed, militant later son Bismarck is of interest. Lassalle protests against Bismarck's "blood and iron" regime. Bismarck, with the later son's keen nose for a power vacuum, had stepped in when the king was on the point of abdicating. In his "blood and iron" policy Bismarck, as Wilson writes:

proceeded to rule for four years without a parliamentary budget, putting through the army program and defying and insulting the parliament, on the pretext that the constitution failed to indicate what was to be done in the event of the King's and the parliament's being unable to agree on the budget. In the meantime, Lassalle's *Workers' Program* had been confiscated by the police as soon as it was published, and Lassalle was being prosecuted "for having pub-licly incited the non-possessing classes to hatred and contempt for the possessing classes."[13]

Lassalle stood trial, verbally assaulted the prosecutor and later organized the general union of German workers after giving them this manifesto:

"A party of labor now exists. This party must be provided with a theoretical understanding and with a practical war-cry, even if it cost me my head three-and-thirty times."[14]

These and other efforts make Bismarck take serious note of Lassalle as a force. Bismarck plays along with him, indulging in Lassalle's wish to be treated like the head of another great power. Wilson writes:

But by January, 1864, the war with Denmark was looming. Lassalle did his best to scare Bismarck into establishing universal suffrage before he committed Germany—declaring that a prolonged war would bring on riot and insurrection at home, . . . But Bismarck, by this time, . . . felt that the power was all on his side, . . ."[15]

Lassalle in hurt pride breaks off diplomatic relations with Bismarck and continues his agitation with the workers:

the workers no longer distrusted him as they had in the early days, because they knew he had the Devil's own courage.[16]

This kind of omnipotent courage, while temporarily successful against Bismarck's iron, was to no avail against the lead of a bullet. In characteristic style, Lassalle goes to his death. As Wilson writes:

She [Helene] writes him [Lassalle] that there can be no question of her marrying him, that she is going to marry a young man, . . . to whom she had formerly been engaged. Lassalle, in his role of reformer, had been opposed to the principle of the duel; but he now challenged both Helene's father and . . . the young Rumanian. . . . Rustow advised his friend [Lassalle] to get in some pistol practice before hand; but Lassalle, in his self-confidence, refused. He was shot to death in his abdomen before he had managed to fire.[17]

Michael Bakunin's story is as illustrative of certain "heroic" undertones. Wilson writes:

Michael was the oldest boy of ten boys and girls, and so was in a position to dominate his sisters by his sex and his brothers by his age. His attitude toward both was protective, and he was their leader in conspiracies against their father. . . ."[18]

Like Lassalle, he became a devotee of Hegelian philosophy. Wilson believed that

The critical turn of his conversion to the revolutionary interpretation of Hegel seems to have come at the moment when he definitely lost his hold over his maturing brothers and sisters.[19]

This threat to his omnipotent feelings was quickly translated into thoughts of world destruction. Unlike Van Doren who confined such notions to his dreams, and Nietzsche who confined them to his writings, Bakunin brought them to life in his action. Wilson writes:

Discussing his character in his later years, he "attributed his passion for destruction to the influence of his mother, whose despotic character inspired him with an insensate hatred of every restriction on liberty." . . . He had visions of ecstatic conflagration: "the whole of Europe, with St. Petersburg, Paris and London, transformed into an enormous rubbish-heap."

And he was always insisting on the importance, in time of revolution, of "unleashing the evil passions."

But he had also the magnanimity of a displaced and impersonal love. . . . He wanted—though in the name of destruction—to embrace the human race, and he was able to arouse in his followers a peculiar exhilaration of brotherly feeling.[20]

As a man of action, Bakunin could not fit in well. Wilson says:

He was condemned to play out his career in a series of unsuccessful attempts to intervene in foreign revolutions. When, for example, in 1848, the February days broke in France, Bakúnin sped to Paris at once and served in barracks with the Workers' National Guard— eliciting the famous verdict of the revolutionary Prefect of Police: "What a man! The first day of the revolution he is a perfect treasure; but on the next day he ought to be shot." And then, as soon as the German revolution had got under way in March, Bakunin moved on to Germany, where he hoped to help the Poles to revolt.[21]

For his part in the Dresden uprising of 1849 he was imprisoned for eight years, first under a death sentence which was commuted, then under another death sentence, again commuted. After the Austrian prison term, he was imprisoned by the Russians, then given exile in Siberia. In 1861, he escaped and was ready again with revolutionary battle-axe.

Bakunin's intemperate passions, so unpredictably useful in cool action, were much more successful in arousing people. There appears to be a strong resemblance to first son Hitler, whom we shall discuss shortly. By 1868 through his secret society work he was becoming for the first time in his life a genuinely formidable power. At the Congress of the International in 1869, Bakunin came into opposition with Marx over the former's wish to abolish the right of inheritance. Wilson quotes Baron Wrangel who was present at once of Bakunin's orations to the Congress:

"I no longer remember what Bakunin said, and it would in any case scarcely be possible to reproduce it. His speech had neither logical sequence nor richness in ideas, but consisted of thrilling phrases and rousing appeals. It was something elemental and incandescent—a raging storm with lightning flashes and thunderclaps, and a roaring as of lions. The man was a born speaker, made for the revolution. The revolution was his natural being. His speech made a tremendous impression. If he had asked his hearers to cut each other's throats, they would have cheerfully obeyed him." For all the futility of his actual enterprises, he had acquired the power of a symbol. There is perhaps something in Bernard Shaw's idea that Wagner's Siegfried, conceived after his experience [with Bakunin] of the Dresden revolution, was based on the character of Bakunin. In any case, despite the practical uselessness and the political inconsistency of Bakunin's defiance of the Prussians, this defiance had come to signify the assertion of the disinterested bravery of the human spirit against self-interest and timidity, just as his survival from the prisons of three despots and his escape which had encircled the world, had demonstrated the strength of that will to be free which Byron had said was "brightest in dungeons." Bakunin appealed to the imagination as Marx had never been able to do: he had the superhuman simplification of a hero of romantic poetry, something very rare and strange in reality.[22]

Wilson's account of Bakunin requires no explanatory notes. Quite evident are the omnipotent and destructive tendencies out of which some kind of creative good may come. Apart from Bakunin's illustrating the heroic attitudes, there is another and more timely reason why we mention him here. His appeal to the imagination as "the superhuman simplification of a hero of romantic poetry" is so strong that he has been recently revived by the U.S.S.R. as a Hero of the Revolution. Any man whose attitude and oratory can convert peace-loving people into cheerful throat-cutters has to be seriously reckoned with.

The discussion of Bakunin's personality provides a good introduction to another violently heroic first son, one more recently emblazoned in memory of man—Adolf Hitler. Our discussion of Hitler will be somewhat meandering because we shall deal not only with his personality but also with men in history who had some influence on him and men who are like him in some respects. We shall find that, for the most part, first son Hitler had a particular affinity for the heroic attitudes of other first sons. Although a rigid generalization cannot be made here, there does seem to be some evidence that it may take an "heroic" to empathize with and understand another "heroic." Previously we noted that first son Van Doren in a bitter melancholy chose

the savagely bitter first son Swift rather than the cheerful later
son Franklin for biographical study. It can be added that of
the three persons mentioned by Wilson as having empathic
insights about first son Bakunin, Shaw, and Byron are first sons
(Wrangel's birth order is unknown). Wilson himself is a first
son.

Inquiring then into the influences on Hitler, we find that
a first son, Nietzsche, and a later son, Wagner, are considered
to be of major import. That demonic first son Hitler was em-
pathically attracted to demonic first son Nietzsche is in keeping
with the trend. But later son Wagner proves a stickler here.
Either Wagner represents a real exception, or Wagner was really
not demonically heroic. Perhaps the matter cannot be decided
here. But it might be useful to view evidence suggestive of the
latter alternative. One bit is contained in Shaw's idea, namely
that it was the Bakunin in Wagner's Siegfried that attracted
Hitler, that it was the heroic men out of Germany's past, drama-
tized by Wagner, rather than Wagner himself, who was Hitler's
inspiration. Even if this is granted, we are forced to account
for Wagner's insight into the past heroes. Is this one heroic's
empathy with another, or is it a cooler utilizing of the stuff of
drama? Eric Bentley may provide an answer here. In his *Century
of Hero Worship* the principal and unequivocal heroic vitalists
are the first sons Carlyle and Nietzsche. Bentley doubts whether
Wagner should be so classified. He writes, "Bernard Shaw was
angry with Wagner for the same reason as Nietzsche. He thought
he had found in Wagnerism an expression of the power-instinct,
only to discover in the end that for Wagner love and not power
was primary."[23]

There is some reason to believe, then, that Hitler, like
Nietzsche and Shaw, read something into Wagner that was not
really there. The need for hero-worship in first sons—a topic
more fully developed in the next chapter—prompts them to see
what they want to see in illustrious figures. Sometimes it is a
lifetime infatuation as between first son Carlyle and later son
Cromwell, but often there is a disillusionment as first son
Beethoven had about later son Napoleon. Hitler's belief in what
he wished to believe seems quite clear. We would classify him
along with Bakunin and Lassalle as heroic men of action, as men
who acted out their consuming demonic passions rather than

coolly and rationally utilizing them. Also along with Hitler we could classify his brother dictator, first son Mussolini—a man whose father was a revolutionary and an admirer of Bakunin and who himself was a disciple of Nietzsche.

A closer study of Hitler, as seen through Bullock's biography, will provide us with illustrations of points that have been made and will be made. First, the omnipotent characteristics of not being able to accept defeat. There were two main periods in which this was shown. The first was during the long years before Hitler came to actual power. He did not accept his personal defeat as an artist, or Germany's defeat in World War I. On the contrary, these rankling defeats stiffened, embittered, and energized him. And just before he became Chancellor the situation for him and the Nazi party was not bright. Alan Bullock writes:

One of the worst difficulties was lack of money. Four elections since March had eaten deep into the Party's resources, and the invaluable contributions from outside had lately begun to dwindle. . . . In the middle of October, Goebbels complained: "Money is extraordinarily difficult to obtain. All gentlemen of 'Property and Education' are standing by the Government."

In these circumstances it was only Hitler's determination and leadership that kept the Party going. His confidence in himself never wavered. When the Gauleiters assembled at Munich early in October he used all his arts to put new life and energy into them. "He is great and surpasses us all," Goebbels wrote enthusiastically. "He raises the Party's spirits out of the blackest depression. With him as leader the movement must succeed."[24]

So far, Hitler's intolerance of defeat does not seem much different from that of other first sons. The sustaining confidence in oneself and one's destiny despite—or even because of—defeats may be seen as was said in first son Churchill's "backs against the wall" heroism. The final exploration of the North Pole by first son Robert Peary after many seeming defeats suggested to his biographer, Fitzhugh Green, the title *Peary, the Man Who Refused to Fail*. In the Civil War, the only Confederate general who did not accept formal defeat and who "surrendered" one year after the war was first son John Mosby. Julius Caesar evidenced this first son pride and undefeatability when he had his statue set up in the temple of Quirinus with the inscription,

"To the Unconquerable God." The most vivid example in recent American political military history of a man refusing to accept failure, adverse opinion, and court martial is that of first son General Billy Mitchell.

To return to Hitler, his persisting against odds so far might be considered within the normal limits for heroically minded first sons. His judgment up to this point was not noticeably impaired by his omnipotent tendencies. He had been able to wait until he obtained power legally. He was more correct than his generals in estimating the will of the other countries to resist. In the situation with Czechoslovakia, however, we can see noticeable beginnings of irrational omnipotent reactions. According to Bullock, Hitler was enraged that the Czech government ordered a partial mobilization which in turn caused Britain and France to warn Hitler they would engage in war if the Germans made any aggressive move against the Czechs. Hitler had to back down:

For a week he remained at the Berghof in a black rage, which was not softened by the crowing of the foreign Press at the way in which he had been forced to climb down. . . .

Hitler never forgave the humiliation. . . . He constantly referred to it in his later speeches, and from it sprang the venomous hatred with which he referred to President Benes, and an inflexible determination to obliterate the very name of Czechoslovakia.[25]

Hitler's rage over this humiliating blow to his omnipotence was such that he was prepared to risk general war in order to punish Czechoslovakia. The general staff was against this move. According to Bullock, General Jodl wrote:

"The whole contrast becomes once more acute between the Fuehrer's intuition that we *must* do it this year, and the opinion of the Army that we cannot do it yet, as most certainly the Western Powers will interfere, and we are not as yet equal to them." General von Wietersheim said that "the western fortifications against France could be held for only three weeks." A furious scene followed, Hitler cursing the Army as good-for-nothing and shouting: "I assure you, General, the position will not only be held for three weeks, but for three years." Jodl added the comment: "The vigour of the soul is lacking, because in the end they (the Staff Officers) do not believe in the genius of the Fuehrer. And one does perhaps compare him with Charles XII of Sweden."[26]

The comparison of first son Hitler to first son Charles XII is, we believe, significant. Charles XII, who in boyhood took first son Alexander the Great as his model, is a classic example of the heroic-minded. His military successes were apparently due more to his heroic megalomania than to military expertise. In his *Fifteen Decisive Battles*, Sir Edward S. Creasy writes:

We must admit that his [Napoleon's] judgment, though severe, is correct, when he pronounces that the Swedish king, . . . knew nothing of the art of war, and was nothing more than a brave and intrepid soldier. Such, however, was not the light in which Charles was regarded by his contemporaries at the commencement of his Russian expedition. His numerous victories, his daring and resolute spirit, combined with the ancient renown of the Swedish arms, then filled all Europe with admiration and anxiety.

But Charles at that time was solely bent on dethroning the sovereign of Russia, as he had already dethroned the sovereign of Poland, . . . Charles himself looked on success as a matter of certainty and the romantic extravagance of his views was continually increasing. "One year, he thought, would suffice for the conquest of Russia. The court of Rome was next to feel his vengeance, as the pope had dared to oppose the concession of religious liberty to Silesian Protestants. No enterprise at that time appeared impossible to him. He had even despatched several officers privately into Asia and Egypt, to take plans of the towns and examine into the strength and resources of those countries."[27]

The comparison can be extended to the Russian campaign of Charles XII and Hitler. Both were frontal and involved the personal honor of the assailants. Creasy writes concerning the decisive battle of Pultowa: "On hearing that the czar was about to attack him, he [Charles XII] deemed that his dignity required that he himself should be the assailant; and leading his army out of their entrenched lines before the town, he advanced with them against the Russian redoubts."[28]

Hitler began the Russian campaign with an unrealistic estimate of how long this would take. Bullock writes:

He [Hitler] was certain that the political weakness of the Soviet régime, together with the technical superiority of the Germans, would give him a quick victory in a campaign which he never expected to last much longer than that in which he had overrun France the year before.[29]

But when the unrealistic estimate was not borne out, Hitler refused to accept the verdict of reality. One step backward meant to him a fatal blow to his omnipotence. Bullock writes:

More and more doubts were felt by commanders as to the wisdom of continuing the attack, but Hitler was insistent: the Russian resistance, he declared, was on the verge of collapse.

Warnings and appeals were of no avail. Hitler categorically refused to admit that he had been wrong. Whatever the cost in men's lives, his armies must make good his boasts, and he drove them on relentlessly.[30]

The last years of Charles XII, after several defeats, bear a marked resemblance to Hitler's last years after the Russian defeat and after the Allied Invasion of Germany. The *Encyclopaedia Britannica* writes concerning Charles XII:

Here it need only be said that Sweden, during the course of the Great Northern War, had innumerable opportunities of obtaining an honourable and even advantageous peace, but they all foundered on the dogged refusal of Charles to consent to the smallest concession to his despoilers. Even now he would listen to no offers of compromise, and after defending Stralsund with desperate courage till it was a mere rubbish heap, returned to Sweden after an absence of 14 years.[31]

Even as early as 1934, Hitler disclosed that he preferred "rubbish heaps to the humiliation of personal defeat." Bullock writes:

Earlier in 1934, when Rauschning asked him what would happen if Britain, France and Russia made an alliance against Germany, Hitler replied: "That would be the end. But even if we could not conquer them, we should drag half of the world into destruction with us, and leave no one to triumph over Germany. There will not be another 1918. We shall not surrender."[32]

In 1945, when defeat was only weeks away,

he [Hitler] issued categorical and detailed orders for the destruction of all communications, rolling-stock, lorries, bridges, dams, factories and supplies in the path of the enemy. Sending for Speer, he told him:

"If the war is to be lost, the nation also will perish. This fate is inevitable. There is no need to consider the basis even of a most primitive existence any longer. On the contrary, it is better to destroy that, and to destroy it ourselves."[33]

It is of interest that, in the last days, Hitler took hope from another first-son refuser of defeat, Frederick the Great. Bullock writes:

Hitler turned for comfort to the example of Frederick the Great, who in 1757, when Prussia was invaded by half a dozen armies and all hope seemed gone, won his greatest victories of Rossbach and Leuthen and routed his foes. He kept Graff's portrait of Frederick hanging above his desk and told Guderian: "When bad news threatens to crush my spirit I derive fresh courage from the contemplation of this picture."[34]

Like Frederick, he found consoling overestimation in the attachment of his dogs to him. A further parallel to Frederick resides in the fact that both men were the first surviving children after two preceding children died in infancy. The intense overestimated connectedness of mothers to their surviving offspring is not without significance here.

The other facet of Hitler's personality which is of interest to us is the method by which he was able to be a man of action. Previously we have indicated that first sons are more often pluralminded and that a certain Hamlet-like indecision interferes with the taking of decisive action. Bullock notes this tendency in Hitler. He writes of Hitler before the invasion of Poland:

At every crisis in his career—in 1932, in June, 1934, September, 1938, as much as now—he had found it difficult to make up his mind, hesitating, listening first to one, then to another, argument, waiting for some sudden impulse to carry him forward.[35]

We do not hear of this type of vacillation in the later-son men of action, Napoleon, Bismarck, Lenin, etc.

One of Hitler's principal methods of overcoming his vacillation appears to be that of self-justification. As a first son, he would be more susceptible to guilt feelings emanating from inner moral voice. To combat his guilt, he must prove to himself that he had been unjustifiably mistreated. His conscience perhaps would not condone his revenging of affronts merely to himself. If he identified himself with a higher, nobler cause, such as the deliverance of Germany, his conscience would accept his retaliatory destructiveness.

To Hitler, the Versailles Treaty was the major unfair treatment of Germany. By dwelling on the injustice of the treaty, Hitler could resolve his guilt conflict and mobilize aggression for action—he could proceed from plural-mindedness to single-mindedness. He indicates in *Mein Kampf* the energizing potential contained in feeling unjustly treated. As Bullock notes:

Hitler in *Mein Kampf* wrote: "What a use could be made of the Treaty of Versailles. . . . How each one of the points of that Treaty could be branded in the minds and hearts of the German people until sixty million men and women find their souls aflame with a feeling of rage and shame; and a torrent of fire bursts forth as from a furnace, and a will of steel is forged from it. . . ."[36]

Bullock comments that almost every speech of Hitler began with a lengthy recital of the wrongs done to Germany:

One of Hitler's most habitual devices was to place himself on the defensive, to accuse those who opposed or obstructed him of aggression and malice, and to pass rapidly from a tone of outraged innocence to the full thunder of moral indignation. It was always the other side who were to blame, and in turn he denounced the Communists, the Jews, the Republican Government, or the Czechs, the Poles, . . . for their "intolerable" behaviour which forced him to take drastic action of self-defence.[37]

Even in Hitler's rise to power in Germany, he was quite careful to acquire it within the law. He waited for the vindication by elections or for the legal transfer of power. The later-son men of action do not dwell so much on the question of legality—whether or not there is a power vacuum is their main consideration. The indications are that, with Hitler, there is not only the obvious "might makes right" but also "right makes might."

A crucial question about Hitler is whether he coolly simulated anger in order to win his point—as Schlesinger believes later-son Jackson did—or whether he was consumed by his emotions. As Bullock says:

The baffling problem about this strange figure is to determine the degree to which he was swept along by a genuine belief in his own inspiration and the degree to which he deliberately exploited the irrational side of human nature, both in himself and others, with a shrewd calculation.[38]

Most of the evidence suggests that though both aspects were present the cool Machiavellian aspect was less prominent. Bullock remarks on Hitler's "extraordinary capacity for self-dramatization."[39] Nevile Henderson called it a capacity for self-delusion. Regarding Hitler's mass meetings, Bullock says:

Paradoxically, the man who was most affected by such spectacles was . . . Hitler himself, . . . and, as Rosenberg remarks in his memoirs, they played an indispensable part in the process of self-intoxication.[40]

We have devoted considerable space to Hitler for several reasons. He illustrates vividly the heroic omnipotence characteristic of first sons, the intolerance to accept defeat which threatens the omnipotence, and the transition from guilty plural-mindedness to self-justified single-mindedness. The other reasons are less theoretical. In these days of diplomacy by terrorization, can we recognize when the threat to drop the atomic bomb proceeds from a cool calculation of the odds involved, and when it proceeds from an irrational megalomaniacal omnipotence? In the former case, raising the odds would be sufficient to deter the potential bomb-dropper. In the latter case, however, increasing the odds might rankle the bomb-dropper sufficiently that he would not care if the whole world became a rubbish heap. Perhaps our study of Hitler may provide more clues about this matter.

That the later sons are not so enamoured of passionate violence as are the first sons is suggested by a review of case excerpts given by the political scientist Harold D. Lasswell in his *Psychopathology and Politics*. Indeed, there appears to be an opposite trend in later sons—toward militant pacifism. Lasswell's excerpts also provide illustrations of other factors we have noted in later sons, e.g., the sense of innocence and certain intellectual tactics.

Early in his career, Lasswell sought to apply not only the insights of Freud, Adler, and Jung to political behavior but also the method of clinical case study to politically active individuals. In three chapters—"Political Agitators," "Political Administrators," and "Political Convictions"—Lasswell presents fifteen case excerpts. In seven of these excerpts the birth order is definitely mentioned—two first sons and five later sons. All of the excerpts are interesting and informative in regard to clinical material.

For our purposes, however, we shall limit ourselves to a rather summary approach.

The two agitators mentioned by Lasswell are both later sons. While we have just considered the "heroic" agitators Lassalle and Bakunin with their theme of violence, here we see the "militant" agitators. They seem to be following the suggestion of later-son Camus that the only way to deal with life is constantly to rebel. This is the kind of militant rebellious agitation shown by Thoreau in his fight against payment of taxes. These agitators, it must be emphasized, are not advocating violence even though their militancy can exasperate others to violence. Lasswell writes:

A's claim to a place among the agitators is not open to question. He was compelled to resign his position when the United States went into the World War on account of the tenacity with which he argued the pacifist position. He had previously run for Congress on the socialist ticket. Suspected of unorthodoxy in the theological school, he steadily became more radical in his views and was expelled from one denomination.[41]

Lasswell quotes his statements to audiences that "capitalism depends on markets, markets ultimately depend on force, and force means war."[42] The intellectual tactics of later sons to upset the composure and theories of the first son are evidenced by Lasswell's writing: "He confesses that he has taken an unmistakable pleasure in 'rubbing the fur the wrong way. . . .' Mr. A prides himself on his ability to cut holes in the logical fabric spun by conspicuous men."[43]

The tactics of deception are seen in:

He had long practice in the art of the impostor. From the plight of his older brother, A learned that he would lose the affection of his father if he was discovered to have indulged in certain practices like masturbation . . . he pretended to virtues which he did not possess. Never once was he found out, and his life was the life of a "model" body and man. . . . He learned to cultivate the mask of rectitude. . . .[44]

The other agitator, later-son B, is also against "bad" things like war:

He [B] has achieved eminence in newspaper work, . . . At twenty . . . B led a fight against the red-light district of the city, exposing the pimps, panderers, and prostitutes in sensational style. He has always responded quickly to the appeal of the underdog and revealed injustices wherever he found them. . . . B has a high reputation for absolute truthfulness and reliability, often carrying his scruples to what his fellow-newspapermen think are unwarranted extremes.[45]

B finally had to be hospitalized because of a paranoid psychosis with homosexual content. B, like A, could not accept the evils in the world, and fought against them militantly in order not to recognize their own "evil." As we indicated earlier, later sons have less of a tendency to see and accept the feeling of personal evil—the most total denial being seen in Christian Science.

In the chapter "Political Administrators," H, a first son (only child), is described in terms recalling our discussion of the threat to inner omnipotence and overestimation. Lasswell writes:

While it is accurate to say that H is diplomatic and seemingly open and frank in dealing with his superiors, it should be added that in situations which involve the fate of his own projects, he is noticeably overtense, and likely to evaluate himself much higher than others. He becomes slightly accusatory if his demands are rejected.[46]

His superiors "felt that H might be entirely broken up if his projects were rudely rejected. . . ."[47] K, the other administrator, a later son, was heavily preoccupied with efforts toward self-mastery and was known for his conscientious efficiency. He would become depressed if he was not able to maintain an over-scrupulous performance of duty. Like A and B, he struggled to abolish the "evil" of personal inadequacy. He had no inner store of omnipotence or arrogance which would vaccinate him against the feelings of inadequacy.

In "Political Convictions," Lasswell begins with later son L who is also against war. "He believes that the United States ought to join the League of Nations and that our government ought to lead the world toward conciliation and peace. . . . He has a strange premonition that if he goes his own way something terrible will happen. Thus L is not only a simple conformer, but a compulsive conformer."[48] P, a first son, is a patriot who proved his patriotism by volunteering in the late war during the course of which he was distinguished for bravery in action. "*His deepest longing is for war to come again* [italics added]. He is in favor of an aggressive foreign policy since it increases the chances of

war, and war he would welcome again as he welcomed it before."⁴⁹ Q, a later son, a contrast to P, is a pacifist. "From an
early age Q showed a morbid fear of blood. Later on, when he
heard that western capitalism meant war and bloodshed, he
expressed a profound emotional revulsion against 'capitalism,'
'imperialism,' and their associated concepts, and called himself a
'socialist,' 'pacifist,' and 'internationalist.' "⁵⁰

Reviewing these excerpts, we find that the five later sons
(A, B, K, L, and Q) appear to be against the evils in the world
and in themselves. They are against the violence of war, rather
than for it. They can be highly energetic in their militant fight
against evil. Of the definitely known first sons, H overestimates
himself and is likely to be irritable if the environment does not
share in his omnipotent self-concept; P is unmistakably in favor
of war. We have not included Lasswell's case O who was probably a first son, inasmuch as Lasswell describes him as an ille-
gitimate child who was brought up and spoiled by an overindul-
gent mother. That O had a "heroic-violent" streak is evident
from Lasswell's description: "O was the young leader of an
anarchist band whose anarchism went beyond precept to dramatic practice. . . . When he realized he had a father who was
still living, . . . his anger boiled up against his mother. . . . O
threw a thick mantle of rationalization over his murderous impulses and criminal acts, seeking to justify coercion in the name
of a coercionless ideal. . . ."⁵¹ Thus, Lasswell's case excerpts
appear to support the prevailing trend for "heroic violence" to
occur more often in first sons.

When we examine action in the military sphere, we are
handicapped because military reputations are difficult to assess
and military historians are not unanimous in their evaluations.
Consequently, what follows in this regard must be considered
as only illustrative and suggestive. In general, the author's impression—despite his inability to demonstrate it convincingly—is
that "heroics" are more frequently found in first sons and cool
militant effectiveness in later sons. The following examples may
help explain the source of this impression.

Perhaps, in the comparison of two ancient generals—first son
Alexander the Great and later son Miltiades, the victor at Marathon—we shall note the heroic first son and the militant, effective

later son. Creasy, in discussing the battle of Arbela, first has to rebut the stock impressions of Alexander, impressions which are close to those about Charles XII and Hitler:

> Until a very recent period, all who wished to "point a moral or adorn a tale," about unreasoning ambition, extravagant pride, and the formidable frenzies of free will when leagued with free power, have never failed to blazon forth the so-called madman of Macedonia as one of the most glaring examples.[52]

Creasy then rebuts the commonplace assertion that Alexander's successes "were the mere results of fortunate rashness and unreasoning pugnacity" by stating that "Napoleon selected Alexander as one of the seven greatest generals. . . ."[53] Without detracting from Alexander's reputation as a military leader, it is possible to state that the heroic elements were pre-eminent in Alexander. The chagrin that his father would leave him nothing to conquer, the impetuousness of a conqueror, cannot be overlooked. And, though Creasy gives it a different interpretation, Alexander's behavior on the night before Arbela certainly lends itself to being described as heroic:

> Darkness had closed over the tents of the Macedonians when Alexander's veteran general, Parmenio, came to him and proposed that they should make a night attack on the Persians. The king is said to have answered, that he scorned to filch a victory, and that Alexander must conquer openly and fairly. . . .
> It was necessary for Alexander not only to beat Darius, but to gain such a victory as should leave his rival without apology for defeat, and without hope of recovery.[54]

Less debatable concerning heroics is Creasy's description of Alexander during the battle: "It was ever his custom to expose his life freely in battle, and to emulate the personal prowess of his great ancestor, Achilles."[55]

If first son Alexander is an example of a heroic general whose military judgment was not impaired by his omnipotent boldness, we find in later son Miltiades cool, effective judgment almost free of heroic omnipotence. Creasy describes him about thirty-eight years before the battle of Marathon. On the death of his older brother, ruler of the Chersonese, Miltiades was sent out to take his place:

We find, in the first act recorded of him, proof of the same resolute
and unscrupulous spirit that marked his mature age. His brother's
authority in the principality had been shaken by war and revolt;
Miltiades determined to rule more securely. On his arrival he kept
close within his house, as if he was mourning for his brother. The
principal men of the Chersonese, . . . went together to the house of
Miltiades on a visit of condolence. As soon as he had thus got them
in his power, he made them all prisoners. He then asserted and main-
tained his own absolute authority on the peninsula. . . ."[56]

Miltiades was not concerned here, as Creasy says Alexander
might have been, that the principal men of the Chersonese might
claim later that they had been defeated by treachery and would
refuse to stay defeated. On the contrary, Miltiades saw a chance
to win and he seized upon it. Later he tried the same technique
on Darius:

When the Persian power was extended to the Hellespont . . . Miltiades . . . submitted to King Darius; . . . Miltiades and the vassal
Greeks of Asia Minor were left by the Persian king in charge of the
bridge across the Danube, when the invading army crossed the river. . . .
On learning the reverses that Darius met with in the Scythian
wilderness, Miltiades proposed to his companions that they should
break the bridge down, and leave the Persian king and his army to
perish. . . .[57]

Later, when Persia sent a naval squadron against the Chersonese,
"Miltiades knew that resistance was hopeless; . . . he loaded five
galleys with all the treasure that he could collect and sailed away
for Athens.[58]

We see Miltiades as a cool-headed, effective predator, fighting when the odds were in his favor and retreating, without
pangs of humiliation, when the odds were against him. At the
battle council before Marathon he advocates a sudden attack:

Acquainted with the organization of the Persian armies, Miltiades
was convinced of the superiority of the Greek troops if properly
handled; he saw with the military eye of a great general the advantage which the position of the forces gave him for a sudden
attack. . . .[59]

Creasy praises his military genius in the battle of Marathon, in
particular his original idea of weakening his center and strengthening his flanks. The later fate of Miltiades is interesting in that

it underlines his cool predatory exploitation of friend as well as foe. After the victory at Marathon, he induced the Athenians to outfit him with galleys and legions so that he could lead this force "to a land where there was gold in abundance to be won with ease."[60] However, he used the expeditionary force in an unsuccessful attempt to settle a private quarrel. "The indignation of the Athenians was proportionate to the hopes and excitement which his promises had raised."[61] In view of his services at Marathon, the death sentence was commuted to a fine.

With these two examples in mind—the heroic, strife-loving first son Alexander and the cool, effective exploiter of weaknesses, later son Miltiades—let us skip over many centuries and view some of the generals in the American Civil War. A general whose heroics are similar to Alexander's is first son "Fighting" Joe Hooker. The nickname given him may be indicative. He is not called "Stonewall" like that later son, nor labeled "Swamp Fox" like later son Marion. What is behind this nickname? Fletcher Pratt gives a clue. Writing about Hooker's frontal heroics he says: "Hooker was . . . a brave, vain, insubordinate man who could lead a charge supremely well." "Hooker was the best assault-commander in the army. . . ."[62] Hooker's omnipotent heroics can be seen at Chattanooga, after he had been minimized by removal from command of the Army of the Potomac. When Sherman pushed across at Missionary Ridge,

Simultaneously Hooker had been ordered to demonstrate at the foot of Lookout. That was too passive a role for Fighting Joe, the vain man; "May I take the height?" he asked. "If I can," said Grant, eyeing him narrowly. He [Hooker] put the whole two corps . . . in the line of battle with an exhortation to remember that the men they were facing had declared they were "Eastern counter-jumpers" whom they could always beat. They stormed that huge mountain in snarling fury. . . ."[63]

Stimulated by Hooker's "Avenge your Honor" appeal, that attack was highly successful. There appears, then, to be sufficient reason for the nickname "Fighting Joe." Whenever Hooker felt belittled, cut down to ordinary, nonheroic size, he became visibly angry and responded with frontal attacks which frequently carried the day on the battlefield. This type of attack can bring consternation in the ranks of the foe, because there seems to be something inhumanly superhuman and weird about it. Thus, Bakunin was possessed with the devil's courage; Charles XII of Sweden had a similar effect on many of his opponents. The most recent example of this kind of violent intimidating heroics might be seen in first son General George Patton. His battlefield speeches to his soldiers, his exposure to danger during frontal attacks, are too well known to require elaboration here. The nickname of "Blood and Guts" seems appropriate. Here is the implication of barbaric emotions—not the implication of rational craftiness as is conveyed by later son Rommel's nickname, "Desert Fox."

These examples from warfare and politics serve to strengthen the author's impression that heroics and militancy tend to be respective characteristics of certain first and later sons in action. This speculative generalization must be qualified by the statement that there are no hard and fast trends. Not all first-son generals are given to heroics—Caesar, Washington, Pershing, and Wavel being eloquent testimony to this fact. And there are not a few instances in which otherwise cool militant later sons have indulged in what seems to be omnipotent heroics—as witness Lee's ordering of Pickett's frontal charge and Admiral Tyron's overestimation of his control of the situation when his flagship was rammed by a sister ship during ordinary maneuvers. Notwithstanding these exceptions, the author's impression is that the rough trends are in the direction stated. Needless to say, much detailed investigation is necessary to substantiate this impression.

To summarize—the purpose of this chapter has been to demonstrate that a certain action type—the heroic—occurs more frequently in the connectedness-prone first son, whereas another action type—the militant—is seen more often in the disconnectedness-prone later son. Although both types are ambitiously striving for conquest and ascendancy, the heroic is concerned especially with proofs of his omnipotence, whereas the militant is preoccupied particularly with attainment of real power. The former's concern with inner omnipotence gives a certain flavor to his actions, a flavor of being more or less violently possessed by his emotions. This characteristic sometimes makes for success in action, sometimes for failure. The latter's concern with real external power makes him more open-eyed, rational, and realistic —a characteristic which more frequently than not makes for success in action.

The larger-than-life-size orientation of the heroic, and the actual-life-size orientation of the militant are, of course, not confined to men in action. Although our main interest in these two chapters has been in action types, the above-mentioned orientations can be basic themes for men of thought. It is this direction which will be pursued as we proceed now to a detailed consideration of Carlyle and Emerson.

CHAPTER V

The Sense of Self

THE "I" AND THE "ME"

THE TWO MEN who will be of principal interest to us now provide a uniquely appropriate bridge between the foregoing and ensuing chapters. We encountered melancholic first son Carlyle and optimistic later son Emerson when we considered prevailing moods; and in tracing the intellectual influences on heroic-minded Hitler, an allusion was made to Carlyle. Now we shall consider these men from a somewhat different viewpoint. To be sure, the new viewpoint will not be totally unfamiliar. Much of what has been said about inner omnipotence and external power is carried over. But, as the chapter heading indicates, the special emphasis is placed on the sense of self. Why this egotistic feeling is subdivided into "I-ness" and "me-ness" will become apparent only gradually.

We shall not rely heavily on the most direct way of investigating the sense of self; that is, ascertaining what introspective thinkers have said about their own selves. Instead, we shall mainly utilize what thinkers have said about other selves, and trust that considerable personal revelation will be forthcoming. This method is especially applicable to Carlyle and Emerson, inasmuch as they both thought and wrote about great men. The excessive credit given to great men by Carlyle is in decided contrast to that given by Emerson, and has made Carlyle in the eyes of the world a prime example and advocate of unbridled egotism. This impression will not be disputed here; Carlyle is an excellent example of aggrandizing I-ness. But little attention has been paid to the more receptively aggrandizing me-ness kind of egotism shown by Emerson.

Some theoretical discussion concerning the self and egotism is necessary before we occupy ourselves with Carlyle and Emerson. A first definition of egotism may be that it reflects what a person wants from life—what will satisfy the ego. From what has been described in previous chapters, it appears that the connectedness-prone first sons tend to wish to satisfy an inner life (inner morality, memories of the past, omnipotence), whereas the disconnectedness-prone later sons tend to wish to satisfy a more immediate outer life (outer morality, current external power). What specific forms these inner and outer gratifications will take is quite another matter. But, as a start, it may be useful to think of a basic source division, inner and outer satisfactions.

Let us consider a homely illustration of this division. Take two sons in a family. The mother, upon leaving for errands, has instructed her sons not to dip into the cookie jar. The cookies are a real, immediate source of enjoyment, and a direct gratification would be to eat them despite the mother's wishes. Another kind of satisfaction—much less direct—would result from not eating them. Instead of the direct oral pleasures, there would be the admiring, approving smile on the mother's face when she returned, or the even less concrete approval from the inner moral voice. Our discussion in the previous chapters would lead us to expect that the son who partook of the immediate outside pleasure would be more often the later son, whereas the son who was content with delayed or inner pleasure would be more often the first son.

These considerations suggest that in terms of egotistic life-aims the first sons are searching for appreciation and admiration, whereas the later sons are desirous of more basic, concrete satisfactions. Put in negative terms, the former are susceptible to the trauma of being demeaned, the latter to the trauma of being deprived. The way of life for the demeanable, with its emphasis on inner nutrition and self value, appears to many to be lacking in practical common sense. Such critics when viewing the situation in India, for example, where sacred cattle roam the streets freely while people die of hunger are likely to comment, "Isn't that going too far from life as it really is?" On the other hand, the way of life for the deprivable, with its emphasis on rather immediate, concrete, external gratifications raises fewer eyebrows.

It is eminently practical and uncomplicated. Nevertheless, a persistent corps of critics throughout the ages have asked, "Is there not more to life than this?"

With this background, we are perhaps better prepared to discuss Carlyle and Emerson. Carlyle will be used to illustrate the connectedness-prone first son who is susceptible to demeanment and who has to do something radically larger than life-size to solve his wounded omnipotence. His psychic nutrition consists principally of appreciation and, thus, he will put a high premium on Man, the source of appreciation supplies, or on an anthropomorphized God, who is a similar source. The overestimation of Man leads to the concept of Superman and the egotism involved is what we are calling I-ness. Emerson, on the other hand, will be used to illustrate the disconnectedness-prone later son whose psychic nutrition depends less on ethereal appreciation and more on tangible satisfaction. He is more susceptible to being deprived than being demeaned. Because his nutritive wherewithal comes from the outside, he feels a reverence for what on the outside produces direct concrete supplies, be it Nature, the social community, or the machine. His kind of receptive egotism—the kind possessed by the hungry man seeking provisions from Nature—is what we are calling me-ness. It should be emphasized that these two kinds of egotism are not mutually exclusive. Indeed, all men possess both kinds. Carlyle had to eat and Emerson required appreciation. The point that we shall be making, however, is that first son Carlyle is principally characterized by I-ness and later son Emerson by me-ness.

The overestimation of man, characteristic in the first son, is disclosed in Carlyle's title *On Heroes and Hero-Worship;* the matter-of-fact estimate by the later son in Emerson's title *Representative Men*. The explanatory note on the back cover of a recent paperback combining the two works gives some background and evaluation:

In 1833, when Emerson and Carlyle first met . . . the meeting gave both men a sense of sympathetic recognition. Early in their conversation it was revealed that they shared a belief in the importance of Great Men. Eight years later, in 1841, *On Heroes* appeared, and its influence on Emerson is undoubted. Within four years he had prepared a set of lectures on what he called *Representative Men*, which complements the Carlyle book. Where the Scot was vehement and dyspeptic, haranguing against democracy and asserting that the history of the world is "at bottom the History of the Great Men who have worked here," Emerson was gently optimistic, with a regard for great men, and, indeed, all men, as "lenses through which we read our own minds."[1]

Examination of the text suggests that the above capsule evaluation is more correct about frontal-attacking Carlyle than about less overt Emerson. Beginning with Carlyle, we shall see many of the characteristics we have described above. He selects for illustration not the simple Pagan Enjoyer of Nature's Provisions but the first Pagan Thinker:

You remember that fancy of Plato's, of a man who had grown to maturity in some dark distance, and was brought on a sudden into the upper air to see the sun rise. What would his wonder be, his rapt astonishment at the sight we daily witness with indifference! With the free open sense of a child, yet with the ripe faculty of a man, his whole heart would be kindled by that sight, he would discern it well to be Godlike, his soul would fall down and worship before it. Now, just such a childlike greatness was in the primitive nations. The first Pagan Thinker among rude men, the first man that began to think, was precisely this child-man of Plato's.[2]

We might imagine the fellowmen of this first thinker saying to him: Why complicate things? That is the sun that keeps us warm and makes things grow. If you must collect all these plural provisions under one name, why not call it nature or mother nature? Why introduce the idea of God and a reality beyond the obvious reality? The first thinker's response might have been along the lines of Carlyle's next comments: "We call that fire of the black thundercloud 'electricity,' and lecture learnedly about it, and grind the like of it out of glass and silk: but *what* is it? What made it? Whence comes it? Whither goes it?"[3] The mere utility of knowledge which makes life more comfortable is not sufficient for Carlyle.

The intimate connection of the worship of a celestial omnipotent being with that of a terrestrial omnipotent man, the "I" self, is seen next in Carlyle:

But now if all things whatsoever that we look upon are emblems to us of the Highest God, I add that more so than any of them is man such an emblem. You have heard of St. Chrysostom's celebrated saying in reference to the Shekinah, or Ark of Testimony, visible Revelation of God, among the Hebrews: "The true Shekinah is Man! Yes, it is even so; it is no vain phrase; it is veritably so. The essence of our being, the mystery in us that calls itself 'I,'—ah, what words have we for such things?—is a breath of Heaven; the Highest Being reveals himself in man."[4]

We later see that Carlyle recognizes with typical exasperation that many critics, instead of making great men larger than life, try to cut them down to life-size:

I am well aware that in these days Hero-worship, the thing I call Hero-worship, professes to have gone out, and finally ceased. This . . . is an age that as it were denies the existence of great men; denies the desirableness of great men. Show our critics a great man, a Luther for example, they begin to what they call "account" for him; not to worship him, but to take dimensions of him—and bring him out to be a little kind of man! He was the "creature of the Time," they say; the Time called him forth, the Time did everything, he nothing—but what we the little critics could have done too![5]

Thus, Carlyle approves of the noble veneration that first son Boswell had for Johnson. If Carlyle had lived much longer, he would have bared his fangs at the miniaturizing biographical sketches written by later son Lytton Strachey. Carlyle's reverent connection with the past is seen in:

Is it [Scandinavian Hero-worship] not as the half-dumb stifled voice of the long-buried generations of our own Fathers, calling out of the depths of ages to us, in whose veins their blood still runs: "This then, this is what *we* made of the world: this is all the image and notion we could form to ourselves of this great mystery of a Life and Universe. Despise it not. You are raised high above it, to large free scope of vision; but you too are not yet at the top. No, your notion too, so much enlarged, is but a partial, imperfect one. . . ."[6]

Here is seen not only the connection with the Past but also the relay baton-passing role of the Present Generation. It recalls first son Einstein's explanation of his creative work: that he was able to stand on the shoulders of past contributors and thus see farther.

Carlyle's actual heroes are for the most part first sons. It is only in considering men of action, in the chapter "The Hero as King," that he limits himself to two later sons, Cromwell and Napoleon. But the chapter "The Hero as Poet" is primarily about first sons Dante and Shakespeare, with some worship of first son Goethe and some criticism of later son Bacon. After extolling Shakespeare, Carlyle writes:

Novum Organum, and all the intellect you will find in Bacon, is of a quite secondary order; earthly, material, poor in comparison with this. Among modern men, one finds, in strictness, almost nothing of the same rank. Goethe alone, since the days of Shakespeare, reminds me of it.[7]

For "The Hero as Man of Letters" Carlyle selects two first sons, Johnson and Burns, whom he rather unqualifiedly admires, and one later son, Rousseau, about whom he is ambivalent. But what he says about Rousseau is pertinent to our point concerning the deprivable later son:

Of Rousseau and his Heroism I cannot say so much. He is not what I call a strong man . . . at best, intense rather than strong. . . .

We name him here because, with all his drawbacks . . . he has the first and chief characteristic of a Hero; he is heartily *in earnest*. . . .

The fault and misery of Rousseau was what we easily name by a single word Egoism. . . . He had not perfected himself into victory over mere Desire; a mean hunger, in many sorts, was still the motive principle of him.[8]

An interesting point is that Carlyle, the ultimate worshiper of the "I" is critical of Rousseau's egoism. One possibility is, of course, that Carlyle may be inconsistent and, like many of us, sees only the mote in the other's "I." But it is also possible that Carlyle is in favor of the egotistical "I" and against Rousseau's egotistical "me." The self as "I" is an organizing, dominating entity—the self as "me" is a more plastic entity which receives supplies from the outside.

Carlyle relates an incident purportedly illustrating how Rousseau was hungry for external plaudits and then one which has a more simple physiological basis. "[A respectful visitor of some rank] finds Jean Jacques full of the sourest unintelligible humour. 'Monsieur,' said Jean Jacques, with flaming eyes, 'I know why you come here. You come to see what a poor life I lead; how little is my poor pot that is boiling there. Well, look into the pot! There is half a pound of meat, one carrot and three onions; that is all: go and tell the whole world that, if you like, Monsieur.' "[9] While there might be some chauvinism in Scotsman Carlyle's ambivalence about Rousseau and two other

French later sons, Voltaire and Napoleon, he does speak admiringly of one Frenchman, first son Mirabeau.

In going now to the more matter-of-fact and practical Emerson, we should keep in mind, for the sake of contrast, Carlyle's
impatience with mere utility. Emerson's first chapter is characteristically titled "Uses of Great Men," and in the very first paragraph the directly useful oral "cookie jar orientation" is revealed:
"It is natural to believe in great men. . . . In the legends of the
Gautama, the first men ate the earth, and found it deliciously
sweet."[10] (Carlyle's first Pagan Thinker would have asked *Why*
is it deliciously sweet?") Emerson's first specific mention of a
kind of Great Man occurs in the fourth paragraph—he is func-
tional rather than speculative. "The knowledge that in the city
is a man who invented the railroad, raises the credit of all the
citizens."[11] The idea of useful supplies from the outside appears
shortly: "Men have a pictorial or representative quality, and serve
us in the intellect. . . . As plants convert the minerals into food
for animals, so each man converts some material in nature to
human use. The inventors of fire, electricity . . . severally make
an easy way for all. . . ."[12]

We have seen earlier that Carlyle would further ask the
inventor of electricity, "What is it," "Where came it?" And
further as to utility we can quote Carlyle:

The uses of this Dante? We will not say much about his uses. . . .
We will not estimate the Sun by the quantity of gas-light it saves
us; Dante shall be invaluable, or of no value. . . .
    Effect? Influence? Utility? Let a man *do* his work; the fruit of
it is the care of Another than he. It will grow its own fruit. . . ."[13]

For Carlyle it is more than "I" who grows the fruit rather than
the "me" who eats it which is important.

To return to Emerson, there can be seen beneath the practical matter-of-factness about great men an impulse to minimize
them, to poke holes in their wide fabric. We mentioned this
tendency in the previous chapter as a later-son intellectual tactic
to produce an equality between himself and the first son. A
rebellious equalization theme with undertones of disconnection
with the past may be seen in Emerson's writing:

Rotation is her [nature's] remedy. The soul is impatient of masters,
and eager for change. Housekeepers say of a domestic who has been

valuable, "she had lived with me long enough." . . . We touch and go, and sip the foam of many lives. Rotation is the law of nature. . . .

Against the best [of our masters] there is a finer remedy. The power which they communicate is not theirs. When we are exalted by ideas, we do not owe this to Plato, but to the idea, to which also Plato was debtor.[14]

In contrast to Carlyle, Emerson would have us revere the idea that the great man happens to possess or represent rather than the great man himself. No idolatry of Man, nor of the self, nor of the "I" for Emerson. To carry this notion so far that little credit is given Plato makes one suspect there might be rivalry beneath the matter-of-factness. This appears to be the case in the following passage:

Every mother wishes one son a genius, though all the rest should be mediocre. But a new danger appears in the excess influence of the great man. His attractions warp us from our place. We have become underlings and intellectual suicides. Ah! yonder in the horizon is our help:—other great men, new qualities, counterweights and checks on each other. We cloy of the honey of each peculiar greatness. Every hero becomes a bore at last. Perhaps Voltaire was not bad-hearted, yet he said of the good Jesus, even, "I pray you, let me never hear that man's name again." They cry up the virtues of George Washington. "Damn George Washington!" is the poor Jacobin's whole speech and confutation. But it is human nature's indispensable defence. . . . We balance one man with his opposite, and the health of the state depends on the see-saw.[15]

For Emerson, individuality is as much not being over-whelmed by a great man as it is the expression of what is within the person. There is a threat to individuality or to self-identity if one gets too intimate with another. This anxiety may lie behind Francis Bacon's disconnectedness advice: "Love your friend as if he were to become your enemy and your enemy as if he were to become your friend."[16] The arm's length, sip-and-run orientation of Emerson again is seen in his: "There is somewhat deceptive about the intercourse of minds. The boundaries are invisible, but they are never crossed. There is such good will to impart, and such good will to receive, that each threatens to become the other; but the law of individuality collects its secret strength; you are you, and I am I, and so we remain."[17] Emerson's use of "I" here seems to issue from defense of self rather than from a dominating self-assertion. It is as though he is saying to the great "I" first son, "Stay at a distance so that my small 'I' already so submerged by my 'Me' needs can have an opportunity to grow—to flourish away from the shadow cast by your 'Great I.' " His feelings about growth and inhibiting shadows come out in:

We have never come at the true and best benefit of any genius, as long as we believe him an original force. In the moment when he ceases to help us as a cause, he begins to help us more as an effect. Then he appears as an exponent of the vaster mind and will. The opaque self becomes transparent with the light of the First Cause.[18]

In a subtle way Emerson carries out his intent to deflate the great men of any original contribution. His first great man is Plato. No one could tell from the opening sentence that Emerson wishes to level Plato to ordinary size: "Among books, Plato only is entitled to Omar's fanatical compliment to the Koran, when he says, 'burn the libraries, for their value is in this book.' These sentences contain the culture of nations; these are the corner- stone of schools; these are the fountain-head of literatures."[19] The later-son tactics, as we saw in military strategy, is not to engage in a frontal attack but to make a deceptive feint. On the second page Emerson begins the covert leveling attack:

This range of Plato instructs us what to think of the vexed question concerning his reputed works,—what are genuine, what spurious. It is singular that wherever we find a man higher, by a whole head, than any of his contemporaries, it is sure to come into doubt what are his real works. Thus Homer, Plato, Raffaelle, Shakespeare. For these men magnetise their contemporaries, so that their companions do for them what they can never do for themselves; and the great man does thus live in several bodies, and write, or paint, or act by many hands: and after some time it is not easy to say what is the authentic work of the master, and what is only of his school.[20]

Emerson continues this leveling theme, along with hungry oral understones, in describing his next great man, "Swedenborg; or The Mystic" (birth order unknown):

As happens in great men, he seemed, by the variety and amount of his powers, to be a composition of several persons,—like the giant fruits which one matured in gardens by the union of four or five single blossoms. . . .

Swedenborg was born into an atmosphere of great ideas. 'Tis hard to say what was his own, yet his life was dignified by noblest pictures of the universe. . . .

Yet the proximity of these [other] geniuses, one or other of whom had introduced all his leading ideas, makes Swedenborg another example of the difficulty, even in a highly fertile genius, of proving originality. . . .[21]

The chapter on "Shakespeare; or The Poet" begins with the sentence: "Great men are more distinguished by range and extent, than by originality."[22] Later: "Great genial power, one would almost say, consists in not being original at all; in being altogether receptive; in letting the world do all, and suffering the spirit of the hour to pass unobstructed through the mind."[23] (Rather than the "I" as author, there is the "me" as receptor.) Emerson does pay the usual homage to Shakespeare, but not the reverent kind expressed by Carlyle who wrote: "I think the best judgment not of this country only, but of Europe at large, is slowly pointing to the conclusion, That Shakespeare is the chief of all Poets hitherto; the greatest intellect who, in our recorded world, has left record of himself in the way of Literature."[24]

Emerson's evaluation of Napoleon is much more sympathetic than Carlyle's, who wrote:

Napoleon does by no means seem to me so great a man as Cromwell. . . . I find in him no such *sincerity* as in Cromwell; only a far inferior sort. . . .

An element of blamable ambition shows itself, from the first, in this man; gets the victory over him at last, and involves him and his work in ruin. . . .

"False is a bulletin" became a proverb in Napoleon's time. He makes what excuse he could for it: that it was necessary to mislead the enemy, to keep up his own men's courage, and so forth. On the whole, there are no excuses. A man in no case has liberty to tell lies.[25]

Carlyle's inner voice of morality which condemns Napoleon's opportunitistic tendencies does not appear in Emerson's reactions. We should not forget that Emerson was the one who declared that consistency is the hobgoblin of small minds and that, consequently, he would not be as revulsed by Napoleon's liberty with the truth. Emerson's tolerance of Napoleon may arise from the latter's "modesty" about his accomplishment. Thus:

Bonaparte was the idol of common men, because he had in transcendent degree the qualities and powers of common men. There is

a certain satisfaction in coming down to the lowest ground of politics, for we get rid of cant and hypocrisy.[26]

Emerson quotes Napoleon:

"They charge me with the commission of great crimes: men of my
stamp do not commit crimes. Nothing has been more simple than
my elevation; . . . it was owing to the peculiarity of the times. . . .
I have always marched with the opinion of great masses, and with
events. . . . My son cannot replace me; I could not replace myself.
I am the creature of circumstances."[27]

One gets the impression that Emerson is easier on those who
admit that "the age made me" rather than on those who claim,
"I made the age." Emerson even goes so far as to describe
Napoleon as original: "This deputy of the nineteenth century
added to his gifts a capacity for speculation on general topics. . . .
His opinion is always original, and to the purpose."[28] With Plato,
Shakespeare, and Goethe, Emerson took special pains to deflate
the notion of originality. But with Napoleon, the spokesman for
the Common Man, Emerson does not strongly challenge his
particular originality.

Emerson's dubiousness about proclaimed outsized greatness
is best seen, however, in his chapter on "Montaigne; or The
Sceptic." Whatever latent sympathy he may have had for
Napoleon, his fullest and most heartfelt allegiance appears to be
with later son Montaigne. The chapter does not begin with the
customary caution that originality may be derivative. Instead, it
begins with a very perceptive description of types, one which
the reader will by now find familiar. Emerson says:

Life is a pitching of this penny—heads or tails. . . . This head and
this tail are called, in the language of philosophy, Infinite and Finite;
Relative and Absolute; Apparent and Real. . . .

Each man is born with a predisposition to one or the other of
these sides of nature; and it will easily happen that men will be found
devoted to one or the other. One class has the perception of difference, and is conversant with facts and surfaces; cities and persons;
and the bringing certain things to pass;—the men of talent and action.
Another class have the perception of identity, and are men of faith
and philosophy, men of genius.

Each of these riders drives too fast. . . . Read the haughty language in which Plato and the Platonists speak of all men who are
not devoted to their own shining abstractions: other men are rats
and mice. The literary class is usually proud and exclusive. The

correspondence of Pope and Swift describes mankind around them as monsters; and that of Goethe and Schiller, in our own times, is scarcely more kind.

(Pope, Swift, Goethe, and Schiller are first sons.)

The trade in our streets believes in no metaphysical causes. . . . Hot life is streaming in a single direction. To the men of this world . . . to the man of ideas appears out of his reason. They alone have reason. . . .
Thus, the men of the senses revenge themselves on the professors, and repay scorn for scorn. The first [professors] had leaped to conclusions not yet ripe, and say more than is true; the others make themselves merry with the philosopher, and weigh man by the pound.[29]

Between these two extremes, Emerson suggests a middle course:

The abstractionist and the materialist thus mutually exasperating each other, and the scoffer expressing the worst of materialism, there arises a third party to occupy the middle ground between these two, the sceptic, namely. He finds both wrong by being in extremes . . . he stands for the intellectual faculties, a cool head, and whatever serves to keep it cool. . . . These qualities meet in the character of Montaigne.[30]

Emerson recounts how his love began and grew for this "admirable gossip." As a boy, Emerson found Montaigne's essays in his father's library: "It seemed to me as if I had myself written the book, in some former life, so sincerely it spoke to my thought and experience."[31] Emerson for the first time then really participated in hero worship, i.e., when he discovered himself in Montaigne. Thus: "Montaigne is the frankest and honestest of all writers. . . ." "The sincerity and marrow of the man reaches to his sentences."[32]

So much for what might be gained by studying Carlyle's and Emerson's writings on the subject of great men. We can learn further about these two thinkers if we consult the writings of later son Henry James. Particularly, we may become more informed about their interaction as friends and as to how such opposite personalities can, in a complementary way, be of benefit to each other. James, though quite aware of their limitations, sees the best of both of them; and, in a characteristic later-son style, does not go overboard in his positive evaluation of these men. The undertone one feels is a calm, rational assessment of the good in Carlyle and Emerson.

"The Correspondence of Carlyle and Emerson" (an essay by Henry James that appeared in the *Century Magazine* in June, 1883, which reviewed the two-volume *Correspondence*) is our source of information. James writes:

Carlyle is here in intercourse with a friend for whom, almost alone among the persons with whom he had dealings, he appears to have entertained a sentiment of respect. . . . It is singular . . . that . . . he never appears to have known the satiric fury [to Emerson] which he directed at so many other objects. . . . Emerson . . . was so much more kindly a judge, so much more luminous a nature. . . . Carlyle was the more constant writer of the two, especially toward the end of their correspondence; he constantly expresses the desire to hear from Emerson oftener.[33]

We may see here some of the first-son desire for intimate connectedness and the later-son desire for disconnected arm's-lengthness. Beneath his savagery, Carlyle wanted the worshiping unity that comes with connectedness; a re-experiencing, perhaps, of the original intense mother-child symbiosis. Because the unity would bear Carlyle's stamp, it would become too oppressive for Emerson who would much prefer to sip from than to be engulfed by a "Great I" personality. From James we get the impression that hero-worshiper Carlyle was in a characteristic way passionately (and perhaps blindly) fond of Emerson, whereas Emerson was characteristically detached, practical, and skeptical. In accounting for why Emerson was not afraid of Carlyle's fury being visited on Concord, James says:

It is true that Carlyle gave him constantly the encouragement of a high and eloquent esteem for his own utterances. He [Carlyle] was evidently a great and genuine admirer of the genius, the spirit of his American friend, and he expresses this feeling on a dozen occasions.
     "My friend, you know not what you have done for me there [in the oration of *The American Scholar*]. It was long decades of years that I had heard nothing but the infinite jangling and jabbering, . . . my soul had sunk down sorrowful and said . . . and lo, out of the West comes a clear utterance, . . . and I *have* a kinsman and brother: . . . I could have *wept* to read that speech; the clear high melody of it went tingling through my heart. . . ."[34]

Emerson, in return, shows little of this passionate need. Not only does he write less often; many of his letters tell of practical business transactions. James writes:

> Emerson took upon himself to present *Sartor Resartus* and some of its successors to the American public, and he constantly reports to the author upon the progress of this enterprise. He transmits a great many booksellers' accounts as well as a considerable number of bills of exchange, and among the American publishers is a most faithful and zealous representative of his friend.[35]

Later:

> Emerson assures him of the growth of his public on this side of the ocean, and of there being many ingenuous young persons of both sexes to whom his writings are as meat and drink.[36]

Emerson appears, then, consistent in his notion about uses. He is practically useful to Carlyle rather than idolatrous. How he uses Carlyle is not so clear as how the latter uses him. Perhaps Emerson sips intellectually from Carlyle and conceals this oral hunger by referring to the "meat and drink" of anonymous "young persons." Perhaps Emerson gains self-stature and power by being the one who sells Carlyle to America.

In general, as was said, James deals rather fairly, objectively, and sympathetically with both men. He notes the pessimism of Carlyle, the optimism of Emerson. He notes their differences in style:

> The violent color, the large, avalanche-movement of Carlyle's style— as if a mass of earth and rock and vegetation had detached itself and came bouncing and bumping forward—make the efforts of his correspondent appear a little pale and stiff. There is always something high and pure in Emerson's speech, however, and it has often a perfect propriety—seeming, in answer to Carlyle's extravagances, the note of reason and justice. "Faith and love are apt to be spasmodic in the best minds. Men live on the brink of mysteries and harmonies into which they never enter, and with their hand on the door-latch they die outside."[37]

But James (perhaps understandably in a later son) does not appear to see the self-justifying, the anti-Great Man undertone in the last quotation. If men die before they unlatch the door to the mysteries, what is the use of their trying? "Be like me or Montaigne," Emerson seems to be saying; "no extremes, no poetic ecstasies or raptures; be of small or spasmodic faith, be detached, because you will never see the promised land." James' empathy with Emerson's viewpoint is suggested by the following:

It must be remembered, of course, that the importance of the individual was Emerson's great doctrine; everyone had a kingdom within himself—was potential sovereign, by divine right, over a multitude of inspirations and virtues. . . .

There was no presumption against even the humblest [the present author would substitute "especially" for "even"], and the ear of the universe was open to any articulate voice. In this respect the opposition to Carlyle was complete. The great Scotchman thought *all* talk a jabbering of apes; whereas Emerson . . . regarded each delivery of a personal view as a new fact, to be estimated on its merits. In a genuine democracy all things are democratic; and this [Emerson's] spirit . . . was the natural product of a society in which it was held that everyone was equal to everyone else. It was as natural on the other side that Carlyle's philosophy should have aristocratic premises, and that he should call aloud for that imperial master, of the necessity for whom the New England mind was so serenely unconscious.[38]

Our extended discussion of Carlyle and Emerson may have served to illustrate the particular thesis of this chapter as well as other matters. In their attitudes toward greatness and bigness, Carlyle shows the connectedness-prone first-son tendency to put Man on a pedestal, to consider admiration of Man a *sine qua non* for life, and to protect against personal demeanment by emphasizing the lordly "I" part of the self. Emerson, on the other hand, displays the disconnectedness-prone later-son tendency to value highly the utilizable external supplies and the comparatively impersonal producers of supplies and to protest against deprivation by emphasizing the receptive "me" part of the self. In the passages quoted, Carlyle reveals himself unmistakably. He is for heroes, for greatness, and for the "I." What Emerson is for is not so apparent. The point made in the foregoing paragraphs is that Emerson is not just neutral and objective about greatness— he is *against* it. But his later-son nonfrontal method of attacking bigness is so disarming, mild, and reasonable that he comes off as an impartial humane person, and Carlyle as an angry, biased one. It seems that Emerson (particularly in his identification with Montaigne) grinds his own axe as much as Carlyle does his. The difference is that the former does it covertly, the latter overtly.

While there is little doubt that Carlyle exemplifies the hypertrophy of the I-self, the evidence introduced so far only hints that Emerson exemplifies the receptive me-self. It is mainly by default, by Emerson's being against the great I-self, that we may suspect that he exhibits a different brand of egotism, one that we are calling me-ness. He is not the best example of me-ness—later son Whitman would be a much better choice. But since Emerson wrote about great men and does exemplify receptive tendencies, he is a fitting contrast to Carlyle. The task of distinguishing I-ness from me-ness still lies ahead of us. A considerable obstacle derives from the fact that very few, if any, thinkers have written about the "me" as such. When they are not proponents of the "I," their opposition takes the form of not emphasizing the "me" but rather of doubting that there is a persistent, organized "I," or emphasizing a more plastic, changing, receptive, and sensual Self.

As has been indicated, an indirect way of evaluating I-ness and me-ness is to ascertain a man's attitude toward Homo sapiens (the reflection of overestimated I-ness) and toward bountiful Nature (a reflection of receptive me-ness). First son Carlyle clearly regards heroic Homo sapiens as the chosen species; later son Emerson is not so sure of this. Before we examine Emerson's attitude toward Nature, let us consider the fruitfulness in this regard of employing the terms Heroic Vitalist and Nature Vitalist. Bentley's two prime examples of Heroic Vitalists were, it will be recalled, first sons Carlyle and Nietzsche. Can there also be a Nature Vitalist? Edmund Wilson in *Axel's Castle* supplies a cue for a Heroic-Nature subdivision. In discussing the Romantic poets, who insist on a vital essence in the world, he writes, "In any case, it is always, as in Wordsworth, the individual sensibility or, as in Byron, the individual will, with which the Romantic poet is preoccupied."[39] Wordsworth, a later son, is perhaps the prime example of the Nature Poet; Byron, a first son, equally so the Heroic Poet. It seems appropriate then to think of two types of vitalists. One type, Byronesque, emphasizes the I-ness involved in the will, the heroic. The other type, Wordsworthian, emphasizes the me-ness involved in the receptive sensibility to outer stimuli, to Nature, the provisioner.

Let us now return to Emerson and see whether there is justification in designating him as a Nature Vitalist. If such be the case, we shall have more warrant in considering him an example of the receptive me-self. Evidence of Emerson's intimacy with Nature (as contrasted with his arm's-length detached relationship with Man) is given by Henry James in another essay on Emerson:

> Courteous and humane to the furthest possible point, to the point of an almost profligate surrender of his attention, there was no familiarity in him, no personal evidity. Even his letters to his wife are courtesies, they are not familiarities. . . .
>
> His observation of Nature was exquisite—always the direct, irresistible impression.
>
> "The hawking of the wild geese flying by night; the thin note of the companionable titmouse in the winter day; the fall of swarms of flies in autumn, from combats high in the air, pattering down on the leaves like rain; the angry hiss of the wood-birds . . ." (*Literary Ethics*).
>
> I have said there was no familiarity in him, but he was familiar with woodland creatures and sounds. Certainly, too, he was on terms of free association with his books, which were numerous and dear to him; though Mr. Cabot says, doubtless with justice, that his dependence on them was slight and that he was not "intimate" with his authors.[40]

One is led to believe that Emerson is afraid of the strong emotions possible to be aroused in him if he were intimate with humans. But with Nature he has no anxiety about being intimate. While others may be drawn to humans by the possibility of a rapturous connection, he is drawn to Nature by the similar possibility. His friend, later son Thoreau, showed the same preferences. Rebellious toward the oppressive Homo sapiens, he easily communed with Nature. As James comments, after noting Thoreau's rebelliously eccentric nonpayment of taxes, the non-wearing of a necktie, etc., "he wrote some beautiful pages, which read like a translation of Emerson into the sounds of the field and forest and which no one who has ever loved nature in New England, or indeed anywhere, can fail to love. . . ."[41]

As was said earlier, it is quite difficult to offer incontrovertible evidence that Emerson exemplifies the receptive me-self. Emerson's well-known remark that consistency is the hobgoblin of small minds strongly indicates that a changing, plastic, receptive self is more to Emerson's liking than a persistent, structuralized, dominating self. Whatever hints we get from later son Emerson are strongly underscored in the case of later son Whit-

man. We have already seen that they have in common an optimism which depends on an ability to disconnect themselves
from evil. The same disconnectedness accounts for their similar
sense of self. Whitman appears to be a marked example of a
highly plastic and highly receptive self. That he had minimal
intuitive feeling of a continuous, predictable, organized I-self is
shown in his remark which goes Emerson's comment on consistency one better: "Do I contradict myself? /Very well then
I contradict myself, . . ."[42] Whitman's receptive me-ness may be
seen not only in the title of the poem "Song of Myself," but also
in the contents which indicate that Whitman's identity is not an
organized "I" but a hungrily receptive repository for all the
stimuli, all the sensations, and all the inhabitants of America.

Our final remarks on the sense of self bring us away from
Carlyle and Emerson to the realm of philosophy. Here we will
have the opportunity to see how among three English empiricists
first sons Locke and Berkeley had a strong intuition of a connected, persistent I-self, whereas later son Hume, with a disconnected view similar to later sons Emerson and Whitman,
doubted the existence of such a phenomenon. C. E. M. Joad's
summary will be quoted at length to this end. He writes
regarding Hume:

The destructive criticism of the commonsense conception of Self
originates, like that of the notion of cause, with Hume . . . it is a
criticism of fundamentally the same order. Just as the criticism of
cause denies the existence of a nexus or a tie binding events and
asserts only a succession of events, so the criticism of the Self denies
a nexus or tie between ideas and experiences and asserts only a succession of ideas and experiences.

[Concerning the common-sense conception of Self]:

Thus a man working at his desk at 10 A.M. is considered by common
sense to be justified in saying, "I am the person who an hour ago
was having breakfast," the word "I" being intended to denote an
entity which remains unchanged, or relatively unchanged in spite of
the difference between its present experiences and its experiences of
an hour ago. . . .
Thus if we think of the ordinary conception of the Self as the
thread of a necklace along which are strung the beads of its psychological states, the effect of Hume's criticism is to affirm the beads
but to deny the thread.[43]

Comparing later son Hume with first sons Locke and Berkeley, Joad summarizes:

"Locke had analysed the process which we call knowledge of the external world into three factors. They were (A), the Self, (B) the experiences of the self which he called ideas, and (C), an external substance *plus* primary qualities which caused the ideas. Berkeley had eliminated (C) and left only (A), the Self, and (B), the Self's ideas. Hume proceeded to eliminate the Self, (A), and left only (B), the ideas or experiences which would normally be said to belong to it.

The universe, then, for Hume, resolves itself into a series of ideas or experiences which only by courtesy are called yours and mine. Indeed, it is only by courtesy title that you and I can be said to exist. More correctly, then, the universe is a series of experiences which are not experiences of anything and do not belong to anybody. They just occur.[44]

In tempered philosophic language, later son Hume has carried to a logical extreme the disconnectedness version of self intuited and written about by later sons Emerson and Whitman. And in similar language first sons Locke and Berkeley have adhered to the connectedness version of self so dramatically and heroically expressed by first son Carlyle. There appears to be no doubt that the connectedness self sense is contained in the word "I." There are many suggestive hints that the disconnectedness self sense is contained in the word "me." More important, however, than the question of whether I-ness and me-ness are the best differentiating terms in this matter is the fact that connectedness-prone first sons tend to have a sense of self different from that of disconnectedness-prone later sons. One of the ways we have tried to describe this difference—apart from I-ness and me-ness—is to have recourse to the terms Heroic Vitalist and Nature Vitalist. Inherent in the term Nature Vitalist is a receptivity to the direct provisions from Nature. It is only in the next chapter that a fuller appreciation of the pertinence of this receptivity will become possible.

CHAPTER VI *Life Aims*

THE CONSERVERS AND THE
CONSUMERS

ASSOCIATED WITH differing senses of the self, two sharply etched alternatives offer themselves in regard to life aims. There are several ways of stating these alternatives. As the chapter subheading indicates, one way is to counterpose immediate gratification of the me-self against delayed gratification of the I-self. Another formulation, more homely but again contrasting vivid immediacy with abstract postponement, resides in the question, "Is it better to eat the bird in hand or to take the risk on the two in the bush?" Still another formulative question is, "Does Man live by bread alone or are spiritual satisfactions quite necessary?" The underlying themes of the foregoing can be consolidated into a question which embodies what we have discussed in previous chapters and indicates all that we will mean, respectively, by "conservers" and "consumers." How important in life are the concrete gratifications received directly and rather immediately from the external environment (hunger assuagement, comfort, and affection), and how important are the more abstract and less immediate gratifications derived from inner sources (ennoblement from reverent worship of heroes and God, peace of mind from obeying the inner moral authority, meaningful completeness from abstract speculation about the world beyond the reality of the immediate senses)?

The thesis of this chapter is that the answers would depend on whether we ask these questions of the disconnectedness-prone later sons or the connectedness-prone first sons. The later son, whom we shall designate as a "consumer," appears more frequently to put the emphasis on the direct, useful, externally provided gratifications of the me-self. The first son, whom we designate as a "conserver," emphasizes the more abstract, internally provided gratifications of the I-self. In documenting this thesis, we shall have to traverse a span of time extending from modern times to antiquity. And we shall eventually come to a consideration of two philosophies, the Stoic and the Epicurean, which exquisitely depict the alternatives we have described above.

Most inquiries into the aims of life begin with a supposedly simple case; namely, primitive society. We shall do the same. But, instead of following the intuitive notions of thinkers about what early primitive life was like, we are on safer ground if we turn to the field anthropologists who study current primitive society. A thorough review of all anthropologists being unfeasible, we shall limit ourselves to one, Malinowski, for a summary statement of the issue of conservation versus consumption. He writes:

Accumulated food can either be squandered or preserved. It can either be an incentive to immediate heedless consumption and light-hearted carelessness about the future, or else it can stimulate man to devising means of hoarding the treasure and of using it for culturally higher purposes. Religion sets its stamp on the culturally valuable attitude and enforces it by public enactment.[1]

It is likely that, if posed with the cookie-jar problem, first son Malinowski would have heeded the wishes of the cookie-provider and foregone the immediate gratification. It is the later son who more often would immediately consume the cookies with a cheerful, "light-hearted carelessness about the future." Malinowski implies that the nonconsumption of food is transformed into a reverent religious feeling. This feeling in turn can fortify a number of different "heroic" activities:

The lover near his sweetheart, the daring adventurer conquering his fear in the face of real danger, the hunter at grips with a wild animal, the craftsman achieving a masterpiece, whether he be savage or civilized, will under such conditions feel altered, uplifted, endowed with higher forces.[2]

This reverent feeling seems similar to that of Carlyle's first Pagan Thinker—whose marvel at God's works prompted speculative intellectual curiosity rather than immediate utilization.

In contrast to first sons Malinowski and Carlyle is the ever sipping, ever hungry later son, Emerson. Although his oral imagery has already been described, the following needs to be quoted in order to see how a large, unsatisfied, direct hunger affects life aims. At the end of his essay on Montaigne, Emerson writes:

The incompetency of power is the universal grief of young and ardent minds. They accuse the divine providence of a certain parsimony. It has shown the heaven and earth to every child, and filled him with a desire for the whole; a desire raging, infinite; a hunger, as of space to be filled with planets; a cry of famine. . . . Then for the satisfaction,—to each man is administered a single drop, a bead of dew of vital power, *per day*,—a cup as large as space, and one drop of the water of life in it. Each man woke in the morning, with an appetite that could eat the solar system like a cake; a spirit for action and passion without bounds; . . . but, on the first motion to prove his strength,—hands, feet, senses, gave way, and would not serve him. He was an emperor deserted by his states, and left to whistle by himself. . . . In every house, in the heart of each maiden, and of each boy, in the soul of the soaring saint, this chasm is found, —between the largest promise of ideal power, and the shabby experience.[3]

Not even in psychoanalytic literature is there a more accurate and vivid description of the basic psychology of oral frustration. The theme is unmistakably, "Is this all that life will provide me—a mere drop in the bucket, a drop which cannot satisfy my tremendous appetite." The image aroused is that of a bottomless pit, never to be fully satisfied. It is reminiscent of Tolstoy in his depression, when he told of the "stupid cheat perpetrated by a parsimonious providence," and his orally colored fable in which the open-mouthed dragon is ready to devour him, the mice are gnawing at the roots, and the unlucky writer is licking drops of honey from the leaves of the bush.

Psychoanalytic theory would account for these feelings of Emerson by saying that the infant, during the oral dependent period, needs constant predictable food supplies from the outside, from the mother. If the mother is in close, predictable, affectionate connection with the infant, then his anxieties will soon be allayed by the presence of the mother (rather than by food from the mother), and still later by the internalized memory

of mother's predictable succorance. Bowlby and Harlow stress
other nonoral satisfactions the infant gets from the affectionate
mother. The infant thus would become dependent on maternal
fondling, smiles and cooing, so that in later periods of deprivation
his imagery would not be exclusively oral. The sequence just
described is most likely to occur with the first son who then is
less susceptible to direct oral supply deprivation, but more susceptible to deprivation of appreciation or admiration. If the
mother is not as closely connected—as more often happens with
later sons—the dependence on concrete outside supplies continues.
The later son has not as large a camel's hump as the first son to
tide him over the rough spots. His cry was not immediately
attended to, and so he is "an emperor deserted by his states, and
left to whistle by himself."

What the deprivables want from life, then, is more and more
direct supplies to allay their basic anxiety and their sense of
powerlessness. Because the supplies are located on the outside,
their interest is focused on the outside. Not sure that satisfaction
will eventually come from the remote two birds in the bush, they
immediately eat the bird in hand. These outer-supply tendencies
bring to mind Riesman's other-directed type. In contrast to the
inner-directed, who get nourishment from within themselves, the
outer-directed are par excellence consumers of externally derived
supplies. Besides the direct enjoyment of these outer supplies,
there is also a status implication about what they are enjoying.
They feel more powerful if they are enjoying what is prestigeful
to enjoy. Thus, we saw how later son Rousseau measured his
status by what was boiling in his pot.

An anxiety about food deprivation has played a leading part
in the social-biological theories of three noted later sons—Malthus,
Darwin, and Veblen. They did not share first son Malinowski's
feeling that enough food would be left over from immediate
needs so that some could be consecrated for higher needs. To
them, Emerson's "cry of famine" was urgently loud. A summary
statement by Riesman indicates their tendencies:

As Darwin took over Malthus' perspective of a bitter race between
man and his means of subsistence—leading Darwin to overemphasize
the adaptation of organism to environment . . . so Veblen along with
many other Social Darwinists underestimated man's ability to survive

in the face of many unproductive, "unreasonable" activities. No matter how bounteous the productivity of the nineteenth century . . . Veblen seems to have strongly felt the precariousness of existence. . . .[4]

This kind of oral dependent anxiety is, of course, at the basis of the question, "Does or does not Man live by bread alone?" Those (like Carlyle and Malinowski) who say Man does not, would point out that a worshipful, religious, reverent feeling also gives nourishment, though of a different kind. Though there are very few thinkers who would say categorically that bread is the sole nutrient of Homo sapiens, there are many (like Malthus, Darwin, Veblen) who believe that it is the first concern or that it should be forthcoming from Providence. A most eloquent statement comes from the pen of later son Fyodor Dostoevski. It is, of course, risky to claim that one particular character in his novels speaks for Dostoevski. But the story of the Grand Inquisitor is at least not inconsistent with his views. The ninety-year-old Grand Inquisitor berates Jesus on his return to the Earth:

Nothing has ever been more insupportable for a man and a human society than freedom. . . . Thou didst reply that man lives not by bread alone. . . . Dost thou know that the ages will pass, and humanity will proclaim by the lips of their sages that there is no crime, and therefore no sin; there is only hunger? "Feed men, and then ask of them virtue!" that's what they'll write on the banner, which they will raise against Thee. . . .[5]

Food, then, as the earliest necessity and satisfaction of life, can be expected to play a prominent role in the imagery with which men speak of life aims. In addition to food, other *externally* derived useful comforts can be emphasized by later sons. One such comfort can be the pleasure derived from contact with other humans. In regard to this we have already seen how Emerson speaks of the uses of great men. And we can add Veblen's need for interhuman succor as revealed in his naming the "parental bent" (the regard for the young) as a primary human interest. More material use-comforts can be seen in Emerson's inventor of the railroad and in Bacon's wish to wrest Nature's secrets from her for the betterment of mankind. Camus' hero is Prometheus, who stole fire from the gods—not to worship it as Carlyle would, but to give it to mankind to use.

Understandably, the nonhuman producers of supplies may become paramount for the disconnectedness-prone later sons. Thus, Whitman and Veblen felt quite positively toward the Machine. Veblen went so far as actually to advocate a society administered by engineers. Riesman's comments about Veblen are pertinent here:

Veblen states in the strongest terms that human nature is not suited to machine industry. . . . And yet it is hard to think of a writer . . . who has welcomed it with more enthusiasm as a tutor which will make men sober, factual, and peaceable. It would appear, taking all of Veblen's work together, that he regarded the machine as compelling an orientation to the external environment, impersonal as nature itself, capable of creating in men a "second nature" entirely methodical and workmanlike, rid of the exuberant animistic projections that might be stimulated by more creative or more artisan-like work. Men would suffer under this tutelage, but they would be safe.[6]

If we follow Riesman in this, later son Veblen would abolish the worshipful, reverent, "exuberant animistic projections" so vital to first sons Carlyle and Malinowski.

So much then for life aims of the later sons, aims calculated to reduce anxiety over deprivation of externally derived supplies. Let us turn now to first sons and see how their particular life aims can be frustrated. We have already found Carlyle complaining that he is living in an age which considers heroes and hero worship unnecessary and undesirable. National characteristics apparently do not affect this frustration, for to a Scot we can add several German first sons. They are discussed by Erich Heller in a book appropriately entitled *The Disinherited Mind*. The men are Goethe, Burckhardt, Nietzsche, Rilke, Spengler, Kafka, and Kraus. The birth orders of Burckhardt and Kraus are not available; the rest are first sons. To them should be added first son Hölderlin about whom Heller says in the "Preface to the Original Edition": "In a way it is even true to say that the silent centre of this book is Hölderlin. . . ."[7] Though Heller writes, "I could have included, without losing sight of the central theme, many more names,"[8] it is noteworthy that he selected these particular first-son Germans as most illustrative and did not include later son Thomas Mann, about whom he wrote a separate book subtitled "The Ironic German."

What is the imagery behind the central theme of *The Disinherited Mind?*" The opening quotations are Rilke's:

Each torpid turn of the world has such disinherited children,
to whom no longer what's been, and not yet what's coming, belongs.[9]

And Kafka's:

Yet I felt no certainty about anything, demanding from every single moment a new confirmation of my existence . . . in truth, a disinherited son.[10]

Here we do not see frank oral hunger, the deprivation of physiologic need. Rather, the loss of a customary connection is seen, the abolition of a previous sovereignty. Cain, Esau, and Hamlet might have felt the same. The long quotation from Hölderlin, which ends the preface, has a Carlyle-like imagery of something wonderful, heroic, Godlike being missing from life—the solution to the loss being in man's dreams:

Now will he strive in earnest to honour the dwellers in Heaven,
Everything living must utter their praise, in word and in deed.

Where, though, where are they, the famous, those crowns of the banquet?

Life thereafter is but to dream of them.

Meanwhile, it seems to me often
Better to Slumber than live without companions, like this,
So to linger, and know not what to begin or to utter,
    Or, in such spiritless times, why to be poet at all?[11]

Only a few quotations from Heller's book are necessary to illustrate in a less poetic way the meaning of a disinheritance from noble omnipotence. First son Goethe's reaction is quite similar to that of first son Lippmann whom we quoted earlier. Thus Heller writes concerning Goethe's feelings five days before his death:

In other words [Heller is quoting Goethe], the Prosaic Age is upon us, with its disenchantment of myth and poetry. . . . It will drag into the vulgar light of day the ancient heritage of a noble past, and destroy not only the capacity for profound feeling and the beliefs of peoples and priests, but even that belief of reason which divines meaningful coherence behind strangeness and seeming disorder.[12]

The more extreme, violent, heroic reaction to this disinheritance is seen in Nietzsche, "who has appealed to what is most immature in the popular imagination of his country, . . ." by "philosophizing with a hammer," proclaiming himself dynamite, preaching the advent of the Superman?[13]

In our discussion of life aims we cannot avoid reckoning with first son Karl Marx, the intellectual father of a system presently contending for worldwide acceptance and adherence. Although the Soviet Union speaks now of Leninism rather than Marxism, it is of interest to know where Marx stood. Was he more the I "Dignity of Man" self kind of thinker, or more the me "Welfare of Man" self kind? Because he was a first son, our thesis would place him in the former category. But is there evidence to substantiate this? We do not mean here the suggestive evidence pointing to his being connectedness-prone—e.g., that in very early youth he considered himself a poet and in later life he was both historian and philosopher. Besides these hints from characteristic first-son fields of interest, do his actual writings support our contention about the I-self predominance? The totality of Marx's writings is beyond the competence of the present author to evaluate. The comparatively short *Communist Manifesto*, however, is more suitable for illustration. The undertone of the *Manifesto*, written in collaboration with first son Engels, is in the heroic tradition. Quite obvious is the frontal attack, the warning of "this is what we think and plan to do, you had better watch out"; and the final battlesong before the assault, a battle cry reminiscent of Lassalle, Bakunin, Hooker, Patton: "Let the ruling classes tremble at a Communistic revolution. The proletarians have nothing to lose but their chains. They have a world to win. . . ." "Working men of all countries, unite!"[14]

For what reason does Marx want the working men to unite? For provision of basic needs which, as Dostoevski's Grand Inquisitor said, would be written on the banners of men? Or for the regaining of self-esteem, or a respected dignity of Man? There seems more in the *Manifesto* pointing to the latter I-self motivation than to the former me-self one. In examining the text of the *Manifesto*, we first come upon the role of the bourgeoisie. They are the new oppressors in the class struggle, just as patricians were in ancient Rome and feudal lords were in the Middle

Ages. But Marx, though giving the bourgeoisie credit for many material advances, seems antagonistic to this kind of new oppressors and nostalgic for the old kind of oppressors:

The bourgeoisie, wherever it has got the upper hand, has put an end to all feudal, patriarchal, idyllic relations. It has pitilessly torn asunder the motley feudal ties that bound man to his "natural superiors," and has left no other nexus between man and man than naked self-interest. . . . It has resolved personal worth into exchange value. . . .
  All that is solid melts into the air, all that is holy is profaned. . . .
  The serf, in the period of serfdom, raised himself to membership in the commune, just as the petty bourgeois, under the yoke of feudal absolutism managed to develop into a bourgeois. The modern laborer, on the contrary, instead of rising with the progress of industry, sinks deeper and deeper below the conditions of existence of his own class.[15]

It is difficult to see in this a Marx who impartially delivers the hammer blow of a plague on both oppressive houses. Mentioning the old oppressors is necessary for a consistent historical development of this theory, but it seems only a mention. As prominent as are the evils of earlier oppression, there are still the connected, "holy" values it gave to life. That the great men, living and dead, are no longer revered is what seems to bother Marx. If he had remained a poet like Hölderlin, he might have been relatively content to dream about the great ones: "Better to slumber than to live without companions, like this." But Marx could not be satisfied in the position of being disinherited. He had to make his dreams come true and, therefore, urged Man to recover his lost dignity and personal worth.

  It would be expected that Marx would not be enamored of the depersonalizing Machine:

Owing to the extensive use of machinery and to division of labor, the work of the proletarians has lost all individual character, and, consequently, all charm for the workman. He becomes an appendage of the machine, and it is only the most simple, most monotonous and most easily acquired knack that is required of him. . . .
  They [the laborers] are daily and hourly enslaved by the machine. . . .[16]

First son Marx does not appreciate the safe, monotonous tutelage that later son Veblen saw as forthcoming from the machine. On the contrary, Marx regrets the absence of "exuberant animistic provocations." Whereas the Grand Inquisitor said "There is no sin, there is only hunger," Marx (and especially Hitler) would have said, "There is no sin, there is only demeanment of self." For Marx's principal humanitarian conclusion as to why the bourgeoisie has to be eliminated is that it lowers Man to the unworthy status of being fed:

It [the bourgeoisie] is unfit to rule, because it is incompetent to assure an existence to its slave within his slavery, because it cannot help letting him sink into such a state that it has to feed him, instead of being fed by him. Society can no longer live under this bourgeoisie; in other words, its existence is no longer compatible with society.[17]

This "dignity of man" motif in Marx is noted also by Camus who wrote:

It has undoubtedly been correct to emphasize the ethical demands that form the basis of the Marxist dream. . . .
He . . . denounced with unparalleled profundity a class whose crime is not so much having had power as having used it to advance the ends of a mediocre society deprived of any nobility. . . .
By demanding for the worker real riches, which are not the riches of money but of leisure and creation, he has reclaimed, despite all appearance to the contrary, the dignity of man.[18]

Later son Lenin, the maker of the revolution was, according to Camus, not given to such misty, sentimental, or omnipotent notions as the dignity of man. As the following quotation from Camus indicates, Lenin was for action, power, food, and the Machine:

If we examine the two works written at the beginning [*What* To Do] and at the end of his career [The Revolution] as an agitator, one is struck by the fact that he never ceased to fight mercilessly against the sentimental forms of revolutionary action. . . . Completely impervious to anxiety, to nostalgia, to ethics, he takes command. . . .
In a lecture . . . Lenin spoke with a precision which left little doubt about the indefinite continuation of the proletarian super-State. "With this machine, or rather this weapon [the State], we shall crush every form of exploitation, and when there are . . . no more people gorging themselves under the eyes of others who are starving, . . . then and only then shall we cast this machine aside."[19]

Up to this point, our survey has revealed a noticeable trend of certain later sons to emphasize the immediate, direct hunger gratification secured by a food supply, and for certain first sons to emphasize rather an indirect kind of nutrition, like that of the self or the spirit, etc. The alternatives were first found in the hypothetical example of the cookie jar, and then in Malinowski's comments about the direct and indirect usages of food by primitive societies. It is to be expected that there are exceptions to this trend. However, apart from the vivid example of biblical first son Esau selling his birthright for a mess of pottage, the author has not been able to find unequivocal exceptions.

Now we shall present some evidence which depends more on inference. The evidence centers around what is perhaps the most explicit set of alternatives known to philosophers and historians. We refer to the opposite philosophies of life available to men after the fall of Athens; namely, the Stoic and the Epicurean philosophies. The choices, upon the deterioration of the Athenian social-political unity and upon the ascendance of the ruling Macedonians, were essentially either to endure life or to enjoy it. Our difficulty here is obvious. We cannot know with any certainty the birth order of the prominent ancient Stoic and Epicurean philosophers. However, by using the philosophical lineage chart provided by Durant, we may be able to see whether first- and later-son philosophers since around 1600 are in the Stoic or Epicurean tradition. Our two sources for the description of these two schools in the fourth century B.C. will be Gilbert Murray's *Five Stages of Greek Religion* and Bertrand Russell's *A History of Western Philosophy*. Though both are later sons, Murray's account seems to have a historian's objectivity and an appreciation of the position of both schools, while Russell appears to be biased against the Stoic and for the Epicurean. Our main interest will be in the views of the two schools. But a subtheme, which will be continued in the next chapter, is the partisan programmatical philosophy of later son Russell.

Murray says:

But the defeat of 404 not only left Athens at the mercy of her enemies. It stripped her of those things of which she had been inwardly most proud; her "wisdom," her high civilization, her leadership of all that was most Hellenic in Hellas. . . .

It is in philosophy and speculation that we find the richest and most varied reactions to the Great Failure.[20]

One kind of reaction was to put the emphasis on how one played the game, rather than on whether the game was won or lost.

Murray then goes on to describe two variants of the emphasis on how one plays the game. The earlier (and more bitter) variant was expounded by the cynics, foremost of whom were Antisthenes and Diogenes; the later (and more mild) variant by such stoics as Zeno, Seneca, and Marcus Aurelius. Common to both variants, however, was the clinging to something not concretely available in the current external world. For the cynics it was the abstract concept of *Aretê*, Goodness, Duty—for the stoics it was the equally abstract (and related) notion of the inscrutable Cosmic or Divine Purpose. Both abstractions appeared to serve as psychic nutriment in the face of disaster. Murray writes of the more bitter cynics:

He [Antisthenes] was defeated with all that he most cared for, and he comforted himself with the thought that nothing matters except to have done your best. As he phrased it, *Aretê is the good,* Aretê meaning "virtue" or "goodness," the quality of a good citizen, a good father, a good dog, a good sword.[21]

Murray goes on:

"He [Diogenes] remains the permanent and unsurpassed type of one way of grappling with the horror of life. Fear nothing, desire nothing, possess nothing; and then Life with all its ingenuity of malice cannot disappoint you. If man cannot enter into life nor yet depart from it save through agony and filth, let him learn to endure the one and be indifferent to the other. . . .

Here, indeed, it seemed, was a way to baffle Fortune and to make one's own soul unafraid. What men wanted was . . . "to be of good cheer"; as we say now, to regain their *morale* after bewildering defeats. The Cynic answer, afterwards corrected and humanized by the Stoics, was to look at life as a long and ardous campaign. The loyal soldier does not trouble about his comfort or his rewards or his pleasures. . . . Only Goodness is good, and for the soldier Goodness . . . is the doing of Duty. That is his true prize, which no external power can take away from him.[22]

About the more humanized Stoic school, Murray writes:

The Stoic School, whose founder, Zeno . . . gradually built up a theory of moral life which has on the whole weathered the storms of time with great success. . . . It lasts now as the nearest approach to an acceptable system of conduct for those who do not accept revelation, but still keep some faith in the Purpose of Things. . . .

The Stoics improved on the military metaphor. . . . Life is not like a battle but like a play, in which God has handed each man his part unread, and the good man proceeds to act it to the best of his power. . . . All that matters is that he shall act his best, accept the order of the Cosmos and obey the Purpose of the great Dramaturge. . . .

The Purpose, though it is not our Purpose, is especially concerned with us and circles round us. It is the purpose of a God who loves Man.[23]

Before taking up the Epicurean response to disaster, let us see how one particular later-son philosopher, Bertrand Russell, views Stoicism as a way of life. We certainly cannot generalize in this matter about all later sons, inasmuch as later son Murray reveals no antipathy toward Stoicism. Murray presents it as one possible life philosophy and, if he has any personal preferences, they do not intrude themselves into his account. Not so, however, with highly militant later son Russell. For him, the Stoic prospect of "they also serve who only stand and wait" is basically objectionable. Russell describes the Stoic outlook:

Since virtue resides in the will, everything really good or bad in a man's life depends only upon himself. He may become poor, but what of it? He can still be virtuous. . . . He may be sentenced to death, but he can die nobly, like Socrates. Other men have power only over externals; virtue, which alone is truly good, rests entirely with the individual. . . .

To a modern mind, it is difficult to feel enthusiastic about a virtuous life if nothing is going to be achieved by it. . . . To the Stoic, his virtue is an end in itself, not something that does good. And when we take a longer view, what is the ultimate outcome? A destruction of the present world by fire, and then a repetition of the whole process. Could anything be more devastatingly futile? There may be progress here and there, for a time, but in the long run, there is only recurrence. . . . Providence, which sees the whole, must, one would think, ultimately grow weary through despair.[24]

Later son Russell complains also about the interpersonal detachment involved in Stoicism, and the lack of such concrete satisfactions as food:

There goes with this a certain coldness in the Stoic conception of virtue. . . . Friendship, so highly prized by Epicurus, is all very well, but it must not be carried to the point where your friend's misfortunes can destroy your holy calm. As for public life, it may be your duty to engage in it . . . but you must not be actuated by a desire to benefit mankind, since the benefits you can confer—such as peace, or a more adequate supply of food—are no true benefits, and, in any case, nothing matters to you except your own virtues . . . love, except in a superficial sense, is absent from his [the Stoic's] conception of virtue.[25]

Russell continues in his rejecting of the abstract nutrition provided by Stoicism:

There is, in fact, an element of sour grapes in Stoicism. We can't be happy, but we can be good; let us therefore pretend that, so long as we are good, it doesn't matter being unhappy. This doctrine is heroic and, in a bad world, useful; but it is neither true nor, in a fundamental sense quite sincere.[26]

And in assessing the total Stoic position, this later son reveals his "stomach" theory of life aims and source of morality:

This [the Stoic answer] is a good answer, up to a point, but it breaks down when we consider the causes of our volitions. We all know, as a matter of empirical fact, that dyspepsia, for example, has a bad effect on a man's virtue, and that, by suitable drugs . . . willpower can be destroyed.[27]

Later son Russell is apparently unable to identify with the inner-connectedness psychology of first son. Anything mystical and animistic seems intolerable to his penetrating, logical mind. Another example of this is his assessment of first son Kepler:

Kepler . . . is one of the most notable examples of what can be achieved by patience without much in the way of genius. . . .

He used them [mystic Pythagorean theories] to suggest hypotheses in his mind; at last, by good luck, one of these worked.[28]

The evaluation of first son Kepler by first son Koestler is, as we shall see later, much more empathic. Russell is so out of rapport with the inner value men that he thought it insincere if one of them talked of frustration arising from anything but an unfed or upset stomach.

We are now, perhaps, in a better position to deal with the Epicurean response to disaster; i.e., a response much the opposite of Stoicism. Murray writes:

The other great school of the fourth century, a school which, in the matter of ethics, may be called the only true rival of Stoicism, was also rooted in defeat. But it met defeat in a different spirit. . . .

Epicurus built up his philosophy, it would seem, while helping his parents and brothers through this bad time. [As refugees] The problem was how to make the life of their little colony tolerable, and he somehow solved it. It was not the kind of problem which Stoicism and the great religions specially set themselves; it was at once too unpretending and too practical. One can easily imagine the condition for which he had to prescribe. For one thing, the unfortunate refugees all about him would torment themselves with unnecessary terrors. The Thracians were pursuing them. The Gods hated them; they must obviously have committed some offence or impiety. . . . It would surely be better to die at once; except that, with that sin upon them, they would only suffer more dreadfully beyond the grave![29]

In a footnote, Murray says:

Epicurus is the one philosopher who protests with real indignation against that inhuman superiority to natural sorrows which is so much prized by most of the ancient schools. To him such "apathy" argues either a hard heart or a morbid vanity. . . . His letters are full of affectionate expressions which rather shock the stern reserve of antique philosophy. He waits for one friend's "heavenly presence." . . . He "melts with a peculiar joy mingled with tears in remembering the last words" of one who is dead.[30]

Epicurus' course of therapy for his followers could be described as soothing and supportive. There is no evil and there is love. This in contrast to the Stoical therapy—there is evil and pain, but one must learn to endure it. Murray describes Epicurus' view:

His first discovery was that men torture themselves with unnecessary fears. He must teach them courage . . . to fear no evil from either man or God. God is a blessed being; and no blessed being either suffers evil or inflicts evil on others. . . . Death is like sleep, an unconscious state, nowise to be feared. Pain when it comes can be endured; it is the anticipation that makes men miserable and saps their courage. The refugees were forgotten by the world, and had no hope of any great change in their condition. Well, he argued, so much the better! Let them till the earth and love one another, and they would find that they had already in them that Natural Happiness which is man's possession until he throws it away. And of all things that contribute to happiness the greatest is Affection. . . .

Like the Cynics and Stoics, he rejected the world and all its conventions and prizes, its desires and passions and futility. But where the Stoic and Cynic proclaimed that in spite of all the pain and suffering of a wicked world, man can by the force of his own will be virtuous, Epicurus brought the more surprising good news that man can after all be happy.[31]

In order to buttress this outlook with theory, Epicurus had recourse to the atomistic idea of Democritus, just as the Stoics relied among others on the ideas of Heraclitus. By separate atoms swerving slightly in their course, they (according to Murray),

"have become infinitely tangled and mingled," and that is "how plants and animals are alive, and how men have Free Will. It also enables Epicurus to build up a world without the assistance of a god. He set man free, as Lucretius says, from the "burden of Religion," though his doctrine of the "blessed Being," which neither has pain nor gives pain, enables him to elude the dangerous accusation of atheism. He can leave people believing in all their traditional gods, including even, if so they wish, "the bearded Zeus and the helmed Athena" which they see in their dreams . . . while at the same time having no fear of them.

There remains the foolish fancy of the Cynics and Stoics that "Aretê" is the only good. Of course, he answers, Aretê is good; but that is because it produces happy life, or blessedness or pleasure or whatever you call it. He used normally the word . . . "sweetness," and counted the Good as that which makes life sweet.[32]

Here seems evident the disconnectedness orientation noted in the later sons. The elimination of evil we have seen in an earlier chapter. William James described the cheerful once-borns as free of the sense of evil and gave as examples later-born Emerson, Whitman, and Mary Baker Eddy. The emphasis of affectionate man-to-man interchange is seen markedly in Whitman. The disconnectedness theme is prominent in the separate atoms which eventually mingle. This is in contrast to the unified and interconnected cosmic whole thought of by the Stoics.

Moreover, the Stoic being unable to disconnect himself from evil must erect a philosophic view which recognizes and somehow absorbs the evil of the world. The strongly connected inner moral authority, which we noted in first sons and which was called the Categorical Imperative by Kant, the conscience by Shaftesbury, the superego by Freud, is designated *Aretê* by the Stoics. Such an indwelling moral authority tends to produce a somewhat grim, if not pessimistic, attitude to life. The good in life tends to be associated with abstract duty and purpose—not with the direct oral sweetness which can make existence happy for Epicurus.

Let us consider for a moment later son Russell's attitude toward the Epicurean response. We must acknowledge that his basic empathy with the Epicurean school certainly does not prevent him from recognizing certain of the faults. But these faults are comprehensible to him. It is more that this way of thinking is not foreign to him as it was in the case of the Stoics. Thus he writes:

Although Epicurus was gentle and kindly towards most people, a different side of his character appeared in his relationships to philosophers, especially those to whom he might be considered indebted. . . . He never acknowledged the extent of his indebtedness to Democritus [or to Leucippus]. . . .[33]

Russell sees another serious limitation:

With this lack of generosity towards other philosophers goes another grave fault, that of dictatorial dogmatism. His followers had to learn a kind of creed embodying his doctrines, which they were not allowed to question. To the end, none of them added or modified anything. . . .

It is no wonder that the Epicureans contributed practically nothing to natural knowledge. They served a useful purpose by their protest against the increasing devotion of the later pagans to magic, astrology, and divination; but they remained, like their founder, dogmatic, limited, and without genuine interest in anything outside individual happiness.[34]

With all this, Russell takes no ascertainable issue with Epicurus' "stomach theory" on which Russell quotes Epicurus: "The beginning and root of all good is the pleasure of the stomach; even wisdom and culture must be referred to this."[35] Furthermore, Russell never accused the Epicureans of being insincere, an accusation which he made concerning the Stoics. Limited and dogmatic, yes—but inhuman, cold and insincere, no. The general impression gained is that later son Russell has much more empathy for the Epicurean response than for the Stoic one.

This account of the Stoic and Epicurean responses to adversity has had a twofold purpose. One was to give the psychological essence of the responses—that of Stoicism to defend against present evil by drawing on inner resources and trusting in the inscrutable and beneficient long-term purposes of God; that of Epicureanism, to deny present evil and to draw on such immediately available short-term gratifications from the external environment as bodily pleasures and the affection of friends. The other purpose was to supply indirect evidence that first sons more frequently have the Stoic and later sons the Epicurean response. Direct evidence, as was said, is impossible to obtain, inasmuch as the birth order of the principal Cynics and Stoics (Diogenes and Zeno) and of the principal Epicureans (Epicurus and Lucretius) is unknown. Some qualitative evidence has been provided by an examination of later son Bertrand Russell's position. Indirect quantitative evidence may be supplied by the table of Philosophic Affiliations contained in Durant's *Story of Philosophy*. The lineage is based on whether philosophical ideas are or are not shared in common. Thus, for example, Locke and Hume are placed together (due most likely to their common empirical outlook) even though, as we noted earlier, these two differ as to whether there is a self. Even so, the table indicates a trend in the direction of the hypothesis. The construction of the table is as follows: There is a center line of philosophers on each side of which are lateral lines of philosophers, with some philosophers between the center line and the lateral lines. We shall be most interested in the philosophers to the left and to the right of center.

Heading the extreme left is Heraclitus with whom the Cynics and Stoics are affiliated; heading the extreme right are Leucippus and Democritus, with whom the Epicureans are affiliated. Though the birth order of these early philosophers is not known, the descriptive names given them are of interest. Heraclitus was called the Dark Philosopher, Democritus the Laughing Philosopher. It will be recalled from a previous chapter that brooding melancholy is more characteristic of sick-soul first sons; cheerfulness more characteristic of healthy-minded later sons. Directly in line from Heraclitus, and to the left of center, are fourteen philosophers, eight of whom lived after the sixteenth century. Birth order is available on seven of these, and they are all first sons (Spinoza, Schelling, Hegel, Schopenhauer, Nietzsche, Croce, and Bergson).

Directly in line from Democritus and to the right of center are twenty philosophers, fourteen of whom lived after the sixteenth century. Birth order is available on eleven of these. Eight are later sons (Bacon, Hobbes, Voltaire, Condilac, Hume, Dewey, Santayana, and Russell). The remaining three first sons are Locke, Mill, and Spencer.

As indicated earlier, the trend is in the direction of the hypothesis. Concerning those philosophers to the left of center, those more affiliated with the Heraclitic Stoic response, there are seven first sons and no later sons. Concerning those philosophers to the right of center, those more affiliated with the Democritic Epicurean response, there are eight later sons and three first sons. If we take Durant's entire table (left, center, and right) after the sixteenth century, there are twenty-eight philosophers; birth order is available on twenty-two: Thirteen are first sons, nine are later sons. This group statistic illustrates the trend described in the introductory chapter, that the philosophers are more often first sons. But, of these philosophers, the greater percentage of first sons appears to be descended from Heraclitus, who has been called the Father of Metaphysics. Metaphysics is the branch of philosophy which has the least to do with immediate or direct usefulness. As Durant defines it, "*metaphysics* . . . is the study of the 'ultimate reality' of all things: of the real and final nature of 'matter' . . . , of 'mind' . . . , and of the interrelation of 'mind' and 'matter' in the processes of perception and knowledge. . . ."[36] The dyed-in-the-wool metaphysician, typically the first son, is then concerned with matter beyond external reality or with matters dealing with the inner mind. The other branches of philosophy—logic, esthetics, ethics, and politics—deal more with actual external reality and, as Durant says, "attempt to coordinate the real in the light of the ideal. . . ."[37] Later-son philosophers like Russell and Dewey are more often engaged in these types of philosophic endeavors.

Our discussion of the Stoic and Epicurean responses to adversity has possibly more fully illustrated what is meant by conserving (and its inherent connectedness) and by consuming (and its inherent disconnectedness). As we close this chapter, we are mindful of the fact that what men want out of life, what substantially they want society to provide them, and how immediately they need these satisfactions, have a most important bearing on how they wish to arrange society. Next we will consider the political repercussions of these different life aims.

CHAPTER VII

Political Directions

CONNECTEDNESS AND
DISCONNECTEDNESS

THIS, THE FINAL GENERAL CHAPTER, gathers up
many of the threads from the previous chapters. For the organization of society or the formation of a state involves the aims
of life, the moral law, and the taking of action. It is fitting, then,
that the chapter subheading should restate the terms of the basic
hypothesis. But there are more specific reasons for using connectedness and disconnectedness. A quite direct reason is that
these terms can refer to how closely or loosely knit are the components of the state. Indirectly, the terms may have something
to do with a paramount political issue—the conserving or the
consuming of goods and property. Indeed, it is held by some
political theorists that the principal function of the state is to
protect accumulated property.

Now let us begin with an inquiry into property and its
accumulation. From the preceding chapter, we might expect that
the Stoic would store up and the Epicurean would use up provisions. For the Stoic's satisfactions are inward and are geared to
a considerable duration of time—"when it was and when it will
be"—whereas the Epicurean satisfactions are outward and are
geared to the present "now it is." We have already learned from
Malinowski that man in primitive society has the choice of heedlessly consuming accumulated food or preserving it. Malinowski's
point about food preservation was, of course, in regard to culturally valuable phenomena, such as religion. But the central
psychological issue can be applied to indirect, delayed gratifications other than religion. Malinowski gives a clue here when
he uses the phrase "devising means of hoarding the treasure."

The treasure then can as well be property and money as it can be religion. Lifting Malinowski's alternatives entirely out of the realm of religion, we can alter his statement slightly to account for more mundane matters. "Accumulated food (or property, or money) can either be squandered or preserved. It can either be an incentive to immediate heedless consumption and light-hearted carelessness about the future, or else it can stimulate man to devising means of hoarding the treasure."[1]

It is perhaps more clear now how the "when it will be" orientation of the Stoic first son may lead to a hoarding of goods and how the "now it is" orientation of the Epicurean later son may result in an immediate consumption of the goods. The "work now enjoy later" first son is more temperamentally equipped to play for the two birds in the bush, for bigger, more omnipotent status, be it the eventual blessings from the Divinity, a Nobel prize, or a million dollars. On the other hand, the "work now enjoy now" later son will tend to play for the one bird in the bush, for the immediate, less risky gratification of pleasure or power. There would perhaps be much less social and political unrest if the two types viewed each other's objectives with detachment. Unfortunately, the delayed satisfaction of the one and the immediate satisfaction of the other are frequently reacted to with mutual resentment. The later son envies the two birds which the first son eventually gains if his omnipotent gamble pays off—particularly so if the later son has not even got his one bird. The first son, who has lost in the gamble, or who has not received the rewards as yet, envies the sure one bird in hand that the later son is enjoying. Little consolation is gained by the first son when he is told "You should have played for smaller stakes," or by the later son when he is informed, "You should have played for bigger stakes."

Continuing in this speculative fashion, and still without introducing evidence, we may go back to the cookie-jar situation. Suppose that the mother offered the sons the choice of a cookie now or a cookie in a few hours. If the later son ate his now, two hours later he would be in the position of a "have not" when the first son was eating. Because of his oral deprivation tendency, he might mildly resent the first son for not sharing the cookie. The resentment would increase if the first son, instead of quietly eating the whole cookie, began to trade on the later son's hunger by offering a piece in exchange for the later son's prized marble. A similar resentment might ensue if the mother had stipulated that if the boys waited until dessert time, they would get two cookies; but if they ate before mealtime, they would get only one. The later son eating his one cookie would in a few hours strongly resent the two cookies the first son got for dessert. The same feeling might result if the mother stipulated that whoever washed the windows would get two cookies—otherwise one cookie immediately. If the later son was hungry enough, he would eat now and afterward envy the toiling first son's two cookies. Out of this resentment and envy, he might begin to have ideas about how goodies or goods should be distributed, to sense "There ought to be a law." The law would most likely emphasize "to each according to his need," that there should be equality in Society's provision of satisfaction, that current human needs have priority over a former contractual stipulation.

What can stimulate resentment in the first son? Perhaps the strongest feelings are aroused by a midstream change in the maternal stipulation. If the mother, out of characteristic sympathy for the younger son, gives him another cookie at dessert time or prevails on the older son to share his dessert cookie with him, the first son may angrily feel that his enduring through immediate deprivation was all for naught. If the two cookies promised for obedience to the rule of not eating between meals came down to one cookie, or if the nontoiling younger son gets two cookies anyhow, the first son can feel enraged at the breaking of the contract. Appeals to the mother may be fruitless, for the maternal instincts would recoil at the first son's demand for his pound of flesh. He might be more successful in appealing to the father who, due to his life among men, tends to be more impartial and less sympathetically softhearted than the mother.

The first son will also feel "There should be a law"—a law most likely emphasizing the sanctity of contracts and the right of a person to whatever he has toiled for and deprived himself of. Occasionally, if he has had plentiful satisfaction and/or his inner conscience (i.e., his identification with parental attitudes) is strong, he may develop a reaction against sadistic revenge—a reaction consisting of pity toward the deprived later son. One should not kick someone who is down, one should be benevolent. Thus the first son may join with the later son in proposing a law

that there should not be gross inequality in the distribution of
life satisfaction. Whereas the later son may advocate such a general law out of identification with other deprived people, the
first son's motive is more complex and includes the reward of
feeling at peace with one's conscience, of feeling virtuous.

The foregoing account represents what tends, on the average, to occur within families. That there are many exceptions
to this is undoubtedly true. The first son may be overindulged
and "contracts" broken in his favor. The father may be sympathetically softhearted and it may be the mother who emphasizes justice rather than mercy. But much more often than
not, the general trends described appear to hold. Usually more
responsibilities and less indulgence constitute the lot of first sons,
and usually it is the fathers who, living competitively with other
men in the extrafamilial environment, are the toughminded ones.
The task now is to provide evidence for these speculations; to
see whether these tendencies of first and later sons as children
within the family carry over to their thoughts, feelings, and
actions as adult men.

We shall begin with some inferential evidence which will
at least provide a background for what follows. The orientation
toward enduring and toiling in the inner moral voiced first sons,
and that toward carefree enjoyment in the outer moral voiced
later sons, may be seen in appropriate quotations from *Roget's
Thesaurus*. There are two aspects: (1) Utility (and Inutility).
(2) Pleasurable Amusement. Synonyms for utility include service-
ability, profitability, value, money's worth, utilitarianism. The
quotations concerning this term (and inutility) are from first
sons (birth orders of Tacitus and Cicero are not available).
"Sensible people find nothing useless" (La Fontaine). "Everything in the world is good for something" (Dryden). "Life, like
every other blessing, derives its value from its use alone" (Johnson). "Nothing can have value without being an object of utility"
(Karl Marx). "Useless as a candle in a skull" (Cowper).[2] The
Stoic and puritanical connotations of the quotations appear to be
that unless one does useful things or makes oneself useful, one
cannot easily justify one's existence. The Epicurean pursuit of
happiness and amusement is not sufficient justification for these
persons. In fact, it is contradictory, for when a thing has been
enjoyably consumed, it cannot be used again. The opposite view

of later sons is seen when we consult the *Thesaurus* in regard to amusement. Among the synonyms are entertainment, fun, play, merriment, frolic. The later son quotations are: "If you would rule the world quietly, you must keep it amused" (Emerson). "Work consists of whatever a body is obliged to do, and Play consists of whatever a body is not obliged to do" (Mark Twain). "Old boys have their playthings as well as young ones; the difference is only in the price" (Franklin). "In Xanadu did Kubla Khan a lofty pleasure-dome decree" (Coleridge). Of the three quotations from first sons, Shakespeare's is neutral while the other two express frank discomfort about sheer pleasure: "He capers, he dances, he has the eyes of youth" (Shakespeare). "A man cannot spend all this life in frolic" (Johnson). "That vague kind of penitence which holidays awaken next morning" (Dickens).[3]

The next inferential evidence concerns the outsized accumulation of money—an accumulation which goes much beyond what could be used for present consumption or enjoyment. Our theorizing would lead us to expect that the serious long-term first sons would more often be hoarders of treasure for later use than would the carefree, heedlessly consuming later sons. This expectation seems to be met, inasmuch as the founders of great fortunes show a marked predominance of first sons. The following list, though certainly not exhaustive, seems fairly representative. First sons: Rockefeller, Morgan, Gould, Du Pont, Krupp, Ford, Guggenheim, Giannini, Getty, Hill, Girard (possible additions are Kress, Cullen, Hearst, and Ivar Kruger). Later sons: Astor, Vanderbilt (possible additions are Baruch and Lasker). It should be mentioned that the most famous female hoarder and money accumulator was a first daughter, Hetty Green. And the principal current female advocate of pecuniary self-interest is first daughter, Ayn Rand.

What goes into accumulating such amounts of money is, of course, a complex matter. It seems safe to say, however, that there must be in these men a stronger interest in money per se than in what money can buy for use. (Such a strong theoretical interest without the feature of hyperaccumulation can be seen in first sons Marx, Keynes, Mitchell.) Money is delayed potential power—one or two steps removed from actual immediate power. One is reminded of the monkeys who learned to get more satisfaction out of collecting counters than out of the original bananas for which the counters could be exchanged. The hyperaccumulation of money by the men mentioned would realize not only the fulfillment of an omnipotent I-wish but also a contractual guarantee that privation or dethronement would never strike oneself or one's descendants. Some of these fortunes were soon or eventually turned to higher cultural purposes—Carnegie's soon, Rockefeller's, Guggenheim's, Ford's later—many others were not. A very superficial examination of the founders and their descendants (an examination needing much detailed study) gives the impression that first-son founders tended to create financial dynasties and to impress the value of money per se on their immediate descendants. This is the situation in the case of Rockefeller, Du Pont, Morgan, Krupp. On the other hand, the outstanding later-son fortune founders, Astor and Vanderbilt, appeared more to use their accumulated money for a higher, rather extravagant standard of living and were not concerned with long-term considerations. As we indicated earlier, the evidence is quite inferential. It and the speculations can be considered only suggestive.

We are on somewhat more solid ground when we consider the writings of a first son who stands out in history as the foremost theoretical exponent of private accumulation—Adam Smith. His *Wealth of Nations* published in the same year as the American Declaration of Independence was a rationale for the economic revolution. Although assuming that economic power is basically motivated by self-interest, he believed that society is ultimately benefited by the whole complex of economic efforts and processes. Thus laissez faire, freedom of trade and enterprise are for the good of humanity. We shall be concerned here with but a small part of his writings, that having to do with how labor and demand determine the price of commodities. Smith begins with:

Every man is rich or poor according to the degree in which he can afford to enjoy the necessaries, conveniences, and amusements of human life. But after the division of labour has once thoroughly taken place, it is but a very small part of these with which a man's own labour can supply him. The far greater part of them he must derive from the labour of other people, and he must be rich or poor according to the quantity of that labour which he can command or which he can afford to purchase. . . . Labour, therefore, is the real measure of the exchangeable value of all commodities.

The real price of every thing, what every thing really costs to the man who wants to acquire it, is the toil and trouble of acquiring it.[4]

It is clear then that Smith, not unlike other writers of that period, stresses the role of labor in determining value. Into this, perhaps, may be read that the man who toils and sweats is the value-producer and thus the valuable man. Although not so stated, an implication would be that coconuts falling onto a beach-comber's lap or manna dropping from heaven are of minimal value because little self-sacrificial labor had been put into them. Smith has often been considered one whose Puritanical conscience demands that some pain should be experienced before pleasure is enjoyed. Feelings toward a younger brother cannot be the case here, as Smith was an only child. More likely, he had identified with the self-responsible attitudes of his parents.

Smith goes on describing how labor, though the real measure, is not always used in establishing value:

It is often difficult to ascertain the proportion between two different quantities of labour. The time spent in two different sorts of work will not always alone determine this proportion. The different degrees of hardship endured, and of ingenuity exercised, must likewise be taken into account. There may be more labour in an hour's hard work than in two hours easy business; or in an hour's application to a trade which it cost ten years labour to learn, than in a month's industry at an ordinary and obvious employment. But it is not easy to find any accurate measure either of hardship or ingenuity. . . . It is adjusted, however, not by any accurate measure, but by the higgling and bargaining of the market, according to that sort of rough equality which, though not exact, is sufficient for carrying on the business of common life.[5]

Smith shows here a characteristic long-term orientation. The "ten years' labor" of learning a trade should, according to Smith, be taken into account and rewarded properly. He probably believed all men to be stoically and long-term oriented and thus what happened in the market was eminently fair. Those who did not go for the long-term stakes were weak and in a way deserved what happened to them. Smith was, therefore, not empathic with the short-term Epicureans who carried on the other side of the "higgling" and "bargaining." They, whose attitudes are more characteristic of later sons, are somewhat at the mercy of their oral deprivation needs. Emerson's cries of famine are quickly translated into urgent demand. Even if the external supply remains constant, the increased demand will force the Epicurean to offer higher prices than he would ordinarily pay. Thus, Manhattan Island was bought for $24. The advantage in the actual marketplace seems to be on the side of the one who can postpone immediate gratification of basic demands, be he buyer or seller. Behind the marketplace, the advantage is not as clear-cut. The long-term risk taker may lose in his gamble—an event which does not move the Epicurean short-termer to excessive tears.

These considerations are relevant to a question in economics —what influences a person to use his income for consumption, as opposed to savings, and vice versa. Keynes called the factor involved "the propensity to consume." Our comments are not intended to dispute Keynes' theory that the poor will have to spend and consume all they make whereas the rich can save from their surplus. Rather they are intended to stimulate inquiry into the psychology of growing rich or remaining poor.

Proceeding backward in time from Adam Smith, we find another first son, John Locke. Among other things, he believed in the institution of accumulated private property. We have already seen how he differs from later son Hume on the issue of the self. Locke's connectedness intuition was of a psychic organization which persisted and endured over a long period of time—the self. Hume's disconnectedness intuition in contrast was almost Epicurean—that the phenomenon which people call the self is here today and gone tomorrow. One is strongly tempted to suggest that the persisting self is perhaps the first instance of privately accumulated property. Locke, of course, has not come down to us as one of the champions of free enterprise. His name is not under a mild cloud as in the case of Adam Smith. Rather he is known to us in political theory as the grandfather of the Declaration of Independence due to his influence on Jefferson. Yet, as we shall see, his emphasis on inner morality and on future rewards for current deprivations moved later son Russell to write, "there is something revolting in a system which recognized prudence as the only virtue . . ."[6] Whereas Russell may have used "revolting" in the sense of "nauseating" others, like later son Rousseau he would use it in the sense of "revolutionary rebelliousness."

In examining Locke's views on property we can easily recognize the theme in Smith that toil should be rewarded. Locke writes in the chapter "Of Property":

Though the earth and all inferior creatures be common to all men, yet every man has a property in his own person; this nobody has any right to but himself. The labor of his body and the work of his hands we may say are properly his. Whatsoever, then, he removes out of the state that nature hath provided and left it in, he hath mixed his labor with, and joined to it something that is his own, and thereby makes it his property.

Though the water running in the fountain be everyone's, yet who can doubt but that in the pitcher is his only who drew it out? His labor hath taken it out of the hands of Nature where it was common, and belonged equally to all her children, and hath thereby appropriated it to himself.[7]

Locke's conscience prevents him from having a predatory "public be damned" feeling. He writes:

It will perhaps be objected to this, that if gathering the acorns, or other fruits of the earth, etc., makes a right to them, then anyone may engross as much as he will. To which I answer, Not so. The same law of nature that does by this means give us property, does also bound that property too. . . . As much as anyone can make use of to any advantage of life before it spoils, so much he may by his labor fix a property in; whatever is beyond this, is more than his share and belongs to others. Nothing was made by God for man to spoil or destroy.[8]

The very same inner moral authority, however, prevents first son Locke from advocating a life of carefree slothfulness and urges him toward a life of constructive toil which can make something his very own:

God, when He gave the world in common to all mankind, commanded man also to labor, and the penury of his condition required it of him. . . . He that, in obedience to this command of God, subdued . . . any part of it [the Earth], thereby annexed to it something that was his property, which another had no title to, nor could without injury take from him.[9]

It is this last phrase, "nor could without injury take from him," which is strongly associated with Locke's theory of civil government. He writes in the first introductory chapter:

Political power, then, I take to be a right of making laws with penalties of death, and consequently all less penalties, for the regulating and preserving of property, and of employing the force of the community in the execution of such laws. . . .[10]

Locke's position, then, is that laws are devised to protect the natural rights to goods which man is entitled to by his *toil*. Though the toiling, accumulating man is morally forbidden to waste this accumulation, Locke does not state that there are natural rights to goods which man is entitled to by his *needs*. First son Locke, like first son Smith, is more empathic with the Stoic than with the Epicurean outlook.

Locke's idea of the state of nature, before the advent of formal law and civil government, is of interest to us. Shortly we will compare it with those of later sons Russell and Rousseau. It is not surprising that first son Locke would intuit an inner moral authority, a categorical imperative belonging even to man in nature:

The state of nature has a law of nature to govern it, which obliges everyone; and reason, which is that law, teaches all mankind who will but consult it, that, being all equal and independent, no one ought to harm another in his life, health, liberty, or possessions.[11]

Since all men are God's property,

Everyone, as he is bound to preserve himself, and not to quit his station wilfully, so, by the like reason, when his own preservation comes not in competition, ought he, as much as he can, to preserve the rest of mankind, and not, unless it be to do justice on an offender, take away or impair the life, or what tends to the preservation of the life, the liberty, health, limb, or goods of another.[12]

First son Locke, thus, believes that men in a state of nature are mindful of mutual obligations without the aid of external social law: "For truth and the keeping of faith belong to men as men, and not as members of society."[13] In this intuition of an inner moral authority, he belongs with the first sons mentioned earlier—Freud, Kant, and Shaftesbury.

Locke's ethics include the altruistic injunction not to despoil, damage, or destroy another man's property (or another man, since he is God's property) and the punitive injunction that such damaging will deservedly be countered by retaliating damaging.

Locke realized that this "eye for eye" justice, though not im-
moral, may not be able to be dispensed wisely by the inflamed,
injured person. Therefore he theorized that men delegated their
natural law punitive rights to a more impartial arbitrator, the
magistrate, or civil government:

> Man . . . hath by nature a power not only to preserve his property
> . . . but to judge of and punish the breaches of that law in others. . . .
> There, and there only, is political society where every one of the
> members hath quitted this natural power, resigned it up into the
> hands of the community . . . and thus all private judgment of every
> particular member being excluded, the community comes to be the
> umpire. . . .[14]

Last to be considered are Locke's ideas about the family
origin of civil governments. The role of the parents and of the
father particularly is to educate and civilize the immature child,
for his eventual adult role where, though still owing some piety
toward his parents, he is independent of their counsel and judgment. In this early parental indoctrination and guidance can be
seen the implementing of the cultural values which we have
called the inner moral voice or superego. When the child comes
of age, he has the parental values within him and can act morally
without the extreme reliance on external moral laws:

> Children, I confess, are not born in this full state of equality, though
> they are born to it. Their parents have a sort of rule and jurisdiction
> over them when they come into the world, and for some time after,
> but it is but a temporary one. The bonds of subjection are like the
> swaddling clothes they are wrapt up in and supported by in the
> weakness of their infancy. Age and reason as they grow up loosen
> them, till at length they drop quite off, and leave a man at his own
> free disposal. . . .
>   . . . when he comes to the estate that made his father a free
> man, the son is a free man too.
>   Thus it was easy and almost natural for children, by a tacit and
> almost natural consent, to make way for the father's authority and
> government. They had been accustomed in their childhood to follow
> his direction, and to refer their little differences to him; and when
> they were men, who fitter to rule them? . . .
>   Thus, the natural fathers of families, by an insensible change,
> became the politic monarchs of them too. . . .[15]

From Locke's chapter "Of Paternal Power" we can see, of
course, the actual political problem he was trying to solve, i.e.,

how can England continue to be governed by a monarch? Locke's intuitive adherence to the idea of a benevolent guiding father would not allow him to dispose of the monarch completely. But he insisted that when men come of age, their judgments become mature and they no longer need the guiding paternal hand. Furthermore, both father and the mature sons are subject to and transmitters of a higher natural moral law, derived from God. Thus, absolute monarchy began to develop, through the Bloodless Revolution, into the constitutional monarchy.

Apart from the actual historical situation we see that first son Locke's ideas about early man in nature have a high degree of connectedness. Early natural man does not roam restlessly and barbarously; he does not require the whip or a Hobbesian sword to hold him in check. Rather he has inner restraints, inner adherence to natural morality. Also, he does not exist in a scattered, atomistic state. Rather he is brought up in an atmosphere of connectedness, in a family by a father who is mainly interested in inculcating the inner moral restraints.

In considering now the political thinking of later sons, we may begin with Bertrand Russell and his discussions of Locke. He much prefers the enlightened social goals of ethics-conscious first son Locke to the inner, mystical, heroic goals of the first sons Byron, Carlyle, Nietzsche, and Hitler. Not that Russell is comfortable with Locke. The emphasis on prudence he finds "revolting." He disagrees with Locke that man lives according to reason in the state of nature: "This is not a description of the life of savages but of an imagined community of virtuous anarchists, who need no police or law courts because they always obey 'reason,' which is the same as 'natural law,' which, in turn, consists of those laws of conduct that are held to have a divine origin."[16] Russell, whom we saw to believe that a dyspeptic stomach causes a weakening of virtue (rather than a mere irritability) seems to have little empathic intuition about a constant inner moral voice.

It is in regard to property rights that later son Russell is unmistakably in opposition to Locke:

Locke's doctrine is, in essence, more or less democratic, but the democratic element is limited by the view (implied rather than expressed) that those who have no property are not to be reckoned as citizens.[17]

Later Russell speaks of

(. . . the absurd lengths to which Locke is driven by his worship of property.) . . .

The principle that a man has a right to the produce of his own labour is in an industrial civilization. Suppose you are employed in one operation in the manufacture of Ford cars, how is any one to estimate what proportion of the total output is due to your labour? . . . Such considerations have led those who wish to prevent the exploitation of labour to abandon the principle of the right to your own produce in favour of more socialistic methods of organizing production and distribution.[18]

The next later son political thinker we shall consider is Hobbes. His position on the outer source of moral authority has already been noted. Like later son Machiavelli, he doubts that man possesses innate morality—only the external sword will enforce moral covenants. There is no natural categorical imperative: ". . . in sum, *doing to others as we would be done to* . . . [is] contrary to our natural passions, that carry us to partiality, pride, revenge, and the like."[19]

Instead of Locke's idea of a state of nature in which most men are innately virtuous and of good will, Hobbes' intuition is that natural man out of self-preservation wants not only to preserve his own liberty but also to dominate others. Rather than the family (as with Locke) being a civilizing influence, it is for Hobbes a school for later brigands:

And in all places where men have lived in small families, to rob and spoil one another has been a trade, and so far from being reputed against the law of nature that the greater spoils they gained, the greater was their honor. . . . And as small families did then; so now do cities and kingdoms, which are but greater families, for their own security enlarge their dominions . . . and endeavor as much as they can to subdue or weaken their neighbors, by open force and secret arts, . . . and are remembered for it in after ages with honor.[20]

These multitudes which oppose and hinder each other are ". . . not only subdued by a very few that agree together; but also when there is no common enemy, they make war upon each other, for their particular interests."[21] The warring multitude needs for the observance of justice "a common power to keep them in awe. . . ."[22] It is not enough to "be governed and directed by one judgment for a limited time. . . ."[23] No, contrary to the

social institution of bees, "men are continually in competition
for honor and dignity. . . ."[24] "Many that think themselves
wiser . . . than the rest; and these strive to reform and innovate,
one this way, another that way; and thereby bring it into dis-
traction and civil war."[25] The agreement between men is only
by artificial covenant, so they need "besides covenant, to make
their agreement constant and lasting . . . a common power, to
keep them in awe, and to direct their actions to the common
benefit."[26]

Thus, to combat this warlike anarchy between men, to make
them behave more like the armies of bees and ants, Hobbes proposes a constant awe-inspiring external authority. Locke believed
that a similar external governing authority would be necessary
until a man became mature. But in Hobbes' version of human
nature a man never becomes that mature, reasonable, or virtuous.
Due to weakness of the many individual wills, the multitudes
should reduce all their wills into one will. In this way, "they
may nourish themselves and live contentedly. . . ."[27] Free "from
the invasion of foreigners and the injuries of one another. . . ."[28]
With this view of the unreasonable mob, the political state is
one that is under continual martial law. The impression of atomistic disconnectedness is strongly gained. Men are freely moving
individual bodies which pursue individual ends. Instead of naturally evolving in the form of a molecule, these atoms continue
to collide randomly with each other. The eventual externally
enforced coalescence does not produce a molecule but rather a
larger atom. Or, to change the metaphor, it produces not a multi-
cellular organism, but rather a larger single cell. The single-
mindedness of the later son is relevant here. Not prone to handle
plural premises and to organize them into an interconnected
whole, he condenses the plurality into a common unity by obliter-
ating the differences between the plural premises. We recall that
Epicurus, the adherent to the atomistic theory, secured this un-
differentiated unanimity among his followers by forcing on them
a dictatorial creed which they were to memorize but not question.
If man is always an immature child at heart, Hobbes is right.
If man eventually matures, Locke is right. If some men remain
immature and some men become mature, both Hobbes and Locke
are partially correct.

Disconectedness in Hobbes is seen in other ways. The connection between a man and his toiled-for property is quite tenuous. The support of the militia by which the sovereign defends the people against foreign invasion requires money. Therefore, Hobbes' sovereigns have to requisition money from their subjects in order to defray the expenses of the militia. Also tenuous is the connection between the people and the sovereign. Although the latter has almost absolute power, his failure to protect and sustain the people is a condition for dissolution of the artificial covenant between them. The people are free to become colliding atoms again, or they can choose a new unifying, protecting leader. Their connected allegiance lasts as long as their lives are protected and their stomachs are fairly full.

Whereas later son Hobbes is not celebrated for his idealism, this is not the case with later son Rousseau. Rousseau's ideas were an inspiration for the French Revolution and somewhat less so for the American Revolution. We have already given evidence of Rousseau's oral deprivation tendencies. We should expect him, therefore, to be Epicurean rather than Stoic in outlook, short-term rather than long-term, a consumer rather than a conserver of provisions, a rejector of contracts which overlook human needs rather than an adherent of contractual property rights. His *Social Contract* appears to bear out these expectations.

Rousseau believed that civil society was founded on the basis of a hoax, the acquisitive taking in the gullible:

The first man who, having enclosed a piece of ground, bethought himself of saying *This is mine*, and found people simple enough to believe him, was the real founder of civil society. From how many crimes, wars and murders . . . might not any one have saved mankind, by pulling up the stakes, or filling up the ditch, and crying to his fellows, "Beware of listening to this impostor; you are undone if you once forget that the fruits of the earth belong to us all, and the earth itself to nobody."[29]

We do not see in this later son the belief we noted in the first sons that a man's labor entitles him to enclose a toiled-upon parcel of common land and to say *"This is mine."* Rousseau's theory about how primitive man got into such sore straits shows strong features of social disconnectedness. In the beginning there seems to have been human atoms interested in self-preservation rather than the closely knit and connected family molecules that first son Locke imagined:

One [appetite] which urged him to propagate his species—a blind propensity that, having nothing to do with the heart, produced a merely animal act. The want once gratified, the two sexes knew each other no more; and even the offspring was nothing to its mother, as soon as it could do without her.[30]

The transition from atomistic disconnection to some type of group living is, according to Rousseau, one in which the rights of atomistic man still have priority over the rights of molecular man. For, although men began to see some advantages of mutual assistance,

they were perfect strangers to foresight, and were so far from troubling themselves about the distant future, that they hardly thought of the morrow. If a deer was to be taken, every one saw that, in order to succeed, he must abide faithfully by his post: but if a hare happened to come within the reach of any one of them, it is not to be doubted that he pursued it without scruple, and, having seized his prey, cared very little, if by so doing he caused his companions to miss theirs.[31]

It is only much later, according to Rousseau, that this basic, disconnected "Man for Man only when it helps the one Man" orientation became recognizably connected. But whatever advantages accrued from a closer family life, they were to be offset by tendencies toward industriousness, leisure time, the making of comparisons, jealous love and unequal accumulations of property: "the fermentation caused by these new leavens ended by producing combinations fatal to innocence and happiness."[32]

These, for Rousseau, are the wages of intimate connectedness. Whereas the Lockean school with its emphasis on self might protest against excessive intimacy on the grounds that it is too encroaching, that it interferes with self-determination, that it wastes precious time, Rousseau's complaint is that it arouses excessive, insatiable passions of love and envy. "Better not try for too much," Rousseau seems to be saying, together with other later sons (Epicurus, Montaigne, and Emerson). And for Rousseau, it is better to return to a life of relatively atomistic contented equality,

so long as they [men] undertook only what a single person could accomplish, and confined themselves to such arts as did not require the joint labour of several hands, they lived free, healthy, honest and happy lives. . . . But from the moment one man began to stand in need of the help of another; from the moment it appeared advantageous to any one man to have enough provisions for two, equality disappeared, property was introduced, work became indispensable, and . . . slavery and misery were soon seen to germinate and grow up with the crops.[33]

Rousseau is out of sympathy with the legitimately rich as well as the illegitimately rich: "Even those who had been enriched by their own industry, could hardly base their proprietorship on better claims. It was in vain to repeat, 'I built this well; I gained this spot by my industry. . . .' "[34] As long as "numbers of your fellow-creatures are starving, for want of what you have too much of?"[35] Rousseau's basic solution is to dissolve the inequality-producing social contracts; to expropriate the rich, and return to simple, happy equality.

Let us now contrast later son Rousseau's political social theories with those of another Frenchman, first son Montesquieu. While the primary purpose is to gain more insight into political connectedness and disconnectedness, a secondary purpose is to show that personality characteristics may transcend national characteristics. We have already seen that French later son Rousseau is similar to English later son Hobbes; we shall see that French first son Montesquieu resembles English first son Locke. The contrast between these two Frenchmen gains added importance in that Durkheim designated them as the forerunners of the science of sociology. Montesquieu shares the idea of first son Locke that the laws of nature are primary, that affiliation between men and justice between men existed before the advent of formal social organization. Durkheim writes, quoting Montesquieu: "Before laws were made . . . there were relations of possible justice. To say that there is nothing just or unjust but what is commanded or forbidden by positive laws is the same as saying that before the describing of a circle all the radii were not equal."[36] It would appear that first son Montesquieu perceives in Man an innate affiliative connectedness and morality prior to the advent of formal social law. What goes on in the individual must for Montesquieu (as for first sons Locke, Kant, Shaftesbury, and Freud) be given as much weight as what goes on in the social organism or body politic. Montesquieu's connectedness is shown also in his postulating that social phenomena obey certain causal laws. He did not share later son Hume's skepticism about deterministic laws; rather, he was more like first sons Kepler, Newton, Marx, and Freud in their intuition that there were such laws. Durkheim believed this to be the main contribution of Montesquieu as the precursor of sociology and wrote, "This idea is stated at the beginning of the [Montesquieu's] book, where we find the famous definition: 'Laws . . . are necessary relations arising from the nature of things.' This definition applies not only to the laws of nature, but also to those that govern human societies."[37]

Rousseau's tendencies toward disconnectedness have already been described. Another evidence of them is the manner in which he disconnects himself from all current notions in order to arrive at a view about what man could be like in a state of Nature. This method of systematic disconnecting doubt was used by another later son, Descartes. As Durkheim says: "One cannot fail to be struck by the resemblance between this [Rousseau's] method and that of Descartes. Both thinkers hold that the first operation of science should be a kind of intellectual purge. . . . Both set out to remove the rubble and uncover the solid rock on which the entire structure of knowledge should rest. . . ."[38]

Rousseau's removal of the rubble led him to the solid rock of atomistic amoral man capable only of sensations and living in perfect dependent equilibrium with a more or less provident Nature. Montesquieu's acceptance of the rubble led him to the notion of a primary affiliative and moral man. There is no doubt that in terms of human infant development Rousseau goes further back than Montesquieu. The former gives a good description of the immature fetus or of the infant up to the age of five months, an infant who knows only the breast and not the mother to whom the breast is attached. Montesquieu's description is more applicable to the infant of the age of six months, one who is attached to the mother as well as to the breast, and who is desirous of her love as well as her milk. Rousseau's aim is to change society so that it approximates the impersonal quality originally found in the state of nature. That is, he wishes the restoration of the early stable equilibrium in which Nature regularly provided sustenance for physical needs. One might say he wishes to restore the early period of dependence on impersonal breast and to avoid dependence on the human being who possesses the breast. (Rousseau, as we know, vigorously asserted that French mothers should nurse their babies.) Society then should become the impersonal breast and there should not be any strong affiliation or connectedness. It is safer to depend on things than upon men. In order to form an impersonal society resembling the former state of nature, Rousseau offers a new social contract by which, according to Durkheim, "each individual will vanishes into a common, general will, which is the basis of society."[39]

This contract is quite similar to that proposed by later son Hobbes—the difference being that with Rousseau the body politic represents the collective will, whereas with Hobbes the absolute monarch represents this. And just as Hobbes stated that under certain conditions, such as need be for self-preservation, the subject could abrogate the contract, so does Rousseau suggest that if the general collective will does not really represent the objectives of the disconnected citizenry, they have a right to disobey the alleged general will. As Durkheim says: "When such violations [of the general will] occur, they are committed, not by the sovereign power but by individuals who have taken its place and usurped its authority. Hence there is no obligation to obey."[40] This view of Rousseau illustrates the later-son tendency to loose contractual ties.

The views of Rousseau and Montesquieu, as well as those of Hobbes and Locke, were available to the Founding Fathers of the United States. And how the American first-son–later-son polarity was influential in adopting or revising certain of these views will be the topic of the concluding part of this chapter.

It is, in a way, appropriate that early history of the United States be the subject of a brief survey. Apart from it being the country with which the author is best acquainted, the more important consideration is that the United States uniquely represents a prolonged experience and experiment in democracy. The earlier antimonarchial attitude developed in time into an anti-aristocratic one. So vigorous has been the national feeling against an aristocratic elite that the United States now gives no titles or official recognition to meritorious achievements of its citizenry. Putting aside a contrast to England with her "Sirs" and "Dames," the equalitarian ethics of the United States overshadows that of Soviet Russia, who now honors her "Heroes of the Soviet Republic." The manner in which we have discussed the European political theorists should prepare the reader that the forthcoming description will cut across the usual way of classifying early American statesmen. Thus, besides the usual contrast of Democrat Jefferson with Federalist Hamilton, there will be a contrast of Democrat Jefferson and Democrat Jackson.

From what we have said about Rousseau, for example, it would appear that political classification may not be a simple task. His statement that man is everywhere in chains prompts one to label him as a lover of freedom. Yet, in spite of his pronounced democratic equalitarianism, his solution—that of having all citizens very dependent on the city-state—suggests that he is willing to substitute state-imposed chains for man-imposed chains. In this solution he is not far from Hobbes and the Leviathan State. Rousseau then appears to be a different kind of freedom-lover than Locke who, though an advocate of some economic inequality, opposed the tyranny of an absolutist central power over individual citizens. Similar nuances will be brought out as we now discuss the early American statesmen.

A logical beginning offers itself in the comparison of first son Thomas Jefferson and later son Alexander Hamilton. According to Charles Wiltse, the intellectual lineages of these two men are in the direction we would expect. "From Hobbes' theory it follows that the end of the State is force, the power to maintain order; and revolution, accordingly, is always wrong. Locke holds, on the contrary, that men enter society for the protection of property, and have consequently a right to change their government, by force if necesary, when it no longer fulfills this purpose. Locke's argument justified the American Revolution; but when it came to establishing a government for the thirteen United States, there were those who placed greater confidence in the opposing view. Outstanding among the champions of Hobbes was Alexander Hamilton, while Locke's basic position was espoused by Jefferson, who added to it certain modifications and distinctions of his own."[41] Thus, first son Jefferson follows first son Locke, and later son Hamilton follows later son Hobbes. One of Jefferson's modifications was to change Locke's "life, liberty and possessions" to "life, liberty and pursuit of happiness." In this Epicurean undertone of Jefferson we encounter a formidable, stickling point in our generalization that first sons are more apt to be Stoic and later sons Epicurean. Jefferson may then be an exception. However, according to Wiltse he is not a pure exception. Jefferson preferred the Stoic doctrine as late as 1785. However, in 1817 his greatest praise was not for Seneca, the Stoic, but for Epicurus. It is Wiltse's opinion that Jefferson is in agreement with Epicurean doctrine as far as the basis of knowledge being sensation and the soul being material.

But of the ultimate dissolution of the soul with the death of the body, he is not so sure as is Lucretius; and when we come to the organization of society and the social compact, the divergence is sharp. . . .

Lucretius finds nature, although governed by law, a chance and purposeless creation; Jefferson never doubts the reasonableness of the world order. . . .

The dictum of Hobbes, who follows Epicurus, that justice [Morality] is based on convention only, Jefferson regards as "Humiliation to human nature."[42]

The evidence seems to point to Jefferson being as much Stoic as Epicurean in his orientation. Apart from these philosophic labels, certainly the inner moral voice is an intuition with him as is his idea that man is basically interconnected with society. He does not believe that most adult men are immature rogues who have to be held in check, but rather, like Locke, he believes that on maturity men no longer need be dictated to. This is why he believed so strongly in the Bill of Rights, and why earlier he opposed the Federal Constitution when it omitted the Bill of Rights.

We shall not go into much detail about later son Alexander Hamilton; a brief quotation from Wiltse will give the flavor of Hamilton's position and his alignment with other later sons:

If Jefferson had been slow to approve the constitution, it was because he feared its centralization of power would rob the common man of his liberty. Hamilton disapproved of it till the day of his death because it did not do that very thing. . . . For Hamilton, under the influence of the two political theorists most distasteful to Jefferson, Hobbes and Hume, was frankly the champion of the Leviathan state. He combined with a deep distrust of democracy a sincere belief that no government could endure which did not identify its interests with the interests of property and wealth.[43]

What in American History follows Jefferson, and Hamilton, is much less agreed upon by the historians. Thus our further remarks will necessarily be quite speculative. Perhaps it would be better to put them in the form of questions. For example, "Is it more than a coincidence that Andrew Jackson was the first later son President?" In speculating that it may be more than coincidence, we shall offer the following considerations. Schlesinger's description of the Jacksonian revolution suggests that it was a political-social movement of the propertyless against the propertied. Jackson then would not be directly in the tradition of later sons Hobbes and Hamilton who wanted a centralized, absolute power and a permanent aristocracy. Rather he would be in the tradition of later son Rousseau who advocated the elimination of inequality. Although in the bank issue Jackson's target is the policy of later son Hamilton, the question arises as to why the preceding first son Presidents did not as effectively combat Hamilton's Federalization. A reading of Schlesinger yields the impression that the preceding Presidents were too identified with the past to fight vigorously for the masses and that it took later son Jackson to activate first son Jefferson's democratic ideals. Schlesinger writes:

Basically, it [Jacksonian democracy] was a revival of Jeffersonianism, but the Jeffersonian inheritance was strengthened by the infusion of fresh influences. . . .

THE NEW INDUSTRIALISM HAD TO BE ACCEPTED: banks, mills, factories, industrial capital, industrial labor. They were all distasteful realities for orthodox Jeffersonians. . . . "The mobs of great cities," Jefferson had said, "add just so much to the support of pure government, as sores do to the strength of the human body."

Jackson himself never betrayed any of Jefferson's revulsion to industrialism. . . .

Jacksonians now tended to exalt human rights as a counterweight to property rights. . . .

In several respects, then, the Jacksonians revised the Jeffersonian faith for America. They moderated that side of Jeffersonianism which talked of agricultural virtue, independent proprietors, "natural" property, abolition of industrialism, and expanded immensely that side which talked of economic equality, the laboring classes, human rights and the control of industrialism. . . .

Jeffersonian democracy looked wistfully back toward a past slipping further every minute into the mists of memory, while Jacksonian democracy came straight-forwardly to grips with a rough and unlovely present.[44]

In Jackson, then, can be seen several later-son characteristics—a military effectiveness, an identification with the deprived
who are beaten down by contractual rights (Jackson himself had
lost considerably at the hands of paper money manipulators),
an acceptance of the Industrial Machine, an addressing of himself to the immediate present rather than to "misty" past. The
question to be put to the historians is, "Did it take a later son to
effect this kind of political social revolution or could the preceding first sons—Washington, John Adams, Jefferson, Madison,
Monroe, and John Quincy Adams—have done it just as well?"
Granted that they were capable of effecting a revolution which
asserted "We are grown men now, England, and no longer need
your paternal supervision." But were they as capable of a revolution which asserted "There are needy, propertyless masses who
deserve a voice in the government and an equal share in the
country's wealth." It is of interest that beginning with Jackson
there were four later-son Presidents in succession (Jackson, Van
Buren, Harrison, and Tyler). Again, this could be a coincidence
or it could reflect a change in national character.

The other speculation to be offered also arises from what
may be merely coincidence. It deals with the topic of secession,
with whether the separate states possess the right to disconnect
themselves from the Union and to pursue their separate exist-
ences. In terms discussed earlier, the question is whether the
states are loosely and atomistically bound in a temporary contract which they can abrogate if they so wish, or are they bound
molecularly and tightly in a contract insuring the intercellular
nature of the whole. As will be recalled, later sons more often
advocate loose contracts, first sons binding contracts. In American political history, this trend seems to be borne out. The most
prominent states' rights advocate was later son Calhoun, whose
position in this much preceded the question of slavery. He is
noted for his proposal that South Carolina nullify the federal
protective tariff law of 1828. And just before the Civil War,
later son Thoreau went even further toward atomism and advocated that individual citizens secede from the state of Massa-
chusetts in order to combat the evil of slavery. "Some are peti-
tioning the State to dissolve the Union. . . . Why do they not
dissolve it themselves . . . and refuse to pay their quota into its

treasury? Do not they stand in the same relation to the state that the state does to the Union?"[45]

The most striking instance, of course, of the right to secession is seen in the Civil War. Appropriately enough, the seceding South prefers the more atomistic name of "The War Between the States." The coincidence resides in the fact that the two principal men who preserved the interconnected Union were first sons, Lincoln and Grant. And the three principal Confederate leaders—Davis, Benjamin, and Lee—were all later sons. And the final unofficial nullification effort came from later son John Wilkes Booth. Again, the historian will have to decide whether this is coincidence or whether it illustrates the disconnectedness tendencies of the later sons.

A discussion of the issues involved in post-Civil War United States history would inordinately prolong this already lengthy chapter. In passing, however, there may be speculatively noted a certain kind of sympathetic identification on the part of *later sons* with the have-nots, with the oppressed needy, which expresses itself in various ways. It can take the form of opposing private, individual "bigness" as in the case of Andrew Jackson, Veblen, Brandeis, and Norris—or in the form of helping the unfortunately deprived (militantly in the case of Garrison, more calmly with Seward and with Hoover). It will be recalled that there were several reformers of social ills among Lasswell's later-son political types. This kind of immediate sympathetic identification appears, to the author, to be different from the more "moral duty," more intellectualized kind of concern with the oppressed and demeaned, as shown by such first sons as Jefferson, Lincoln, Holmes, Wilson, and the two Roosevelts.

With these impressions and speculations we conclude this chapter and the first section of the book. Considerable territory has had to be traversed in this general section in order to demonstrate, through first- and later-son polarities, the various ramifications of connectedness and disconnectedness. In a certain way, the journey has completed a full circle. We began with the sources of moral authority and we now end with them. Earlier we considered the individual and sometimes clinical repercussions of inner and outer moral authority. And in this chapter we have dealt with their political-social repercussions. Whereas earlier the sense of evil and innocence and the mood of melancholia or cheerfulness were the prime considerations, now the significant matter is the nature and purpose of the political state. If the source of moral authority is inner, then the state need not function as an external policeman. But if there is little or no inner source, such a policeman is very necessary to quell riotous disorder.

A clue to the family origins of connectedness and disconnectedness has been supplied by what first- and later-son political theorists have speculated concerning the birth of society. First son Locke gives a picture of an originally closely knit family, of the father quite active in inculcating reason and morality in his son. The result is that the mature son no longer requires paternal direction; he has made his father's doctrines his own. A similar connectedness, inner-moral authority view is shared by other first sons—Freud, Kant, Shaftesbury, Montesquieu, and Jefferson. Later son Rousseau offers an opposite picture, that of individuals atomistically or disconnectedly interested in their own welfare, weakly bound into a family unit, perpetually on the verge of violent wrongdoing, and thus constantly requiring of the political state the exercise of its police power. Views of this disconnectedness, outer-moral authority nature have been held by other later sons—Machiavelli, Hobbes, Hamilton, and Russell.

Political considerations other than moral authority have of course been treated in this chapter. The principal one is the matter of property. We have attempted to show that the connectedness-prone first sons tend to operate in the Stoic tradition of conserving and accumulating for future rewards. They see the police power of the state being exercised to protect those future rewards for past toil and abstinence. The disconnectedness-prone later sons tend to operate in the Epicurean tradition of consuming present supplies. They see the state not only as the external policeman but also as the external provider and equal distributor of these supplies. The chronic controversy about what property belongs to whom can be seen in first sons Locke and Jefferson championing the right of a man to the fruits of his labor, and later sons Rousseau and Jackson regarding the needs of men as the paramount factor in political matters.

We have limited ourselves to eminent men in the remote past and in the comparatively recent past. This was done in order to submit evidence which fairly well has stood the test of time. The political-social issues raised in this chapter are, however, still very much alive. We shall reserve for the final chapter some speculative comments on the contemporary scene and on the first and later sons involved.

PART TWO *Special Considerations*

CHAPTER VIII *Tendencies in Literature*

THIS SECTION is devoted to rather special aspects of the personality. It will be much shorter and more speculative than the long first section, principally because the author's clinical experience is not an aid in evaluating the new topics. The matters discussed in the first section—morality, action, power, omnipotence, life aims, etc.—are those which come under the psychoanalyst's close and frequent scrutiny. Insights gained from this scrutiny may with comparative assurance be applied to the thoughts, feelings, and actions of eminent men. But when such topics as literature, history, and science are considered—as they will be in these chapters—the psychoanalyst cannot borrow easily from his clinical experience and thus must remain only descriptive, suggestive, or speculative. Furthermore, the speculations are derived mainly from reading of secondary sources rather than from reading of the original text. The author's wish, then, in this new section is to communicate impressions regarding the application of the connectedness-disconnectedness hypothesis to particular topics—impressions that clearly need evaluation by the appropriate specialists.

Beginning with literature, we should come to closer grips with a matter that has been alluded to throughout the book—the predominance of first sons among eminent poets. First, we should demonstrate in a general way that dominance does exist. The trend appears quite marked in poets who are not Americans. The lists, without specification as to major and minor poets, are first sons English (19): Browning, Burns, Byron, Cowper, Donne, Dryden, Gray, Housman, Hulme, Keats, Kipling, Marlowe,

[171]

Milton, Pope, Shakespeare, Shelley, Sidney, Spenser, Yeats. Later sons English (8): W. H. Auden, Beaumont, Blake, Coleridge, Cowley, Goldsmith, Tennyson, Wordsworth. First sons (non-English and non-American) (13): Baudelaire, Claudel, Dante, Goethe, Heine, Hölderlin, La Fontaine, Lorca, Pasternak, Pushkin, Rilke, Rossetti, Schiller. And later sons (non-English and non-American) (2): Ronsard and Tagore. To the list of first son poets may be added the name of the early Greek poet Hesoid whom most accounts give as a first son, who had an inheritance dispute with his younger brother. The American poets do not show this marked trend. First sons (10): Aiken, W. R. Benét, Hart Crane, Field, Frost, Lindsay, Christopher Morley, Pound, Whittier, and William Carlos Williams. Later sons (8): S. V. Benét, T. S. Eliot, Longfellow, Lowell, Poe, Riley, Robinson, and Whitman. This lack of trend is pointed up in the fact that of two brothers, later son Stephen Vincent Benét is more renowned than first son William Rose Benét. What accounts for these national differences is a question better left to poets, critics, and culture historians.

If it is granted that first sons generally predominate among the poets, the question is, "What has poetry to do with first sons," or rather "What has it to do with connectedness?" Susanne K. Langer's writings may supply some clues. If a poetic predilection consists in part of an ability for abstract symbolization of language, her comments on early child development are pertinent. She writes that first the infant makes "idle experiments in vocalization. . . . If, now, his audible acts wake echoes in his surroundings—that is to say, if his elders reply to them—there is a growth of experience; for the baby appears to recognize, gradually, that the sound which happens there and comes to him, is the *same* as his lalling. This is a rudimentary abstraction. . . ."[1] It follows from Langer that this "rudimentary abstraction" depends on parental attentiveness and responsiveness to the infant—on a mother-child connectedness which tends to occur more often with the first born, or first born of the sex. If the elders do not reply as constantly to the child (as happens more frequently with later borns) the child may continue in experimental vocalizing or, as Langer suggests, he shifts more quickly in growing up from "subjective, symbolic, to practical associations."[2]

We have noted, it will be recalled, a greater practicality in later sons and a greater dreamy speculativeness in first sons.

So far, Langer's views account only for a symbolic language propensity which could manifest itself in fiction as well as in poetry. Granted that the first son may more frequently possess a strong subjective, symbolic layer arising out of parent-child connectedness, how may this lead to the making of poetry? Again Langer suggests an answer. In following Langer now in her differentiation of carefree fairy tales from serious myth we should keep in mind the light-heartedness and need for quick gratification in later sons and, in contrast, the serious moral undertones of the stoical first sons:

The difference between the two fictional modes—many scholars to the contrary notwithstanding—is a crucial one. For the fairytale is irresponsible; it is frankly imaginary, and its purpose is to gratify wishes. . . . The end of the story is always satisfying, though by no means always moral; the hero's heroism may be slyness or luck quite as readily as integrity or valor. The theme is generally the triumph of an unfortunate one—an enchanted maiden, a youngest son . . . over his or her superiors, whether these be kings, bad fairies . . . stepmothers, or elder brothers.

Myth, on the other hand . . . is taken with religious seriousness, either as historic fact or as a "mystic" truth. Its typical theme is tragic, not utopian; and its personages tend to fuse into stable *personalities* of supernatural character. . . .

Fairytale is a personal gratification . . . a compensation for the shortcomings of real life, an escape from actual frustration and conflict. Because its function is subjective, the hero is strictly individual and human. . . .

Myth, on the other hand . . . is a recognition of natural conflicts, of human desire frustrated by non-human powers, hostile oppression, or contrary desires. . . . Its ultimate end is not wishful distortion of the world, but serious envisagement of its fundamental truths; moral orientation, not escape. . . . Moreover, because the mythical hero is not the subject of an egocentric day-dream, but a subject greater than any individual, he is always felt to be superhuman, even if not quite divine. . . .

The great step from fairytale to myth is taken when not only social forces—persons, customs, laws, traditions—but also cosmic forces surrounding mankind, are expressed in the story; when not only relationships of an individual to society, but of mankind to nature, are conceived through the spontaneous metaphor of poetic fantasy. . . .

There is something to be said for the contention that mythology is made by the epic poets. . . .

For it [the epic] demands not only personification, not only some sort of rise and fall in heroic action, but *poetic form*, a unity above the separate incidents, a beginning, climax, and solution of the entire mythical drama. . . .

The origin of myth is dynamic, but its purpose is philosophical. It is the primitive phase of metaphysical thought, the first embodiment of *general ideas*. . . . When this [mythical] mode is exhausted, natural religion is superseded by a discursive and more literal form of thought, namely philosophy.[3]

Langer's views supply, it would appear, a serviceable explanation of why the connectedness-prone first sons tend to express themselves in poetry. Familiar characteristics of the first sons are seen in the makers of epic poetry—the seriousness, the taking myth as historical fact, the two-self conflict of contrary desires, moral orientation, the hero as superhuman, the plural considerations of cosmic forces, and a connecting or unifying of separate incidents. And in the fairy-tale makers are seen some characteristics we have noted in later sons—the wish gratification, the happy ending, the lack of emphasis on morality, the hero as merely human, as a younger son fighting off the yoke of the elder brother, as succoring the deprived and unfortunate.

If we turn to what first and later son poets have said about poetry, we may see some support of the foregoing speculations. Sir Philip Sidney, a first son, wrote *An Apologie For Poetrie* which Smith and Parks, compilers and editors of the anthology *The Great Critics*, describe as one of the first pieces of formal criticism written in England. Sidney stressed the ennobling, utilitarian value of poetry; not, as we shall find with some later-son writers, the sheer pleasure and delight obtained from it. Smith and Parks state: "Sidney . . . bases his position . . . on the educational value."[4] They note with reservation his Aristotelian-like "careful divisions of poetry into types,"[5] and they say, "we are out of accord with the rigidity of his arguments from authority. He 'looks merely at the stop-watch.' Theocritus did not do it; Virgil did not do it; . . . therefore Spenser must not do it." [Saintsbury: *History of English Criticism* . . . .].[6]

We see in Sidney the first-son seriousness and the intimate, almost subservient connectedness to past time. It is interesting

that Sidney speaks of the Philosopher-Historian-Poet triad for
which first sons have a predilection, and of how the poet can
be a better educator than the philosopher or historian:

> The Philosopher therefore and the Historian, are they which would
> win the gole: the one by precept, the other by example. . . . For the
> Philosopher . . . is so hard of utterance, . . . that one that hath no
> other guide but him, shall wade in him till hee be olde, before he
> shall finde sufficient cause to bee honest. . . .
>
> On the other side, the Historian wanting the precept, is so tyed,
> not to what shoulde bee, but to what is, to the particuler truth of
> things, and not to the general reason of things, that hys example
> draweth no necessary consequence and therefore a lesse fruitfull
> doctrine.
>
> Nowe dooth the peerelesse Poet performe both [functions]. . . .[7]

Other first-son poets and critics also propose the notion
that poetry should have an ennobling, serious, moral, tradition-
connecting purpose. Pope, according to Smith and Parks, was
"strongly desirous . . . to be the lawgiver for manners and morals
to his time. . . ."[8] And he believed in a stoical subordination of
instinct to an inner voice of morality and reason:

> But the phrase "follow nature" did not mean "to abandon yourself
> to your instincts . . . but to subordinate yourself to the commands of
> the one thing which was the same in all men—the reason. . . ."[9]

Schiller stresses also the moral element in poetry:

> Though man by the freedom of his imagination and of his under-
> standing departs from simplicity, from truth, from the necessity of
> nature, not only a road always remains open to him to return to it,
> but, moreover, a powerful and indestructible instinct, the moral
> instinct, brings him incessantly back to nature; and it is precisely the
> poetrical faculty that is united to this instinct by the ties of the
> closest relationship.[10]

Samuel Johnson exhibited a similar moral orientation together
with an omnipotent connectedness which, à la Hegel, takes in
all of time:

> He [the poet] must write as the interpreter of Nature and the legis-
> lator of mankind, and consider himself as presiding over the thoughts
> and manners of future generations, as a being superior to time and
> place. . . . "Poets are the unacknowledged legislators of the world."[11]

In Shelley we also may see clearly the first-son characteristics of connectedness. From his *A Defense of Poetry*:

In the infancy of society every author is necessarily a poet, because language itself is poetry; and to be a poet is to apprehend the true and the beautiful, in a word, the good which exists in the relation, subsisting, first between existence and perception, and secondly between perception and expression. . . .

But poets, or those who imagine and express this indestructible order, are not only the authors of language and of music, of the dance, and architecture, . . . they are the institutors of laws . . . and the teachers, who draw into a certain propinquity with the beautiful and the true, that partial apprehension of the agencies of the invisible world which is called religion.[12]

As we pass now to the later sons, we are not struck as much by the vast, connected synthesis of the true, good, and beautiful emphasized by first sons. With later sons, the aim is much more modest—to entertain, simply to write a poem, to give pleasure, to make the poem short and sweet, to show power. Ronsard shows the later son's pragmatic concern with method, with how to invent a poem, and an aversion to the melancholic. Reminiscent of Descartes' *Discourse on Method*, he begins his *A Brief on the Art of French Poetry*: "Although the art of Poetry can be neither learned nor taught by precept, . . . I wish to lay down some rules by which one day you may be able to reach the first order of skill in this happy calling. . . ."[13] Later he says, according to Smith and Parks:

Since the Muses are not willing to reside in a soul unless it be kindly, saintly, virtuous, you should act always with kindness, never with meanness, sullenness, or chagrin. . . .

When I bid you invent fair things and great, I do not mean inventions fantastic and melancholic. . . .[14]

The impression gained from Ronsard is that the poet should not become emotionally involved; that he should stand at a safe distance and go through some imitation of feelings. Like Descartes and Montaigne, he distrusts excesses and would prefer to be nearly right rather than all wrong. This is an impression opposite to the one gained for first sons. With the latter, we feel that there are pent-up emotions bent on finding some symbolic outlet that will morally synthesize their inner conflict.

Wordsworth, according to Smith and Parks, is noted for his rebelling against binding, overconnected traditionalism:

The *Observations Prefixed to the Second Edition of Lyrical Ballads* has had a various treatment. It has been regarded in certain quarters as a declaration of literary rights, a powerful document in the liberating of letters from bondage; . . . whatever sort of *thing* the document was, it raised a wall between the Eighteenth and Nineteenth Centuries; it dated a new era. . . . We do not often have such dividing walls.[15]

Whereas the first son endeavors to make a synthesis of the thesis and antithesis, respectively represented by past tradition and present exigency, the later son, less connectedly bound, can with little psychic effort make a clean break. Thus Wordsworth here behaves like the present-minded, like such strippers-away of the past as Voltaire, Bacon, Rousseau, Lenin, etc. Wordsworth is oriented toward free instinctual pleasure:

It is desirable that such readers . . . should not suffer the solitary word Poetry, a word of very disputed meaning, to stand in the way of their gratification; but that, while they are perusing this book, they should ask themselves if it contains a natural delineation of human passions, human characters, and human incidents; and if the answer be favorable to the author's wishes, that they should consent to be pleased in spite of that most dreadful enemy to our pleasures, our own pre-established codes of decision.[16]

In the last sentence we see that for later son Wordsworth, "that most dreadful enemy . . . the pre-established codes" was vanquished with as much ease as later son Jacob vanquished the Angel of God in a wrestle. The inner moral voice—the superego—does not have the supremacy over the later sons that it has for the first sons.

Later son Poe not only is pro-pleasure but he is against anything of epic proportion, against anything plural which will dilute the single power effect. Smith and Parks quote Norman Foerster's summary of Poe's aesthetic beliefs:

"The end of art is pleasure, not truth. In order that pleasure may be intense, the work of art must have unity and brevity." . . . his [Poe's] ideas were drawn . . . above all, from Coleridge, his chief master in criticism. . . .[17]

(Coleridge is a later son.) The penetrating, precise exploration of a single part and the military orientation—both characteristic of later sons—may be seen in their quotation from Poe: "We now demand the light artillery of the intellect; we need the curt, the condensed, the pointed, the readily diffused." [Marginalia].[18]

In *The Poetic Principle*, Poe inveighs against the long epic: "The value of the poem is in the ratio of this elevating excitement. But all excitements are, through a psychal necessity, transient. . . . after a lapse of half an hour . . . it [the excitement] flags—fails—a revulsion ensues—and then the poem is, in effect, and in fact, no longer such."[19] Whatever first son Milton believed he was achieving toward a large-scope interconnected unity in *Paradise Lost*, Poe's opinion is that if it is read that way, the effect is lost:

> This great work [*Paradise Lost*] . . . is to be regarded as poetical, only when . . . we view it merely as a series of minor poems. If, to preserve its Unity—its totality of effect or impression—we read it (as would be necessary) at a single sitting, the result is but a constant alternation of excitement and depression. . . .
>
> In regard to the "Iliad," . . . granting the epic intention, I can say only that the work is based on an imperfect sense of art. . . . If, at any time, any very long poems *were* popular in reality—which I doubt—it is at least clear that no very long poem will ever be popular again.[20]

Regarding didactic morality, later son Poe discusses it like later son Bacon discussed the idols which interfere with scientific discovery:

> While the epic mania . . . has, for some years past, been gradually dying out of the public mind, by mere dint of its own absurdity, we find it succeeded by a heresy too palpably false to be long tolerated. . . . I allude to the heresy of *The Didactic*. It has been assumed . . . that the ultimate object of all Poetry is Truth. Every poem, it is said, should inculcate a moral. . . . [But I believe that] there neither exists nor *can* exist any work more thoroughly dignified—more supremely noble than this very poem— . . . this poem written solely for the poem's sake.[21]

Poe also is against the intense poetical, emotional involvement: "We must be simple, precise, terse. We must be cool, calm, unimpassioned. In a word, we must be in that mood, which, as nearly as possible, is the exact converse of the poetical. . . . He must be theory-mad beyond redemption who . . . shall still persist in attempting to reconcile the obstinate oils and waters of Poetry and Truth."[22]

The question of what is poetry, of what is its aim, as the foregoing would indicate, is not an easily answered one. Much less difficulty would be encountered if the question were "What are poetries?" For in writing about the subject the poets themselves appear to form a familiar polarity—the first sons nearer the Stoic connectedness pole, the later sons nearer the Epicurean disconnectedness pole. The difference of opinion arising from this polarity certainly may add to the feeling of an individual poet that he is out of joint with his time. There may be not only a generalized public indifference to a general poetic expression but also a rejection by the in-group critics of a specific kind of poetry. The critical ban placed by first sons Pope and Johnson on any spontaneous poetry that did not have moral undertones can be just as frustrating as the critical ban placed by later son Eliot on poetry which has excessive feelings or which estimates man excessively as heroic.

All that has been discussed here about poets and poetry may be applied to literature in general. Throughout this book, the field of literature has been resorted to in order to illustrate some repercussions of the connectedness-disconnectedness hypothesis. One point deserves further amplification. We have repeatedly seen that the first sons have a predilection for larger-than-life-size heroic themes with later sons are inclined to life-size average man views. Thus, the heroic, ennobling features were strikingly seen in first son Carlyle; the leveling, average man features in later son Emerson. And we alluded to the fact that in biography hero-appreciating first son Boswell differed from miniaturizing later son Strachey. In amplification we shall now mention other examples of contrasting attitudes to the proper size of Man.

There have been several literary works by later sons which can be interpreted as designed to topple man off his lofty over-estimated "arrogant" perch. The phrase "interpreted" is used advisedly, inasmuch as these works have ambiguous meanings. A factor which may throw an interpreter off is the later son's unconscious method of indirection, of nonfrontality. In short, frequently it is hard to pin down a later-son writer as to his intentions. Without it being said in so many words, the heroic,

serious man comes off, in the hands of the later sons, as a somewhat ridiculous figure. Infrequently will there be anything as
overt as later son Russell's speaking of being revolted by prudence as a cardinal rule of life. More often, it appears, there is a
light, darting, comic ridiculing, as evidenced by later son Oscar
Wilde's handling of the trait of earnestness. This is brought out
by Eric Bentley in his comparison of two masters of comedy,
the more frontally direct first son Shaw and the more elusive
later son Wilde. He writes:

> *The Importance of Being Earnest* . . . is a variant . . . of farce, a
> genre which, being the antithesis of serious, is not easily put to serious
> uses. . . .
>   Wilde proclaims that earnestness is less praiseworthy than the
> ironic attitude to life which is regarded as superficial. . . . Wilde is as
> much of a moralist as Bernard Shaw but . . . instead of presenting the
> problems of modern society directly, he flits around them, teasing
> them, declining to grapple with them. . . .
>   What begins as a prank ends as a criticism of life. What begins
> as intellectual high-kicking ends as intellectual sharp-shooting.[23]

The lighter, the more indirect touch of the later son can
obscure his intentions, just as a good guerrilla warfare leader is
not anxious to have his plans known. Wilde used elusive non-
serious farce, whereas Shaw's satiric bite is more recognizable.
Irony is too light a term to describe Shaw's involved seriousness—
as it is much too light to do justice to first son Swift's savagery
and first son Mencken's battle-ax. It appears to be a much more
appropriate term for later sons, such as Montaigne and Emerson.
Erich Heller, it will be recalled, treated later son Thomas Mann
separately as the Ironic German rather than including him in his
collection of disinherited minds who were mostly first sons.
Later son Veblen's ridiculing of the American businessman,
though sharp, does not have the heaviness of Mencken's term
"boob." Though more will be said about this subject later, at
this point it will suffice to indicate how a light, indirect method
of attack may conceal the fact that an attack is going on.

The foregoing consideration may be applied to the works
of later sons Cervantes and Melville. There is no unanimous agreement that they are attacking the lofty perched, serious, heroic
man. Much more unanimity obtains in the cases of later sons
Rabelais, Voltaire, and Mark Twain that they are, by satire,

irony, or comedy, cutting down to size romantic, heroic, out-sized men and customs. Mark Twain's *Huckleberry Finn* is often interpreted this way; *A Connecticut Yankee in King Arthur's Court* invariably so; and his privately published work on flatulence at the court undoubtedly so. But in the case of *Don Quixote*, critics are divided as to whether Cervantes was attack-ing what Don Quixote represented, or whether he identified with chivalrous, romantic attitudes. Whatever the answer really is, the bare text of Cervantes' work which puts Don Quixote in a comic light and practical Sancho in a wiser light moved first son Byron to say that Cervantes smiled away Spain's chivalry. It is of note that the major recent attempt to revive Spain's chivalry, heroic traditions and customs was carried out by first son Hemingway.

The case of *Moby Dick* is even less obvious. The character who attempts outsized tasks is Captain Ahab—his fate in relent-lessly pursuing the impossible is that which is attached to hybris, man's conceit that his omnipotence can challenge that of the gods. The reader is left with more sympathy for Ishmael and Moby Dick than for the power-crazed Ahab. The latter is foolish if not irrational. One does not get the same feeling when reading Hemingway's *Old Man and the Sea*. In this analogous situation of trying to land the fish the task is depicted heroically so that one empathizes with the old man. One feels he had to do what he did even though he comes out sadder and wiser.

The speculation that Herman Melville is attacking or at least not identifying with the epic myth-making hero can be sup-ported by Melville's overt feelings about his mother preferring his older brother and by certain trends in his works as seen in Newton Arvin's critical biography. As a background we learn, incidentally, from Arvin that Melville did not begin as a man of words, of symbolic language, but rather, reminiscent of Bacon and Descartes, as a man of action:

The need for movement, for flight, for the coarse stuff of experience was stronger in him in his earliest youth than the need for expression. The germ of what was creative in him needed to ripen, not in solitude nor in intellectual labor, but in the push and stir of action. In the beginning, for Melville, was decidedly not the word, but the deed.[24]

The later-son tendency toward practicality rather than toward poetic myths is indicated by Arvin's writing: "*Typee* and *Omoo* owe much of their vitality to their apparently unpoetic ballast of facts."[25]

In Melville, we do not see Santayana's solution for the future poet, that of rising vertically to an elevated throne and making the grand epic synthesis, imperturbed by the flux and mutation on the horizontal level; Melville plunged rather into the horizontal flux. This may account for Melville's greater success in prose than in poetry, even though he devoted much of his adult life exclusively to poetry. Arvin writes: "if Melville's poems have a strongly prosaic quality, this is their distinction, not their defect."[26] Later on he says: "Romantic as his mind in its deepest reaches was, it had always had, like most powerful minds, the other bias too, the bias toward 'facts,' toward materiality, toward the unromantic impermeability of things."[27] We should not expect, then, that Melville would be especially sympathetic to the kind of romantic heroics fanatically expressed by Ahab. Besides obviously missing in practicality, it may remind him of his older brother's lofty position in the family circle. Arvin takes note of a comic ridiculing of highly placed figures in *Omoo*: "The play of fantasy in *Omoo* takes the form not of night-marishness or even of daydreaming but of an easy and emotionally liberating current of humorous narrative, always slightly in excess, as one sees with half an eye, of the sober autobiographical facts. It usually has the satisfactory effect of throwing a ludicrous light on the representatives of order and authority—captains and mates, consuls and missionaries . . . we take our own revenge on respectability by contemplating the discomfiture of the feeble Captain Guy and the bullying consul Wilson. . . ."[28]

The question arises whether Melville takes revenge on his brother through the fate of Captain Ahab. About an earlier novel, *Redburn*, Arvin comments that the central character's social humiliation issues from wearing "the old gray shooting-jacket that Redburn's elder brother gives him as he sets out from home. . . ."[29] We would anticipate that somewhere in *Moby Dick* Melville's feelings about his brother would appear. Arvin, however, does not point this out. His interpretation of how Melville feels about Ahab is sufficiently positive in tone that one has the same inquiry as about Cervantes and *Don Quixote*—is he for or against the central heroic character? Perhaps the answer is that Melville is ambivalent—as is Cervantes. The heroic older brother is needed, is held up as well worthy of love, but is resented. Arvin regards Ahab as more than an example of clinical grandiosity:

Ahab is not only the sick self; he is, for his time and place, the noblest and most complete embodiment of the tragic hero. . . .

He calls himself "proud as a Greek god," and indeed his pride is noble enough to endure the comparison. . . .

Yet even as he pronounces his great tirade [against the flaming corposants] Ahab is dimly and bitterly aware that what he says is not true: what stands there is not, in the high sense, a personality, but only a proud and defiant will. . . . He has ceased to be anything but an Ego; a noble Ego, to be sure; a heroic one; but *that* rather than a Self. He is no longer a free mind: his thought has become the slave of his insane purpose. . . .

There is something of Prometheus, of Agamemnon, of Oedipus in Ahab: he is guilty of an inflated arrogance similar to theirs, a similar conviction of his superiority to the mass of ordinary men.[30]

If we follow Arvin, we can suppose that Melville had ambivalent feelings toward Ahab. But which side of the ambivalence is stronger—is Melville more for or more against? The ending of *Moby Dick* indicates that, using Langer's criteria, Melville leans more to the wishful fairy tale than to the tragic myth; that he uses the story as a compensation for life's shortcomings, that *Moby Dick* depicts a victory of the nobody, younger brother Ishmael over the somebody, dominant older brother Ahab for the love and possession of the mother; Arvin writes of the ending:

Ahab is dedicated now to mere destruction, and he ends by attaining his suicidal wish and meeting his death in water. Ishmael, thanks to his rejection of mere hatred, survives the wreck; is picked up before he drowns by "the devious-cruising *Rachel*," the vessel that is itself a symbol of bereaved motherhood.[31]

It certainly appears that the story ends more favorably for Ishmael than it does for Ahab. Ishmael gets the mother and Ahab goes to his death. The moral seems to be reflective of American equalitarianism, a theme also voiced by later sons Emerson, Whitman, Veblen, and Dewey. Not the favored arrogant, superior ones will inherit Mother Earth; no, they have had their chance— now it is the turn of the meek, of the ordinary man. In this context, Melville's poem about the partial mother may be re-quoted:

> When boys they were I helped the bent;
> I made the junior feel his place,
> Subserve the senior, love him, too;
> And sooth he does, and that's his saving grace.
> But me the meek one never can serve,
> Not he, he lacks the quality keen
> To make the mother through the son
> An envied dame of power, a social queen.[32]

Melville, it would appear, has finally turned the tables.

The contrast between larger-than-life-size first sons and actual life-size later sons would be expected to manifest itself in a subject especially conducive to larger-than-life-size overestimation—namely, romantic love between the sexes. The following will indicate that the first sons, who had a greater connectedness with the mother, more frequently are exponents of intense feelings to women than are later sons. Melville may serve as a starting point. Arvin writes:

> ... There was doubtless, in his feelings for Lizzie [his wife], a very large strain of the brotherly, even of the filial. . . .
> There is always a certain factitiousness or unreality in Melville's characters, except when . . . they are middle-aged or elderly. And he is always at his easiest and most unconstrained when he can leave the land and the world of women quite behind him and launch himself upon the high seas in the midst of men and boys exclusively.[33]

The above can serve as an initial contrast to what is found in first sons. The greatest romantic worship of Woman has been given by the mother-connected first sons—Abélard of Heloïse, Dante of Beatrice, Shakespeare of Juliet. The essence of the intense feeling is the search for *the* woman, *the* girl of one's dream. With later sons who have written about love between the sexes, the impression gained is about *a* man and *a* woman—as in Tolstoy's *Anna Karenina* or Lawrence's *Lady Chatterley's Lover*. The intense overestimation seems not to be present in the later sons—one woman, from a more practical viewpoint, is indeed not that different from another one. It is unlikely that a later son could write an epic heroic poem about a woman whose face launched a thousand ships. In psychoanalysis, the contrast may be seen between first son Freud and later son Adler. It is not surprising that Freud, who could write as late as 1931, "Deeply embedded in me there still lives on the happy child of Freiberg, a youthful mother's first-born son," should have stressed the erotic nature of the child, libido theory, and the Oedipus complex which presupposes that a boy is so desirous of his mother that he would wish to kill his father. Adler, on the other hand, placed minimal emphasis on the vicissitudes of heterosexual love as a mainspring for neurosis. While his opposing theory of a drive for power accounted for several phenomena not readily explainable by the libido theory, the power theory received a blow when first son King Edward VIII abdicated his throne in order to marry the woman he loved. First son Proust's attachment to a mother-connected childhood was as deeply embedded as Freud's, and more noticeable. Memories of childhood tantrums when his mother did not come to kiss him good night were not put to one side. So great was the connectedness to that special period and that special woman that he devoted almost all of his creative talent to an artistic reliving of the things past. The other side of the intense-feeling coin is represented by the leading mysogynist, first son Schopenhauer. Here it is not a case of little involvement, it is a case of love turning to fury. A similar chain of events occurred with first son Milton, who reacted intensely to the ego-wound of his young wife's deserting him, defended in his pamphlets the right to divorce such a wilful, contrary woman, and when these pamphlets were in danger of being considered heretic he wrote his famous *Areopagitica*.

The attitude of later sons to women seems comparatively lukewarm, neither very much for or against. Bacon regarded connectedness toward the wife and children as "hostages to fortune." The contrast between later son Eliot's no-excessive emotions and first son Yeats' overestimation can be seen in MacNeice's saying that Eliot's "Portrait of a Lady" throws a cold, cruel light on the sort of woman whom Yeats described as a masterpiece of civilization. Later son Dreiser's practical handling of a man-and-woman relationship in *An American Tragedy* is in great contrast to the intensely romantic love themes of first sons as in Hemingway's *Farewell to Arms* and Fitzgerald's *Tender Is the Night*.

A revealing illustration of tepid romantic feelings is provided by a later son, Sören Kierkegaard. Though he has been known as a passionate man, the impression gained from his *Diary of The Seducer* is that the passion is not directed toward women.

His lack of fervent impetuousness, his vacillation, may be contained in the opening sentences of the *Diary*. The words are directed toward the young lady but they seem more applicable to his own state of mind: "Caution, my beautiful unknown! Caution! To step out of a carriage is not so simple a matter, sometimes it is a very decisive step. I might lend you a novel of Tieck's in which you would read about a lady who in dismounting from her horse involved herself in an entanglement such that the step becomes definitive for her whole life."[34] In the later interaction it is difficult to know whether Kirkegaard is afraid of women or afraid of sex. For example: "I have witnessed a rendezvous where although the girl was charming and the man handsome, the total impression was almost disgusting, and the meeting itself was far from beautiful, although I suppose it seemed so to the lovers. . . . I am vexed when I see a man with such an opportunity, so upset that mere love gives him delirium tremens. It is caviar to the general. Instead of having enough discretion to enjoy her disquiet, to allow it to enhance and inflame her beauty, he only produces a wretched confusion, and yet he goes home joyously imagining it to have been a glorious experience."[35] On the fourteenth day Kierkegaard seems to be attaining serenity amidst the waves of passion: "I scarcely recognize myself. My mind is like a turbulent sea, swept by the storms of passion. . . ."[36] "Roar on, ye wild forces, ye powers of passion! Let your dashing waves hurl their foam against the sky. You shall not pile up over my head; serene I sit like the king of the cliff. . . ."[37] On the sixteenth day, Kierkegaard is sufficiently in command of his passions that he can begin to view the whole matter intellectually: "How beautiful it is to be in love, how interesting to know that one is in love."[38] On the nineteenth day he uses as the criterion that he is really in love the fact that he barely feels it: "That I am really in love I can tell among other things by the reticence with which I deal with this matter, even to myself."[39]

The caution behind Kierkegaard's advances may be seen in his later remarks: "Although she must belong to me, it must not be identical with the unlovely idea of her resting upon me like a burden. She must neither hang on me in the physical sense, nor be an obligation in a moral sense."[40] His aversion to any binding connectedness is seen earlier in *Either/Or*. He speaks like Bacon

who advised treating your enemy like your friend and your
friend like your enemy; or Rousseau advocating no ties between
individuals:

One must guard against *friendship*.
    But because you abstain from friendship it does not follow that
you abstain from social contacts.
    The essential thing is never to stick fast.
    One must never enter into the relation of *marriage*. Husband and
wife promise to love one another for eternity. This is all very fine,
but it does not mean very much. . . .
    Husband and wife are indeed said to become one, but this is a
very dark and mystic saying. When you are one of several, then you
have lost your freedom; you cannot send for your traveling boots
whenever you wish. . . .
    . . . for woman is and ever will be the ruin of a man, as soon as
he contracts a permanent relation with her.[41]

Kierkegaard's adverse attitude toward binding, intimate connections such as marriage between individuals had its philosophic
counterpart in his hatred of Hegeleanism. Hegel's marriage of
opposites into a synthesis, his principle of "both-and" stirred
Kierkegaard into a declaration of disconnectedness and atomism,
of two mutual objects, in *Either/Or: A Fragment of Life*. He
says: "Either/or is the key to heaven." . . . "Both—and is the
way to hell."[42]

    So in romantic love as in hero worship and as in morally
tinged tragedy, the disconnectedness-prone later sons are not
given to the same enlargement or overestimation that is found in
the connectedness-prone first sons. Obviously, not all of the possible examples can be given to this trend. Nor will space permit
all possible selected quotations from other eminent critics bearing on this point. For the most part, we have attended to what
the first- and later-son *poets* have had to say about poetry and
literature. When we turn to other eminent critics who function
almost exclusively as *critics*, we are faced with the problem of
not knowing their birth order. It will be helpful, however, to
give some illustrations of how these critics view first- and later-
son writers. Those illustrations are selected which support the
connectedness-disconnectedness hypothesis. To be sure, due to
differences in opinion and taste, there are many critical writings
which cannot be viewed as supporting the hypothesis. Thus, the
aim can be to show only that some critics think in this fashion.

The first illustration is Bentley's comparison of first son Ibsen and later son Wagner. He brings out the contrast between being individual or group minded (seen also in first sons Montesquieu and William James, and later sons Rousseau and Dewey) and the intrinsic romanticism of Ibsen as opposed to the intrinsic realism of Wagner. Eric Bentley says: "Wagner and Ibsen differ as dramatists above all in their utterly different presentation of human nature. Wagner is not interested in the individual; Ibsen is seldom interested in anything else. Wagner's characters are incarnations of qualities and instincts, or representatives . . . of groups. Humanity comes into Wagner only through the musical presentation of crude impulses, chiefly sexual. For Ibsen on the other hand, the individual is not indeed all, but he is certainly the beginning and the end."[43] On another page he says: "one might say that Ibsen, the great man of the modern and realistic tradition, was perhaps even more deeply a romanticist, and that Wagner, the great man of the fancy and anti-realistic tradition, was at heart a rather crude realist. In different terms, Ibsen was a realist outside, a fantasist inside; Wagner was a fantasist outside, and a realist inside."[44]

The second is Lionel Trilling's comparison of first sons Hemingway and Faulkner with later sons O'Neill and Wolfe (though Trilling includes Dos Passos with the latter two, his birth order is not available to the present author). Trilling's analysis of these writers in *The Liberal Imagination* represents a highly cogent account of the inner workings of plural-minded, conflicted first sons and of the single-minded, gratification-desiring later sons. In "The Meaning of a Literary Idea" he says: "In any extended work of literature, the aesthetic effect . . . depends in large degree upon intellectual power, upon the amount and recalcitrance of the material the mind works on, and upon the mind's success in mastering the large material."[45] It is to be noted that Trilling is speaking of the extended literary work, of something of epic-length proportions, not of something briefer as Poe advocates. The mastery or synthesis of such plural factors and premises is, as we have seen, more the penchant of first sons. Trilling goes on:

It is customary to say of Thomas Wolfe that he is an emotional writer. Perhaps: although it is probably not the most accurate way to describe a writer who could deal with but one emotion; and we feel it is a function of his unrelenting, tortured egoism that he could not submit his mind to the ideas that might have brought the variety and interest of order to single, dull chaos of his powerful selfregard, for it is true that the intellect makes many emotions out of the primary egoistic one.[46]

Trilling is impressed by the striving toward intellectual synthesis in Hemingway and Faulkner, and critical that O'Neill and Wolfe have stopped short:

We feel that Hemingway and Faulkner are intensely at work upon the recalcitrant stuff of life. . . . The opposite is true of Dos Passos, O'Neill, and Wolfe; at each point of conclusion in their work we feel that *they* feel that they have said the last word, and we feel this even when they represent themselves, as O'Neill and Wolfe so often do, as puzzled and baffled by life.[47]

We have noted with other later sons that their last word is sufficient for the present or near-future situation; it need not be the very last word, in fact it is preferable that it not be, for then, as Descartes, Kirkegaard and Emerson suggested, one would be blindly committed and not free to change one's mind. For existentialist Kierkegaard, eternity was not spread out over all of time; rather it was condensed into one moment. Kierkegaard and other later sons thus could be eternally right, inasmuch as eternity was the instantaneous moment. Conflict between past and present would be minimal because the past could be easily erased.

The task of first sons Hemingway and Faulkner is, according to Trilling, not simple. Time has duration, a conflicting past and present which require synthesis:

What comes into being when two contradictory emotions are made to confront each other and are required to have a relationship with each other is . . . quite properly called an idea. . . . And it can be said that a work will have what I have been calling cogency in the degree that the confronting emotions go deep, or in the degree that the old pieties are firmly held and the new exigencies strongly apprehend. In Hemingway's stories a strongly charged piety toward the ideals and attachments of boyhood and the lusts of maturity is in conflict not only with the imagination of death but also with that imagination as it is peculiarly modified by the dark negation of the modern world. Faulkner as a Southerner of today, a man deeply implicated in the pieties of his traditions, is of course at the very heart of an exigent historical event which thrusts upon him the awareness of. . . .

. . . willingness to remain in uncertainties, mysteries, and doubts.[48]

Trilling feels that O'Neill and Wolfe were passive in the face of knotty intellectual problems and adopted the simple, easy answers:

The passivity of Thomas Wolfe . . . led him to that . . . simple affirmation, recorded in *You Can't Go Home Again*, that literature must become the agent of the immediate solution of all social problems and undertake the prompt eradication of human pain. . . .[49]

Trilling obviously is not neutral in his evaluation of these writers. He prefers the working out of the inner conflict with tragic undertones of death and violence to the single-minded optimistic Yea Sayer exemplified by Wolfe and Whitman. He does not, as Kazin and Wilson do, point up the particular brand of egoism that Hemingway possessed. But the empathy with the conflicted heroic plural-minded enables him to give a psychologically accurate analysis of what goes on in some first sons.

More neutral is F. O. Matthiessen's comparison of first son Yeats and later son Eliot as to their sense of the tragic. It is of special interest because it describes the relationship of tragic to heroic in Yeats, and the relationship of tragic to deprivation and suffering in Eliot. In *The Responsibilities of The Critic* (Essays and Reviews by F. O. Matthiessen selected by John Rackliffe) Matthiessen says:

Yeats' view of tragedy . . . is based on his belief that antithesis is the law of life. But where he throws his emphasis is not in the disaster that inevitably springs from the conflict, not on the tragic loss but on the heroic affirmation. . . .

Division between the two kinds [of tragedy] is not to be made absolute, as Yeats himself indicated, but the great difference in tone between Yeats' poetry and Eliot's may be attributed to the different quality each has stressed at the heart of the tragic experience. . . . Yeats' distaste for "passive suffering" would doubtless extend to "Gerontion" as well as to "The Hollow Men," and the intermingled doubt and faith of Eliot's later poems would fall far short of the affirmation Yeats demanded. . . .

His [Yeats'] most characteristic expression is not tragedy, but a special product of the tragic attitude, the "zest" of the hero. . . .[50]

The reader may wonder why we have not yet dealt squarely with T. S. Eliot, who is perhaps the most influential modern poet-critic. One reason is purely mechanical—a discussion of him is more appropriate at the end of this kind of a chapter than at the beginning. The other is that Eliot is difficult to discuss. Either he is a very complex person who defies easy categorization or, due to the elusive later-son tactics, he is hard to break down. The present author's main (but not exclusive) impression is that he is elusive; that he persuades a reader to drop his guard so that he can make a sudden point. Eliot's lack of bombast, his tongue-in-cheek playful seriousness, and his professed humility induce a reader to feel that here is a nonthreatening man without an ax to grind and who is on the side of the better things. Thus in an essay on Shakespeare, included in the expanded edition of his *Selected Essays*, he writes: "My own frivolous opinion is. . . ."[51] and "I admit that my own experience, as a minor poet. . . ."[52] In this critical method, one of nonfrontal sniping, he is reminiscent of later son Wilde who turned from "intellectual high-kicking to intellectual sharp-shooting."

T. S. Eliot gives a good description of the difficulties involved in trying to get a direct bead on an elusive later son. The description concerns later son Montaigne:

Of all authors Montaigne is one of the least destructible. You could as well dissipate a fog by flinging hand-grenades into it. For Montaigne is a fog, a gas, a fluid, insidious element. He does not reason, he insinuates, charms, and influences; or if he reasons, you must be prepared for his having some other design upon you than to convince you by his argument. . . . Pascal studied him with the intention of demolishing him. . . . Indeed, by the time a man knew Montaigne well enough to attack him, he would already be thoroughly infected by him. . . .

But what makes Montaigne a very great figure is that he succeeded, God knows how—in giving expression to the scepticism of *every* human being.[53]

Eliot may be linked with later sons Montaigne and Emerson as very able guerrilla warriors who, operating under a cloak of amiability and humility, began to sharpshoot or to bring up the "light artillery" of Poe. In sharp contrast is the battle-ax direct frontality of two first sons, Hulme and Pound, who are acknowledged to be the two principal influences on later son Eliot. Hulme is similar to Bakunin and Lassalle in his open advocating of Sorel's revolutionary violence. Pound's affinity with another lover of direct violence, first son Mussolini, is well known. His frontality in taking on the entire United States as his opponent is in the style of first son John Brown.

Whatever Eliot's intellectual or poetical affiliations are with Hulme and Pound, he does not share their need for excessive, violent feelings, for grandiosity, or for heroic largeness. The "heroic" affirmation response to a tragic loss—the response of first son Yeats—leaves Eliot rather cold. In his essay on Shakespeare, Eliot puts this stoic response in a ridiculous light by equating it with "cheering oneself up." He writes:

There is, in some of the great tragedies of Shakespeare, a new attitude. It is not the attitude of Seneca, but it is derived from Seneca . . . it is modern, and it culminates, if there is ever any culmination, in the attitude of Nietzsche. . . . It is the attitude of self-dramatization assumed by some of Shakespeare's heroes at moments of tragic intensity.[54]

Of the last great speech of Othello he says:

It is usually taken on its face value, as expressing the greatness in defeat of a noble but erring nature. . . .
What Othello seems to me to be doing in making this speech is *cheering himself up*. He is endeavouring to escape reality, he has ceased to think about Desdemona, and is thinking about himself. Humility is the most difficult of all virtues to achieve; nothing dies harder than the desire to think well of oneself. . . . He [Othello] takes in the spectator, but the human motive is primarily to take in himself.[55]

There is no doubt that Eliot is correct in saying that the affirmative, heroic, stoic response to tragic adversity is designed to cheer oneself up. We have seen that this response is more characteristic of first sons who mourn the loss of their early connectedness to the mother and need to feel and behave heroically in order to assert that, though their omnipotence has been bent, it has not been broken. But Eliot is not equally perceptive about the other way of cheering oneself up, the Epicurean denial of adversity which is more characteristic of later sons. In his account of larger-than-life Stoicism we see that, by default, actual life-size Epicureanism becomes the right way to meet life: "A man does not join himself with the Universe so long as he has any-thing else to join himself with; men who could take part in the life of a thriving Greek city-state had something better to join themselves to; and Christians have had something better. Stoicism is the refuge for the individual in an indifferent or hostile world too big for him; it is the permanent substratum of a number of versions of cheering oneself up. Nietzsche is the most conspicu-ous modern instance of cheering oneself up. The stoical attitude is the reverse of Christian humility."[56]

It does appear that this is a one-sided account of the human dilemma after the fall of the Greek city-states. A reader's nose is not rubbed by Eliot in the Epicurean solution, nor is his mouth forced open so that he must swallow it. The solution is not even mentioned directly by name. Instead, by a Cartesian elimination of Stoicism on to the "false" pile, the only thing left is humility, i.e., Epicureanism. Eliot's dim views of Hamlet's trying to master his conflict is the opposite of Trilling's high estimate of such an attempt. The latter, it will be recalled, believes that a mastery of conflicting emotions is a sign of intellectual power and ac-tivity; those who stop short with simple, *ad hoc* answers, are taking the easy way out. Not so with Eliot. He believes that Hamlet (and Shakespeare) should not have taken on such a large, complicated problem and because they did so, they failed:

Hamlet (the man) is dominated by an emotion which is inexpressible, because it is in *excess* of the facts as they appear. And the supposed identity of Hamlet with his author is genuine to this point: that Hamlet's bafflement at the absence of objective equivalent to his feelings is a prolongation of the bafflement of his creator in the face of his artistic problem. . . .

The intense feeling, ecstatic or terrible, without an object or exceeding its object, is something which every person of sensibility has known; it is doubtless a subject of study for pathologists. . . . We must simply admit that here Shakespeare tackled a problem which proved too much for him.[57]

In Eliot we see a good illustration of one kind of superior intelligence, the precise, penetrating kind. His insistence on exact objective equivalent to feelings is quite similar to Descartes' obtaining a sense of location when lost in the forest by following a dim objective light, or his use of objective coordinates to locate a number, and similar also to Bacon's emphasis on the more vivid sensory experience as a guide to the exact truth. It is a different approach from multipremised Einstein's more abstract truth-seeking which emphasizes meaningful comprehensibility rather than sensory certainty. While searching for the interconnected meaning, the first son must live in mysteries and doubts as Trilling described concerning Hemingway and Faulkner. They must have what first son Keats described as "negative capability," the ability to live and think amidst uncertainty. Certainly Shakespeare tackled a problem which may have been too big for him (or for anyone). From the first son's connectedness viewpoint it is an admirable attempt to seek permanent truth; from the later son's disconnected viewpoint it is impractical or it lacks humility.

One final comment about Eliot. Since he is a major modern poet and since poets are uniquely sensitive to their times (if they are not the unacknowledge legislators), it is of interest to know what Eliot thinks is amiss with the world. Frequently in this chapter we have commented on the tragic sense, the sense of what is depressing about life. In earlier chapters we have called attention to the inner pain of first sons whose omnipotence has been demeaned by actual life—they feel, as Heller suggested, disinherited. And we have noted the inner pain of later sons who feel deprived and who express the frustration in oral terms. The two types of psychic pain find their expression and solution philosophically in Stoicism and Epicureanism—in Heraclitean connectedness and in Democritean disconnectedness. In political social terms, the two types of frustration are solved by emphasis on the individual's welfare and by emphasis on the group's welfare. In literature, imaginative and imaginary solutions are provided to the demeanable first sons by the ennobling epic myth, and to the deprivable later sons by the gratifying fairy tale.

When we inquire in Eliot's type of poem and his type of solution, we find some obstacles and some clues. The principal obstacle is that arising from special literary considerations. Thus, though our hypothesis would tend to place this later son as a deprived fairy taler, he is better known from "The Waste Land" as a worker in the mythic method. How much this is due to Pound's influence and example is certainly a fair question. Shapiro believes that the mythic method is not in character for Eliot, that it reflects Eliot's search for a proper form to reach the mystical experience. Certainly, from what we have seen about Eliot's aversion to outsized heroics, he cannot be designated a pure example of the ennobling epic myth-maker. Whether Eliot merely uses myth, or whether he has a different mythical feeling, or whether the essential imaginative solution is in the direction of fairy tale rather than myth is a debatable issue.

There is evidence from "The Waste Land," however, which suggests that Eliot is more safely described as deprived than as demeaned. If deprivation is his principal psychic pain, we would expect that the wish-gratifying fairy tale would dominate over the epic-myth as a solution. Edmund Wilson's essay points up Eliot's deprivation. To be sure, the following passage, though not taken out of context, does not represent the entirety of Wilson's evaluation of Eliot as a poet. We are only quoting now what is pertinent to the topic of deprivation. The reader may keep in mind other later sons: Tolstoy's licking the drops of honey, Emerson's cry of famine and complaining of the one drop of water, Coleridge's "Water, water, every where, nor any drop to drink." In *Axel's Castle* Wilson comments about "The Waste Land" and other of Eliot's works: "The water for which he [the poet of 'The Waste Land'] longs in the twilight desert of his dream is to quench the spiritual thirst which torments him in the London dusk; and as Gerontion, 'an old man in a dry month,' thought of the young men who had fought in the rain, as Prufrock fancied riding the waves with mermaids and lingering in the chambers of the sea, as Mr. Apollinax has been imagined drawing strength from the deep sea-caves of coral islands—so the poet of 'The Waste Land,' making water the symbol of all freedom, all fecundity and flowering of the soul, invokes in desperate need the memory of an April shower of his youth, the song of the hermit thrush with its sound of water dripping and the vision of a drowned Phoenician sailor, sunk beyond 'the cry of gulls and the deep sea swell,' who has at least died by water, not thirst. The poet, who seems now to be traveling in a country cracked by drouth, can only feverishly dream of these things."[58]

The foregoing provides an appropriate stopping point for this chapter. Our aim has been to provide illustrations suggesting that the connectedness-disconnectedness hypothesis (with its birth order indicator) may be applied to literature. Though we have dwelled occasionally on the aspect of literary form (e.g., myth or fairy tale), our main emphasis has been on the personality of the writer. What has emerged from our discussion is what has been the theme of the previous chapters. Namely, that there is not one kind of poet or prose writer, there are at least two types; that, despite the pronouncements of whoever occupies the chair of official criticism, it would be quite difficult to prove that one kind of poet or one kind of poetry is superior to, or more mature than, another kind. Rather it seems that the safer criterion is whether the writer has expressed what happens to be his inner self in an artistic way. This criterion of artistry has not been mentioned here for the obvious reason that it is beyond the competence of the author to discuss. It is also for this reason that the application of the hypothesis to artistic endeavors such as music, painting, and architecture will not be attempted. The application to literature—though beyond the author's usual scope—is more feasible because it depends on the written word, or communication through language. But even this application—descriptive, suggestive, and speculative in nature —requires working through on the part of those with more special expertise.

CHAPTER IX

Tendencies in History

HISTORY—LIKE SCIENCE (which is treated in the next chapter)—is too specialized a subject to be handled by the author in anything other than a suggestive way. Whereas literature deals with the gamut of emotions and thoughts familiar to the psychoanalyst, history and especially science have many concepts and phenomena which are outside the direct experience of the clinician. If the psychoanalyst or psychologist is to talk about history, it will have to be in terms of types of historians rather than types of histories. As we will soon see, even types of historians will be too difficult a subject to handle.

In the introductory chapter we mentioned that the gross survey revealed a preponderance of first sons as historians. There are, however, some difficulties involved in using this as a reliable guide. First, biographies with birth orders are not available on enough eminent professional historians to provide a good sampling. The second difficulty is not being able to determine whether a man should be included as a historian. Because of these difficulties we shall not restrict ourselves to historians per se, but shall consider any historically minded man, be he a historian, philosopher, writer, scientist, etc. (As a matter of fact, relatively little attention will be paid to professional or academic historians.)

If history, broadly conceived, is concerned with the past, with what has happened, then a first definition of a historically minded person may be that he is one who is interested in discovering what really happened in the past. Johan Huizinga speaks of "the impulse toward the past."[1] In discussing the criterion by which a pursuer of history can be distinguished from a pursuer of literature, he writes: "If the all-predominating need for 'genuineness,' the deeply sincere desire to find out how a certain thing 'really happened,' is lacking as such, he is not pursuing history."[2] A slight hint that first sons may more often be the "genuine" pursuers of history is given by Huizinga when he says that history must remain stoic: "The populace is always antistoic. Great waves of emotion, floods of tears, and excesses of feeling have always been breaks in the dikes of the popular soul. . . . With Rousseau . . . the anti-stoic intellectual attitude triumphed for good. . . . History may become democratic, but it must remain stoic."[3]

It is, however, when Huizinga describes the deep psychology of historical understanding that the hint about first sons becomes even stronger:

And now comes the core of the question. There is a very important element in historical understanding which might best be indicated by the term "historical sensation." One might also speak of "historical contact." . . . The German term . . . "presentiment," which was already used by Wilhelm von Humboldt [a first son] in this connection, would express it almost completely, if it were not worn a bit too threadbare in other contexts. This not completely reducible contact with the past in an entry into an atmosphere, it is one of the many forms of reaching beyond oneself, of experiencing truth, which are given to man. . . .

This historical sensation is apparently so essential that it is felt again and again as the true moment of historical cognition.[4]

Huizinga, after quoting first sons Michelet and Taine on this subject, writes: "In their vagueness, these two statements are more usable than careful definitions in the theory of knowledge. . . . It [the historical sensation] is a resurrection that takes place in the sphere of the dream, a seeing of intangible figures, a hearing of half-understood words."[5]

Let us assume for the moment that having this historical sensation is an important component of historical-mindedness, and that it is characteristic of first sons. By this assumption we can account for the impulse to the past and the notion of extended, continuous time seen frequently in the connectedness-prone first sons, e.g., Carlyle, Hegel, Marx, Proust, Bergson, etc. The assumption helps us explain why later son Camus was hostile to history, and later son Kierkegaard thought of eternity as compressed into a single moment rather than extended in time. It can lead to the speculation that just as later son Descartes had a special sense for location in space, first son Einstein had such a sense for time. The assumption is also useful in accounting for the differences toward the past shown by Adler, Freud, and Jung. Later son Adler's therapy was almost entirely geared to the present; first son Freud required an emotional reliving of childhood traumata; first son Jung went even further back than did Freud in his postulating in archaic, racial unconscious. Finally, the assumption fits very neatly with the myth that Clio, the Muse of history, was the *eldest* daughter of Memory.

The phrase "assume for the moment" was used advisedly because, as we shall learn now from Huizinga, a later son's penetrating, precise handling of a part may lead to a more accurate reconstruction of the past. He writes: "The more clearly they [the great culture historians] define those forms the better they succeed. A general question can only lead to a general answer."[6] He mentions several overgeneralized formulations which have become outdated and speaks favorably of later son Leslie Stephen: "Hardly outdated at all is the work of a third historian . . . too little known outside England, Leslie Stephen. . . . Leslie Stephen's was not a constructive mind. His *English Thought in the Eighteenth Century* avoids general theses and almost never leads to general conclusions. But it is precisely for that reason that his work has suffered very little at the hands of time."[7]

The dangers (as well as the advantages) of mystic overgeneralization by such first sons as Spengler and Hegel are brought out by Huizinga in the following:

Can cultural history . . . escape the danger of its morphology degenerating into mythology?

Oswald Spengler used the words "morphology of world history" in the subtitle to his *Decline of the West*. Perhaps in the future it will be said of Spengler, as Meinecke once said in passing of Taine, that he was among those "who have done more for scholarship by means of great errors than others by means of small truths. . . ." If so, it will be because of the depth of Spengler's insight, his masterly combination of dissimilar things under a single denomination, his violent clarification of our historical thinking. It will not be because of the system he constructed. After one decade his pattern of world history stands as an uncompleted and abandoned mausoleum.[8]

Later, speaking of Hegel's anthropomorphic *Weltgeist*, Huizinga writes: "The fault . . . lies in the fact that the scholar has staked out too large a claim for his thinking. He wants to have a view of the pattern of a vast complex and describe a general morphology without having become sufficiently familiar with the structure of its parts. The result is what [later son] de Tocqueville saw happening. . . . A vague, indeterminate, historical concept takes form, with all sorts of heterogeneous notions loosely associated in it. The whole can only be grasped and expressed by applying a striking metaphor to it. The vaster the complexes the historian wishes to fathom, the greater the danger of such hypostatizations."[9]

We see in the foregoing some familiar characteristics of first and later sons. Though perhaps possessing the "historical sensation," the connectedness-prone first sons attempt to make a synthesis of plural parts; this larger-than-life attempt frequently does not come off even though it can be quite stimulating. The disconnectedness-prone later sons, though not psychologically drawn toward the past, handle one thing at a time in a precise way—their limitation is not in the realm of inaccuracy but rather in that general syntheses are not attempted.

Apart from professional historians, there is the more general subject of personalities affected by history. Here Huizinga is again instructive in his essay *Historical Ideals of Life*. In his initial example, first son Charles the Bold, we see the first-son attraction to the heroic past: "Charles the Bold, Duke of Burgundy, had, like so many of his contemporaries, an unbridled craving for glory and a vast admiration for the generals of antiquity—Caesar, Hannibal, Alexander—whom he strove consciously to resemble and imitate. He had in his mind's eye an exalted image of ancient grandeur, and he attempted to live in accordance with that image. In other words, Charles had an historical ideal of life.

"It is about such historical life-ideas that I wish to speak: about the manner in which historical concepts may influence, and sometimes perhaps dominate, the evolution of a culture, a state, or an individual; about how such historical concepts sometimes present themselves as direct examples to be imitated, sometimes more as inspiring cultural symbols; and the way mankind, looking upward and backward to an illusory perfection in the past, attempts to advance itself by means of such an ideal, or dreams its time away in such a delusion."[10]

The two other examples Huizinga gives as being so affected are both first sons, Charles XII of Sweden and Louis XVI of France. Though kings are more likely to be first sons, we have noted the same glorification and emulation of the past in the first sons Heroic Vitalists who are not kings, from Carlyle through Nietzsche to Hitler. It is quite likely that the "historic sensation" was prominent in these first sons without the necessary refining feature of accuracy. Huizinga writes appropos of this: "I shall here consider as historical concepts both those based on historical research or substantiated tradition and those that are creations of mythological fancy. The historical accuracy of a concept is for the moment of no importance; the only thing that matters is whether it appeared to its advocates to be the true picture of a past reality. Not even that is utterly necessary, in fact: it is sufficient that the concept can be conceived of as living reality—even a fictional character in a romance or novel can do service in this respect as an historical concept. Hence an historical life-ideal may be defined as any concept of excellence man projects into the past."[11]

The very general way in which Huizinga defines historical life-ideal allows room for "concepts of excellence" other than that of omnipotent heroics. And we do find him describing two ideals, the bucolic and the chivalric—which may correspond, respectively, to the later son's Nature Vitalism and the first son's Heroic Vitalism. Regarding the bucolic he writes:

No other single illusion has charmed humanity for so long with such an ever fresh splendor as the illusion of the piping shepherd's pipe and surprised nymphs in rustling woods and murmuring brooks. The concept is very closely akin to that of the golden age, and constantly overlaps it: it is the golden age brought to life.

. . . from antiquity to Rousseau the notion of the natural state derived its strength and vitality from the concept of the golden age and the bucolic idyl.[12]

We recognize here not only later son Rousseau's Man in Nature but also later son Wordsworth's nature poetry, and the themes of later sons Tolstoy and Whitman.

As for the chivalric ideal, Huizinga regards it as more real and as possessing more historical context than the bucolic. From his description the chivalric, with its self-denial, can be equated with the morally obligated Stoic—and the bucolic with the emphasis on simple pleasures with the Epicurean:

> Even in its first development as an actual way of life, in the twelfth century, chivalry displayed the characteristics of a renascence, a conscious revival of the romantic past, whether that past was sought in antiquity, in the times of Charlemagne, or, above all, in King Arthur's circle.
>
> Compared with the bucolic ideal, then, the chivalric ideal had in the first place more historical content. The chivalric tradition had much more basis in a real past and was much more open to historical specification than the vaguely described, never-changing image of happiness in the pastoral poem. A more profound difference is the following: In the concept of the golden age and the bucolic fantasy the ideal of happiness predominated over the ideal of virtue—virtue was there negative, primarily innocence, the lack of a stimulus to sin in the state of simplicity. . . . In the chivalric ideal, on the other hand, the aspiration toward virtue outweighed that toward happiness.
>
> . . . chivalric virtue was basically not only altruistic but also ascetic. The ascetic basis manifested itself clearly in the strange, barbaric appearing chivalric vows to deny oneself rest or comfort until a certain heroic feat had been accomplished.[13]

As Huizinga continues, we see not only the violent, heroic vitalism characteristic of first sons but also that other feature of overestimation, romantic love of women:

> Self-sacrifice was rooted in the deep erotic soil of the chivalric ideal. It cannot be brought enough to the fore that the chivalric ideal found its highest expression in the tournament. . . . The essential element in both the tilt and the chivalric vow was the presence of the women under whose eyes the man shed his blood or displayed his bravery and strength. This sexual element was clearly seen and expressed throughout the Middle Ages. From it sprang the whole romanticism of chivalry: the motif of the knight who freed the maiden. . . .
>
> Kings exposed themselves to the danger of the most violent battles.[14]

The chivalric ideal was, of course, too strenuous and demanding an ideal to continue as a general cultural phenomenon. It fell, according to Huizinga, not only of its own weight but also from the barbs of ridicule. He would tend to agree with Byron that later son Cervantes smiled Spain's chivalry away.

Those who upheld the chivalric ideal were aware of its falsity, and it is for this reason that—almost from the very beginning—there was a tendency for the ideal to deny itself from time to time in irony and satire, parody and caricature. *Don Quixote* was merely the last, supreme expression of that irony. . . . The bucolic ideal was safe-guarded from such constant decay much more than the chivalric ideal because it had fewer points of contact with reality. Cervantes himself still took the pastoral seriously.[15]

Huizinga has been quoted at length in order to show that the views of at least one cultural historian are supportive of the connectedness-disconnectedness hypothesis. Many strands from previous chapters can now be gathered together. Those men prone to connectedness (usually first sons) carry the past within themselves. The impulse to the past, or the historical sensation, or the sense of time duration, is thus more or less natural to them, inasmuch as the indwelling past is just as real as the external present. Their pasts are variously composed—in some it is the original omnipotence that stands out, in others it is the intense erotic connectedness to the mother, in others it is the inner voice of morality. Depending on what component stands out, they can be described as heroic, chivalric, romantic, stoic. On the other hand, those men prone to disconnectedness (usually later sons) are more absorbed with the immediate present; though they may have an intellectual interest in past events, there are fewer intense, psychological connections with the past. The "historical sensation" and the sense of time duration would be some-what out of character for them. Their present gratification needs might lead them to invent an illusory golden past rather than to revive a real past. They can be described as Nature Vitalists, bucolic, Epicurean.

Emerging from this summary are some possible generalizations about the truthfulness of historical accounts. On a simple, intellectual mechanics basis, the plural-minded who attempt a broad synthesis of many parts may be less successful than the single-minded who, avoiding general conclusions, deal precisely with the one part. On this mechanical basis, the former may frequently be less accurate than the latter. Thus, one way of defining truthfulness is to equate it with accuracy. Among actual historians, first son Spengler's stimulating but inaccurate broad interconnection of historical events can be contrasted with later son Bancroft's insistence on accurate recourse to original documents. One may say that Bancroft is more truthful than Spengler. The usual way of putting this, however, is that Bancroft is more accurate than Spengler.

While the foregoing deals with intellectual preferences or cognitive styles, what we now must consider is the effect of more subjective motivations, of wishful thinking. The connectedness-prone first sons who carry the past with them cannot escape from the real past. They may distort it, they may emphasize certain aspects at the expense of others, but they cannot deny or negate something so intimately connected with their selves. This is what Huizinga referred to in saying that the chivalric ideal had more real historical content than the bucolic. The disconnectedness-prone later sons—not so intimately connected with the past—can more easily deny the real past. If the needs of the present dictate that a certain past is needed to provide rational justification of the present, that particular past can be invented. In this sense of truthfulness, the wishful thinking of the connectedness-prone is likely to be closer to the truth than the wishful thinking of the disconnectedness-prone. The former have to play by a certain rule, e.g., that every imaginative reconstruction has to have at least a kernel of truth. Hitler's "Big Lie" technique always had a noticeable enough nucleus of truth—(it *was* true that Germany was the only nation that kept to the Versailles Treaty by disarming). But later son Lenin did not have to keep to this rule—he could abolish past history, rewrite it according to the needs of the present, and go to the lengths of claiming that Russians rather than non-Russians were the originators of certain ideas and inventions. If Hitler's liberties with the truth derived from an heroic, epic-myth tendency, Lenin's liberties derived from a fairy-tale tendency. And appropriately enough in terms of size, the epic myth may be called the Big Lie, and the fairy tale the Little Lie. By its partial foundation in the real past, the epic falsehood is more credible than the fairy-tale falsehood.

These generalizations find some support in Bronislaw Malinowski's observations about the myths of origin in his *Magic, Science and Religion*. Though myth in general is defined by him as "a narrative resurrection of a primeval reality,"[16] a principal difference between the myth of origin and the other two types of myth is that, whereas in myths of origin there need not be adherence to what actually happened in the past, in myths of death and in myths of magic the adherence must be much stronger. In other words, myths of origin tend to be less historical, less rooted in a real past than the other two types. The reason why myths of origin may be nonhistorical is that their sociological function is frequently that of justifying and rationalizing the conqueror's right to certain territories and privileges wrested from the original owners. Malinowski writes:

This violation [of traditional precedent and charter] always takes place when the local claims of . . . a clan which has emerged on the spot, are overridden by an immigrant clan. Then a conflict of principles is created, for obviously the principle that land and authority belong to those who are literally born out of it does not leave room for any newcomers. . . . The result is that there come into existence a special class of mythological stories which justify and account for the anomalous state of affairs.[17]

Thus, myths of origins, myths about how things were at the beginning, frequently require the erasure of the actual past and the rewriting of history to justify current needs. There is here no impulse toward the past; rather there is a power-status-gratification impulse in the present which invents historical traditions. Such fabricated myths of origin are understandably more of a necessity to the later son than to the first son. The first son does not have to fabricate a myth; he did come first and thereby enjoyed certain privileges. If the later son is to dispossess the privileged first son and still appear legal, he has to invent an appropriate myth of origin. The notion of the original Man in Nature was invented by later son Rousseau in order to justify a dispossessing attack on the oppressive privileged classes. Later son Emerson disputed the originality of eminent men, emphasizing frequently that creativity was derivative. Later son Jacob's dispossession of Esau's birthright received a mythological justification from later son Thomas Mann.

In the actual example given by Malinowski, there can be seen the dispossession of the first born by later borns: "The problem of rank which plays a great role in their sociology [of the Trobrianders] was settled by the emergence from one special hole. . . . This event was notable in that, contrary to the usual course (which is: one original 'hole,' one lineage), from this hole . . . there emerged representatives of the four main clans one after the other. Their arrival, moreover, was followed by an apparently trivial but, in mythical reality, a most important event. First there came the . . . (iguana), the animal of the Lukulabuta clan, which scratched its way through the earth as iguanas do, then climbed a tree, and remained there as a mere onlooker, following subsequent events. Soon there came out the Dog, totem of the Lukuba clan, who originally had the highest rank. As a third came the Pig, representative of the Malasi clan, which now holds the highest rank. . . . The Dog and Pig ran around, and the Dog, seeing the fruit of the *noku* plant, nosed it, then ate it. Said the Pig: 'Thou eatest *noku*, thou eatest dirt; thou art a low-bred, a commoner; the chief . . . shall be I.' And ever since, the highest subclan of the Malasi clan, the Tabalu, have been the real chiefs."[18] Thus, the rewriting of history through a myth of origin legalizes the later-borns' right to conquered territory.

The foregoing exposition may serve as a background for considering later son Tolstoy's philosophy of history as discussed by Isaiah Berlin in his essay *The Hedgehog and the Fox.* Apart from considerations of history, the essay is pertinent inasmuch as the title proposes a personality typology similar to the connectedness-disconnectedness typology. Berlin opens the essay with: "There is a line among the fragments of the Greek poet Archilochus which says: 'The fox knows many things, but the hedgehog knows one big thing.' . . . But taken figuratively, the words can be made to yield a sense in which they mark one of the deepest differences which divide writers and thinkers, and, it may be, human beings in general. For there exists a great chasm between those, on one side, who relate everything to a single central vision, one system less or more coherent or articulate, in terms of which they understand, think and feel—a single, universal, organizing principle . . . and, on the other side, those who pursue many ends, often unrelated and even contradictory, connected, if at all, only in some *de facto* way, for some psychological or physiological cause, related by no moral or aesthetic principle. . . ."[19]

Although this typology reads remarkably like the typology offered in this book, certain considerations prevent them from being readily equated. If Berlin's hedgehog knows one big thing because he has interconnected many parts into a synthesis, the hedgehog personality can be equated with our connectedness personality. But if the one big thing is known from an intense, single-minded focus on one part of the whole, then the hedgehog personality is more like our disconnectedness personality. Similar considerations are involved in the question of what is meant by the knowing of many things. Before the full discussion of Tolstoy and his type, Berlin does give a list of whom he considers to be hedgehogs and foxes. Hedgehogs: Dante, Plato, Lucretius, Pascal, Hegel, Dostoevski, Nietzsche, Ibsen, Proust (six first sons, two later sons, one unknown). Foxes: Shakespeare, Herodotus, Aristotle, Montaigne, Erasmus, Molière, Goethe, Pushkin, Balzac, Joyce (six first sons, one later son, three unknown). It can be seen that Berlin's listings do not show birth order predominance; and it is quite likely that his typology is not identical with the connectedness-disconnectedness one.

Berlin then proceeds to Tolstoy: "The hypothesis I wish to offer is that Tolstoy was by nature a fox, but believed in being a hedgehog; that his gifts and achievement are one thing, and his beliefs, and consequently his interpretation of his own achievement, another; consequently his ideals have led him, and those whom his genius for persuasion has taken in, into a systematic misinterpretation of what he and others were doing or should be doing. . . . But the conflict between what he was and what he believed emerges nowhere so clearly as in his view of history to which some of his most brilliant and most paradoxical pages are devoted."[20]

The main impression obtained by the present author from Berlin's later discussion is that later son Tolstoy fits rather well into the category of rewriters of history, of inventors of myths of origin; the category whose sociological motivation is to dispossess the privileged on the behalf of the underprivileged. Berlin first tells what other critics have thought of Tolstoy: "Contemporary historians and military specialists, at least one of whom had himself fought in 1812, indignantly complained of inaccuracies of fact; and since then damning evidence has been adduced of falsification of historical detail by the author of *War and Peace*, done apparently with deliberate intent, in full knowledge of the available original sources and in the known absence of any counter-evidence—falsification perpetrated, it seems, in the interests not so much of an artistic as of an 'ideological' purpose."²¹ On another page Berlin writes: "Something is surely amiss here: Tolstoy's violently unhistorical and indeed anti-historical rejection of all efforts to explain or justify human action or character in terms of social or individual growth, or 'roots' in the past; this side by side with an absorbed and life-long interest in history, leading to artistic and philosophical results which provoked such queerly disparaging comments from ordinarily sane and sympathetic critics—surely there is something here which deserves attention."²²

About Tolstoy's attitude to the past, we learn from Berlin that it is not so much an impulse to the past, but rather an interest in origins. "Tolstoy's interest in history began early in his life. It seems to have arisen not from interest in the past as such, but from the desire to penetrate to first causes, to understand how and why things happen as they do and not otherwise. . . ."²³ He did not share with first sons Bakunin and Lassalle their admiration for first son Hegel. Rather his attitude— ". . . in one of his letters he described Hegel's writings as unintelligible gibberish interspersed with platitudes"²⁴—is one very much like that of later sons Kierkegaard and Camus.

An Emersonian reshuffling of merit in which the credit is taken away from the hero general and given to the humble soldiers can frequently be seen in Tolstoy. Berlin writes that the arrival on the battle scene of the great soldier, Prince Bagration:

puts heart into his subordinates; his courage, his calm, his mere presence create the illusion of which he is himself the first victim, namely, that what is happening is somehow connected with *his* skill, *his* plans, that it is *his* authority that is in some way directing the course of the battle. . . . The dispatches which will duly be written later will inevitably ascribe every act and event on the Russian side to him and his dispositions; the credit or discredit, the victory or the defeat will belong to him, although it is clear to everyone that he will have had less to do with the conduct and outcome of the battle than the humble, unknown soldiers who do at least perform whatever actual fighting is done, i.e. shoot at each other, wound, kill, advance, retreat, and so on.²⁵

Later son Tolstoy is clearly hostile to heroics. In 1812, "Those who went about their ordinary business without feeling heroic emotions or thinking that they were actors upon the well-lighted stage of history, were the most useful to their country and community, while those who tried to grasp the general course of events and wanted to take part in history, those who performed acts of incredible self-sacrifice or heroism, and participated in great events, were the most useless."[26]

In Huizinga's terms, later son Tolstoy is with later son Cervantes in attacking the Stoic chivalric ideal and in preserving, in his later return to the soil and the peasants, the Epicurean bucolic ideal. If historical-mindedness is at all based on the concept of causality, on the concept that what did happen has an influence on what is happening, then Tolstoy appears not to have been historically minded. His disconnected view of the battle-scene as seen through the eyes of Pierre Bezukhov is almost identical with later son Hume's skeptical, atomistic attitude about interconnected causality. Berlin writes:

Pierre Bezukhov wanders about, "lost" on the battlefield of Borodino, and looks for something which he imagines as a kind of set piece; a battle as depicted by the historians or the painters. But he finds only the ordinary confusion of individual human beings haphazardly attending to this or that human want. That, at any rate, is concrete, uncontaminated by theories and abstractions; and Pierre is therefore closer to the truth about the course of events—at least as seen by men—than those who believe them to obey a discoverable set of laws or rules. Pierre sees only a succession of "accidents" whose origins and consequences are, by and large, untraceable and unpredictable; only loose strung groups of events forming an ever varying pattern, following no discernible order.[27]

We have quoted Berlin extensively more to learn about Tolstoy's philosophy of history than to inquire into Berlin's typology. His hedgehogs and foxes constitute a typology of cognition, of world views. Though at points it may overlap with our typology it cannot coincide, inasmuch as the connectedness-disconnectedness typology is more protean and includes, besides cognitive thinking, ways of feeling and acting. Though Berlin is quoted extensively, he is not quoted in entirety. Some of his views on Tolstoy and some of the parallels he draws between eminent men cannot be used to illustrate our hypothesis. Others can be used very well. Thus, Tolstoy as a penetrating perceiver of differences:

His genius lay in the perception of specific properties, the almost inexpressible individual quality in virtue of which the given object is uniquely different from all others.

It is in analysing, identifying sharply, marking differences, isolating concrete examples, piercing to the heart of each individual entity *per se*, that Tolstoy rises to the full height of his genius.[28]

Tolstoy as a Deweyan individualist who wants tastes disputed so that a simple social norm be established:

Tolstoy's genius lies in a capacity for marvellously accurate reproduction of the irreproducible, the almost miraculous evocation of the full, untranslatable individuality of the individual. . . . But then this same writer pleads for, indeed preaches with great fury, particularly in his last, religious phase, the exact opposite: the necessity of expelling everything that does not submit to some very general, very simple standard: say, what peasants like or dislike, or what the gospels declare to be good.[29]

Tolstoy's affinity with Rousseau:

It is a commonplace that he owed a great deal to Rousseau. . . . He remained an admirer of Rousseau, and later in life still recommended *Emile* as the best book ever written on education. Rousseau must have strengthened, if he did not actually originate, his growing tendency to idealize the soil and its cultivators—the simple peasant, who for Tolstoy is a repository of almost as rich a stock of "natural" virtues as Rousseau's noble savage.[30]

Tolstoy as a Cartesian systematic doubter who tries to reduce plurality by casting almost everything on the "false" pile:

Tolstoy can only say what it is not. His genius is devastatingly destructive. He can only attempt to point towards a goal by exposing the false signposts to it; to isolate the truth by annihilating that which it is not. . . .[31]

To appreciate Tolstoy as an historian or as a philosopher of history, it is clearly necessary to know Tolstoy as a man. The observations of Isaiah Berlin have helped in this regard. The matter may properly be generalized. It is clearly necessary to know the historian as a man in order to understand why he writes the type of history he does. The personal element is perhaps not quite so important in the case of academic or professional historians who are under the common discipline of a calling; the common discipline tends to evoke nonpartisan and supra-personal attitudes; one and one are two, regardless of personal subjectivities. But in the case of historical writers, or those influenced by a historical ideal, the personal viewpoint appears highly important. In inquiring into Tolstoy's historical writing we have found that he can be variously described as antiheroic, antichivalrous, antistoic, anticausality; or pro-common man, pro-bucolic, pro-Epicurean, pro-accidental occurrence. For our immediate purposes, he can be described as interested in myths of origin. He is too involved in the horizontal level where human and social frustrations exist to take a detached attitude about what the real past origins were; such an attitude would legitimize present inequalities. Rather, he must be partisan and rewrite history. Even though he runs the risk of fabricating the past, he, like Rousseau, must do all he can to redistribute merit; to take it away from the heroes who have more than they need and give it to the nonheroic common men who have less than they need. His partisanship is more open than Emerson's but in a similar direction. Due to his extremism, Tolstoy is much less credible than Emerson, who uses a Montaigne-like fog. Equally partisan and extreme is first son Carlyle who, as we said earlier, insists on giving all of the credit to the heroes, to his in-group. Though currently discredited, his views possessed considerable credibility because they were based on actual past events. Though his (and Nietzsche's) views were one-sided, the nucleus of truth was sufficient to influence strongly a number of men, of whom Hitler and Mussolini are notable examples.

Let us consider now how the past was treated by two men in recent political history. They are first son Justice Holmes and later son Harold Laski. Our source is Edmund Wilson's essay *The Holmes-Laski Correspondence*. In Holmes, we may see how a man views events from the vertical level—a level made possible not only by heroic aristocratic tendencies but also by the lofty position of the Supreme Court. In Laski, we may see how a man, who by temperament and calling operates on the horizontal level of programmatic socialism, treats past and present events. Our quotation from Wilson will be rather full in order to see the full personalities of these men. Wilson, after writing "These letters . . . throw into relief, I believe, certain aspects of Holmes and Laski in a way that nothing else has yet done, and they stimulate long-range reflections on the characters and careers of

the two men"[32] then goes on to the point that is pertinent to
our discussion. "The great scandal about Harold Laski, regretted
by all his friends and sometimes used against him by his enemies,
was his habit of unscrupulous romancing. He would freely invent
stories that had often no basis whatever in fact about people he
did not know but whom he claimed to have met and talked with,
exploits that he had not performed, scenes that had never
occurred and books that he had never read. It is obvious that
these falsehoods of Laski's represented a genuine aberration, because they were entirely gratuitous. Laski *was* on confidential
terms with distinguished and famous people; he *did* have a phenomenal memory and he *was* immensely learned; he *did* have
an uncanny knack of picking up unsuspected treasures from the
shelves of secondhand-book dealers. From what motive, then,
could he have allowed himself to bewilder and trouble his friends,
to leave traps for his biographers and editors, and to make himself ridiculous in retrospect by providing in his personal letters
so much evidence against himself?"[33]

Wilson suggests various motivations for Laski's aberrations,
a major one being that elfish Laski was engaged in a manipulative
power struggle against the smugly self-important, prosperous
class and needed to build up himself and his socialist program
and to downgrade those in his path. His leveling method was not
the violent tearing-down of Tolstoy who was also a social reformer but more like Oscar Wilde's spoofing or like the leg-
pulling mischievousness of other later sons—Mark Twain, H. H.
Munro, Stephen Leacock, Robert Benchley, James Thurber.
Wilson actually writes: "He was almost elfishly small . . . his
appearance was perennially youthful, as of a schoolboy who was
stumping his elders or innocently waiting for someone to pick
up one of those buzzing matchboxes that give the effect of an
electric shock. I was told years ago by a friend who had crossed
on a boat with Laski of his method of dealing with a man who
was boring the other passengers by his pompousness and self-
importance. Laski sat down and wrote this man a note that purported to come from the captain, apologizing for not having
realized before that there was so distinguished a person aboard . . .
and inviting him to dine with him [the captain] that evening
tête à tête in his cabin."[34]

The small boy at a disadvantage, who, puny of physique, had pitted his will against the steam-rollering vested interests of orthodox Judaism, one-hundred-per-cent Americanism and the formidable class structure of the British Empire had made of his intellect an instrument that could analyze and estimate these great social entities as few members of them could do for themselves. . . . He not only watched politics intently, he bet on and worked for those movements and groups that he thought would help to realize his vision. . . .

Yet in Laski's imagination—for all his considerable shrewdness—lay his weakness as well as his strength. . . . In some sense, Laski lived in a dream—a dream full of actual data, with its foundations in a real grasp of history, and made vivid with first-hand impressions of a variety of modern societies, but a dream that did not, nevertheless, quite make the right contact with life. . . . In his rallying to Soviet Russia at the time when the Stalinist Terror had made the regime least defensible, his capacity for fantasy became quite alarming. . . .—and he went around abroad making speeches in which he promised a number of things that he and other Leftists wanted but that neither Bevin or Attlee had any intentions of granting, till the latter had to cut him short and rebuke him for his "irresponsible statements."

[Yet] He had always been a dedicated man. . . . his complete lack of snobbery—. . . . Harold Laski was genuinely kind. . . .

Mr. Martin has done well to minimize them [Laski's delusions and croppers] and to emphasize that Laski's career was brilliant, courageous and useful, and had behind it a backbone of hard work that contradicted his apparent facility.[35]

Wilson's multifaceted nonpartisan approach when discussing later son Laski is duplicated when he describes first son Holmes. One gains from Wilson the impression that Holmes was a man of aristocratic, stoic, heroic tendencies whose austere sympathy for other men derived from a puritanical inner conscience controlling his violence rather than from immediate identification with the unfortunate—as a man whose vertically positioned, long-term outlook gave him a distaste for the partisan action connected with social reform. The preference for humanity in the large, historical sense rather than for the individual common man can be seen in the following. Concerning interconnected humanity, Holmes regarded the law "not merely as a sacred code, which had simply to be read correctly, but as a complex accretion of rules accumulated through more than a thousand years and representing the needs and demands of definite groups of people existing in particular places at particular periods of history."[36] Quoting Holmes: "One doubted oneself how it [the law] could be worthy of the interest of an intelligent mind. And yet one said to oneself, law is human—it is a part of man, and of one world with all the rest."[37] As profoundly humanistic as this side of Holmes is, it can scarcely be equated with being sentimental or ardently democratic. As Wilson writes, quoting Holmes: " 'I repeat my old aphorism . . . that everything is founded on the death of men—society, which only changes the modes of killing—romance, to which . . . generations, of dead, on the memorial tablets of a great war are necessary.' "[38]

This undercurrent of attraction to violence is further emphasized in Holmes', according to Wilson, "always insisting that the right to kill to enforce authority by violent means . . . is of the essence of any sovereign power. . . ."[39] And in Wilson's statement:

Nor had the war made him more democratic; he was far from having been so favorably impressed by any of the common men with whom he had been thrown in the Army as Tolstoy's Pierre, in *War and Peace*, was by the peasant Karataev. "It's odd," he had written his parents, "how indifferent one gets to the sight of death—perhaps, because one gets aristocratic and don't value much a common life. Then they are apt to be so dirty it seems natural—'Dust to Dust'— I would do anything [for them] that lay in my power but it doesn't much affect my feelings."[40]

What apparently held in check his violent, heroic tendency was his inner moral voice. Wilson describes him as a man "who was scrupulous about every word he wrote, and who did not, until he was over ninety, allow himself the self-indulgence of dropping a book he had once begun."[41] Wilson speculates that "his new [liberal] friends had been working on his conscience,"[42] and so influenced his dissent in the Abrams case. When in addition to moral considerations there was a heroic, historic principle involved, Holmes could empathize with democratic aims. Wilson quotes Holmes: " 'All my life . . . I have sneered at the natural rights of man, and at times I have thought that the bills of rights in Constitutions were overworked—but these chaps . . . remind me, if I needed it . . . that they embody principles that men have died for, and that it is well not to forget in our haste to secure our notion of general welfare.' "[43] It was perhaps this historical heroic, moral component that explains why Holmes "holding these unpopular opinions, to which he gave frequent expression, he should have devoted himself to the service of the democratic government for which he had fought, attempting to interpret the will of the people in measures which he often disapproved. . . ."[44]

First son Holmes and later son Laski illustrate, then, two ways of treating the past. The former, predisposed to connectedness, took the past quite seriously; so much so that not only was he scrupulous about every word he wrote but also he was fundamentally conservative rather than liberal in his political and legal thinking. Though this was a slight distortion of the past, his moral sense and rationality prevented him from giving the past the great distortion we see in the cases of Carlyle Nietzsche, Hitler, etc.

Justice Oliver Wendell Holmes, because he was up on the vertical level, did not have a bet going on the horizontal level outcome; he could be nonpartisan and not given to wishful thinking. Laski, however, was betting heavily on the outcome of his political wager on Socialism. Partisan on the horizontal level, he was susceptible to taking great liberties with the past, making fabrications even when seemingly unnecessary.

The essay not only instructs us about Holmes and Laski but also tells us something about first son Wilson. It has been mentioned that he gives multifaceted, nonpartisan pictures of both Holmes and Laski. Although he is judiciously impartial to Laski, the impression is gained that he is psychologically more identified with Holmes and probably, in general, with those who are prone to connectedness. It is noteworthy that the *Eight Essays*—consisting of essays hand-picked by Wilson from all the essays he has written—is almost exclusively concerned with first sons: Shaw, Theodore Roosevelt, Dickens, Housman, Lincoln, Holmes, Hemingway. The only later son is Laski. (The birth order of Marquis de Sade is not available.)

First son Wilson's personality and historical attitude are especially pertinent to us now, inasmuch as he is to be compared with later son T. S. Eliot. Though not historians, both men are highly influential literary critics who are especially characterized by the historical approach. The principal question will be, "Are these approaches identical or do they differ along the lines we have seen in first and later sons?" Because Eliot's psychology has been discussed in the previous chapter, we shall concentrate here more on Wilson. The particular flavor of Wilson's personality can be gained from a rather full quotation from another eminent literary critic, Alfred Kazin. In *On Native Ground* he writes: "At a time when so many writers had either wearied of criticism or corrupted it, a time when the very exercise of criticism seemed peculiarly futile and isolated, Wilson continued to write criticism as a great human discipline, a study of literature in its relation to civilization that sacrified nothing to closeness of observation, yet kept its sights trained on the whole human situation."[45] On another page he says:

In Sainte-Beuve's phrase, Wilson was rather a "naturalist of souls," a critic in whom judiciousness and sympathy became illumination, the kind of critic who can exploit every auxiliary field of knowledge and become the partisan of none. As a critic, therefore, he became associated with no particular doctrine, canon of taste, or normative zeal.

Wilson called himself a historical critic in the tradition that stems vaguely from Vico and Herder through Taine and Marx. . . . F. Scott Fitzgerald once called Wilson his intellectual conscience; but Wilson was, even more, the conscience of two intellectual generations. . . . By the catholicity of his interests, the freshness and directness of his performance, he seemed more than any other critic in America the experimentalist who worked with the whole tradition of literature in his bones.

He was above all the spectator, the bookman of active humility and detachment. . . .

Wilson became . . . a spectator in the social sense, a spectator between two worlds. It was for this reason that one always saw the density of the past in his work, the underground sense of history and curiously aloof sympathy with the present. . . . His student's mind was something more than an aptitude and a gift of balance; it was the exercise of his sense of history, the very groundwork, as it were, of the open-mindedness and elegiac resignation. . . .

What one missed in this criticism, of course, was a positive affirmation, the intensity of a great conception.

Yet . . . what Wilson had to give, always, stood best revealed in his own words, as when he said in a lecture that the object of any intellectual activity is to give meaning to experience. . . . This, as he said, was the great achievement of the historical interpretation of literature; it was certainly his special triumph.[46]

From Kazin, one sees some connectedness characteristics in Wilson that we have encountered in other first sons. Perhaps the main one is the solution on the vertical level (Santayana's phrase). From this vantage point, a man could more easily be the objective, reflective spectator. As in a space ship one can view the continent as a whole, Wilson can, as Kazin says, keep his "sights trained on the whole human situation." The spectator thus can make a synthesis out of the plurality, "a spectator between two worlds." If he were intensely interested in programmatic action on the contemporaneous horizontal level, he could not be as nonpartisan. Like the first-born iguana who was a spectator up in a tree, he must maintain at the most "a curiously aloof sympathy with the present." This aloof interest enables him to be an accepting naturalist of souls like first sons Montesquieu, William James, Frazer, and Freud (and first daughters, Margaret Mead and Ruth Benedict). Certainly the prime requisite for taking action is not the important thing for Wilson as it would be, for example, for later son Descartes who needed to know his location in the horizontal level flux. Wilson, like Einstein, knows pretty well where in space he is at the moment—he is up in the tree. For him and Einstein, the problem is not to attain location point certainty but rather to achieve comprehension, to know what everything means. Not only the meaning of the plural activities down below—but also the meaning from the viewpoint of time. Relatively satisfied as to where in space he is at the present, he, with an underground sense of history, now tries to comprehend where he was or where he was going—or where the people down below were and where they will be going. In this state of seeming ruminative doubt, of negative capability, a leading guide as to origins and ends is the inner moral voice. Thus, like Lippmann, he can become the conscience of two (or more) intellectual generations. The guide supplied by conscience has long-term time aspects; it has stoical undertones of "elegic resignation." This guide, coupled as it frequently is with plurality, conflict, abstraction, and even resignation is no manual for action on the horizontal level. There in the chaotic flux one may be more helpful if, like later sons Descartes, Rousseau, and Dewey, one is single-minded, doctrinal, and disputes tastes in order to establish stabilizing social norms.

As for Eliot, however, it cannot be easily said that he has no "canon of taste or normative zeal." As we will see shortly, he is uniquely distinguished as an arbiter of taste. In spite of this partisanship, he is also known for his traditional or historical approach. The partisan feeling certainly would interfere with a disinterested desire to know the past as it really happened. It would, however, reinforce another historical approach—that of creating new myths of origin. Certain evidence and opinions strongly suggest that this is indeed Eliot's historical approach. We shall not find him fabricating the past out of whole cloth; such a gross method would bring down on him the strong disbelief meted out to Tolstoy and Laski. Instead, there is a subtle redistribution of merit, similar to the procedure followed by Emerson in *Representative Men*. By adhering to real men in the past, Eliot achieves the credibility usually accorded to the historical overemphasis of first sons. The resulting new myths of origin give us a new set of Literary Founding Fathers. As with the Trobrianders in whose myth of origin the pig became the chief after pointing out to the dog that the latter ate dirt and was thus low bred, so with Eliot who, in the minor aristocratic tradition, points out that so-and-so ate the vulgar dirt of excessive feelings and is, therefore, not a fit literary figure to emulate. The credibility of Eliot's new set of Founding Fathers is put under great strain, however, when for example he deposes Shakespeare and tries to enthrone a minor figure.

Eliot's historical attitude has been under attack by various critics, perhaps most heatedly by Shapiro. In *Axel's Castle* Wilson is critical of Eliot's disconnected, atomistic, unhistorical method. He writes: "T. S. Eliot has undertaken a kind of scientific study of aesthetic values: avoiding impressionistic rhetoric and *a priori* aesthetic theories alike, he compares works of literature coolly and tries to distinguish between different orders of artistic effects and the different degrees of satisfaction to be derived from them. And by this method, Eliot has done more than perhaps any other modern critic to effect a revaluation of English literature."[47]

Later on, Edmund Wilson says: "Now this point of view . . . seems to me absolutely unhistorical—an impossible attempt to make aesthetic values independent of all other values. Who will agree with Eliot, for example, that a poet cannot be an original thinker. . . ."[48]

The serious, stoically minded Wilson cannot accept poetry taken out of intellectual and historical context, cannot accept Eliot's Epicurean ideas that the true, pure, and exalted function of poetry is to afford a superior amusement. Thus, though Wilson praises Eliot's successful attempt to find absolute values through the comparison of the works of different periods, he is overtly critical of Eliot's disconnection of poetry from intellect and history.

A penetrating discussion of Eliot as a critic is given by Stanley Edgar Hyman in *The Armed Vision, A Study in the Methods of Modern Literary Criticism.* Hyman carefully distinguishes traditional from historical (the chapter is titled "T. S. Eliot and Tradition in Criticism"), and in general reaches conclusions similar to those offered by the present author. He opens with:

T. S. Eliot's contribution to the new criticism has been chiefly, as John Crowe Ransom once phrased it, "the recovery of old criticism." His influence in this direction has been very great, and although it is hard to tell how much of this is the influence of the criticism itself and how much is respect for his authority as one of the foremost living poets, Eliot is undoubtedly our chief spokesman for a critical viewpoint that can be roughly called "traditional."[49]

Eliot's function as an arbiter of tastes is seen in Hyman's writing that Eliot believes that there are two functions of criticism: "one function 'the elucidation of art and the correction of taste,' the other 'to bring the poet back to life.' "[50] Hyman points out that: "Actually Eliot's 'tradition' is a utilitarian concept, and he constantly emphasizes the *using* of the tradition."[51]

Sometimes this use is "in a relatively pure literary sense. . . ."[52] But: "A different and more characteristic use of tradition, this time for essentially nonliterary ends, is found in such essays of Eliot's as the ones on Bishop Andrewes and Archbishop Bramhall . . . where he attempts to refurbish, amplify, and even artificially provide an Anglican literary tradition. He claims that Andrewes's sermons 'rank with the finest English prose of their time, of any time,' and are superior to Donne's because Donne's motives are 'impure' and he lacked 'spiritual discipline' a deficiency that has had the effect of making Donne's sermons more widely known. Thus, at one blow, Eliot establishes a literary tradition on the basis of criteria that are wholly ethical, attacks a great writer *as writer*, with a whispered hint of apostasy or at least careerism in his clerical profession, and exalts a right relation to the English Church as the fount not only of salvation in a future life but of the best prose here and now."[53]

Hyman continues his discussion of Eliot by stating:

Sometimes Eliot writes passages that appear to be entirely meaningless manipulations of terms cloudy enough to give the semblance of conveying a critical judgment. . . .

Even at its broadest . . . Eliot's tradition is highly exclusive. It seeks out the classic and excludes the romantic. . . . Eliot in general sees his task in the substitution of his "tradition" for theirs [that of others] . . . and in general reversing the nineteenth century's hierarchy.

It [Eliot's prose style] gives the effect, frequently delusive, of being far removed from the tawdry concerns of the present in a concentration on the timeless. . . .

Principally as a result of Eliot's use of terms like these, almost every writer who has ever discussed his criticism has caught him in contradictions.[54]

The crucial question of whether Eliot is really historically minded is brought up by Hyman. He first quotes Eliot:

The historical sense compels a man to write not merely with his own generation in his bones, but with a feeling that the whole of the literature . . . from Homer and within it the whole of the literature of his own country has a simultaneous existence and composes a simultaneous order. This historical sense, which is a sense of the timeless as well as the temporal and of the timeless and of the temporal together, is what makes a writer traditional.[55]

Then Hyman writes:

Eliot is using "historical" here in a curious sense, and the ambiguity of the word has made for something of a critical controversy over whether or not Eliot's critical method is "historical." Edmund Wilson . . . has discussed Eliot as the very type of the unhistorical critic, one who treats all literature as though it coexisted simultaneously, comparing and judging it by absolute standards, in a temporal vacuum. John Crowe Ransom, on the other hand, chose Eliot as his example of "The Historical Critic" in *The New Criticism*, pointing out that Eliot "uses his historical studies for the sake of literary understanding." Obviously, the parties in the controversy are using "historical" in two different senses: Wilson meaning the use of contextual or relative criteria, Ransom (and apparently Eliot himself) meaning historical knowledge or awareness of the past. . . .

. . . it might be suggested as a tentative resolution of the controversy that Eliot does not know enough history, in Ransom's sense, to be a consistent historical critic in Wilson's sense.[56]

If both sides in this controversy are credited with good intentions, the answer to the opposing views may rest in different notions of time. As we have indicated, time as an extended reality having duration is keenly sensed by the connectedness-prone first sons, the best examples being Einstein and Bergson. Time and other phenomena are seen in contextual interrelation. Time is not for them a disconnected "now." Moments for them become minutes, hours, days, years, centuries, light years. When they think in such long-term views they are frequently considered to be "timeless." But there is a different sort of timelessness possible when one thinks principally of new nows, or past, present, and future being telescoped into a simultaneous coexistence. This kind of timelessness of nonextended time is more characteristic of the disconnectedness-prone later sons, a notable example being Kierkegaard. The past does not have to be rigorously erased; it was not written down indelibly in the first place. Thus Hume did not recognize the past "I." Whitman could forget the past "I" and say, "Do I contradict myself? Very well, then I contradict myself." Descartes' coordinates make no provisions for when an event took place, only where it took place.

If Eliot is really on the horizontal time level (in spite of the vertical level trappings), his historical attitude will be quite different from Wilson's. On the horizontal level, time intervals between mutating events are much shorter. Here short-time history is being made, whereas "up in the tree" long-term history is being observed and comprehended. It is, then, not surprising to find Eliot saying, according to Hyman: "Whoever has approved this idea of order, of the form of European, of English literature, will not find it preposterous that the past should be altered by the present as much as the present is directed by the past."[57] Eliot is admittedly from this statement an alterer of the past. He is as much a maker of history as the later sons we saw to be successful leaders of revolutionary mass movements—Cromwell, Lenin, Napoleon, Brigham Young, Gandhi, etc.

Also characteristic of later sons, Eliot is anti-heroic. Like Emerson and Tolstoy he believes that the common man, the man without demonic, omnipotent, heroic tendencies is the principal contributor to historically important events. Hyman quotes Eliot: "The poet must be very conscious of the main current, which does not at all flow invariably through the most distinguished reputations."[58] His structures against willful arrogance are continued in his advice: "What happens is a continual surrender of himself as he is at the moment to something which is more valuable. The progress of an artist is a continual self-sacrifice, a continual extinction of personality."[59] It may be, as Hyman suggests, that "Eliot has a positive terror of personality, including his own, and the overpowering discipline of a literary tradition is his refuge from it."[60] At any rate, his group-minded proposal of a single guiding dogma to hold in check and to make meek the individual unruly self-assertive man is strongly reminiscent of such later sons as Hobbes and Hamilton. As Hyman quotes Eliot:

What I have been leading up to is the following assertion: that when morals cease to be a matter of tradition and orthodoxy—that is, of the habits of the community formulated, corrected and elevated by the continuous thought and direction of the Church—and when each man is to elaborate his own, then *personality* becomes a thing of alarming importance.[61]

It is fitting that we should close this chapter with the comparison of first son Wilson and later son Eliot. More accessible to personality exploration than professional or academic historians, their functioning as critical literary historians has allowed us to view the attitudes toward the past of a connectedness-prone first son and a disconnectedness-prone later son. Put in brief and condensed terms, the former, sensitive to the extended duration of time, strives to make the past and present meaningful; the latter, sensitive to the simultaneity of time, strives to make the knowledge of the past useful for present purposes.

It is understandable that the special focus on history would inevitably lead us back to the many aspects of the personality discussed in previous chapters—the orientation toward individual and group morality, the plural- and single-mindedness, the heroic and the militant, etc. For, though the focus has been seemingly special, the field of history is or can be sufficiently broad that all aspects of human thought and behavior can be encompassed under its rubric.

CHAPTER X *Tendencies in Science*

THE RATHER GENERAL systematic treatment given to previous topics cannot be accorded to the subject matter of this chapter. The lack of carryover from clinical experience to science prevents the author from offering more than a few scattered observations and speculations. Only the necessity of testing the connectedness-disconnectedness hypothesis in every possible field motivates the writer to approach this technically difficult subject. Our attention will of course be on the scientists rather than on their scientific productions. And we shall endeavor to see whether what we have discussed heretofore may have any application to the new subject.

An appropriate beginning can be made with the theory of evolution. Its appropriateness rests on the fact that it is intimately associated with biology and man; that it has a definite relation to the topics of the previous chapter—time, history, and origins; that the centuries which had to elapse before it was definitively formulated and the resistance it met when finally proposed indicated that the theory went counter to some deep psychological needs of mankind. We shall find that of all the men sufficiently aware of the facts to arrive at the theory, only certain men appeared able to do so. That these men were predominantly later sons (Darwin is the prime example) either is a remarkable and misleading set of coincidences or, as we shall speculate, constitutes some support for the connectedness-disconnectedness theory.

Before discussing the men involved, it would be well to examine the psychological aspects of the theory. Little emotional comfort is seemingly derived from a theory which strikes such a severe blow at the omnipotence of Man. Not only is Man taken off the lofty throne of being God's kinsman and, instead, given kinship with the lowly animals, but also the causal necessity for God is removed. There is here little chance for individual ennoblement or for ennoblement through reverence of an omnipotent God. Appropriately enough the theory is deflatingly entitled The Descent of Man—rather than the Ascent of Man.

Particularly bleak and chilly would be the theory for those with heroic and stoic tendencies; thus, one would not expect first sons to formulate this theory. Whereas the chill for the heroically minded is obvious, that for the stoic may require some amplification. The stoic, it will be recalled, is able to put up with short-term adversity because there is a long-term Divine Plan or Intelligence at work. Even if there be no personal immortality, there is at least an everlasting God who has inscrutable purposes. These cosmic, Divine purposes give meaning to life; they causally or teleologically connect Man's short existence to something higher and of permanent duration. Without this long-term reward for his moral obeisance and his enduring, the stoic would become depressed; he could not feed himself; he would cease being interested in what happened long ago or what is going to happen in the far, far future. He would write neither histories nor epic poems.

The question naturally arises, "For what manner of men might the theory of evolution not be so chilling?" It will be recalled that Epicurus comforted the common people by informing them that there was no life after death; that they need not fear punishments from God, because on death they would be disconnected from Divine retribution. Enjoy the pleasures of life on this earth, because there is no hereafter. The Epicurean guarantee that people were individual atoms not masterminded by Divine Intelligence was comforting to those who considered existence on a short-term terrestrial basis. It would not then be surprising that the disconnectedness-prone later sons would either not be repulsed by the theory of evolution or actually be attracted to it. What matter if there be a final extinction of the esteemed heroic "I?" Hume was skeptical that there was such a phenomenon, and Eliot strongly recommended that even during life there should be an extinction of the personal Self.

We come now to the men involved in the evolutionary theory. The foremost of these was, of course, later son Darwin. It needs to be pointed out that he was an investigator of Nature rather than of Mankind. If first sons Wilson, Montesquieu, Frazer, Freud, and Malinowski in their study of man may be called "naturalists of souls," then Darwin may simply be designated as a naturalist, or a naturalist of the flora and fauna. This distinction is pertinent inasmuch as it was another later-son naturalist of plants and animals, Lamarck, who earlier had constructed an evolutionary theory. Because Darwinism and Lamarckism are sometimes thought to be contradictory, it must be pointed out that in his *Origin of Species* Darwin accepted the Lamarckian idea of the inheritance of acquired characters as partially contributing to evolution. It is also of interest that Lamarck did not call upon the Divine Intelligence or design to explain the formation of new organs. The explanation was much less aristocratic. Rather, the new origin was a repercussion of unsoulful bodily needs—a principal one being the oral need, which we have noted often in later sons. Thus, the giraffe stretches its neck in order to feed higher and higher on the tree leaves; as a result of this habit, the giraffe's neck and fore limbs eventually grow longer. The underlying theme is that if animals are left to themselves, they will evolve in an adaptive fashion without the intervention of God.

The naturalist orientation is clearly evident in two other later sons intimately associated with evolution, Alfred Wallace and Thomas Huxley. None of the men so far mentioned gave his investigative attention to man—or even to the anthropoid apes. Darwin studied the Crustacea; Lamarck, originally a botanist, made his great contribution on the Invertebrata; Wallace, also a botanist, studied insects principally, and Huxley investigated sea polyps. To this list of later sons must be added the name of an economist, Malthus. His theory was one of the bases of Darwin's theory. As the *Encyclopaedia Britannica* note reads: "Upon reading in Oct. 1838, T. R. Malthus' *Essay on the Principle of Population*, his own observations having long since convinced him of the struggle for existence, it at once struck Darwin 'that under these circumstances favorable variations would tend to be preserved, and unfavourable ones to be destroyed. The result of this would be the formation of new species. Here, then,

I had . . . a theory by which to work.' "[1] Malthus of course cannot be called a naturalist in the strict sense. But his emphasis on basic biological needs, on the possibility of men starving, certainly excludes him from the category of "naturalist of souls."

In order to assert conclusively that the theory of evolution is a later-son production, we may be called upon to show that first sons had a chance to formulate it but did not do so. This would be a very difficult if not impossible assignment. What can be offered instead are some suggestive instances. The first involves Agassiz who, though a great naturalist, somehow paid some attention to the "soul." This first son was viewing the same phenomena that Darwin and Wallace were viewing and at about the same time. Yet not only did he not arrive at the theory of evolution but he was coldly unsympathetic to Darwinism after the theory was announced. When asked why he rejected it he gave a few technical reasons but most important to him was the fact that Darwinism conflicted with his philosophy. Typical of many first sons, he could not do without an interconnecting Divine Intelligence. Each specimen of plant or animal was "a thought of God." Their basic unities were "association of ideas of the Divine Mind." Like first son Pascal, he could not drift in a sphere of disconnected uncertainty. Like first son Einstein he must maintain that God does not play at dice.

The other instance involves first son Charles Lyell, the geologist. Here we do not see a sharp rejection of Darwin—in fact, Lyell was quite friendly to Darwin and urged him to publish his work. Whether Lyell was in an investigative position to originate the theory is of course debatable. The *Encyclopaedia Britannica* note on Darwin reads: "The great naturalist [Darwin] appeared in the ripeness of time, when the world was ready for his splendid generalizations. In the preparation for Darwin Sir Charles Lyell's *Principles of Geology* played an important part, accustoming men's minds to the vast changes brought about by natural processes, and leading them, by its lucid and temperate discussion of Lamarck's and other views, to reflect upon evolution."[2]

It is possible that in spite of this intellectual awareness, Lyell's interest in man may have diverted him from viewing certain phenomena or, if he did view them, may have prevented him from building an evolutionary hypothesis. For, though he was first interested in limestone formation and then in marine remains, his third great work was the *Antiquity of Man*. Further evidence of Lyell's pro Homo sapiens orientation is supplied, according to Loren C. Eiseley, by Darwin himself. Eiseley writes: "Darwin did not wish to leave man an exception to his system, but he was content to consider man simply as a part of that vast, sprawling, endlessly ramifying ferment called 'life.' The rest of him could be left for the philosophers. 'I have often,' he once complained to a friend, 'been made wroth (even by Lyell) at the confidence with which people speak of the introduction of man, as if they had seen him walk on the stage and as if in a geological sense it was more important than the entry of any other mammifer.' "[3]

Once the theory had been proposed by those able to originate it, most thinkers—scientific, philosophic, and literary—accepted it eagerly. The theory had the effect of opening a door to new vistas or of making meaningful a previous miscellany of phenomena. As usually happens, once the idea was taken up it underwent various personal modifications so that the term "evolutionist" became less precise. It became hard to determine whether the thinker was a true Darwinian evolutionist, or a neo-evolutionist, or a pseudo-evolutionist. For this reason, there would be considerable difficulty in demonstrating a later-son—first-son predominance in men who incorporated the theory of evolution into their thinking. We shall, however, give some suggestive illustrations of a possible trend. For comparison purposes, first it is necessary to see approximately what kind of evolutionist Darwin was. In his Conclusion to the *Origin of Species*, Darwin's essential point seems to be that the Divine Creator's role in evolutionary development was limited to placing no more than a few prototypes (perhaps just one) on earth. From this point on, the biological organism was on its own, its evolutionary development depending mainly but not exclusively on natural selection. The minimal role of the creator is seen in Darwin's writing: "A celebrated author and divine has written to me that he has gradually learned to see that it is just as noble a conception of the Deity to believe that He created a few original forms capable of self-development into other and needful forms, as to believe that He required a fresh act of creation to supply the voids caused by the action of His laws."[4] And again, later: "It is so easy to hide our ignorance under such expressions as the 'plan of creation,' 'unity of design,' &c., and to think that we give an explanation when we only re-state a fact."[5]

That Darwin's self-esteem as a human being seems to be enhanced by *minimal* Divine interaction is seen on a later page: "When I view all beings not as special creations, but as the lineal descendants of some few beings which lived long before the first bed of the Cambrian system was deposited, they seem to me to become ennobled."[6] Once left on their own, the organisms do encounter a hard struggle for life and existence. A principal hardship is of an oral character (". . . from the war of nature, from famine and death. . . .").[7] What happens in natural selection is "Extinction of less-improved forms."[8] This last phrase is pertinent because it is milder and has a nuance different from "survival of the fittest," a phrase contributed by Spencer.

Disregarding other more technical aspects of the theory, we might say that Darwin is predominantly (though not exclusively) on the side of disconnectedness. If we were to transpose the entire biologic evolution to the development of a human being, Darwin would concede that conception by the parents, intra-uterine existence within the mother, and a short postnatal oral dependence are what the individual owes to his antecedents. From then on, he is on his own in the struggle for existence. The connected dependency of child upon parents—prolonged much after birth—is a phenomenon mentioned by many writers as being uniquely human. Darwin, however, does not seem to think along those lines. For him there is a rather early disconnection of the ties to the original parental sources. In this respect he is much like later son Rousseau who believed that man in Nature began disconnectedly without many parental ties and finally evolved into a somewhat reluctant participant in the connectedness inherent in the state. As Rousseau says in *The Social Contract*, "Hunger and other appetites made him (man) at various times experience various modes of existence, and among these was one which urged him to propagate his species—a blind propensity that, having nothing to do with the heart, produced a merely animal act. The want once gratified, the two sexes knew each other no more, and even the offspring was nothing to its mother, as soon as it could do without her."⁹

With Darwin's underlying motif in mind, we can view the thinking of first son Herbert Spencer. He thought of himself and others have thought of him as the principal philosopher of evolution. Quite intimate with Darwin and Huxley, he thought along the lines of evolutionary theory and used it for other hypotheses. Yet the question arises: "Is he a Darwinian type of evolutionist as far as disconnectedness is concerned?" The answer appears to be in the negative. This theory was attractive to him mainly because it described how the grand plan of progress is made possible in *Social Statics* he argues teleologically that "the greatest happiness is the purpose of creation." His inability to do without a *persisting* connectedness to some mystical power is seen in his formulation of the Unknowable. His stoic and heroic attitude may be reflected in the fact that he contributed the phrase "survival of the fittest." The use of the superlatives— Darwin uses the comparative phrase "extinction of less-improved forms"—we have found rather characteristic of omnipotent first sons. "Survival of the fittest" can be used, as indeed it was used, to support the laissez-faire economists who were mainly first sons—and to support the creation of an elite of Heroic Supermen, as we saw in Carlyle, Nietzsche, and Hitler.

Quite a different perspective is evidenced by later son John Dewey in his essay *The Influence of Darwinism in Philosophy*. The disconnecting features of the theory appealed to him because they did away with binding traditional permanence and allowed the individual the opportunity for self-development. Especially welcome to Dewey was the evolutionary theory's elimination of a metaphysical first cause or final end. And he takes Spencer to task for reintroducing such a shopworn notion. The following quotation illustrates Dewey's antagonism to any binding design and also his emphasis on immediate concrete goals in the horizontal level of flux and mutation. Darwin will be quoted rather fully here in order that our previous references to him acquire some substance. There will be an opportunity to compare Dewey, a very practical pragmatist, with first son James, a speculative pragmatist who was sufficiently unconcrete to investigate varieties of religious experiences and to write an essay on the problem of being, on why anything should be what it is. Most important, however, are the differences between later son Dewey and first son Spencer.

Dewey wrote:

In laying hands upon the sacred ark of absolute permanency, in treating the forms that had been regarded as types of fixity and perfection as originating and passing away, the "Origin of Species" introduced a mode of thinking that in the end was bound to transform the logic of knowledge, and hence the treatment of morals, politics, and religion. . . .

The conception of . . . species, a fixed form and final cause, was the central principle of knowledge as well as of nature. . . . Change as change is mere flux and lapse; it insults intelligence. . . . Since, however, the scene of nature which directly confronts us is in change, nature as directly and practically experienced does not satisfy the conditions of knowledge.[10]

The influence of Darwin satisfies the conditions of knowledge:

The influence of Darwin upon philosophy resides in his having conquered the phenomena of life for the principle of transition, and thereby freed the new logic for application to mind and morals and life."

The design argument thus operated in two directions. Purposefulness accounted for the intelligibility of nature and the possibility of science, while the absolute or cosmic character of this purposefulness gave sanction and worth to the moral and religious endeavors of man.

This philosophy remained . . . the official and the regnant philosophy of Europe for over two thousand years. . . .

The Darwinian principle of natural selection cut straight under this philosophy. . . .

When Henry Sidgwick casually remarked in a letter that as he grew older his interest in what or who made the world was altered into interest in what kind of a world it is anyway, his voicing of a common experience of our own day illustrates also the nature of that intellectual transformation effected by the Darwinian logic. Interest shifts from the wholesale essence back of special changes to the question of how special changes serve and defeat concrete purposes. . . .

. . . shifts from an ultimate goal of good to the direct increments of justice and happiness that intelligent administration of existent conditions may beget and that present carelessness or stupidity will destroy or forego. . . .

. . . many moralists and theologians greeted Herbert Spencer's recognition of an unknowable energy from which welled up the phenomenal physical processes without and the conscious operations within. Merely because Spencer labeled his unknowable energy "God," this faded piece of metaphysical goods was greeted as an important and grateful concession to the reality of the spiritual realm. Were it not for the deep hold of the habit of seeking justification for ideal values in the remote and transcendent, surely this reference of them to an unknowable absolute would be despised in comparison with the demonstrations of experience that knowable energies are daily generating about us precious values.[11]

The discussion of Spencer and Dewey may illustrate how, by personal modifications, certain ideas in the theory of evolution can be congenially incorporated into the minds of diverse thinkers. This perhaps explains why in the twentieth century this theory, though not held to explain everything, has been generally accepted by scientists and the informed laity. Spencer and Dewey also illustrate respectively the connectedness and disconnectedness version of the theory, with Dewey being closer to Darwin's designless notion. An illustration of a more marked divergence (either a support of our hypothesis or a remarkable coincidence) may be seen in the celebrated Scopes trial in Dayton, Tennessee. Though the year was as late as 1925, the attack on the Godless and designless evolutionary theory was led not by some anachronistic Rip Van Winkle but by a man who was thrice a presidential candidate and once a Secretary of State—first son William Jennings Bryan—and the militant defense of Darwin's theory was upheld by later son, Clarence Darrow.

Our discussion of the theory of evolution has two purposes. First, if the essential theory is the correct one—that is, that evolution can and does proceed on a chancy natural selective basis without the design or intervention of a Divine Intelligence or Inscrutable Power—then the discussion may illustrate how the connectedness-prone first sons, out of a need to cheer themselves up, refused to look at the facts squarely and to draw necessary unheroic conclusions. On this view, the disconnectedness-prone later sons are more objective (at least in this particular area) and are closer to the cheerless truth. Second, if the essential theory is one of several possible explanations (Divine Intervention or some teleological factor being another possible explanation)—then the discussion may illustrate how the connectedness-prone and disconnectedness-prone differ in their areas of observation and/or in their myths of origin. On this view, neither is wholly correct. The first sons, training their eyes on man and what is vertically above him, see only a part of the truth; they are motivated to establish the omnipotence of man and of anthropomorphic God; thus they cheer themselves up with their partial truths. Similarly the later sons, focusing on the animal side of man and what is below him, see only one part of the truth. They are motivated to dethrone the arrogant omnipotent heroes and restore the determination of destiny to the individual biological atom. In such a fashion, they cheer themselves up. Concerning the second alternative, the present author is inclined to minimize the possible effect of wishful thinking. Although an effort to cheer oneself up by means of various myths may initially impel an investigator in one direction rather than another, the requirements of one's own rationality and that of the general scientific discipline sift out the purely personal wishful thinking components, leaving public conclusions that have a high degree of probability. Thus, in regard to the theory of evolution, the second alternative is better couched in terms of: "Neither is wholly correct for the reason that each has restricted his observation to a particular parcel of reality."

One biological entity about which differences in observations might be highly important for man is that organism which man lives by and with in varying degrees—namely, woman. Differences here are highly involved with our birth-order indicator of connectedness and disconnectedness. We have already noted that first sons tend to overestimate or to romanticize women, whereas later sons tend to have a more practical attitude. This trend was pointed out in literature and also in depth psychology. It does not seem wise to minimize the power of this overestimation or to write it off as simply irrational. As we saw, Freud made this intense erotic need for the mother a principal base for his theory. Those who are skeptical that a little boy may be driven to the lengths of wishing to kill his father in order to possess his mother may be more impressed with the fact that, before the advent of economic determinism, tournaments were fought during the age of chivalry in order to gain the favor of a lady, and that Helen's face launched a thousand ships. If there is a grain or two of truth in this launching of a thousand ships, then we may have a potential power source similar to that of the atom.

Because scientific investigators are usually too cautious to reveal their attitudes toward women, it is difficult to show, quantitatively, any first-son or later-son polarity. However, we have two men who may illustrate the trends described. They are later son John Burroughs and first son Havelock Ellis. Burroughs is known as a naturalist, or as a nature writer. He is a naturalist of plants and animals, as were the originators of the theory of evolution. The quote below illustrates his direct sensory contact with life, uncomplicated by abstractions or other secondary considerations. His attitude toward women is revealed more by what he does not say. But it seems safe to conclude that he would describe the breast merely as a milk-giving organ. Not so, however, with Ellis who wrote the many-volumed studies on *The Psychology of Sex.* As we shall see in his "What Makes a Woman Beautiful," the milk-giving function of the breast is conspicuous by its absence. Instead, there is the aesthetic overestimation which very well could explain the launching of so many ships.

John Burroughs begins his essay *Science and Literature* by acknowledging his affinity for the lower forms of life: "I seldom . . . go into a natural history museum without feeling as if I were attending a funeral."[12] He finds poetic elements in those men who are close to nature, even in Darwin: "Thus all Darwinian books have to me a literary or poetic substratum. The old fable of metamorphosis and transformation he illustrates afresh in his 'Origin of Species,' in the 'Descent of Man.' "[13] Burroughs does not find Darwin's ideas bleak and chilling. On the contrary, though acknowledging that Darwin "is said to have lost his taste for poetry, and to have cared little for what is called religion"[14] he says:

His sympathies were so large and comprehensive . . . that both his poetic and religious emotions, as well as his scientific proclivities, found full scope, and this demonstration becomes almost a song. . . .

Flowers, trees, rivers, lakes . . . are far more . . . to our natural lives, and serve as vehicles for the expression of our natural emotions. . . . The farmer is dearer to literature than the merchant . . . the drover, the herder . . . are more interesting to her than the man of more elegant and artificial pursuits.

The reason of all this is clear to see. We are embosomed in nature; we are an apple on the bough, a babe at the breast. In nature, in God, we live and move and have our being. Our life depends upon the purity, the closeness, the vitality of the connection. We want and must have nature at first hand; water from the spring, milk from the udder, bread from the wheat, air from the open. Vitiate our supplies, weaken our connection, and we fail. . . . Keep me close to nature, is the constant demand of literature; open the windows and let in the air, the sun, let in health and strength; my blood must have oxygen. . . . I cannot breathe the cosmic ether of the abstruse inquirer, nor thrive on the gases of the scientist in his laboratory; the air of hill and field alone suffices.[15]

Burroughs' paen to Mother Nature rather than to human mother is not the kind of song Ellis sings. Although the scientific attitude prevents him from being as lyrical as Burroughs, in the opening paragraph it is clear that he is talking about the human mother:

The beautiful woman is one endowed, as Chaucer expresses it,
    "With buttokes brode and brestës rounde and hye"; that is to say, she is the woman obviously best fitted to bear children and to suckle them.[16]

The breast for Ellis is obviously not just a detachable, milk-giving organ; it is connected to a beautiful mother. Whereas Burroughs found religion in nature, Ellis can find it in sex:

There is, indeed, a general tendency for the sexual functions to take on a religious character and for the sexual organs to become sacred at a very early period in culture. . . .
    The special characteristics of the feminine hips and buttocks become conspicuous in walking and may be further emphasized by the special method of walking or carriage. The women of some southern countries are famous for the beauty of their way of walk; "the goddess is revealed by her walk," as Virgil said.[17]

We need not quote Ellis extensively to get the strong undertones of his special interest. The following captures in essence how he considers the breast: "the beauty of a woman's breasts, and of any natural or artificial object which suggests the gracious curves of the bosom, is a universal source of pleasure."[18]

We have quoted later son Burroughs and first son Havelock Ellis at some length not only to show a different attitude to women but also to illustrate how one can have a very special viewpoint toward human nature. We can understand why scientific investigators, who are impelled like Ellis to concentrate on the human being, would be less able to originate a theory of evolution—and why investigators, who are impelled like Burroughs to focus on the infrahuman organisms, would be less able to originate a psychological theory like Freud's based on an erotic attraction between the sexes and on the abstruse complexities of the psyche. If nature is considered in its entirety, it should include the human being as well as the infrahuman organisms—the complex, abstraction-oriented as well as the simple, sensation-oriented—the twice-born as well as the once-born. Not that one person can necessarily encompass both aspects in his investigation or in theory building. We are grateful enough that these partial viewpoints have been forthcoming and it is much safer to say that the limitations reside only in the partiality—to bring in improper motivation as a source of error is decidedly risky. For if one says Freud's theory is wrong because Freud was fixated on his mother, one would have to say Darwin's theory was wrong because he had a less than normal connection to his mother.

We turn now to a more precise field of science—mathematics. One would not ordinarily expect subjectivity to play much of a role here. Yet it was Bell's description of the low-keyed debate over the continuous versus the discrete which originally influenced the present author toward the connectedness-disconnectedness hypothesis. The pertinent passage from Bell needs to be requoted:

So we may state here briefly what the main guiding clue through the whole history of mathematics is.

From the earliest times two opposing tendencies, sometimes helping one another, have governed the whole involved development of mathematics. Roughly these are the *discrete* and the *continuous*.

The discrete struggles to describe all nature and all mathematics atomistically, in terms of distinct . . . elements. . . . The continuous seeks to apprehend natural phenomena—the course of a planet in its orbit . . .—in the mystical formula of Heraclitus: "All things flow."

We should expect from the reference to Heraclitus that the adherents of the continuous and of the discrete would differ not only cognitively but also emotionally. For Heraclitus may be called the Father of Stoicism as well as of Metaphysics; and

Democritus the Father of Epicureanism as well as of Physics. A hint as to subjectivity, as to rivalry for role of king to the queen of sciences, is supplied by first son Pascal who said that the mind which can comprehend many premises is the "mathematical" intellect—the mind which penetrates the discrete part being called the precise intellect. If Bell is correct in saying that there are discrete- as well as continuous-minded mathematicians, then Pascal's assertion must be questioned. But let us inquire more into Bell's observations, using Pascal's claim and our birth-order indicators as reference points.

Among Bell's *Men of Mathematics*, birth order is available on twenty-one mathematicians (we are not including the Bernoulli family). Eleven are first sons, nine are later sons. Certainly, there is no trend here toward first-son preponderance, toward the multipremised connectedness we have described in Pascal and other first sons. There may, however, be some support for Pascal's statement if he is referring to the most outstanding mathematicians. Bell lists Archimedes, Newton, and Gauss as the three greatest mathematicians the world has ever known. Of the others, he gives special merit to Henri Poincaré. He calls him "The Last Universalist" and says of him, "he might have made a fourth with the uncomparable three . . ."[20] Though the birth order of Archimedes is not known, Newton, Gauss, and Poincaré are first sons. Thus, if Bell is accepted as a neutral judge (and we of course cannot be sure of this), Pascal's claim may have some foundation.

Bell supplies a cue for determining whether a mathematician is oriented toward the continuous or toward the discrete. The "continuous" mathematicians have made unique contributions to calculus and analysis; the "discrete" mathematicians to algebra, the theory of numbers, and symbolic logic. Both kinds of mathematicians have made contributions to geometry. Using Bell's criteria, there seems to be some support for our birth-order hypothesis. Thus, those mathematicians with marked creativity in the continuous, and minimal creativity in the discrete, show a preponderance of first sons. (First sons: Newton, Cauchy, Weierstrass, Poincaré, Cantor; later son: Dedekind.) Those with minimal work on the continuous, and notable work on the discrete, show a preponderance of later sons. (Later sons: Cayley, Sylvester, Russell, Whitehead; first son: Galois.) Those making special contributions to geometry are about evenly divided as to birth order. (First sons: Pascal, Gauss, Poincaré, Riemann; later sons: Descartes, Cayley, Lobachewsky.) Thus the first-son–later-son ratios in the continuous, continuous-discrete, and discrete categories are, respectively, 5 to 1, 4 to 3, and 1 to 4. (We are not considering those mathematicians who have made contributions in both the continuous and the discrete; Russell and Whitehead are taken from Bell's article in the *Encyclopaedia Britannica*.)

Apart from Bell's criteria, the present author gained some informal general impressions. A distinguishing characteristic appears to be that first sons were much more frequently interested in the largest whole—the entire universe—rather than just in a part like the earth or pure mathematics. Thus, six of the eleven first sons were preoccupied in varying degrees with the movements of the heavenly bodies (Newton, Lagrange, Gauss, Cauchy, Riemann, and Poincaré). Only one of the nine later sons, Hamilton, was similarly preoccupied. (Interest in the celestial bodies is also seen in the first-son mathematical physicists, Galileo, Kepler, and Einstein.) As for the unique mathematical contributions of later sons, we can offer only hesitant impressions. The orientation to the part or atom can be seen in the remarks of J. J. Sylvester: "it [mathematics] is as incapable of being . . . reduced to definitions of permanent validity, as the . . . life, which seems to slumber . . . in every atom of matter, in each leaf. . . ."[21] To the detail in Cayley: "It is difficult to give an idea of the vast extent of modern mathematics. The word 'extent' is not the right one: I meant extent crowded with beautiful detail. . . ."[22] The attention to part and detail may be a characteristic of what Pascal calls the penetrating precise intellect. If "point" can be considered equivalent to part and detail, the contributions of Descartes and Lobachewsky concerning how one travels geometrically from point to point would support our hypothesis.

One other impression about later-son mathematicians is perhaps worth mentioning. They seem better able than first sons to disconnect themselves from customary views. Being less traditional, they can take the opposite point of view or reverse the customary sequence. Lobachewsky's theory contradicted an axiom "whose necessity is based only on a prejudice sanctified by thousands of years."[23] Jacobi and Abel departed from the traditional by simply inverting the terms of a hypothesis. Thus, it seems possible that the later sons' relative freedom from connectedness allows them to take one part at a time, penetrate it, turn it this way and that, stand it on its head, if need be, in order to understand the complete essence of that part. This is in contrast to the forte of the first sons who try to make coordinated connected sense out of many diverse parts by finding a common denominator. Einstein's $E = mc^2$ is perhaps an outstanding example of this.

A final note on Bell's mathematicians refers to their personalities. Just as Pascal may have spoken like a dominant superior first son in saying his type of intellect was the true mathematical one, we see in J. J. Sylvester the later son's tendency to rise up and supplant the older or first born. In an inaugural lecture at the age of seventy-one, he offered a new theory. Bell quotes him: "The theory I am about to expound or whose birth I am about to announce, stands to this ('the great theory of Invariants') in relation not of a younger sister, but of a brother who, though of later birth . . . is entitled to take precedence over his elder sister, and exercise supreme sway over their united realms."[24]

A more general view of the field of science can be obtained from the book *Lives in Science* published by *Scientific American*. The book is additionally useful for our purposes because it makes some very pertinent observations about the history of science and the scientist as a man. The editors write in the Introduction: "The history of science is an unfortunately neglected aspect of history. The situation is explained, no doubt, by the impenetrability of that ivy-clad academic wall which sets the humanities apart from the sciences. . . . The historical approach shows, first of all, that science is only incidentally an accumulated body of knowledge. The making of observations, the collecting of data—the fact finding process that is so plainly identified as 'scientific' appears as an adjunct to a more significant enterprise. The scientist wants to make sense out of what he knows. . . . This is a far cry from the popular image of the scientist as a digger of hard facts from some rich mine of certainty. The work of the scientist is seen to be more like that of the artist."[25] If the scientist is indeed somewhat of an artist, we should expect that subjectivity would enter the picture, at least in different cognitive styles if not also in different emotional attitudes.

The problem of which of these scientists in *Lives in Science* to select to illustrate our hypothesis is not an easy one. Birth orders are available on fifteen of the eighteen men presented. A discussion of each of the fifteen would inordinately prolong this chapter. The solution we shall adopt is to concentrate on the men in two sections: "The Great World System" and "The New World System." At the risk of going considerably outside his sphere, the present author will offer his impressions—a better term would be reactions—as to the relationship of the connected-ness-disconnectedness hypothesis to the works of these men. The impressions are given partly for the sake of completeness and partly to decrease the "impenetrability of that ivy-clad academic wall."

The main point to be developed about the Great and the New World Systems is that the men involved in the rather law-ful, regulated Great World System were predominantly first sons: Galileo, Newton, Laplace (Hooke was a later son), whereas the two men involved in the tradition-breaking New World Systems were both later sons: Hamilton and Fitzgerald. We have frequently noted that later sons appear better able to dis-connect themselves from the past, and thus more apt to take a fresh, "modern" viewpoint. Bacon, Voltaire, and Descartes are frequently described as the heralds of the modern world. We have speculated that this disconnecting ability was present in the later-son mathematicians Lobachewsky, Abel, and Jacobi. To this list we can easily add the later son Copernicus whose departure from tradition cut man and his planet down to life-size.

Beginning with the Great World System, we obtain from I. Bernard Cohen a valuable description of Galileo's aim and methods. The aim appears to be a synthesizing connectedness—the method consisting of perception of resemblances and second-order abstractions rather than direct observations.

By showing the similarity between the earth, moon and planets, which indicated they must obey the same laws, Galileo brought ter-restrial and celestial phenomena within one universal physics. . . .
Here we have a typical example of Galileo's method in physics: Imagine the conditions of a given situation, make a mathematical formulation and derive the reasonable consequences, then make a rough check, if it seems necessary, to be sure that the result is correct. His experimental test involved a brass ball rolling in a groove. . . . In "experiments near a hundred times repeated," Galileo found that

the times agreed with the law, with no differences "worth mentioning." His conclusions that the differences were not "worth mentioning" only shows how firmly he had made up his mind beforehand, for the rough conditions of the experiment would never have yielded an exact law. Actually the discrepancies were so great that a contemporary worker, Père Mersenne, could not reproduce the results described by Galileo, and even doubted that he had ever made the experiment. . . .

Galileo liked to use what we may call "thought experiments," imagining the consequences rather than observing them directly. . . .

Galileo's writings abound with references to the facts of experience, of direct observation. In this sense, Galileo built his science on a somewhat empirical basis. But he was in no sense such an empiricist as the nineteenth-century writers attempted to make him out. He was not a careful experimenter, though he was a keen observer, and it is only the fallacy of writing history backwards that has made us visualize him as a patient investigator who only reluctantly drew conclusions after long tests. The latter picture describes a much later kind of scientific man, of whom the prototype may well have been Robert Boyle.[26]

Departing for a moment from *Lives in Science*, it is of interest that the other kind of scientific man, Robert Boyle, was a later son. Boyle's adherence to direct observations is in line with what we have seen in other later sons, such as Descartes and Bacon, who drew certainty from direct sensory experience and are skeptical about metaphysical abstractions. Galileo apparently relied on his abstract mathematical intuition that a combinatory fit was present, the derived certainty being equal to the later son's direct sensory certainty. This certain mathematical intuition was also present in first son Kepler even though it led to many false trails. Koestler's account of him in *The Watershed* is illuminating in regard to Kepler's speculative, pattern-finding tendencies. Though upholding Copernicus' theory, he could not tolerate the uncaring disconnectedness involved in the idea that the earth was just a planet revolving around the sun. There must be some relationship. He never gave up hope that he would discover through astrology in what way "the sky does something to a man." We learn from Koestler how this desire for connectedness combined with mathematical intuition:

These cosmological speculations were becoming both more intense, and more mathematical in character. . . . On July 9, 1595 . . . an idea suddenly struck him with such force that he felt he was holding the key to creation in his hand. . . . The idea itself was completely false; yet it led eventually to Kepler's Laws . . . and the birth of modern cosmology.[27]

As we return to *Lives in Science* we find similar tendencies toward mystic patterning in first son Newton. Apparently Newton did not share Burrough's need for the oxygen of the fresh air and did not walk and travel as Descartes did when he wanted to collect his thoughts. A contemporary wrote that he never knew Newton "to take any recreation or pastime either in riding out to take the air, walking, bowling, or any other exercise whatever, thinking all hours lost that were not spent in his studies."[28] And that: "When reminded that he had not eaten, he would go to the table and 'eat a bite or two standing.'[29] What was going on under the absent-mindedness was not always pure rational thinking. Cohen writes that though "Newton is often described as the inaugurator of the 'Age of Reason' . . . the late Lord Keynes called attention to another side of Newton: his quest for an answer to the riddle of existence. . . ."[30]

First son Newton had an interesting scientific contact with the next figure in the "Great World System"—later son Robert Hooke. Cohen's account is as follows: "Halley and Hooke had concluded from Johannes Kepler's accounting of planetary motions that the force of the attraction must vary inversely with the square of the distance between the planet and the sun. But they had been unable to prove their idea. 'What,' Halley asked Newton, 'would be the curve described by the planets on the supposition that gravity diminished as the square of the distance?' Newton answered without hesitation: 'An ellipse.' How did he know that? 'Why,' replied Newton, 'I have calculated it.' These four words informed Halley that Newton had worked out one of the most fundamental laws of the universe—the law of gravity."[31] Apparently Hooke did not have the mathematical "continuous" intellect, the "calculus" type that would have answered his own question. E. N. da C. Andrade writes: "If Hooke himself had been able to deduce mathematically the consequences of his principles where planetary orbits were concerned, he would have solved the great problem of the solar system which it was Newton's glory to settle. How near he came, with his instinctive sense of scientific truth!"[32]

The question arises whether we are dealing here with a situ-

ation similar to that of the theory of evolution. There we speculated that a disconnectedness-prone mind would have the best
chance to originate that particular theory. Here we wonder
whether only a connectedness-prone mind would originally formulate the law of gravity. From what Andrade tells us about
Hooke, he would seem to have the precise mind, penetrating the
part rather than the broad, synthesizing mind. He was a magnificent experimentalist in the fashion of Boyle whose assistant he
was. Like the later-son naturalists, he was primarily interested in
less-than-life-size phenomena, whereas first son Newton devised
a telescope better to see the heavens. "Hooke was then a great
pioneer in microscopy, distinguished alike as a designer of the
instrument and its adjuncts, as an observer and as an interpreter
of what he saw."[33] Later: "his figures of the louse, the silverfish
insect and the flea . . . are extraordinary in their accurate detail."[34]

The last of the men of the Great World System is first son
Laplace. The similarity to Newton is the first point brought out
by James Newman: "Historians of Science have rightly called
the Marquis de Laplace the Newton of France. He earned the
title for his immense work on celestial mechanics, which capped
the labors of three generations of mathematical astronomers and
produced a universal principle that has been applied to almost
every field of physics." Like Kepler, he appeared to want to
believe that there was an order in the heavens which was bene-
ficially interested in Man, ". . . that nature arranged the operation of the celestial machine 'for an eternal duration, upon the
same principles as those which prevail so admirably upon the
Earth, for the preservation of individuals and for the perpetuity
of the species.' "[36]

Laplace preferred not to give the name of God to this
benevolent attentiveness from the heavens. Newman tells of a
purported incident involving first son Laplace, later son Napoleon, and first son Lagrange (Newman believes he was a greater
mathematician than Laplace): "Napoleon on receiving a copy of
the *Mécanique céleste* protested to Laplace that in all its vast
expanse God was not mentioned. The author replied that he had
no need of this hypothesis. Napoleon, much amused, repeated
the reply to Lagrange, who is said to have exclaimed: 'Ah, but
it is a beautiful hypothesis; it explains many things.' "[37]

We should not expect man-of-action Napoleon to need such

an interconnecting hypothesis; Lagrange's use of it would be in character. Laplace's notion of an ideal deterministic intelligence equals that attributed to omniscient God. Newman quotes Laplace: "Given for one instant an intelligence which could comprehend all the forces by which nature is animated and the respective situation of the beings who compose it—an intelligence sufficiently vast to submit these data to analysis—it would embrace in the same formula the movements of the greatest bodies of the universe and those of the lightest atom; for it, nothing would be uncertain and the future, as the past, would be present to its eye."[38]

This passage illustrates par excellence the multipremised comprehender of everything. It is similar to Pascal's saying that he cannot understand the whole without knowing the parts and vice versa, and to Einstein's aversion to a dice-playing God. Yet the theme contained in it (and in Laplace's actual life) lacks the reverence and humility expressed by Pascal and Einstein. For the passage ends with more than a hint of Man finally possessing this heroic outsized intelligence—a hint that would have prevented Laplace for ever authoring the *Descent of Man*. "All these efforts in the search for truth tend to lead it (the human mind) back continually to the vast intelligence which we have just mentioned, but from which it will always remain infinitely removed. This tendency, peculiar to the human race, is that which renders it superior to animals; and their progress in this respect distinguishes nations and ages and constitutes their true glory."[39]

As for the two later sons concerned with the New World System, a general impression can best be gained from the Introduction to *Lives in Science*: "In the triumph of the Enlightenment, there was scarcely any doubt that calculus would encompass all that could be known. Yet before the last volume of *Mécanique céleste* came from the printer, Laplace had found a discerning and critical young reader. William Rowan Hamilton, at the age of sixteen, was enthralled by the vision, but he was challenged also by the difficulties which Laplace was content to gloss over and conceal. Hamilton did not succeed in constructing a new celestial mechanics. He did, however, discover a strange new algebra, in which ab may not at all times be equal to ba. Noncommutative algebra is used today to describe events in physics not dreamed of in the calculus."

"George Francis FitzGerald is another radically original figure whose true stature could not be measured until the twentieth century. He suggested the insouciant notion that the yardstick might be contracted and the clock slowed down in order to make the equations of motion come out right. Today everybody appreciates the common sense of this suggestion in a world where we know that $E = mc^2$ and where it has been shown that short-lived particles actually live longer when they are accelerated close to the speed of light."[40]

To go beyond this general statement into the technicality of Whittaker's articles is decidedly outside the present author's competence. A few general reactions to Hamilton may, however, not be out of place. First, apparently there can be cognitive preferences and even fashions in mathematics. Perhaps the preference for the continuous universalist type of mathematician obscures the valuable insights provided by the discrete type. Thus, about Hamilton, Whittaker writes: "After Isaac Newton, the greatest mathematician of the English-speaking peoples is William Rowan Hamilton. . . . His fame has had some curious vicissitudes. During his lifetime he was celebrated but not understood; after his death his reputation declined and he came to be counted in the second rank; in the twentieth century he has become the subject of an extraordinary revival of interest and appreciation." Later he says: "he started a glorious school of mathematics, though it was not to come into full flower for another half-century. I remember discussing in 1900 with Alfred North Whitehead whether quaternions and other noncommutative algebras had much of a future as regards application to physics. Whitehead remarked that while all the physics then known could be treated by ordinary algebra, it was possible that new fields in physics might some day be discovered for which noncommutative algebra would be the only natural representation. In that very year this anticipation was started on the road to fulfillment. Thus the Hamiltonian ideas on dynamics began to come into prominence. But very slowly. When my book *Analytical Dynamics* was published in 1904, I was criticized severely for devoting a large part of it to such topics as the co-ordinates—momentum duality, action and other Hamiltonian ideas. The critics called them mere mathematical playthings."[42]

A passing comparison of later son Hamilton and first son

Newton may be fruitful. Though both men entered college at the same age, eighteen, according to Cohen, "In his early years at the University he [Newton] was not outstanding in any way."[43] Whereas according to Whittaker, the progress of " 'Hamilton the prodigy' . . . was brilliant, not only on the examinations but also in original research."[44] The slower development of the more inward and absent-minded Newton is reminiscent of Einstein's celebrated slowness in the early school years. The lonely meditation about the complexities of the universe and of existence, the attempt to find a meaningful connection between all the plural considerations, frequently do not manifest themselves in early intellectual flowering.

Hamilton appears to have been more practical, more close to immediately useful ideas. Whittaker writes: "The boy loved the classics and the poets, but at the age of fifteen his interests, and the course of his life were completely changed when he met Zerah Colburn, an American youngster who gave an exhibition in Dublin of his powers as a lightning calculator: 'For a long time afterwards,' wrote Hamilton later, 'I liked to perform long operations in arithmetic in my mind, extracting the square and cube root and everything that related to the properties of numbers.' "[45] It would seem that Hamilton enjoyed the exercising and the functioning of his intellectual processes. The direct satisfaction of a good intellectual workout was sufficient; abstract rumination about final ends was not necessary. This may explain Hamilton's focus on method, function, action—a focus we have seen in other later sons. His law was not that of binding interconnections; rather it was "the law of varying action," which he called the "characteristic function."[46] His ambition was not noticeably less than Newton's but was of single-minded disconnectedness-action permitting type rather than the plural-minded connectedness-action inhibiting type.

Newton and Hamilton can also be compared as to their attitudes toward live, moving Nature. We have already seen that Newton was so absent-mindedly inward that he would sometimes forget to eat and also that he eschewed the fresh air. Cohen further relates that Newton's mother ". . . conceived the idea of making him a farmer, but the experiment proved an unqualified failure. Newton found farming totally distasteful. Instead of attending properly to his chores he would read, make wooden models with his knife, or dream. Fortunately for science, his mother gave up the attempt. . . ."[47] Hamilton presents a different attitude to Nature. Though not as lyrical as Burroughs about the bucolic or as curious as Hooke about microscopic life, he does show the familiar attitude about milk from the breast. Whittaker writes: "The countryside was full of stories about him. One of them concerns his administration of the seventeen acres of farmland around Dunsink Observatory, of which the Royal Astronomer has control. Hamilton, who was town bred, knew nothing of farming but in order to supply his household with milk he bought a cow. After some time, in the ordinary course of nature, the yield of milk began to fall off."[48] The story ends with Hamilton, having been informed by a farmer that the cow was lonely, paying the farmer to have the latter's cattle graze in the pastures and thus keeping his cow company.

We have to conclude our abbreviated discussion of *Lives in Science*. The purpose has been merely to illustrate how the connectedness-disconnectedness hypothesis may be applied. Toward this end, we have limited ourselves to scientists involved in the Great World System and those in the New World System. There seems to be suggestive evidence that first sons are better able to view the reality in its connectedness aspects, the later sons in its disconnectedness aspects—the better abilities being respectively related to a once-removed abstract cognition and to a first-hand, sensory cognition. The significant difference between the Great World System and the New World System resides in the maximum emphasis placed on causal connectedness in the former system, and the large emphasis placed on relatively free movements of ultimate particles in the latter system.

Arthur S. Eddington notes this contrast in his essay *The Decline of Determinism*. Although first son Eddington does not find indeterminism as displeasing as did first son Einstein, he is not eager to throw away traditional determinism. He writes: "Ten years ago practically every physicist of repute was, or believed himself to be, a determinist, at any rate so far as inorganic phenomena are concerned. He believed he had come across a scheme of strict causality regulating the sequence of phenomena. . . . Then rather suddenly determinism faded out of theoretical physics. Its exit has been received in various ways. Some writers are incredulous and cannot be persuaded that deter-

minism has really been eliminated from the present foundation
of physical theory. Some think that it is no more than a domestic
change in physics, having no reactions in general philosophic
thought. Some decide cynically to wait and see if determinism
fades in again. The rejection of determinism is in no sense an
abdication of scientific method. It is rather the fruition of a scientific method which had grown up under the shelter of the old
causal method and has now been found to have a wider range.
It has greatly increased the power and precision of the mathematical theory of observed phenomena. On the other hand I cannot agree with those who belittle the philosophical significance
of the change. The withdrawal of physical science from an attitude it had adopted consistently for more than 200 years is not
to be treated lightly; and it provokes a reconsideration of our
views as to one of the most perplexing problems of our existence."[49]

Eddington's balanced attitude is similar to that of first son
Niels Bohr, whom Eddington quotes in a preface to the essay:
"While the feeling of free will dominates the life of the spirit,
the regularity of sensory phenomena lays down the demand for
causality. But in both domains simultaneously the point in question is an idealization whose natural limitations can be more closely
investigated and which determine one another in the sense that
the feeling of volition and the demand for causality are equally
indispensable in the relation between subject and object which is
the kernel of the problem of perception."[50]

In Eddington and still more in Bohr we may see a first-son
connectedness tendency to accept the two aspects as given and—
instead of letting them remain disconnectedly separate but equal
as in Descartes' mind-body dualism—to try to combine them in
some ideal abstract synthesis. It may be that some first-son
mathematical physicist will eventually supply the kind of combined solution that first son Kant had to make in the case of
later son Hume's skepticism about causality. The point is that
the rival points of view of what reality really is have been in
evidence from earliest history. Not only in mathematics, as Bell
showed, but also in philosophy.

It is perhaps fitting that we should conclude this chapter with
more than a passing reference to philosophy, that field of inquiry
once so intimately related to the sciences and now in the position

of a parent who has seen her specialized offspring grow up and leave the nest. And since the scientist uses his mind as a perceptive and cognitive instrument, it is appropriate that we pay attention now to the contrasting notions of the mind as proposed by later son Hume and first son Kant. Though we have mentioned these two men from time in previous chapters, a more direct comparison of some of their ideas may be useful.

Hume, the great empiricist, believed that man learns only through experience, that it is the vivid perceiving of separate sensations which impress us as believable and give us the true knowledge of reality. He was like later son Francis Bacon who de-emphasized the contribution of the reflective component of the mind, which combines, synthesizes, and integrates these separate sensations into ideas. According to Hume, such connective and unifying concepts as "cause and effect" or the "self" are not necessarily true and are due rather to our tendency to "feign."

It was Kant who rescued metaphysics as a possible science and buttressed man's confidence in beliefs intuitively arrived at independent of or prior to experience. While knowledge gained from experience might be subject to error, pure or a priori knowledge had the connective features of necessity and universality, and this pure knowledge was possible through a combining or synthesizing power of the mind.

The flavor of Hume's and Kant's different orientations can be seen from the following. Hume on the abstract, metaphysical approach: "but [these philosophers] proceeding from particular instances to general principles, they still push on their inquiries to principles more general, and rest not satisfied till they arrive at those original principles by which, in every science, all human curiosity must be bounded."[51] Later on he says: "But this obscurity in the profound and abstract philosophy, is . . . the inevitable source of uncertainty and error."[52] Kant says: "against this [Hume's] assertion, destructive to all pure philosophy, we would have been guarded, had he had our problem before his eyes in its universality."[53] Hume on the earthly immediate versus the celestial remote: "And shall we esteem it worthy the labor of a philosopher to give us a true system of the planets, and adjust the position and order of those remote bodies; while we affect to overlook those, who, with so much success, delineate the parts of the mind, in which we are so intimately concerned?"[54] Kant on the same:

"the charm of widening the range of our knowledge is so great, that unless we are brought to a standstill by some evident contradiction, we hurry on undoubtingly in our course."[55] Elsewhere he says: "and so there has ever really existed in every man some system of metaphysics. It will always exist, so soon as reason awakes to the exercise of its power of speculation."[56] Hume on the parts and the whole: "Complex ideas may, perhaps, be . . . nothing but an enumeration of those parts or simple ideas, that compose them."[57] Kant on the whole and the parts: "The conception of twelve is by no means obtained by merely cogitating the union of seven and five. . . ."[58]

We may see from Hume and Kant that in philosophy as well as in science thinking men have been divided on the question of how much connectedness there is in reality. It is a division which cuts across the field of activity. We are forced to dissent from the implications of what Pringle-Patterson asserts in the *Encyclopaedia Britannica* on the separate pursuits of philosophers and scientists: "Philosophy claims to be the science of the whole; but if we get the knowledge of the part from the different sciences, what is there left for philosophy to tell us? To this it is sufficient to answer generally that the synthesis of the parts is something more than that detailed knowledge of the parts in separation which is gained by the man of science."[59] And: "By the gradual sifting out of the special sciences, philosophy thus came to embrace primarily the inquiries grouped as 'metaphysics.' . . ."[60] The fact of the matter rather seems to be that the orientation toward connectedness and disconnectedness is no respecter of fields. There are physical scientists and metaphysical scientists—physical philosophers and metaphysical philosophers.

In closing, it is necessary to re-emphasize that connectedness-proneness and disconnectedness-proneness are ways of designating preponderances along a continuum. The situation is not one of either/or but rather one of more or less, since all men have both psychic tendencies. The "more or less" may be relatively immune to further change or may be capable of change. If in science or philosophy we have first son Einstein chronically near the connectedness pole, and later son Russell similarly so near the disconnectedness pole, we do find first sons Eddington and Bohr preparing partially to embrace indeterminism, and the notable example of later son Alfred North Whitehead leaving the company of Russell and seriously considering, in what he called his *"Adventures of Ideas,"*[61] the deterministic notion of God and the Heraclitean and Hegelian notion that "a clash of doctrines is not a disaster—it is an opportunity."[62]

This is the final chapter dealing with evidence in the public domain. In all these chapters, the present author has exceeded his particular expertise in venturing to discuss and speculate about nonclinical matters. Perhaps, in this particular chapter, the exceeding has been most pronounced. The rationale for such a procedure has been, as stated previously, to subject the hypothesis to as much testing as possible. By bringing the hypothesis in contact with nonclinical material, there may be less chance that what J. Robert Oppenheimer calls a "self-sealing system"[63] will develop. And through this public domain evidence, there may be accomplished what Oppenheimer says the whole point of science is: "to invite the detection of error and to welcome it."[64]

CHAPTER XI

Experimental Results

and Theoretical Concepts

Fresh from a discussion of scientists and their tendencies, the reader may well feel that it is time for the connectedness-disconnectedness hypothesis to be scrutinized from the more customary scientific point of view. Hopefully, he has patiently given his attention to the presentation of impressionistic evidence, and has been persuaded that there is sufficient evidence of this kind to warrant the formulation of a hypothesis. If he has been so persuaded, the author's principal objective will have been accomplished.

The tough-minded reader, however, may require more persuasion. He may have found the evidence up to this point to be "soft" (qualitative and impressionistic) rather than "hard" (quantitative, rigorously sampled as well as statistically supported). In short, he would like to see evidence appropriate to the testing of the hypothesis.

The author shares this wish; but he also believes that, for some considerable time to come, the behavioral sciences cannot afford to give up the qualitative case-study approach in their search for truth, and that an exclusive reliance on quantitative methods of the more precise sciences would sacrifice knowledge for certainty. However, because he does share some of the tough-minded reader's attitude, the author would now like to present some quantitative, experimental results which may help to support the contents of previous chapters.

Obtaining "hard" evidence in the area of birth order is no problem. The problem arises rather in deciding what quantitative results to rely on. For the scientific literature frequently contains conflicting reports about the association of a particular trait with birth order, this despite the scientific and statistical respectability of each of the conflicting studies. Thus, subjective factors of selectivity and interpretation are called for in evaluating these "hard" experimental results. The author's selectivity will be seen in the fact that he has put major reliance on the findings of Helen L. Koch, who is generally regarded as having done one of the most (if not *the* most) carefully controlled experimental studies of birth order. Her work, carried out on five- and six-year-old children of both sexes (coming from two-children families), takes into consideration factors which the author was forced to neglect in the investigation of eminent men. Thus, Koch considers not only whether the child is first-born or second-born, but also the sex of the other sibling and the time-spacing between the births. Her findings will be described presently.

There are two major facets noted in the eminent men which are seemingly supported by experimental findings. The first does not lend itself easily to precise definition and will require preliminary discussion. It has to do most directly with the function of language and was alluded to in the chapter on "Literary Tendencies." There, reference was made to Susanne K. Langer's notion about speech or language development, i.e., that there is an earlier stage in which speech is experimental or emotionally expressive, and a later stage in which speech is used to communicate thought and meaning. A similar view is seen in neurophysiologist R. W. Gerard's statement in "The Biological Basis of Imagination" that "Language is man's main symbolic system. . . ."[1] Later, in commenting about the theory of A. Pick, who worked in the field of aphasia, Gerard writes: "But, in man, language (with mathematics as one form of language) remains an especial index to the workings of mind; and Pick, combining philological study with his clinical observations, has formulated a series of stages in language use, which may be interrupted anywhere by the aphasic slash. On the sensory or receptive side there is, first, the perception of speech as distinct from mere sound. There follows the recognition of words as separate entities and then of the 'musical' parts of speech, cadence, and intonation. Only then comes an awareness of meaning, followed by full understanding of sentences with their proper word relations and emphases."[2]

The pertinence of the above to the connectedness-disconnectedness hypothesis is that the more the child is exposed to and confronted by adult verbal discourse (as more frequently happens with first-born children) the more likely he will be especially concerned with the meaning of his speech and language. The adult environment requires of him that he leave the speech developmental stage in which he croons to himself or later engages in separate monologues with a playmate (as Piaget has described). The requirement now is that he be able to engage in a dialogue which is intelligible and meaningful to his adult conversational partner. From this requirement issues a certain kind of abstract comprehensiveness, a predilection to find meaningful connections between events or phenomena. The later-born, not under such adult pressure and stimulation, can be more comfortable with a disconnectedness shown in self-expressive musical monologues, or in considering the directly sensed event quite apart from the abstract, meaningful connections.

It should be emphasized that this author does not go along with the implication that, in itself, the capacity for abstract, meaningful dialogue is a direct reflection of the maximal stage of cognitive or symbolic development. His personal opinion is that maximal development is reflected by an optimal interplay of all levels of language or symbolic development. An unhealthy preponderance of the abstract, meaningful tendency can lead to intellectual sterility; such a preponderance in the other direction can issue forth in chaotic babble. What the author is attempting to describe are divergent developmental paths rather than superior and inferior paths.

Perhaps an excerpt from literary criticism will help to illustrate what has been set forth. A. E. Housman, in *The Name and Nature of Poetry*, has compared the poetic tendencies of first son Shakespeare and later son Blake. In this comparison we shall find the meaningfulness of the connectedness-prone first son and the shear musicality of the disconnectedness-prone later son: "For me the most poetical of all poets is Blake. I find his lyrical note as beautiful as Shakespeare's and more beautiful than anyone else's; and I call him more poetical than Shakespeare, even though Shakespeare has so much more poetry, because poetry in him preponderates more than in Shakespeare over everything else, and instead of being confounded in a great river can be drunk pure from a slender channel of its own. Shakespeare is rich in thought, and his meaning has power of itself to move us, even if the poetry were not there: Blake's meaning is often unimportant or virtually non-existent, so that we can listen with all our hearing to his celestial tune."[3] (It should be mentioned that Blake's meaning possibly escapes Housman who, as a first son, would tend to think of meaning in a more abstract sense.)

Housman's reference to the confounding "great river" and to the pure "slender channel" can be applied to the polarity mentioned in an earlier chapter, "The Plural Minded and the Single Minded." In examining the cognitive styles of great thinkers, a differentiation was made between Pascal's multipremised type who interconnects many ideas, and the precise type who trains his discriminating intellectual activity on one thing at a time—the former resembling a confounding river, the latter a pure channel. If we follow Gerard's idea that mathematics is one form of language, we may see in first son Einstein and later son Descartes the mathematical repercussions of language development—Einstein's approach being that of seeking by interconnection to comprehend various ideas and concepts issuing originally from sensory impressions; Descartes' approach being that of eliminating the more vague abstraction until he found a directly and vividly sensed certainty upon which he could logically build a system.

The reader, in possession of the preceding background information, may now be in a better position to see the pertinence of the experimental results to be described. These results are principally concerned with a certain abstract language proclivity in first-borns and, in order to indicate steps in the author's thinking, the description will be presented more or less chronologically.

It will be recalled that quite early in the investigation the author was interested in the phenomenon of intellectual creativity. From his study of learning problems in school boys it appeared that first-born sons were less susceptible to learning problems than were later-born sons. The question had arisen: were first sons indeed more creative than later sons? The coming upon Pascal's typology and the subsequent investigation gave, of course, a negative answer to this question—the differences appeared to be those of kind rather than of degree.

Soon after the initial development of the hypothesis, a noteworthy reinforcement of the idea of differences in kind came from Morris Stein's investigation of creativity in industrial chemists. Stein took a large group of intellectually superior industrial chemists and endeavored to separate them into two groups on the basis of their creative ability. Utilizing the evaluations of the particular chemist's superiors, peers, and subordinates, he was able to set up two groups: the creative, and the not-as-creative. The two groups were then investigated for statistically significant differences in family background, personality characteristics, and intellectual functioning. Though Stein's positive findings are of considerable interest, they are not as germane to our discussion as are his negative findings and some unpublished results.

The pertinent negative finding was that there was *no* relationship between birth order and the quantity of creativity as so defined. In response to the present author's query as to whether birth order manifested itself in any possible way, Stein kindly went over his data and reported that there were significant differences—not between the creative and the not-as-creative groups, but between the first-borns and later-borns as to their score on the Miller Analogy Test. On this test, used to ascertain abstract verbal ability and the facility in making connections between seemingly dissimilar notions, first-borns scored significantly higher than later-borns. This finding led the present author more strongly to the basic hypothesis: the abstract, analogy-making propensity was seen as a characteristic of connectedness, of Pascal's multipremised type that perceives interrelating resemblances.

It was not until three years later—after considerable involvement with the thought and actions of eminent men—that the author once again reviewed scientific literature on birth order. Whereas previously this literature (perhaps due to the many conflicting reports) had made little impression on him, at this subsequent point some of it appeared to have considerable pertinence to the cognitive aspects of the connectedness-disconnectedness hypothesis; and of greatest pertinence were the studies done by Helen L. Koch.

Koch's research design consists essentially of the study of 384 five- and six-year-olds of both sexes, from intact families in which there were two children. The total group was broken down into 24 subgroups on the basis of birth order, sex of sibling, and spacing between siblings; for example: boys with younger brothers, less than two years' difference in age; boys with an older sister, two to four years' difference in age; boys with an older brother, four to six years' difference in age, etc. Information about the child's personality was gathered from interviews with child and parent, from tests of the child, and from teachers' ratings of the child's behavior in the classroom situation. Of interest are the results of the administration of the SRA Primary Mental Abilities Test, Primary Form. With regard to the total test, second-borns scored somewhat higher than first-borns. But with regard to two of the subtests—the Verbal Test and the Perceptual Speed Test—birth order trends are seen which are in the direction of our basic hypothesis. Thus, those first-born sons who are two to four years older than their siblings score significantly higher on the Verbal Test which, according to Koch, "is heavily saturated with Thurstone's Factor V (Verbal Meaning). . . ."[4] Koch comments on this finding in her paper on "The Relation of 'Primary Mental Abilities' in Five- and Six-Year-Olds to Sex of Child and Characteristics of His Sibling": "It is possible that if a child has his parents' undivided attention for more than two years before the sib arrives and at a time when he is making most rapid progress in acquiring speech that he will be relatively more influenced by their verbal and intellectual stimulation than one would be whose sib follows close on his heels. There is evidence that parents talk to and instruct their second-borns less than they do to their first-borns. Hence, one might expect first-borns, especially at the wider spacings, to score higher on the Verbal Test than second-borns."[5]

On the Perceptual Speed Test, however, Koch finds that first-borns are "consistently less discriminating than second-borns."[6] Her comment on this is: "The second-born, we suspect, though he receives less verbal stimulation and instruction from his parents than the first-born, is challenged in a concrete way more by the sib than is the first-born. The duration of the interaction with the sib is also longer for the second-born. . . . The challenge given the second-born by his older sib makes the former more observing and alert to details."[7]

Koch's findings on these two subtests represent, in the present author's opinion, some experimental support for the ideas expressed earlier. There appears to be in the young children a rough cognitive style differentiation highly similar to that described in eminent men—the first-born showing a proclivity in abstract, meaningful, verbal language; the later-born a proclivity in precise, discriminating perception of the detail. Other findings by Koch—without the qualifying remarks about age spacings—additionally support the verbal, abstract inclination of first borns. Thus Koch in a paper titled "Sibling Influence on Children's Speech" reports a broad finding: "First-born children articulate consistently better than do second-born children."[8] And in "Children's Work Attitudes and Sibling Characteristics" she states: "First-borns scored higher than second-borns in curiosity."[9]

As the foregoing indicates, there seems to be a high probability that, because of early verbal discourse with the adult parents, the first-born or first of a sex tends to have a particular affinity for language and the abstract cognition entailed in it. This affinity is not necessarily shown in the ability to learn many languages—an ability which may have an instrumental, practical motivation—but rather in an abstract absorption in the structure and process of language. For them it may well be that, in the beginning, there was the Word and that after this beginning an autonomous inner world of words and their abstract, cognitive interconnection evolved. Using the terms of the Semanticists, first sons tend to be absorbed in a "verbal world," later sons in an "extensional world."

These rather schematic insights, derived from experimental studies on children, may have greater significance if we again refer to eminent men. There are many examples of a first son's abstract interest in language. Due to space limitations, the author can only note in passing such an interest on the part of Samuel Johnson and H. L. Mencken as exemplified, respectively, in *A Dictionary of the English Language* and *The American Language*. And the author must resist the temptation to dwell on the philological work of Karl Wilhelm Humboldt—tempting because the abstract verbal orientation of this first son can be contrasted with the precise perceptiveness of his famous younger brother, naturalist and traveler Alexander Humboldt.

But it may not be superfluous to pause for a moment and consider the example provided by Peter Mark Roget. This first son, after a highly productive career as a physician and scientist, became absorbed during his fifties in compiling his *Thesaurus of*

English Words and Phrases. His abstractness is further evidenced
by the fact that he begins the *Thesaurus* with a section devoted
to abstract concepts. His remarks in the "Introduction" are most
illustrative of a first son's high estimation of language. He says:
"The use of language is not confined to its being the medium
through which we communicate our ideas to one another; it
fulfills a no less important function as an *instrument of thought.*
. . . Metaphysicians are agreed that scarcely any of our intellectual operations could be carried on, to any considerable extent,
without the agency of words. . . . Words are the instruments by
which we form all our abstractions, by which we fashion and
embody our ideas, and by which we are enabled to glide along a
series of premises and conclusions with a rapidity so great as to
leave in the memory no trace of the successive steps of the
process. . . ."[10]

One would never guess from Roget's account that words
once had a fresher and more sensory symbolism; that in early
childhood the word "dog" denoted and symbolized not a member
of the canine family but a four-legged, hairy creature that sniffed
and barked. This earlier symbolism appears to be more frequently
accessible to the disconnectedness-prone later sons. If later son
Blake exemplifies the musicality of early speech, later son Sherwood Anderson—whose literary affiliations are, according to
Horace Gregory, with later sons Emerson, Whitman, Thoreau,
Melville, and Mark Twain—uniquely illustrates the direct sensory
imagery. We shall see in Anderson's impressions of Gertrude
Stein that, for him, words are more the edible staff of life and
much less instruments of abstract thought. In a sketch originally
published in *The New Republic* and later incorporated in *The
Portable Sherwood Anderson,* he says: "Miss Stein is a worker
in words with the same loving touch in her strong fingers that
was characteristic of the women of the kitchens of the brick
houses in the town of my boyhood. . . . She is laying word
against word, relating sound to sound, feeling for the taste, the
smell, the rhythm of the individual world. . . . She is making
new, strange and to my ears sweet combinations of words."[11]

It seems that in symbolic, cognitive activity the connectedness-prone first son tends to be *more distant,* the disconnectedness-
prone later son *less distant* from immediate sensory perception.
As a correlate, or consequence, the first son is not apt to react

to the uniqueness of individual phenomena. He will be more alert to the connecting resemblances between one phenomenon and another; and will seek to abstract from the variety a common denominator or an organizing principle. He tends to feel as first son Henri Poincaré did about mathematics: "A mathematical demonstration is not a simple juxtaposition of syllogisms, it is syllogisms *placed in a certain order*, and the order in which these elements are placed is much more important than the elements themselves. If I have the feeling, the intuition, so to speak, of this order, so as to perceive at a glance the reasoning as a whole, I need no longer fear lest I forget one of the elements, for each of them will take its allotted place in the array, and that without any effort of memory on my part."[12]

On the other hand, the disconnectedness-prone later son, being closer to the senses, does react to and appreciate the individual uniqueness of phenomena. He may protest as Bacon did against the uniqueness being lost sight of under the abstracting rubric, or as later son Kierkegaard did against being a mere paragraph in first son Hegel's abstract system. Whereas the first son may see fifty roses and be satisfied at designating them as a collection of roses, or as representing a stage in botanical development, the later son might insist that each rose be considered separately. Later son Emerson expresses it that there is simply *the* rose.

Of course, even more to the point is the attitude of the cook in Anderson's kitchen, Gertrude Stein, a later daughter and youngest of five children. Her statement "A rose is a rose is a rose is a rose"[13] constitutes the essence of particularizing, individualizing, sensory oriented disconnectedness. John Malcolm Brinnin writes in his perceptive biography *The Third Rose*: "In a writing career that lasted more than forty years, Gertrude Stein separated literature from history, from sociology, from psychology and anthropology, even from knowledge itself. As a poet, she destroyed the connecting tissues that hold observed realities together and, as a writer of novels, she attempted to remove from the body of literature the very sinew and bone of narrative."[14]

The evidence suggests that there is an abstract-sensory continuum, and that on it the connectedness-prone first sons are closer to the abstract pole, the disconnectedness-prone later sons closer to the sensory pole. The abstract-sensory continuum, to be sure, has long been of interest to psychologists and neurophysiologists investigating the processes of cognition and perception. Among the principal questions of these investigators has been the one asking how much a perception is influenced by what goes on centrally, within the higher centers of the brain; and how much goes on in the sense organs, sensory nerves, and the lower centers of the brain. A monograph by Abraham S. Levine dealing with *"Perseveration"* or *"The Central Factor"* is relevant. Levine proposes that: "Since the term 'perseveration' has acquired many confusing connotations, it is considered advisable to substitute for it the term 'central factor.' "[15] He defines this factor as "the capacity for establishing and maintaining set."[16] And he says: "This list is extended by Hebb . . . to include Pavlov's and Hull's stimulus trace, Beach's central excitatory mechanism, Morgan's central motive state, and Kleitman's 'interest.' All of these terms according to Hebb have a common element: That element is recognition that responses are determined by something else besides the immediately preceding sensory stimulation. . . . All such terms then, are a reference to the *'central process'* [italics in original] which seems relatively independent of afferent stimuli. . . ."[17]

In summarizing his thinking, Levine refers to Stern's analytic-synthetic typology, a typology almost identical with Pascal's precise and multipremised intellect, and which was illustrated in later son Descartes and first son Einstein. Levine writes: "As translated by Spearman, the core description [of Stern's typology] runs as follows: 'The former (analytic type) inclines to regard details in isolation from each other, to draw boundaries, and to detect faults. The latter (synthetic type) inclines rather to bring what is separate into a single view, to connect the remote, and to arrange the chaotic, whilst often deficient as regards the truth in detail and sharpness in single judgments. . . .' It may be hypothesized that the common thread running through this diversity is a ratio of central factor to certain peripheral factors."[18]

The question arises as to how the preponderance of the central factor originates. The author believes that the Freudian theory, as postulated by David Rapaport, and the social-psychological theory of Neal E. Miller, may be quite helpful in attempting to answer this question. Rapaport stresses that the origin of thought processes is intimately related to a delay in gratification of basic drives. Thus, when the hungry nursing infant is deprived of the breast he will hallucinate that the breast is present. This hallucination constitutes the primordial thought or idea. For some time in the infant's development the thought processes are closely related to the drives, to memories of how the drives were satisfied, and to wishes about how the drives may be satisfied. This urgent, wishful, cognitive activity constitutes the primary process and is seen particularly in dreams. Gradually—and for reasons not clearly understood—the thought processes become less concerned with immediate gratification of the drive, less based on the sheer pleasure principle. The energy of the thought processes undergoes modulation and taming, by virtue of such mechanisms as repression and countercathexis which operate from growing central components, the ego and the superego. The energy investments of cathexes take on the feature of being bound rather than of being freely mobile. This more modulated and regulated cognitive activity constitutes the secondary process and makes abstract thought possible.

Now it is apparent that, although externally produced delay in gratification may give rise to the primordial thought-hallucination, in itself it has little effect in producing the ultimate, modulated, secondary process type of cognition. If it did have a substantial effect, all that would be needed to produce a population of abstract thinkers would be a systematic frustration or delayed gratification of the basic drives of children. What frustratingly delayed gratification usually leads to is impulsive, sensory-bound thinking and behaving. On a less intense level, it can produce the type of thinking and imagery contained in Emerson's orally frustrated account of the emperor left to whistle by himself, his cry of famine unheeded.

What psychoanalytic theory (as initially stated by Freud and developed by Rapaport) has in mind is, rather, that the child develops the ability to delay his gratifications. This ability, in turn, depends on the child's predictable nurturing connection with the mother, the need-satisfying object. As Rapaport writes in regard to the development of the more modulated secondary process: "In this new organization of memory, the transition from one idea to another was no longer determined by a belongingness to the same drive, but rather by a *connectedness along*

the pathways in reality toward the need-satisfying object. . . .
The cathexes operating within this new memory-organization,
limited in displaceability and amount and not striving toward
direct and complete discharge, were conceptualized as *bound
cathexes*" [italics in original].[19]

The pertinence of the above to the connectedness-disconnectedness hypothesis requires no belaboring. The first born, or
first of a sex, usually receives enough intense nurturing from
the mother so that integration of the memory traces of this predictable mothering decreases the need for more primitive wish-
fulfillment thinking. The child can wait; he can withstand some
short-term postponement of need-gratification because he can
depend that the need will soon be gratified. Therese Benedek
has discussed this sequence in her analysis of the origins of confidence. Thus, from a connectedness of mother with child there
can issue an internalization of the mother, a central ego and
superego factor that, by countering direct drive gratification,
makes abstract thinking possible.

Miller's social-psychological theory, now to be discussed,
should not be thought of as antagonistic to the one just described.
Because it is concerned with the ways older children learn, it
represents rather a theoretical approach, supplementary to the
psychoanalytic one which applies more to infants and small
children. An additional attractive feature of this theory is that
it grew out of experimental investigations and is capable of further experimental testing. Miller described two main types of
social learning: One is called matched dependent behavior. Essentially, this is the imitation of a knowledgeable or prestigeful
person by a less knowledgeable or less prestigeful person. In the
family, the imitation would proceed upwards. Thus, the youngest
child would imitate the middle child, who would imitate the
oldest child who, in turn, would imitate the parents. This process
of imitation does not guarantee meaningful or intelligent behavior. The imitated person knows why he is performing an
action; the imitator can perceive only the action and not the
thinking and judgment that precedes the action. Thus, to take an
extreme example, the son may see the father scratch his head
while thinking out the solution to a problem. The son may imitate the head-scratching with the hope that his action will lead
to the solving of a problem.

The other process of social learning is what Miller calls copying. The one who is being copied has a strong interest that the person who is copying him has done it accurately. If the copying person makes a mistake, he is punished by the copied person in some way—disapproval, scolding, coolness. If the copying person does well in his task, he is rewarded by the copied person in some way—smiles, warmth, approval. By the cues of punishment and reward, the copying person finally succeeds in learning the exact way; he has made it his own and is no longer dependent on the original model for guidance.

The essential difference between Miller's two processes rests in the activity of the person who is being copied. In imitation, this person supplies no cues to the imitator; whereas in copying, he supplies constant evaluations as to whether the copier is on or off the target. In imitation, the shadow of the copied person falls quite lightly on the imitation. Though the imitator continues to be dependent on outside sensory cues, he is more free to experiment, less bound to an internalized, definite right-or-wrong way. In copying, the shadow of the copied person falls heavily enough on the copier so that a part of the copied person becomes an internal part of the copier. Though much less dependent now on external sensory cues, he is much less free to experiment because he is bound strongly to an internalized right way; his cues are more likely to be abstract, intellectual stimuli, than direct, sensory ones.

Miller's finding that the oldest children in the family are more frequently copyists and the younger siblings more often imitators is not surprising. All other things (aptitude, vigor, intelligence) being equal, the first son more often comes under the vigilant, somewhat anxious eyes of his parents. If the father—as did the fathers of J. S. Mill and Mozart—hopes to perpetuate his own skills and knowledgeability, it is more frequently the first son whom he selects as the instrument of his perpetuation. While all sons strive toward masculine adequacy by imitation and by trial-and-error experimentation, the first son is in the position, for better or worse, of having within the family an actively interested tutor in the person of the father. In other areas of the personality, the molding activities of the interested mother can be highly tutorial.

It seems likely that certain cognitive processes cannot be

considered apart from the extent of the father's and the mother's interest—wholesome or overanxious—in the son's following his precepts, his hopes, his accumulated wisdom. The first son is likely to receive a larger dose of this than is a later son. Through punishment-reward conditioning, there has been added to the first son's psyche an indwelling critic, who constantly informs the son when he is approaching or deviating from the precepts of the father and the mother. Thus he is bound to the past in a much stronger way than a later son. Memory influences his thinking and actions as much as does current, vivid sensory perception. The later son, who tends to be more an experimental imitator than a memorizing copyist, is more oriented to the "now" than to the synthesis of the "then and now."

Further possible repercussions of what is involved in copying and in imitating may be seen as we consider now another major trend noted in eminent men. This concerns the feeling about the self—with the intuition of first sons (as Locke, Berkeley, Carlyle) that there *is* a continuous core of self-identity; and the opposing intuition of later sons (as Hume, Emerson, Whitman) that there *is not necessarily* such a persevering identity. It is, of course, possible to account for the identity trend without bringing in Miller's theory. One could use the abstract-sensory polarity hypothesis and say that first sons make an abstract generalization about the self of last week, the self of yesterday, and the self of today—the common denominator being the "I"— whereas later sons particularize each such state and discover no continuous core. But, using Miller's theory, one would be inclined to expect that memorizing copyists would have a more persistent feeling of self-identity than would experimental imitators. The former are comparatively more bound to and stimulated by their internalization (a summation of which may be the self), whereas the latter are comparatively more receptive to experimentation with new, externally derived identities.

Some support of the foregoing appears to be provided by the experimental work of Helen L. Koch. She found that the younger of two brothers (when younger by less than two years) "most frequently of all comparable close-spacing groups, expressed the desire in the interview to become the sib. The younger boy sees himself as somewhat like the sib, of similar age and same in sex. He identifies with the sib, looks up to him and wants to be like him. . . . As examples of the younger boy's respect for his slightly older brother and of his own inferiority feeling, . . . let me quote the remarks of a few [of his group]. 'Bill (older brother) does most of the good work. I never do and that's why I'd like to be Bill, if I could.' 'I would like to be Curt. Then I could beat him up.' 'I would like to be Tom cause he can read and write.' "[20]

As a possible explanation of this trend, Koch notes that these later sons most often felt that the mothers preferred their first sons. This state of affairs—which we have seen to exist in the cases of later sons Alfred Adler and Herman Melville—is not conducive to a feeling of confidence about one's self-identity. Rather, it leads to feelings of identity-inferiority and to attempts to enhance one's self-image by being like or imitating those who have been successful in winning the favor of mother or of society. Thus there appears to be an intimate relationship between the copying mode of learning and a confidence in self-identity on the one hand and the imitating mode of learning and a dissatisfaction with and an inconstancy of self-identity on the other.

We have already indicated (concerning family learning climates) that, if the father hopes to perpetuate his own skills and knowledgeability, he more frequently selects the first son as an instrument of this perpetuation. In such cases, the father sees himself in his son, or sees in the son what he could have become. Similarly, the mother can realize her aspirations through the son. Out of these identifications of parents with their son arises the energy necessary for the parents to act tutorially, to stimulate, correct, and guide the copyist son. Because they themselves are realized, the parents are likely to be rivalrous with the son or jealous of his attainments. An example of this situation among eminent men may be seen in K. R. Eissler's psychoanalytic study of first son Goethe, "The Environment of a Genius" which appeared in *The Psychoanalytic Study of the Child*. Here the activity of the father as well as the resultant effects on Goethe's sense of identity are stressed.

In the case of Goethe we see a good example of the connectedness of the adult parents with the first son—a pedagogized copyist's connectedness with the father, a more emotional one with the mother. Eissler writes: "The father's life was so organized that he could regard the rearing and education of his children as his main and principal function. He was hardly distracted by other activities from full concentration on his son, who at an early age was given the opportunity of sharing the main part of his father's daily activities and thus of familiarizing himself thoroughly with the adult world."[21] Eissler's opinion is that the son was an extension of (the father's) own self and also that the son was the father's most beloved object. We note here the tutorial father who will correct the copyist son, and the inevitable adult world orientation of the son. Eissler believes that various paternal and maternal influences gave Goethe a strong inner identity: "Combined with a core of basic, close, and unambivalent contact with the world there is also encountered in Goethe a core of solid sense of identity. . . . Out of exuberance and abundance he was a man of many shapes, but never out of a basic dissatisfaction of a weakness of sense of identity."[22]

Any initial feeling that here, indeed, may be *the* recipe for producing a genius is soon dissipated when one views the childhood of Rousseau and Melville. Whereas Goethe's needs were amply and consistently gratified, Rousseau and Melville were so deprived that oral-dependent needs and loud cries of famine became their principal characteristics. Charles Kligerman writes of Rousseau (in his article entitled "The Character of Jean Jacques Rousseau"): "Rousseau's father appears to have been a psychopathic character. He drank, brawled, was inconsistent, of violent temper, and fond of wandering. Despite the varied ministrations of female relatives and nurses, this inadequate father seems to have furnished the only fairly constant relationship with the young Jean Jacques. The relation consisted of seductiveness, overprotectiveness, severity, and finally abandonment."[23]

The father apparently did not see himself in his son but rather his dead wife. As Kligerman writes: "Rousseau tells us almost initially: 'In me he thought he saw her he so tenderly lamented, but could never forget that I had been the innocent cause of his misfortune, nor did he overembrace me.' . . ."[24] The father did participate in educating Rousseau, but the method could hardly be considered tutorial or grooming for further responsibility: "Quite early Rousseau was taught by his father to read, and every night after supper they would read romances which had belonged to the mother. Often they would become so enraptured as to read the entire night."[25] The resulting sense of identity was weak. Kligerman believes that, in Rousseau's case, there was "a series of fluctuating ego states in a loosely organized personality."[26]

Kligerman writes in his article "The Psychology of Herman Melville": "Probably the best avenue of approach to an understanding of Melville's character is the Ishmael legend. . . . The arresting opening of *Moby Dick* 'Call me Ishmael' has been quoted by all the critics, who did not fail to note that Melville was early buffeted, that he felt rejected 'like an infant Ishmael with no material Hagar to accompany him.' . . . In the case of Melville we see at once a typical background of such oral frustration and neglect. As the third of eight children, he was early forced to relinquish his mother's side and experience five times the pain of seeing his mother favor a smaller child at the breast."[27] In an earlier chapter, we have seen what Melville felt about his mother's preference for his older brother; Kligerman puts it that the mother "was a cold, proud, narcissistic woman who had much to demand but little to give to a small boy."[28] With no strong inner core, Melville continued to feel unfed. In his dependence on women and men he was always on the verge of swallowing them up, and thereby merging identities.

Kligerman writes about this aspect of Melville: "It was during this pregnancy (his wife's first) that the first signs of Melville's disintegration appeared. . . . In effect, then, Lizzie betrayed Melville just as his mother had earlier betrayed him. She fed the younger child, and he again felt rejected like the infant Ishmael. . . . His confidence in mothers once more shattered, Melville was again in a receptive mood to turn to a father, this time Hawthorne."[29] Melville simply engulfed Hawthorne and fused their egos.

From these psychoanalytic impressions we might expect that those with a weaker sense of continuous self-identity would be prone to engage in experimental imitations, to rely somewhat on incorporated borrowings from other men. Some literary criticisms appear to support this idea. Thus Newton Arvin in discussing *The Whale* states that in addition to relying on reminiscence Melville had an "extraordinary dependence on the writings of other men."[30]

Perhaps a more striking example is seen in Edmund Wilson's appraisal of T. S. Eliot. Later son Eliot's experimental borrowings moved first son Wilson to some sharpness in an otherwise appreciative appraisal. In *Axel's Castle* Wilson writes: "And Eliot had, in his early poetry, introduced phrases from Shakespeare and Blake for purposes of ironic effect. He has always, furthermore, been addicted to prefacing his poems with quotations and echoing passages from other poets. But now, in 'The Waste Land,' he carries this tendency to what one must suppose its extreme possible limit: here, in a poem of only four hundred and three lines . . . he manages to include quotations from, allusions to, or imitations of, at least thirty-five different writers . . . as well as several popular songs. . . . We are always being dismayed, in our general reading, to discover that lines among those which we had believed to represent Eliot's residuum of original invention had been taken over or adapted from other writers. . . . Yet Eliot manages to be most effective precisely . . . where he might be expected to be least original. . . ."[31]

Suggestive evidence concerning imitativeness and identity weakness in the disconnectedness-prone later-borns come from a study of histrionic, role-playing personalities. In "Contemporary Conversion Reactions," F. J. Ziegler, J. B. Imboden, and E. Meyer suggest—after recalling Sydenham's comment that conversion hysteria "imitates almost every disease which befalls mankind"[32] —that the term *histrionic personality* is more accurate than *hysterical personality*. They write: "In the histrionic personality, the role playing shifts and varies conspicuously with cues from the audience of the moment, indicating an inability to maintain stable personal and social identities. . . ."[33] They stated: "We investigated the sibling position in a group of 100 consecutive patients belonging to the present series of conversion reactions."[34] Following certain cues, they found "that a significantly greater proportion of our patients had occupied the position of the youngest child, or the youngest child of one sex in the family than would have been expected by chance alone."[35]

Because of conflicting reports in the literature we cannot of course lean too heavily on the findings of these investigators as providing proof for our speculations. More important perhaps is the concept of the histrionic personality and its relation to imitation. The concept is comparatively new and may not mean the same thing to all investigators. As described above, there is an atomistic, disconnected, contemporaneous undertone, i.e., "the role playing shifts and varies conspicuously with cues from the audience of the moment." Following Neal E. Miller's concept, we could call the histrionic personality an experimental trial-and-error imitator, possessing a Humean discontinuity in self-identity. What the histrionic personality may have to be distinguished from is the self-dramatizing personality. Returning to eminent men, we would ask: "are Bakunin and Hitler to be considered histrionic personalities because they were able to sense the mood of the audience, or are they better described as self-dramatizing personalities, with a continuous self-core, who stirred up themselves as well as the audience with their passions?" and "is sentimental, dependent Rousseau a better example of the histrionic personality that responds to the audience of the moment?" Although these questions cannot receive a definite answer here, it is important that the distinction be made.

One bit of evidence about contemporaneous role-playing comes from existentialist later son Camus. It is more revealing than any clinical description. We wish to bring out here an illustration not of psychopathology or of the florid histrionic type but, rather, an insight into a personality that is in close perceptive contact with urgent, existing reality, and an insight into his solution of role-playing. The abolition of a continuous, rational self-core is seen in these quotes from *The Myth of Sisyphus and Other Essays:* "what Kierkegaard calls for quite plainly is the third sacrifice required by Ignatius Loyola, the one in which God most rejoices: 'The sacrifice of the intellect.' "[36] This step—advocated by later sons Camus, Kierkegaard, and Loyola—is echoed by later son Eliot when he calls for an extinction of the personality. Camus states in an Epicurean fashion that "what counts is not the best living but the most living. . . . The present and the succession of presents before a constantly conscious soul is the deal of the absurd man. . . . The actor's realm is that of the fleeting. . . . Of all kinds of fame the least deceptive is the one that is lived. . . . Hence the actor has chosen multiple fame, the fame that is hallowed and tested. From the fact that everything is to die someday he draws the best conclusion. . . . For that is his art —to stimulate absolutely, to project himself as deeply as possible into lives that are not his own. . . . He will die in three hours under the mask he has assumed today. Within three hours he must experience and express a whole exceptional life. That is called losing oneself to find oneself."[37]

Reflections of later son Camus, a playwright and philosopher on personal identity, are matched by the reflections of a distinguished actor, later son John Gielgud. His views on acting and on "losing oneself to find oneself" are given by Lillian Ross in one of a series of "Profiles" that appeared in *The New Yorker* under the general title *"The Player."* Of all the actors and actresses interviewed for these articles, Gielgud's account of himself seems to be most revealing with regard to identity-inferiority and imitative borrowings. The youngest of three sons—there was also a younger sister—Gielgud says: "I am the only actor in my immediate family. . . . I've never known whether one becomes the part or the part becomes one. My own personality is so mercurial that I react strongly to a sad part. But I don't think a part has ever taken me over. When I first played Hamlet, I was self-conscious. I worried about the audience's knowing it was I. When I stopped trying to disguise myself in the part, I worried about the terrible qualities in me that the audience might not like. . . . There's life for an actor in the characters he plays. Being another character is more interesting than being yourself. It's a great pleasure to me. I love putting on the costume, putting on the makeup. . . . You constantly catch yourself trying to study how people really feel emotion. You store it up for future use; you reproduce it later in other forms. If I see a bad accident, I watch the expressions on the faces of the people."[38] Gielgud concludes with: "I find everything I love in the theatre. When I go into a theatre and get into a dressing room, it's like going into a safe place that I know, without thinking, is mine. It's like going home."[39]

This discussion of self-identity brings to a close a long and rather complex inquiry. If there is one general thread running through this inquiry, it is the polarity in regard to cognition—the connectedness-prone first sons appearing to possess an abstract-cognitive tendency, the disconnectedness-prone later sons a sensory-cognitive tendency. Because this polarity is based on theoretical inference rather than on concrete evidence, the terms *abstract* and *sensory* can be considered only suggestive. What the experimental and impressionistic evidence actually points up is the tendency of first-borns, or first sons—in contrast to later-borns, or later sons—to have a proclivity for language and a constancy of self-identity. To account for this double tendency the author has theorized that first sons—due to a connected parental nurturing—have developed comparatively persistent, central psychic components. From these persisting components issue intrapsychic stimuli which may offset stimuli coming through the sense organs from the external world. Such a more or less *closed*, intrapsychic system provides the soil for the particular kind of abstractness involved in language and self-identity. On the other hand, later sons—due to a disconnected nurturing—have comparatively less persistent central components, are more receptive to stimuli from the external world and, with this more or less *open* system, are not as given to the abstractness inherent in language and in the sense of persisting self.

For the link between the kind of nurturing and the resultant kind of cognition, the author has had recourse to theories arising from psychoanalytic observation and psychological experimentation. The Freudian thinking, as espoused by David Rapaport, indicates that the closer the connectedness of child with mother (or mother with child), the greater the growth of central components such as the ego and superego which, by inhibiting immediate gratification and stimulus-bound behavior, make abstract thinking possible. Neal E. Miller's social-psychological theory that arose from experimental procedures gives a picture of the interpersonal mechanism involved in learning which is more capable of experimental verification. It is true that Miller's theory is not directly concerned with abstract versus sensory styles. Some inference is necessary to conclude that the strong tutorial connection between the copied person and the copier gives rise to abstract thinking; whereas the weak connection between the imitated person and the imitator does not do so. The inference can be bolstered by recalling Piaget's observations, mentioned earlier, that the abstract *whys* do not, normally, enter a child's conversation unless he has been frequently questioned by grown-ups. It seems safe to assume that tutorial questioning by interested or overinterested parents forces the child to think along such abstract lines as cause and effect.

Other theories bear on self-identity and imitation, but they do not consider the role of the parent and thus will not be discussed systematically. Such a theory, for example, is that of Jean Piaget. His two primary functions involved in cognitive adaptation, namely assimilation and accommodation, are pertinent to our thesis. Assimilation, according to Piaget, is the function whereby parts of the external environment are ingested, digested, and restructured to become included in the self system. Accommodation is the function whereby the individual, in coming to grips with the outside object, changes his self-organization in order better to apprehend the object. Assimilation, so to speak, is inner-directed, and effects a restructuring of the object; accommodation is outer-directed and effects a restructuring of the self. One would expect then a more persistent sense of self in those predominantly engaged in assimilation, a more plastic sense of self in those primarily given to accommodation.

That assimilation is akin to the self-absorbed, abstract connectedness tendency and accommodation to the imitative, perceptually alert disconnectedness tendency is suggested by John H. Flavell in *The Developmental Psychology of Jean Piaget*:

In play [or make-believe] the primary object is to mold reality to the whim of the cognizer; in other words to assimilate reality to various schemas with little concern for precise accommodation to that reality. . . . In imitation, on the other hand, it is accommodation which reigns supreme. All energy is focused on taking exact account of the structural niceties of the reality one is imitating and in precisely dovetailing one's schematic repertoire to these details. In other words, as in play the primary concern is to adapt reality to the self (assimilation), in imitation the paramount object is to adapt the self to reality (accommodation).[40]

The reader will no doubt recognize in play assimilation the dreamy synthesizing of the connectedness-prone first son (e.g., Einstein) and in imitation-accommodation the precise analyzing of the disconnectedness-prone later son (e.g., Descartes). As indicated earlier, Piaget does not attribute these cognitive preferences to any family experiences or parental activities.

Up to this point, we have restricted ourselves to particular facets of the connectedness-disconnectedness hypothesis—to those facets which appear most supported by work done by investigators other than the author. Not that we have mentioned all the work carried out in the area of birth order. A systematic review would necessarily include the experimental contributions of Stanley Schacter, C. MacArthur, Robert Sears as well as the case-study investigations of W. Toman. Though many of their findings and theories could be marshalled in support of the basic hypothesis, space does not permit such an elaboration.

The remainder of this chapter will be given over to some quantitative trends found by the author that possibly bear on the relationships of certain basic psychoanalytic concepts to the connectedness-disconnectedness hypothesis.

The best known of these is the Oedipus complex. We have stated earlier that first sons more frequently than later sons show the kind of intense, romantic overestimation of a woman that could lead to death wishes toward the father, the sexual possessor of the mother. And we have speculated that, because Freud was a first son, he gave his special attention to the Oedipus complex and to the libido theory. Also contained in the Oedipal situation is its resolution. In this resolution, the boy gives up crude sexual desires toward the mother and identifies with the father and his prohibitions. This identification with the father is the basic factor in the final integration of the superego, the entity we have referred to as the inner moral voice. In previous chapters we have called attention to the inner moral voice as being more characteristic of first sons than of later sons.

The question arises: "is there any quantitative evidence indicating that first sons, more than later sons, manifest the Freudian Oedipus complex?" Because the complex is, indeed, quite complex and more suitable for a qualitative analysis, it is difficult to select any single phenomenon which can be strictly equated with the whole Oedipus complex and then handled quantitatively. A possibility, however, may lie in the examination of dreams of death of the parents. For it was in regard to such dreams that Freud made his first mention of the Oedipus complex. He wrote in "The Interpretation of Dreams" that "we may be guided by our knowledge that the very great majority of dreams of the death of a parent refer to the parent of the same sex as the dreamer, so that a man generally dreams of the death of his father, and a woman of the death of her mother. I do not claim that this happens constantly; but that it happens in a great majority of cases is so evident that it requires explanation by some factor of general significance. Broadly speaking, it is as though a sexual preference made itself felt at an early age, as though the boy regarded his father, and the girl her mother, as a rival in love—by whose removal he or she could but profit."[41]

With the idea, then, that if any single, well-defined, easily countable phenomenon may reflect the entire Oedipus complex, it would be a man's dream of his father's death, the present author reviewed the dreams elicited from a large number of military neuropsychiatric patients he had seen during World War II. In a much earlier study of these dreams the writer had reported that, contrary to Freud's impression, these men dreamed of the death of the mother more often than of the death of the father.[42] The later review, however, took into account the birth order of these men and endeavored to see whether dreams of the father's death were more frequent in the first sons. To reduce the number of variables, the investigation was restricted to those men who came from families of no more than three children. Five groups were established (a) only children (35); (b) first-born (74); (c) first sons with an older sister (32); (d) middle sons (31); (e) last-born sons (38).

Although only a minority of these patients recalled having ever dreamed of the death of a parent, a trend was evident in the direction of the hypothesis. Generally stated, the trend was that dreams of father's death—as compared to dreams of mother's death—diminished as the boy was farther removed from the direct authority of the father. Thus, the father-death dream was comparatively more frequent in the only child who had no other rival for the mother (six father-death dreams, five mother-death dreams); next in the first-born son (six father-death dreams, eleven mother-death dreams); next in the first son (two father-death dreams, six mother-death dreams); and least frequent in the last-born son (one father-death dream, seven mother-death dreams).

If the five groups are consolidated into two large groups, 141 first sons and 69 later sons, it would seem that, though dreams of mother's death occur with about the same frequency in both groups (16 and 17 per cent, respectively), dreams of father's death occur about three times more frequently in first sons (10 per cent) than in later sons (3 per cent). If a man's dream of his father's death, as Freud suggested, is an indicator of the Oedipus complex, the results just described support our hypothesis that first sons tend early in life to be erotically connected with the mother, to be jealously hostile to the father and, subsequently, to resolve and control this turbulent situation by developing a strong inner moral voice, the superego.

This trend, coupled with other evidence from eminent men, suggests strongly to the writer that this particular portion of Freud's theory—the Oedipus complex—stems from the fact that Freud was a first son. In his self-analysis he naturally gave priority to theoretical concepts which explained his personality to himself. If he had been a later son, perhaps he would have been attracted to a different myth—possibly one involving a mother-goddess. But of all the Greek myths available, the one concerning Oedipus must have had special significance for him. If the Oedipus complex is not universally valid it is not, as sometimes claimed, because Freud represented only a viewpoint of Viennese patriarchal middle-class society; Freud was not a local or contemporary type. Rather, the Oedipus complex can be lacking in universality because it explains one type of man better than it does another type. Freud's contribution to depth psychology does not rest merely on his postulates of the Oedipus complex, however. The originality and richness of his insight into the unconscious workings of the mind is beyond argument.

That his insight has provided and still provides a bountiful reservoir for his followers, and has led to the most enduring and encompassing school of depth psychology, is either a reflection of Freud's particular genius and/or a repercussion of his early life situation. For, although Freud was the first son of his mother and could write: "A man who has been the indisputable favorite of his mother keeps for life the feeling of a conqueror, that confidence of success that often induces real success,"[43] he was also able to appreciate what it may feel like to be a later son under the domination of a first son. In Freud's case the first son was his nephew John, who was one year older than Freud. John was the first son of Emanuel Freud, who was the first son of Sigmund Freud's father by an earlier marriage. Ernest Jones writes in his biography of Sigmund Freud: "There is every reason to think that the most important person in Freud's early childhood was, next to his parents, his nephew John, a boy only a year older than himself. . . . He wrote later, when speaking of his boyhood ideals, Hannibal and Marshall Masséna: 'Perhaps the development of this martial ideal may be traced yet farther back, to the first three years of my childhood, to wishes which my alternately friendly and hostile relations with a boy a year older than myself must have evoked in the weaker of the two playmates. . . .' 'At times he must have treated me very badly, and I must have opposed my tyrant courageously. . . .' "[44] It may not be accidental, then, that Freud's first-son and later-son experiences in childhood contributed to the breadth of his insight.

We shall consider the typical anxiety dreams as the concluding topic. The author's interest in these dreams has extended over the past twenty years, and culminated in a conceptualization very similar to, if not identical with, the connectedness-disconnectedness hypothesis. In 1942–43 he noted that the two most common anxiety dreams reported by a very large number of prospective soldiers at an induction station were: (1) dreams of being attacked, chased, or threatened by an external object—hereafter called the attacked dream—and (2) dreams of falling from heights —hereafter called the falling dream. Furthermore, it was found that there were individual differences concerning these two kinds of typical anxiety dreams: some reported that they had the attacked dream but never the falling; some the falling but never the attacked; while the majority reported the occurrence of both types of dreams but differed as to which type was the more unpleasant or anxiety producing. The same individual differences in dreaming were observed later in military neuropsychiatric patients, in children and parents at a child guidance clinic, and in men and women in psychoanalytic practice.

Curiosity as to whether these individual differences were a reflection of basic personality differences led, over the years, to a series of observations and a series of speculations. Finally, in a paper published in 1960,[45] the writer—on the basis of certain evidence—offered the hypothesis that the falling dream was reflective of an anxiety present in the first five or six months of infancy, e.g., a period of dependency on *a* mother who provides food, warmth, and contact; whereas the attacked dream was reflective of an anxiety present after six or seven months, e.g., a period of dependency on *the* mother who provides *herself* as well as providing food, warmth, and contact. In the earlier period, the hungry infant can be satisfied by food regardless who it is that gives the food. Mother figures can be interchanged, as long as hunger and other elemental needs are gratified. In a later period, when "stranger anxiety" appears (the infant cries if the face seen is not his mother's), the person of *the* mother (not merely *a* mother) is as important as—if not more important than—the food. The transition from the earlier to the later phase is made possible by the identification, or involvement, or connection that the mother has with the infant. The greater the connection involved, the more the infant would have anxiety over separation from *the* mother; the lesser the connection, the more the infant would have anxiety over separation from *a* mother. This tendency is exemplified by the so-called anaclitic depression experienced by infants in the tenth and eleventh month if separated from their mothers for a long period of time. The infant declines food, pines away, and recovers only if the mother is brought back. It is highly significant that this sequence of events upon separation occurs only if there has been a previous close connection between infant and mother. When there has not been such a connection, the anaclitic depression does not take place.

Quite apart from the matter of typical anxiety dreams, it can be seen that the above represents the theory behind the connectedness-disconnectedness hypothesis. The connectedness-prone are attached to *the* mother who, incidentally, provides food; the disconnectedness-prone are attached to the food supplies which, incidentally, are provided by *a* mother. The theory allows us to better understand the intense oral cravings noted in later sons. It also accounts for the first son's overestimation and attachment to the human mother, and the later son's attachment to the impersonal Mother Nature who gives out of her bounty. Other extensions of the theory—particularly concerning identification—are too complicated to discuss here. Interested readers are referred to technical articles.

Much of the evidence relating typical anxiety dreams to this developmental theory of anxiety is too qualitative and inferential to be gone into now. We shall mention, however, one quantitative trend which supports the idea that the falling dream is reflective of the disconnected, separation-from-*a*-mother phase; and the attacked dream a reflection of the connected, separation-from-*the*-mother phase. The trends are found in data about a highly potent source of a feeling of disconnection, dislocation, or discontinuity—the source is the early loss of a parent. The writer stated that among military selectees—a "normal" sample of the male population—the falling dream was the predominantly unpleasant anxiety dream of those who lost their mothers at an early age. (Of 174 selectees who lost their mothers by death or separation before the age of six, 66 per cent had predominantly falling dreams, and 34 per cent had predominantly attacked dreams. However, in 206 cases where loss of mothers occurred between the ages of six and thirteen, the percentages were about reversed—31 and 69 per cent, respectively). In a previous communication, the author discussed this trend in the following way: "before the strands of the weblike matrix between child and parents have had a fair chance to grow strong, before the knowable image of the parent has become internalized in the child, there has been a disruption, a discontinuity of the parent-child relationship. The anxiety stimulated by the potential discontinuity is possibly reflected in the falling dream."[46]

The foregoing suggests that connectedness and disconnectedness may be roughly indicated by the typical anxiety dreams as well as by birth order. To put it somewhat differently, connectedness and disconnectedness are much more complex phenomena than an exclusive reliance on the crude birth order indicator would suggest. This is why the author has repeatedly stressed throughout this book that the basic hypothesis has to be considered somewhat apart from its convenient but rough indicator. Although eminent man can be studied from the viewpoint of their birth order only (their anxiety dreams being only rarely available), it is clear from these comments on typical anxiety dreams that not all first sons, nor all later sons, are alike; that their inner anxieties, as reflected by dreams, may modify their proneness to connectedness and disconnectedness.

One would be interested in the possibility of using both indicators (birth order and dreams) to establish a connectedness-disconnectedness continuum. The only substantial data available to the author are those from the military psychiatric patients. Of 340 patients from homes of no more than five children, 121 men (Group A) possess two indicators of connectedness—they were first sons and reported the attacked dreams as more unpleasant; 154 men (Group B) constitute a mid-group possessing one indicator of connectedness and one of disconnectedness, e.g., first-son–falling dream, or later-son–attacked dream; 65 men (Group C) possessed two indicators of disconnectedness—they

were later sons and reported the falling dreams as more unpleasant. If we consider Groups A, B, and C as representing a
connectedness-disconnectedness continuum, certain trends appear
to support what we have described earlier about the presence
or absence of inner regulatory mechanisms. Limiting ourselves
only to those personality features which show a straight-line
increase or decrease from Group A through Group B to Group
C, we find that connectedness (Group A) differs from disconnectedness (Group C) in the following way: Marked childhood
temper tantrums and enuresis past the age of twelve rise in frequency from the connectedness to the disconnectedness groups.
(Tantrums 24 per cent in Group A; 33 per cent in Group B;
37 per cent in Group C). (Prolonged enuresis 9 per cent in Group
A; 16 per cent in Group B; 18 per cent in Group C). The inability to regulate rage or urination—perhaps due to the lack of
an internalized parent—is evident here.

Another way of describing this tendency in the disconnectedness group is to say that the gratifications of the immediate
impulse take precedence over longer-term gratifications arising
from postponement of the impulse. We have pointed out in
previous chapters that the disconnectedness-prone are geared to
the present and have an Epicurean orientation, whereas the connectedness-prone are geared to the past as well as to present and,
in a Stoic fashion, are prepared to endure present discomfort to
obtain future rewards. These considerations may help explain the
other trend noticed in Groups A, B, and C: Scholastic achievement and military rank achievement were highest in Group A
and lowest in Group C. (24 per cent of Group A had some
college education; 21 per cent of Group B; and 6 per cent of
Group C). Inversely, as to not finishing the eighth grade, 10
per cent of Group A, 15 per cent of Group B, and 23 per cent
of Group C). The greater achievement in Group A may be due
to a greater ability to tolerate immediate sensual frustration, or to
more of an ability to be gratified by remote or abstract pleasures.

The application of the combined indicator to eminent man
is virtually impossible except in an anecdotal fashion. Two instances, however, may be used for illustration. The first concerns
Freud. As a first son of his mother, he was exposed to potential
displacement of disconnectedness at the birth of each of his five
younger siblings. Yet, perhaps due to the constancy of his par-

ents' involved connection with him, he never experienced a falling dream. He wrote in "The Interpretation of Dreams": "Of
other typical dreams, in which one flies with a feeling of ease
or falls in terror, I know nothing from my own experience. . . ."[47]
Freud, then, would be classified by the combined method as
connectedness-prone.

The second illustration pertains to later son Herman Melville. Newton Arvin, in his critical biography, calls attention to
Melville's literary preoccupation with the sensation of falling,
and quotes from Melville's *Redburn*: "For a few moments (after
climbing the main mast) I stood awe-stricken and mute. I could
not see far out upon the ocean, . . . and from my lofty perch
the sea looked like a great, black gulf, hemmed in, all round, by
beetling black cliffs. I seemed all alone; treading the midnight
clouds; and every second, expected to find myself falling—falling
—falling, as I have felt when the nightmare has been on me."[48]
Later Arvin discusses this tendency and, significantly enough,
finds it in later son Poe: "the nightmarish image of falling to
one's destruction from a high place had appeared before in his
own writing, and what psychiatrists call hysophobia was as characteristic for him as it was for Poe."[49] The falling-dream–later-
son combined disconnectedness may account for what Arvin says
about Melville: "For the better part of five years, from the day
he joined the crew of the *St. Lawrence* to the fall of 1844, Melville was to lead a life of constant movement, strenuous action,
and sometimes irresponsible vagabondage."[50]

A study of typical anxiety dreams may also be useful in the
investigation of spurts of creativity. Although these dreams are
better known clinically for their association with emotional disturbance yet, as the following will indicate, they may preface a
creative intellectual production. Thus Martin Buber opens his
book *Between Man and Man* with a description of a dream he
had, which influenced his philosophical and theological thinking.
In this variant of the attacked dream, a piece of flesh is bitten
out of his arm by a wild animal. Descartes describes three dreams
—one neutral, one a long dream of the falling variety in which
he is losing his balance, and a very brief attacked variety dream
involving a frightening noise—which immediately preceded his
coming upon "I think, therefore I am." Further research of these
dreams may be fruitful in regard not only to the connectedness-

disconnectedness hypothesis but also to creativity—a subject implicit in this book on eminent men, but one which is as yet baffling.

Further discussion of dreams and other phenomena, possibly related to the connectedness-disconnectedness hypothesis, would lead us too far from the particular objective of this chapter. Our concern here has been primarily to ascertain how the basic hypothesis can be tested. To this end we have emphasized the quantitative approach and have discussed experimental results, experimental procedures, and underlying theoretical concepts which may be supportive of or pertinent to the hypothesis. The author hopes that it is clearly evident that an investigatory task of considerable magnitude still lies ahead, a task which will require both qualitative and quantitative methods.

PART THREE *Summation*

CHAPTER XII *Coda*

BEFORE ANY FURTHER DISCUSSION, clearly the first
order of business is to restate the salient points of this complex
investigation—points that may have become blurred even for the
most patient and discerning reader. And it is not only for the
reader's benefit that this is done. Understandably, the author
would be keenly disappointed if he had failed to make himself
understood, or worse, if he had succeeded in making himself
misunderstood. The chances for blurring and misunderstanding
are greatly increased when, as has happened here, many areas
are covered and many ideas developed. At the risk, then, of
some repetition, a brief restatement will be offered which proposes to indicate where the author has firm opinions and where
he is only suggestive or speculative.

The most salient point is the basic hypothesis which states
that there are two inherent psychic tendencies, connectedness
and disconnectedness, whose accentuation is at least in part
causally related to the psychological intensity of the parent-child
interaction. The wording allows for the possibility that predominance of these tendencies can also be causally related to
hereditary factors. As will be recalled, this was not the author's
initial working hypothesis; rather it was a terminal hypothesis
arrived at inductively. The initial hypothesis was concerned with
birth order and, in effect, stated that certain personality factors
are causally related to order of birth. This proving to be too
crude a way of accounting for the phenomena, the expanding
hypothesis took the form that "certain personality factors are
causally related to some factor contained or reflected by order

of birth"—the "some factor" eventually becoming the psychological intensity of the parent-child interaction.

There is, to be sure, another important factor contained in birth order which is not mentioned in the basic hypothesis. We refer to sibling interaction, to the way older brothers deal with younger brothers, and vice versa. Not that we have ignored this factor. On the contrary, much in the preceding chapters has been concerned with sibling interaction. It is not referred to in the basic hypothesis for the simple reason that no clear-cut evidence has been offered by the author in its support. This does not mean that the author doubts its importance. Rather, the author, believing in its importance, doubts that the evidence he has gathered can be brought to bear crucially on this question. The evidence derives from a comparison of first sons and later sons. The first sons are a much more heterogeneous group than are the later sons. The former include first-born first sons, later-born first sons, first sons with younger brothers, first sons without brothers, and first sons without brothers or sisters. The later sons at least have in common that they are all later-born and they all have had older brothers. If the eminent first sons had been restricted to those who were first sons and who had at least one younger brother, opinions about sibling interaction could have been offered by the author with somewhat more confidence. Since this was not done, what has been said on this score must be considered suggestive and designed only to give a fuller picture of the family situation.

The evidence, however, is more pertinent to the parent-child interaction factor. The comparison of first and later sons rests on the assumption that the first-born of a sex encounters a nurturing experience with the parents which differs in quality and quantity from that encountered by the later-born of a sex. Of all that enters into the nurturing experience, we have focused on the degree of psychological connectedness existing between the parent and the child. And we have postulated that, for better or worse, the first-born of a sex encounters more psychological connectedness in his nurture by his parents than does a later-born of the same sex.

It was this feature in the nurturing experience which influenced the author to choose the terms *connectedness* and *disconnectedness* to describe the resultant psychic tendencies. The choice was made over equally applicable terms which, though more sharply describing the psychic tendencies, gave no clue as to what they may have related. It was for this reason that Piaget's terms *syncretism* and *juxtaposition* and the mathematical-philosophical terms *continuous* and *discrete* were not adopted. Other sets of terms, while catching well a particular psychological facet, did not seem comprehensive and general enough to account for all the phenomena. Thus, passed over were such sets of terms as *past* and *present-minded*, *general* and *particular-minded*, *synthetic* and *analytic-minded*, *plural* and *single-minded*, *abstract* and *concrete-minded*, *deterministic* and *nondeterministic*, *molecular* and *atomistic*, *introvert* and *extravert*, *inner* and *outer-directed*. The advantages of using the terms *connectedness* and *disconnectedness* may be offset by what is hoped will be only a temporary disadvantage. This is the possibility that for some people *disconnectedness* may have a comparatively negative connotation. At first blush, it may seem better to be *connected* than *disconnected*. It is hoped that the preceding chapters have demonstrated that there are as many disadvantages to *connectedness* as there are to *disconnectedness*, and that the ability to disconnect is as important as the ability to connect.

It is time now that we deal squarely with the most crucial question concerning this investigation: has the author succeeded with the evidence offered in demonstrating the probability of the basic hypothesis being valid? This is a question which, of course, each reader will reserve the right to answer for himself. But it may be of interest to the reader to know how the author himself would answer it. He would say that the evidence and clinical observations gathered by him, the quantitative evidence gathered by research psychologists (referred to in the preceding chapter), and the qualitative assessments of eminent men made by authorities in fields outside the author's direct scope, lead him to the conclusion that the various trends cannot be attributed to coincidence or chance, and that there is a good probability that the basic hypothesis is valid. Though this may seem a cautious statement, it has certain affirmative implications. It makes the hypothesis a serious one and, at least for the author, it shifts the burden of proof on to those who would assert that there is a low order of probability.

What would sway the author from his opinion is another

hypothesis which would more adequately account for all the evidence presented. He would not be swerved by having it pointed out to him that here and there he has been in error. He is well aware that the considerable scholarship necessary to avoid inaccuracies in the many areas covered is beyond his scope. Thus he is prepared to learn that a few of the eminent men who have been listed as first sons are really later sons, and vice versa. He also would not be appreciably swerved if one or two of the several secondary hypotheses could be disproved. Thus, for example, it would not be fatal to the hypothesis if first sons were shown to be more adept at algebra than at calculus, or if later sons were shown to be uniquely drawn to making epic myths rather than to the making of fairy tales. However, if more than one or two of these secondary hypotheses should be disproved, the inferential evidence for the basic hypothesis would be seriously weakened.

The foregoing touches on the question of the source of error, an important question to every investigation. The author is of the opinion that the sampling procedure constitutes the least source of error. The considerable number of eminent men, activity fields, historical periods, and political-social environments reduce the chance that an atypical sample is present. Most of the men generally regarded as highly eminent have been dealt with in some way or other. When they have not been mentioned, or have been mentioned only sparingly, it is because there was some uncertainty about their birth order, or because they would constitute an unnecessary additional illustration of a point already made, or because an interpretation of their works along the lines of the particular subhypothesis might necessitate an inordinately prolonged discussion.

A much more important source of error is the kind that stems from the subjective bias of any investigator and that quite unconsciously presses him to select only those bits of evidence which are favorable to his hypothesis. Thus there is the possibility that, in spite of the representative sampling, the author has unwittingly restricted himself to those excerpts from the works and actions of a particular eminent man, and to those views of authorities concerning the eminent man, which best support his theory. The author has consciously tried to guard against this possibility. How successful he has been in this effort must be left to the reader and to the experts in the various fields to decide.

Proceeding with the restatement, it would be well to emphasize again what assumptions should *not* be made about the findings. Perhaps the leading misassumption would be that all first sons believe and think in a way that is different from all later sons; or that there is more in common between any first son and any other first son than there is between any first son and any later son. If the hypothesis were worded in terms of birth order, the foregoing might not be an unreasonable assumption. But since birth order is only a crude indicator of connectedness and disconnectedness, it may happen occasionally that a particular later son has been exposed to more parental connectedness than has a particular first son. Thus, exceptions here and there are to be expected. This statement does not conflict with what the author stated in the introductory chapter, and will state again: *the basic hypothesis must stand or fall upon the use of birth order as an indicator in sizable groups of individuals.*

Contributing also to possible misassumptions on this score is the fact that basic connectedness and disconnectedness have a variety of surface manifestations. One first son may show poetic inclinations, another a metaphysical bent, another a drive toward heroic action. Similarly, one later son may exhibit a genius for algebra, another for scientific inventiveness, another for militant social action. Thus, one should not expect all first sons and all later sons to resemble each other outwardly. In several instances, some outward resemblance may lead one to link a later son with a first son rather than with another later son. A case in point, and one which we have dwelled on considerably, is that of later son Hume. Outwardly he appears to resemble first sons Locke and Berkeley, in having in common with them an empirical philosophical orientation; inwardly, his disconnectedness more closely resembles that of later sons Bacon, Descartes, Dewey, and Russell. Similarly, first son Theodore Roosevelt might be linked on the surface with later son Andrew Jackson as a man of action. Inwardly (to make positive linkages) Theodore Roosevelt may be more like Lincoln, Andrew Jackson, more like Gandhi. To make negative linkages, Theodore Roosevelt could be more like Hitler, Andrew Jackson more like Borgia.

There is no doubt that the use of basic connectedness and disconnectedness may produce some exceedingly strange bedfellows. While no one would lift an appreciable eyebrow at the linkage of first sons Milton and Shakespeare, Locke and Jefferson, or of later sons Emerson and Walt Whitman, and Richelieu and Bismarck, many would strongly protest if it were suggested that there was something in common between first sons Einstein and Hitler, or between later sons Gandhi and Cesare Borgia. We have, indeed, suggested something of this sort—not with the purpose of degrading those worthy of respect, but with the aim of finding some very basic common denominators. An analogous situation exists in zoology. The common-sense view accepts easily the linkage of a perch, a salmon, and a shark as fish denizens of the water. But when the zoologist proposes the idea that a large water-dwelling whale has more in common with a little land-dwelling mouse than it has with a large water-dwelling shark, that the whale and the mouse both belong to the class Mammalia, then the common understanding is, at least initially, strained to the point of incredulity.

Another possible misassumption—which may still persist in spite of the author's efforts—is one referred to before; namely, that connectedness is better than disconnectedness, or vice versa. It should be acknowledged that the author began this investigation with certain intellectual opinions and prejudices in favor of the connectedness orientation. And the perceptive reader will have long ago recognized this enterprise as an example of wide synthesis, of connectedness. Thus, it is only fair to raise the question of how a connectedness-prone investigator of human nature can do justice to the disconnectedness side. Perhaps the author has not been as impartial as he would like to think; perhaps it is inevitable that some subjective bias has crept in. All that can be said is that after this long investigation the author feels he has arrived at the stage of intellectual impartiality. He has become greatly impressed by the type of thinking and action which may issue from a disconnectedness-prone person. He hopes the reader will dismiss as invalid any statements of the author which appear to deviate from intellectual impartiality.

The author's position in this matter may be better described by likening it to the position taken by Santayana in his assessments of Lucretius, Dante, and Goethe. Santayana is a later son but somewhat atypical in that, though he was the later son of his mother, he was the first son of his father, and experienced a highly connected nurturing from a much older half-sister. He shows both disconnectedness and connectedness features, with the predominance being to disconnectedness. His account of how the philosopher-poet has to rise to the vertical level above the flux and mutation on the horizontal level has abstract connectedness features. On the other hand, he classes himself and has been classed by others as being in descent from such materialistic philosophers as Democritus, Epicurus, and Lucretius. Furthermore, in his Introduction to *Three Philosophical Poets* he shows the familiar oral usefulness that we have seen in disconnectedness-prone later sons: "The sole advantage in possessing great works of literature lies in what they can help us to become. . . . It is this continual digestion of the substance supplied by the past that alone renders the insights of the past still potent in the present and for the future. . . . Regarded from this point of view, as substances to be digested, the poetic remains of Lucretius, Dante, and Goethe . . . afford rather a varied feast."[1]

How, it can be asked, is it possible for later son Santayana to be impartial toward first son Dante, the supernaturalist, and first son Goethe, the romanticist, when his deepest empathy is with Lucretius, the materialist? Yet Santayana does achieve an intellectual impartiality. He continues in the Introduction: "In their doctrine and genius they may seem to be too much opposed to be at all convergent or combinable in their wisdom. Some, who know and care for one, perhaps, of these poets, may be disposed to doubt whether they have anything vital to learn from the other two. . . . without any vagueness or doubleness in one's criterion of taste one may admire enthusiastically the poetry of each in turn; and that one may accept the essential philosophy, the positive intuition, of each, without lack of definition or system in one's own thinking."[2]

Finally, in his Conclusion, Santayana states: "It may be possible, after studying these three philosophical poets, to establish some comparison between them. By a comparison is not meant a discussion as to which of our poets is the best. Each is the best in his way, and none is the best in every way. To express a preference is not so much a criticism as a personal confession."[3] The intellectual position taken by Santayana is one to which the present author fully subscribes.

The remaining possible misassumptions can be dealt with briefly. (a) Though concerned almost exclusively with highly creative men, this investigation throws absolutely no light on why some men are creative and others are not. No assumptions are possible about the origin of creativity or the quantity of creativity. What has been pointed out is that, given a creative man, the direction of his creativeness may be explained on the basis of connectedness or disconnectedness. (b) There is no intention of creating a new theory of psychoanalysis. To point out that first son Freud would be attracted to the superego concept of inner moral authority and to sexuality, and that later son Adler would be attracted to the theory of inferiority and drive to power, was not done to detract from their intuitions but to understand the source of the intuition. Though not sharing Jung's particular views about the psyche, the author does share his view that Adler as well as Freud had valuable truths to offer about human nature. Furthermore, the author believes that the theoretical contributions contained in this book are in the mainstream of Freudian psychoanalysis—if not the current narrowed mainstream, surely in the mainstream of a half century ago when divergent views were more frequent and welcome. Thus the synthesis of the theories of Freud and Adler under a predominantly Freudian rubric need not be thought of as a building block for the formation of a new psychoanalytic theory. (c) Closely connected with the preceding is the question of innovation in psychotherapy. As noted earlier, this is not a study of clinical cases—rather it is an investigation of personality styles. It is not intended that the clinical methods be changed on the basis of what has been set forth here. What may be intended in this direction is that the additional diagnostic insights about the patient might aid the therapist in further individualizing his treatment.

Almost all the foregoing has been concerned with the restatement and clarification of the basic hypothesis. Only scant mention has been made of the several secondary hypotheses, any one of which may seem to the reader to be as significant and intriguing as the basic one. The author shares some of this feeling.

But because he ascribes to each of these hypotheses a lower order
of probability than he does to the basic hypothesis, he will not
offer a careful, systematic restatement of them.

The remainder of this chapter will be devoted to a partial
review of the secondary hypotheses and some speculations about
the current world situation. Toward this end, a fitting departure
point is provided by Alexis de Tocqueville and his *Democracy
in America*. In these troubled times, when we are trying to see
into the murky future, it may be profitable to consult again this
political theorist who was prophetic enough in the early nineteenth century to foresee that the United States and Russia would
emerge as rivals for world power. The discussion of Tocqueville
at this point is fitting also in terms of the chronology of this
book. For it was after the investigation had been completed and
all of the previous chapters written that the author read Tocqueville's two-volume work in its entirety. He was struck not only
by the astuteness of this political observer and theorist but also
by the close parallels between Tocqueville's theoretical deduc-
tions about aristocracy and democracy and the present author's
ideas about political connectedness and disconnectedness. It appeared that the same forces making for national character were
operative in the formation of individual character. For several
reasons, then, *Democracy in America* was uniquely attractive as
an initial text for the conclusion of this chapter.

Tocqueville, a later son, appears at first blush to be much
more an abstract thinker than, for example, first son James Bryce,
the other noted European observer of America. Granting this
difference, there is, however, suggestive evidence that Tocqueville, like the later sons, excels at a single-minded, programmatic
penetration of the part whereas Bryce, like other first sons, excels
at a complex, plural-minded approach. Commager's assessment
bears on the above. He writes: "Where Tocqueville sifted all his
evidence through the sieve of Democracy, rejecting all else as
dross, Bryce has no master-key to American development, but
gave equal consideration to environment, institutions, and mechanics. Tocqueville was interested in the American experiment
because he was sure that it prefigured European experience and
he wanted to guard against it. . . . But Bryce thought the United
States interesting in its own right . . . and he concluded dis-
passionately that 'the examination and appraisement of the insti-

tutions of the United States is no doubt full of instruction for Europe . . . but its chief value lies in what may be called the laws of political biology. . . .' "4

The two authors may be directly quoted in this matter. Tocqueville, in his Preface to Volume I of the twelfth edition of *Democracy in America*, writes that his "work was written fifteen years ago, with a mind constantly occupied by a single thought—that the advent of democracy as a governing power in the world's affairs, universal and irresistible, was at hand."5 Bryce, at the end of his Introductory to *Reflections on American Institutions*, writes: "I have attributed less to the influence of democracy than most of my predecessors have done. . . . Some one has said that the end of philosophy is to diminish the number of causes. . . . But it is an end not to be hastily pursued. A close analysis of social and political phenomena often shows us that causes are more complex than had at first appeared. . . ."6

We have dwelled briefly on the intellectual contrasts between Tocqueville and Bryce in order both to understand Tocqueville better and to restate certain points. Thus, Tocqueville displays the penetrating single-mindedness and the programmatic "what do we do with the knowledge" orientation we have seen in disconnectedness-prone later sons. In being programmatic, he is in a certain sense less abstract than Bryce who, as such connectedness-prone first sons as Newton, Montesquieu, and Freud, was searching for the basic (and somewhat deterministic) lawfulness beneath phenomena. The two men—later son and first son—again illustrate Santayana's remarks about comparative excellence: "Each is the best in his way, and none is the best in every way."

Tocqueville's *Democracy in America* was a pioneer effort, a "first" in political writing. John Stuart Mill called it, according to Phillips Bradley, "the first philosophical book ever written on Democracy as it manifest itself in modern society . . . M. de Tocqueville has endeavoured to ascertain and discriminate the various properties and tendencies of the Democracy . . . he has earned the double honor of being the first to make the attempt, and of having done more towards the success of it than probably will ever be done again by any one individual."7

The present author is of the opinion that it would take a disconnectedness-prone later son to be the first in this area.

When intellectual creativity calls for a rather complete break with past tradition, it is the disconnectedness-prone man of genius who comes forward. Thus, later sons Francis Bacon, Descartes, and Voltaire were the particular heralds of modern times—later sons Copernicus and Darwin dealt vigorous blows to the traditional concepts of the central position of the earth and of man—later-son scientists G. F. FitzGerald and William Rowan Hamilton were the spokesmen of the nondeterministic New World System. In Tocqueville's case, though he was an aristocrat and his family had suffered under the guillotine, he did not attempt to turn the clock back. He was not described, as many traditionalists have been, as having one of the finest minds of the previous century. In his appreciation of democracy or equality as the wave of the future he was thoroughly a modernist, in touch with the immediate present.

The disconnectedness-prone genius of Tocqueville may account for what is generally thought to be his one outstanding failure in prediction. Though he was much more often correct than incorrect—as witness the predicted emergence of the United States and Russia as two rival world powers—he did not expect that the federal system would be preserved. As Phillips Bradley writes: "He makes some shrewd observations on its operation, but does not altogether foresee the shifting balance of power between the states and the Federal government which was even then impending. He anticipated that the strength of the Federal government was likely to decrease, that of the state governments to increase."[8]

Commager writes: "It was not at all remarkable that a European observer, weighing all considerations in the balance of history, should conclude that the Union could not last and that democracy would become the tyranny of the majority, though it was perhaps a bit surprising that so perspicacious a critic as Tocqueville should have come to this conclusion."[9]

It has been pointed out that it is characteristic of the disconnectedness-prone to think in terms of separate components, in terms of discrete atoms rather than of interconnected molecules. In mathematics, the later-son's creativity was seen in the *discrete*, the first-son's in the *continuous*. Later son John Dalton's atomic theory is still another case in point. Politically, later sons Rousseau and Hobbes thought of society as being composed of colliding, self-interested, individual humans. And later son John C. Calhoun was the principal advocate of states' rights. In general, the disconnectedness idea is not in the direction of binding, abstract, contractual commitments. Tocqueville, then, would be expected to see the loosely connected, discrete, political atoms more easily than the strongly interrelated political molecule. And he does begin this study with Chapter 5 of Volume 1, entitled "Necessity of Examining the Condition of the States before that of the Union at Large," in which he writes: "In short, there are twenty-four small sovereign nations, whose agglomeration constitutes the body of the Union . . . the Federal government, . . . is the exception; the government of the states is the rule."[10]

Tocqueville goes even further in the atomistic approach by considering first and foremost the individual township, giving comparatively little attention even to the sovereign state government. His doubts about the strength of the Federal Union appear to stem from his feeling that the influence of the states is direct, real, immediately sensed, whereas the influence of the Union is abstract and thus weak. He says in Chapter 8: "The sovereignty of the Union is an abstract being, which is connected with but few external objects; the sovereignty of the states is perceptible by the senses, easily understood, and constantly active."[11] It does not appear that Tocqueville was swept along into this opinion by the opinions of other observers; rather it seemed to issue from his particular observational tendencies. For he wrote in Chapter 18: "Many people in France imagine that a change of opinion is going on in the United States which is favorable to a centralization of power in the hands of the President and the Congress. I hold that a contrary tendency may distinctly be observed. So far is the Federal government, as it grows old, from acquiring strength and from threatening the sovereignty of the states that I maintain it to be growing weaker and the sovereignty of the Union alone to be in danger."[12]

In tracing Tocqueville's predictive error to his disconnectedness tendency, the aim is not to detract from his great contribution, but rather to understand better what was possible and not possible for him to apprehend with his particular cognitive style. The probing, clear view of the operations of a single phenomenon—democracy—was explicitly appropriate to his cognitive style. Bryce, in evaluating Tocqueville, comments on his strong and penetrating intellect, and on the elegant precision of his reasoning. These are the characteristics of what Pascal called the precise intellect, the mind which penetrates to the part. Pascal's other type of intellect—the multipremised—which attempts to get a wide, interconnected bird's-eye view of the whole, is better illustrated by first son Bryce: "He who regards the wide land-scape from a distant height sees its details imperfectly, and must unfold his map in order to make out where each village lies. . . . But he catches the true perspective of things better than if he were standing among them."[13] If there is any object-lesson in this, it might be that the limitation as well as the strength of a cog-nitive style must be taken into account in evaluating the observa-tion and prognostication of a man—be he connectedness-prone or disconnectedness-prone.

So much, then, for Tocqueville's type of thinking. Of equal or greater pertinence to our hypothesis are his views on the origins, workings, and possible repercussions of democracy. In Chapter 3 of the same volume, "Social Condition of the Anglo-Americans," Tocqueville places unique emphasis on the sociolegal aspect of birth order, the law of primogeniture. He believes that the abolition of this law paved the way for democratic equality; that the breaking of the family inheritance into equal parts for the children rather than all of it going to the first son was nec-essary to establish social equality. The inheritance is no longer a family molecule, aristocratically preserved in time by the first son; it is reduced to equal, democratic atoms. As a result, the family connectedness suffers. It is no longer the closely-knit family intuited by first son Locke; it is more the collection of individuals intuited by later son Rousseau.

Tocqueville expresses it as follows:

But the law of inheritance was the last step to equality. I am surprised that ancient and modern jurists have not attributed to this law a greater influence on human affairs. It is true that these laws belong to civil affairs; but they ought, nevertheless, to be placed at the head of all political institutions; for they exercise an incredible influence upon the social state of a people, while political laws show only what this state already is. . . . When the legislator has once regulated the law of inheritance, he may rest from his labor. . . . When framed in a particular manner, this law unites, draws together, and vests prop-erty and power in a few hands; it causes an aristocracy, so to speak, to spring out of the ground. If formed on opposite principles, its action is still more rapid; it divides, distributes, and disperses both property and power. . . . But the law of equal division exercises its influence not merely upon the property itself, but it affects the minds of the heirs and brings their passions into play. These indirect consequences tend powerfully to the destruction of large fortunes, and especially of large domains.

Among nations whose law of descent is founded upon the right of primogeniture, landed estates often pass from generation to generation without undergoing division; the consequence of this is that family feeling is to a certain degree incorporated with the estate. The family represents the estate, the estate the family, whose name, together with its origin, its glory, its power, and its virtues, is thus perpetuated in an imperishable memorial of the past and as a sure pledge of the future.

When the equal partition of property is established by law, the intimate connection is destroyed between family feeling and the preservation of the paternal estate; the property ceases to represent the family; for, as it must inevitably be divided after one or two generations, it has evidently a constant tendency to diminish and must in the end be completely dispersed.[14]

Again, we must pause to point out that this kind of insight into the effects of property division is more possible for a later son like Tocqueville than for a first son. While the first son is more acutely sensitive to the trauma of being displaced, or of being deprived of the reward for his toil, the later son is keenly aggrieved if he senses an unequal distribution of goods and power. Thus later son Adler was more perceptive than first son Freud concerning the power inequities among siblings. And we have seen later son Melville's anguish that his mother bestowed more favor on his older brother than on him. Aristocratic involvement with the family tradition, with its glory, power, and virtues is more characteristic of the first son, and has been depicted in literature, among others by first son John Galsworthy in his *Forsyte Saga*, and by first son William Faulkner in the Sartoris family.

Let us return to Tocqueville's *Democracy in America*. His description of the alternative life orientations inherent in an aristocracy and in a democracy are almost identical with the alternatives seen in first son Carlyle and later son Emerson, and with the alternatives described by the present author in the chapter on "Conservers and Consumers." The aims of the connectedness-

prone first son are in the direction of glorious, heroic ennoblement; those of the disconnectedness-prone later sons in the direction of practicality and well being. Tocqueville writes:

We must first understand what is wanted of society and its government. Do you wish to give a certain elevation to the human mind
and teach it to regard the things of this world with generous feelings,
to inspire men with a scorn of mere temporal advantages . . . and
keep alive the spirit of honorable devotedness? Is it your object to
refine the habits, embellish the manners, and cultivate the arts, to promote the love of poetry, beauty, and glory? Would you constitute a
people fitted to act powerfully upon all other nations, and prepared
for those high enterprises which, whatever be their results, will leave
a name forever famous in history? If you believe such to be the
principle object of society, avoid the government of the democracy,
for it would not lead you with certainty to the goal.

But if you hold it expedient to divert the moral and intellectual
activity of man to the production of comfort and the promotion of
general well-being; if a clear understanding be more profitable to man
than genius; if your object is not to stimulate the virtues of heroism,
but the habits of peace . . . if, in short, you are of the opinion that
the principal object of a government is not to confer the greatest
possible power and glory upon the body of the nation, but to ensure
the greatest enjoyment and to avoid the most misery to each of the
individuals who compose it—if such be your desire, then equalize the
conditions of men and establish democratic institutions.[15]

Tocqueville likens (in Chapter I of the First Book of Volume 2, "Philosophical Method of the Americans,") the American
philosophical method to that of later son Descartes, whom we
have seen to be a single-minded stripper-away of complicating
traditions and nonessentials, who relied upon what was clearly
and strongly sensed by him as an individual. Tocqueville writes:

In most of the operations of the mind each American appeals only to
the individual effort of his own understanding. America is therefore
one of the countries where the precepts of Descartes are least studied
and are best applied. . . . In the midst of the continual movement that
agitates a democratic community, the tie that unites one generation to
another is relaxed or broken; every man there readily loses all trace
of the ideas of his forefathers or takes no care about them. . . . As it
is on their own testimony that they are accustomed to rely, they like
to discern the object which engages their attention with extreme
clearness; they therefore strip off as much as possible all that covers
it. . . . In the 17th century Bacon, in the natural sciences, and

Descartes, in philosophy, properly so called abolished received formulas, destroyed the empire of tradition. . . .[16]

Another close parallel between Tocqueville's ideas and those of the present author may be seen in Tocqueville's Chapter 10 of the same Book. We shall not be confined to the specific point indicated in this chapter, "Why the Americans are More Addicted to Practical than to Theoretical Science." For our purposes, a better title would be "Scientific tendencies issuing from equalitarian disconnectedness," and we shall use this opportunity to enlarge on matters insufficiently discussed previously.

The later-son distrust of conclusions which are not reached by a clear, vivid sensory experience has been noted in Bacon, Descarte, and Hume. Tocqueville writes:

Those who cultivate the sciences among a democratic people are always afraid of losing their way in visionary speculation. They mistrust systems; they adhere closely to facts and study facts with their own senses. . . .

In America the purely practical part of science is admirably understood, and careful attention is paid to the theoretical portion which is immediately requisite to application. On this head the Americans always display a clear, free, original, and inventive power of mind. But hardly anyone in the United States devotes himself to the essentially theoretical and abstract portion of human knowledge. . . . A desire to utilize knowledge is one thing; the pure desire to know is another. . . .[17]

In explaining the divergency in scientific attitudes, Tocqueville calls attention to heroic conserving and the militant consuming orientations which we had noted in first and later sons. "In aristocratic societies the class that gives the tone to opinion and has the guidance of affairs, being permanently and hereditarily placed above the multitude, naturally conceives a lofty idea of itself and of man. . . . In aristocratic ages vast ideas are commonly entertained of the dignity, the power, and the greatness of man. These opinions exert their influence on those who cultivate the sciences as well as on the rest of the community. . . ."

"Men of science at such periods are consequently carried away towards theory; and it even happens that they frequently conceive an inconsiderate contempt for practice." On the other hand, Tocqueville sees in democratic states that: "The greater part of the men who constitute these nations are extremely eager in the pursuit of actual and physical gratification. As they are always dissatisfied with the position that they occupy and are always free to leave it, they think of nothing but the means of changing their fortune or increasing it. To minds thus predisposed, every new method that leads by a shorter road to wealth, every machine that spares labor . . . every discovery that facilitates pleasures or augments them, seems to be the grandest effort of the human intellect. . . . In aristocratic ages science is more particularly called upon to furnish gratification to the mind; in democracies, to the body."[18]

Our own data, of course, do not bear on national climates as a determinant of scientific attitudes. But the data on family climates affecting first and later sons strongly support certain of Tocqueville's ideas. A proclivity for ingenious or practical inventiveness appears to be more frequent in later sons than in first sons—regardless of the country of origin. Later sons of this type include Alfred Nobel, Guglielmo Marconi, Nikola Tesla, Benjamin Franklin, Alexander Graham Bell, the Wright Brothers, John Ericsson, and Irving Langmuir. It is noteworthy that the largest industrial organization devoted to the applied knowledge of electricity, the General Electric Corporation, was formed by the merger of two companies founded by the combined inventive genius of two later sons, Thomas A. Edison and Elihu Thomson. The number of first sons of this type is much smaller and, for the moment, seems to be limited to S. B. Morse, George Eastman, and Lee De Forest. What needs to be mentioned to offset Tocqueville's general statement about practicality is that disconnectedness-prone later sons are also theorists—but of a type different from connectedness-prone first sons: their theories are based on the discrete rather than on the continuous.

Further reference to Tocqueville has to be limited, for reasons of space, to a summary mention of one issue. Regarding our findings that first sons are drawn to poetry of the epic, heroic variety, and later sons to nature poetry, Tocqueville states:

"Aristocracy naturally leads the human mind to the contemplation of the past and fixes it there. Democracy, on the contrary, gives men a sort of instinctive distaste for what is ancient. In this respect aristocracy is far more favorable to poetry; for things commonly grow larger and more obscure as they are more remote, and for this twofold reason they are better suited to the delineation of the ideal. . . . When skepticism had depopulated heaven, and the progress of equality had reduced each individual to smaller and better-known proportions, the poets, not yet aware of what they could substitute for the great themes that were departing together with the aristocracy, turned their eyes to inanimate nature. As they lost sight of gods and heroes, they set themselves to describe streams and mountains."[19]

Hopefully, our discussion of Tocqueville has served to review many of the secondary hypotheses and to indicate close parallels between the genesis of national character and the genesis of individual character. Tocqueville is, of course, calling attention to the weighty and pervasive influence of a general, sociopolitical climate. Though we are in agreement about many of the reasons behind the influence, we cannot concur that the social climate by itself will be weighty. For, as previously indicated, aristocratic first sons are continually being produced whether the age of the nation is aristocratic or democratic—and similarly with democratic later sons. The social climate has been the usual reference point in explaining the differences between Carlyle and Emerson; Carlyle living in an aristocratic nation, Emerson in a democratic one. This author has added to this explanation by emphasizing that Carlyle is aristocratic due to a first-son connectedness, Emerson democratic because of a later-son disconnectedness.

From what Tocqueville observed, the United States could be designated as a later-son disconnectedness-prone society. While this may be the most striking social characteristic, is it a characteristic which is to be found in the majority of individuals comprising the society? Tocqueville cannot be used to answer this question, inasmuch as he rarely gave an illustration of the thinking of an eminent American. This author is tempted to conclude that the actual Americans who gave European observers this impression were disconnectedness-prone later sons.

Bearing on this point is Bryce's considering that later son Emerson was more characteristically American than first son Hawthorne (in spite of the fact that both were influenced at the same time by the same New England social climate). Bryce wrote: "American imagination has produced nothing more conspicuously original than the romances of Hawthorne. If any one says that he finds something in them which he remember in no previous English writer, we know what is meant and probably agree. But can it be said that there is anything distinctively American in Hawthorne, that is to say, that his specific quality is of a kind that reappears in other American writers? Few will affirm this. The most peculiar, and therefore I suppose the most characteristically American school of thought, has been what used to be called the Concord or Transcendental school of forty years ago; among the writings produced by which those of Emerson are best known in Europe."²⁰ And it should be mentioned in this connection that the American President whom Tocqueville encountered was Andrew Jackson, the first later-son President.

These considerations suggest that, if it helps a person not to be out of joint with his times, the disconnectedness-prone later sons in the United States enjoy more support from the disconnectedness social-intellectual climate than do the connectedness-prone first sons, and whatever supportive advantages accrue from being known by fellow Americans as being typically and familiarly American, this advantage is possessed by later son Emerson and not by first son Hawthorne; by later-son scientist Benjamin Franklin and not by first-son scientist Willard Gibbs; by later-son poet Walt Whitman and not by first-son poet Robert Frost.

To many first sons this disadvantage may be only a mild one, to others the disinheritance may give sufficient anguish that they may feel as Friedrich Hölderlin did—"Why be a poet at all in these times"²¹—or sufficient bitterness that they may be bent on some world destruction. These remarks are not intended to elicit pity for the disinherited first sons. They have had their golden age and now it is the others' turn. The remarks are intended to elicit concern for the situation because the first-son contributions are vital for the world, and there is no guarantee that the first son will behave like dispossessed first son Esau; he might behave like Cain.

With this background we can move to the present and consider, first of all, the late President of the United States, later son John F. Kennedy. He is selected not only because he was the leader of one of the world's great powers, but also because his personality characteristics have been sufficiently in view that we can use them to test our hypotheses. The question is: Is John F. Kennedy more classifiable as a militant than as a heroic man of action? As a single-minded rather than plural-minded? As practical rather than theoretical? As democratic rather than aristocratic?

According to our hypothesis, his birth order would lead us to answer in the affirmative to the former rather than to the latter of these choices. The following brief discussion will indicate that, in the main, this expectation is borne out.

For the hypothesis it may be said that during the presidential campaign many observers felt that later son John F. Kennedy and later son Richard Nixon were much alike in their cool aggressivity. Kennedy's campaign could be characterized as a militant, single-minded effort which used power skillfully and exploited to the full any weakness his opponent showed (the personality characteristics of the even later-born son Robert Kennedy are quite pertinent here). The same use of power, together with a decided hint of antibigness motivation, was seen later in the handling of the situation with U.S. Steel Corporation. Kennedy's manner in speechmaking was not the dramatic, excitement-arousing kind possessed by first sons F. D. Roosevelt, Hitler, Churchill, and Mussolini. His rather clipped, terse, matter-of-fact, almost monolevel speech had its effect by revealing the inner conviction of the speaker—reminiscent of those produced by later son Lenin. During the early months of John F. Kennedy's administration many observers commented on the practical, *ad hoc* atmosphere. And for some time he was thought of as a man of activity rather than a man of action.

There are certain offsetting features which seemingly go against the hypothesis. We are not referring here to John F. Kennedy's keen intellectual interests which, though quite different from those of later sons Richard Nixon and Dwight D. Eisenhower, were not atypical for later sons. His cognitive style seemed to be of the penetrating, probing kind, and he has been described as employing the Cartesian method of systematic doubt. The offsetting features we are referring to are a possible heroic component as seen in the *Profiles in Courage* and his orientation to history. There would be considerable difficulty in proving conclusively that the late President showed more features of disconnectedness than of connectedness in these areas. The following will indicate what suggests to the present author that this is the case.

The impression is gained that John F. Kennedy was more

interested in the practical usefulness of heroic examples and of
the past than in heroism and in the past per se. That heroic examples can be used as identification models we have learned not
only from later son Emerson but also from later son Santayana,
who were quoted earlier in this chapter regarding the philosophical poets: "The sole advantage in possessing great works of
literature lies in what they can help us to become." This practical, useful attitude came through most vividly in the small part
President Kennedy played in Mrs. Jacqueline Kennedy's tele-
vised tour of the White House. There could be seen the contrast
between the first born Jacqueline Bouvier Kennedy's fascinated
absorption in the past as a thing in itself without a lesson learned
thereby, and later son John F. Kennedy's matter-of-fact attitude
which consisted, in essence, of saying that the study of the past
is useful because it informs us that this nation has weathered
previous crises and will most likely weather this one.

Kennedy's essential disconnection from the past is evidenced
also in the political changes following his assassination. Before
his death, the United States was expecting a 1964 presidential
campaign in which the country could choose between a past-
minded candidate, Goldwater, and a present-minded one, Kennedy. First son Barry Goldwater's attachment to what used to
be is striking enough that it is easily caricatured. In its essential
conservatism, however, it is much like that of first son Senators
Taft and Byrd. Goldwater wished to offer the voters a contrast
between himself and later son Kennedy in the Democratic Party
(and later son Rockefeller in the Republican Party). But the
assassination and the elevation to the Presidency of Lyndon
Johnson have blurred the picture. First son President Johnson,
with an old-fashioned respect for property rights and the profit
motive (a la first sons John Locke and Thomas Jefferson), has
succeeded while endorsing liberal measures in drawing conservative support away from the conservative first son Goldwater.
Johnson then is not the polar opposite to past-minded Goldwater
that present-minded Kennedy would have been.

A question can be asked as to whether a man with other
personality characteristics—say those of connectedness—could
have been elected President in 1960. The naval historian, Admiral
Samuel Eliot Morison, suggested recently that the late President's
deceased older brother, Joseph, could have been elected had he

lived, or that he would have made an equally good President. This author would like to present now some inferential evidence indicating that, despite all the backing, vigor, and power of the strongly connected Kennedy family, and despite the qualifications of their first son, it would have been unlikely for the connectedness-prone first son to be elected to the presidency.

First, it should be mentioned that the 1960 presidential campaign was the *first* in the twentieth century in which both candidates were later sons. There were in this century many first-son–later-son contests, and at least four first son–first son contests (Taft-Roosevelt, Wilson-Hughes, Coolidge-Davis, and Truman-Dewey). Perhaps all this should be attributed to mere coincidence. But there is also the possibility that this is a sign of the times. We recall that the basic democratic movement encompassing the masses rather than just the individual landowners was not accomplished under the first son Presidents (Washington, Adams, Jefferson, Madison, Monroe, and Adams) but under the seventh President (later son Andrew Jackson). And Jackson was followed by three consecutive later-son Presidents.

Further suggesting that the times may call for a particular kind of personality is the recent first son-later son distribution among leaders of the great powers. At one time during this writing, the leaders in the Western World were almost exclusively later sons (Kennedy, Macmillan, DeGaulle, Adenauer, Khrushchev). This was not the case during World War II, when first sons F. D. Roosevelt, Churchill, Hitler, and Mussolini were in power.

This author's belief is that the Western World is frightened by the atomic bomb and wishes to repose leadership in those men who are guided by practical survival motivations, rather than by idealistic, heroic ones. The Western World has rejected the aristocratic alternative mentioned by Tocqueville ("Would you constitute a people fitted to act powerfully upon all other nations, and prepared for those high enterprises which, whatever be their results, will leave a name forever famous in history?"). The results of the atomic bomb are too costly a price to pay for a name forever famous in history. The Western World has chosen, instead, Tocqueville's democratic alternative (". . . if your object is not to stimulate the virtues of heroism, but the habits of peace . . ."). Understandably, it would recoil from the destruc-

tive heroics of a Hitler or a Mussolini. But it even draws back
from the last-ditch heroics of a Churchill, and is only faintly
attracted by the idealistic loftiness of an Adlai Stevenson.

What we have said about the Western World does not seem
to apply to the East. There the principal leaders are first sons
Mao Tse-tung and Jawaharlal Nehru in the Far East, and Nasser
in the Near East. Let us dwell for a while on Mao Tse-tung, the
leader of the most populous nation in the world and the philosopher of the type of Communism which contends, or may con-
tend, with Soviet Communism. There is, first, an obvious
intellectual contrast between Mao and later son Khrushchev, his
Soviet opposite number. Mao Tse-tung was steeped in books from
early boyhood and later became a teacher—Khrushchev was an
indifferent student, whose older brother had been a teacher. The
revolutionary impetus also seems different in the two men. With
Mao Tse-tung, family poverty could not have been the stimulant,
inasmuch as his father was a rich peasant. He seems to have been
led into the movement by certain intellectual convictions, similar
to those which prompted first son Karl Marx. Khruschev's family, however, was quite poor and the resulting inferiority may
be what led him into such ferocious dispossessing attacks on the
rich kulaks that he was censured by the party early in his career.
It is of interest that Mao Tse-tung never engaged in similar leveling attacks on the Chinese kulaks. While this may be mainly due
to the peculiarity of Chinese economics—the dependence on
agriculture rather than on industrialism—some of it may be accounted for by the first son's tendency to believe in a man's right
to the fruits of his toil.

Going into more detail about Mao Tse-tung, we find that
books and thoughts rather than real events have played a pre-
dominant role in his life. He had to fight his father in order to
attend school; after resigning from the Army he, according
to Anne Fremantle (who drew on Edgar Snow's biography of
Mao), "spent the next six months reading by himself in the
Hunan Provincial Library. Daily, from the moment it opened
until closing time, Mao would devour books 'like an ox loosed
in a vegetable garden.' "[22] That Mao Tse-tung became a Communist through his readings and reflections rather than through
actual poverty is indicated by the following passage from Anne
Fremantle's *Mao Tse-tung: An Anthology of His Writings*. She

says in her Introduction: "It was during the winter of 1920-21 that Mao read *The Communist Manifesto*, translated into Chinese by Chen Wang-tao. This was the first Marxist book ever to be published in China. By the spring of 1921, Mao considered himself a Marxist."[23]

While first son Mao Tse-tung certainly had read later son Lenin's manuals on revolutionary tactics and had been exposed to Lenin's doctrine that anything goes, that every means, fair or foul, must be employed to win the end, he did not fully absorb this doctrine. Instead, on and after the Long March he insisted that the soldiers observe some chivalric, Marquis of Queensberry rules of conduct. Anne Fremantle writes: "He enforced three rules on all Red soldiers: prompt obedience to every order; no confiscation from peasants; prompt delivery to headquarters of all goods confiscated from landlords. To these three were added the Eight Points, which still have to be memorized by every Red soldier, and repeated daily, as well as being frequently sung as a Red Army song."[24] (Some of the Eight Points are: Be courteous and help out when you can. Return all borrowed articles. Pay for all articles purchased.) And Mao takes pride in his assertion that the Reds had never killed a prisoner of war in their twelve years of war with Japan. As for the disloyal Chinese, these, he said, when captured were re-educated and liberated. If caught again, the process started a second time and, if necessary, a third time.

It is of more than academic interest to know which of Tocqueville's alternatives Mao would select. The foregoing description and his being a first son would lead us to expect that he would choose the heroic-aristocratic over the democratic alternative. The expectation that he would like to leave a name forever famous in history appears to be borne out. For Mao Tse-tung himself wrote of the Long March:

"Speaking of the Long March, I should like to ask, 'What is its significance?' We say that the Long March is the first of its kind ever recorded in history. . . . Since P'an Ku divided heaven from earth and the Three Sovereigns and Five Emperors reigned, has there ever been in history a long march like ours? For twelve months we were under daily reconnaissance and bombing from the air by scores of planes. . . . The Long March is also a manifesto. It proclaims to the world that the Red Army is an army of heroes."[25]

The heroic theme, against odds, is almost identical with first son Churchill's "we will fight on the beaches . . ." and "never have so many owed so much to so few. . . ."

Since creating a name famous in history may involve the customary method of attaining national fame—namely war—the crucial question is how war-minded Mao is. The burden of evidence points to his being more warlike than devoted to the habits of peace; that he is not only not averse to a righteous, heroic war but also psychologically receptive to it. In his *Strategic Problems of China's Revolutionary War*, Mao says: "War, this monster of mutual slaughter among mankind, will be finally eliminated through the progress of human society. . . . But there is only one way of eliminating it, namely, to oppose war by means of war . . . and to oppose counter-revolutionary class war by means of revolutionary class war. There are only two kinds of wars in history, just and unjust. We support just wars and oppose unjust wars. . . . A war which will be waged by the overwhelming majority of mankind and of the Chinese people will undoubtedly be a just war—it will be incomparably the most honourable undertaking for saving mankind and China, and will form a bridge leading world history into a new era."[26]

We see here that Mao, in a fashion typical of some first sons, does not restrict himself to his part of the world, China, but rather aims at a broader area, mankind. In this he differs sharply from later sons DeGaulle and Adenauer who are first and foremost, respectively, for France and for Germany. In this broad, grand objective he differs also from later son Khrushchev who is prepared to accept peaceful coexistence in order to preserve the Soviet Union. To Mao, peaceful coexistence would appear to be an unrighteous, *ad hoc* betrayal of principle.

We are not attempting to predict whether Mao would actually risk a nuclear war in order to maintain his theoretical principles. Rather, we are suggesting that his heroic-idealistic tendency makes him a personality type who would not shrink from a "just" war, a war that would preserve the world for Communism. In this tendency he is not much different from first sons Woodrow Wilson and Abraham Lincoln. It was the latter's determination to preserve the Union which involved the United States in a bloody, fratricidal war. Mao may have become more conservative as he has grown older, but the seeds of aggressive heroism were distinctly present not too long ago. Even if we discount as adolescent exuberance a diary entry,

> To struggle against Heaven, what joy!
> To struggle against Earth, what joy![27]

and a poem which reads in part:

> I opened the casement of a solitary tower
> And inquired: Who, on the immense planet
> Decides the fate of creatures? . . .[28]

we have to consider seriously the undertones in his best-known poem "The Snow," written in 1945. The theme is heroic, romantically sexualized, and harks back to the times of the medieval tournament where men fought for a lady's favor, to the rivalry which was smiled away by later son Cervantes, and whose essence is quite foreign to the recent leaders of the Western world, John F. Kennedy, Macmillan, Adenauer, De Gaulle, and Khrushchev. The poem reads in part:

The earth is so charming,
Like a red-faced girl clothed in white.
Such is the charm of these rivers and mountains,
Calling innumerable heroes to vie with each other in pursuing her.[29]

The conclusion seems inescapable that Mao would be inclined to choose Tocqueville's aristocratic alternative, which requires now a partial requoting from his first volume: "Do you wish to give a certain elevation to the human mind . . . to inspire men with a scorn of mere temporal advantages. . . . Is it your object . . . to promote the love of poetry, beauty, and glory? Would you constitute a people fitted to act powerfully upon all other nations, and prepared for those high enterprises which, whatever be their results, will leave a name forever famous in history?"

If the leadership is reflective of national psychology, it would appear that the East is more prepared for "those high enterprises" than is the West. Why there is this difference is not clear. One may speculate that the inwardness and traditionalism of the Indian and the Chinese peoples—together with their fatalistic attitude toward death—make a nuclear holocaust a less unnerving prospect than it is to the Western peoples. The realization has not come home to the East as it has to the West that Man may have finally overreached himself. Whatever the basic reasons are for this difference, the fact remains that first sons Mao Tse-tung and Jawaharlal Nehru are personality types not readily found among the recent national leaders of the West.

These later-son Western leaders have, in this author's opinion, been selected by their peoples because they are highly sensitive to the concrete realities of the situation rather than to the abstract reality—because they are militantly rather than heroically aggressive—because they follow later son Descartes' maxim which consists of avoiding the extreme position so that, if one is wrong, one will not be totally wrong. While this maxim affords little opportunity of being totally right, the nuclear age does not require total rightness. It is quite sufficient if the national leaders are not totally wrong. What has been said does not imply that the leader who would be the first to give the order to drop the bomb would most likely be a heroically minded first son. While he may order it for reasons which appear idealistic and overly zealous, the militant later son might be inclined to order it if he detected any weakness in the enemy. (Later son MacArthur is a case in point.)

Thus it is just as possible, if not probable, that nuclear warfare could be started by an irrationally heroic first son like Bakunin or Hitler as by a coolly and rationally militant leader later son like Napoleon.

It may seem that the author is suggesting that the best interests of mankind during the nuclear crisis are served by having the leadership in the hands of the more practical later sons, and that everyone could breathe more easily once the East followed the example of the West. Only in part would this be a fair assumption. While it may be true that later sons with their single-mindedness may be better equipped to find the way out of the Cartesian forest in which we seem to be lost, there is another side to the coin. The connectedness-prone first sons tend to be more deeply committed to the preservation and continuation of those traditional values which to many are not mere anachronisms but, rather, represent the sublime, noble essence and achievements of the human race. On this aristocratic view, Homo sapiens is not just one of the many animal species who come on and off the stage of the evolutionary process. On the contrary, he is God's chosen species, closer to God than to the beast—and as such is decidedly worth preserving as he is and as he has become. Later sons do not typically share this view. For Copernicus, Earth was not God's chosen planet; for Darwin, Man was not God's chosen species. And we have also seen the contrast between later son Emerson's cool appraisal of Man and first son Carlyle's intense admiration of him.

It is this intense commitment of first sons to the somewhat abstract and elevated notion of Man which is the counterbalancing feature. The labor and energy they will expend in behalf of this concept should not be underestimated. To the "blood, toil, tears, and sweat" of first son Churchill, first son Faulkner in his Nobel prize acceptance speech has added "agony" as another sacrificial ingredient necessary that man will not only endure but also prevail. This commitment to the preservation of Man acts, then, to offset somewhat the heroic aggressiveness that first sons tend to employ toward this end. They cannot easily damage that which they love. Furthermore, their particular commitment increases the chances that, when and if Man survives the nuclear crisis, Man will be quite recognizable as a continuation of his previous self; he will have preserved his acculturation, his time-accumulated identity. We have seen how during the hectic days of the Long March and the Revolutionary Wars Mao Tse-tung had the inclination, time, and energy to insist on the soldiers' memorizing the Eight Points. An American counterpart may be seen in first son General Maxwell Taylor's emphasizing, during his tenure as Commandant of West Point, the necessity of classical education. These are not single-minded efforts to win the war—they are plural-minded efforts, directed toward the peace after the war.

This analysis of the world crisis should not be thought of as an attempt at a speculative prediction. Rather it is an examination of the value issues inherent in the situation. For many people, the issues are not debatable. For some, the Scylla of mass survival without preservation of traditional values is much less frightening than the Charybdis of survival of comparatively few who will carry on the torch of civilization as we have known it—a few who might say in dedicated inspiration as Lincoln did at Gettysburg that these honored dead have not died in vain. For others,

the Charybdis is decidedly less threatening than the Scylla. But
for those who occupy the middle position the choice is not easy.
And, understandably, they hope that some sort of compromise
can be reached—not the usual one as between butter and cannon,
but as between butter and traditional values—between consuming
and conserving.

It is hoped that what has been suggested concerning the
birth orders of these leaders will not be taken too literally. The
reader is reminded (no doubt unnecessarily) that birth order is
but a crude indicator of basic connectedness and disconnectedness. Particular first sons and later sons may be almost indistin-
guishable in their conduct and policies as national leaders. The
author has attempted to account for group trends—the difference
between national leader birth order in World War II and that
of the present, and the difference between the national leader
birth order of the West and that of the East. The excursion into
the present world crisis was not done for the purposes of testing
the basic hypothesis but rather in the hope that some speculative
analysis might contribute additional insights into the personality
styles of those national leaders upon whom the fate of the civilized world may depend.

The time has come for a final summing up—hopefully, in a
few additional paragraphs the author can convey to the reader
what he regards as the gist of this long communication. He has
already stated that he is strongly persuaded by the totality of
evidence that there is a good probability that the basic hypothesis
is true, i.e., that differences in the intensity of parental nurturing
do indeed accentuate inherent tendencies toward connectedness
and disconnectedness. These two terms, elusive of exact definition, are approximately described as a tendency to relate one
thing to another (connectedness), and a tendency to consider a
thing by itself, apart from context and relations (disconnectedness). The greater the parental involvement with the child (as
frequently occurs in children who are the first-born, or first-born
of a sex), the more the accentuation of the tendency toward connectedness. The lesser the parental involvement (as frequently
occurs in children who are not the first-born, or first-born of a
sex) the more accentuation of the tendency toward disconnectedness. From these two basic tendencies springs a variety of
phenomena in the areas of thinking, feeling, and acting.

Most of the evidence for the hypothesis has been gathered not from controlled experimental investigation but rather from experiments in nature, from the creative thoughts and actions of a large number of first sons and later sons whose talent or genius has made them pre-eminent in Western civilization. The advantages of this kind of evidence are that one gains access to an atypical but extremely important sample of men (access not possible if there is exclusive resort to normal, average samples), and that one can better appreciate certain subtleties and nuances which are not always reducible to the proportions necessary for controlled experimentation. The disadvantage of this type of evidence clearly resides in its imprecision. The imprecision is enhanced when an attempt has been made here to investigate not just a few but many men and in many fields of endeavor. The author, in pursuing the task to completion, has felt that the advantages outweigh the disadvantages. Moreover, he feels that certain safeguards have been provided against imprecision. Not only have numerous caveats been extended to the reader concerning the author's restricted expertise and scholarship in matters outside his particular scope, but also—and more important—the evidence is quite public in nature. Thus, there are no obstacles to the detection of error.

There is a related consideration which comes much closer to the heart of this book. It revolves around the question of how one knows he is speaking the truth about human nature. In the introductory chapter, a statement was made to the effect that a psychological theory of types automatically includes the investigator of human nature. Because he is a certain type, the microscope he uses is not wholly objective, but rather slanted in the direction of his subjective bias or his cognitive style. However successful this author may have been in appreciably reducing his subjective bias, he doubts very much that his cognitive style has undergone any change. The book in its wide, interrelating scope is a characteristic example of a connectedness-prone cognitive style; human nature has been reviewed with this kind of microscope.

How, then, does one square this with speaking the truth? The author has done the squaring by thinking of the impossible task asked of a witness who takes the oath to tell the truth, the whole truth, and nothing but the truth. The task appears impossible for the reason that one cognitive style—connectedness-prone—is better at telling the whole truth; the other cognitive style—disconnectedness-prone—is better at telling nothing but the truth. The author has resolved the dilemma for himself by trusting that his attempt to tell the whole truth will be complemented by the attempts of others to tell nothing but the truth.

If the book offers any practical conclusion it would reside in this implied division of labor and style. Repeatedly the author has been impressed by the fact that particular insights into human nature and particular truths about reality may issue forth only from a particular type of intellect: That what may be possible for a disconnectedness-prone mind to see and develop may be impossible for a connectedness-prone mind, and vice versa. However desirable it would be to have a mind equally and powerfully discerning in both directions, the evidence suggests that this is an unrealizable hope. Santayana voices a similar opinion in the Conclusion of his essay on Lucretius, Dante, and Goethe by stating: "Who shall be the poet of this double insight? He has never existed, but he is needed nevertheless. It is time some genius should appear to reconstitute the shattered picture of the world. . . . We may hail this needed genius from afar. . . . But this supreme poet is in limbo still."[30]

The picture that emerges is that the potentiality of mankind for double insightedness will depend not on the one supreme poet or genius, but rather on the coordination of particular single insights. It should be emphasized that by coordination is meant a later fusion of two different views and not such an early, premature fusion that there is no real substance and sturdiness to the separate views. An analogy to this may be seen in the functions of the eye. Two slightly different images of the external world are perceived by the right and left eyes; the coordination of these retinal images takes place in the brain. Only by means of this binocular vision are we able to perceive depth, to have a three-dimensional perception of reality.

It seems necessary for the attainment of full-dimensional truth that there be a coordination of the connectedness and disconnectedness insights. As long as first and later sons are born into the world, we shall have a bountiful supply of connectedness-prone and disconnectedness-prone individuals. The coordination, however, is quite a different matter. We have already ruled out the possibility of a perfect coordination taking place in one person. Even if it were possible, it might be fatal to genius to insist on rounding off its jagged predilections so that a well-balanced Golden Mean results.

The solution would seem to be in the direction of individuals preserving their psychological styles and pronenesses, and at the same time being intellectually aware of matters beyond their psychological scope. While this kind of detachment is not possible for everyone, it is possible (and almost mandatory) for the leaders of the peoples, whether they be in politics or in science. It *was* possible for Santayana, who said one could enjoy the three poets without any doubleness in one's criteria of taste. If it is objected to that such impartiality is only possible for a contemplative philosopher, let us consider Holmes and Nobel. We have already seen how first son Justice Holmes, despite a strong aristocratic bent, allowed himself to be educated by later-son Justices into an intellectual awareness of the social needs of the underprivileged, an awareness which influenced his decisions. With later son Alfred Nobel, whose practical inventive talent produced high explosives, we find not simply an intellectual impartiality toward the dreamy, speculative, creative men, but an actual solicitude, concretely expressed in Nobel prizes.

It is feasible, then, to think of the double insights issuing from a more or less objective communication between men who are subjectively predisposed to their separate and single insights. As the examples illustrate, it does not go against human nature for a man to rise above his bias or even his principles and to consider viewpoints which are not natural for him. If minds are not immediately changed in the process, at least windows are opened. For a fruitful communication to take place it is imperative that there be sturdy, vigorous communicants. If we liken the situation to a two-party system, either party—be it the connectedness-prone or the disconnectedness-prone—when out of power must act energetically to preserve its own identity against the potentially suffocating influence of the other. When in power, each party must realize intellectually, if not emotionally, that its own absolute power would not only corrupt absolutely, it would cripple by limiting mankind to one-eyed vision. Being a Cyclops is only slightly less bad than being eyeless in Gaza. Each party needs some area in the general political-social-intellectual atmos-

phere in which it can breathe and flourish. An oversupply of a
particular psychological oxygen is not necessary. Indeed, an oversupply might block an opportunity to enjoy some of adversity's
sweet uses. But a severely protracted undersupply would de-
vitalize one of the communicants in this fruitful dialogue, and
deprive mankind of the rewards of a division of labor and style.

What, it may be asked, would motivate men away from a
partisan attitude toward a coordinated, bipartisan one? Certainly
a common danger, such as nuclear warfare, would motivate many
men in this direction. For others, the good will necessary to par-
take in the dialogue requires that their basic needs be first gratified. For still others, the idealistic good will is already a fixed
part of their personalities and requires little reinforcement. Whatever the motivation might be, the consequent dialogue would
have to be meaningful and intelligible. Certainly this requirement
—that Man ultimately behave like Homo sapiens—is not beyond
his biological scope. Though the thinking component of Man
has recently been obscured by his feeling and acting components,
it is still present in reserve. Because it is most powerful when
fully informed, there should be no relaxation in educational
efforts to open up the minds of men.

The reconstitution of Santayana's shattered picture of the
world may depend on something over and above good will and
the use of the intellect. It may depend on an all-embracing
religious concept which integrates the various aspects of the
world. Until recent times, the Fatherhood of God served as such
a concept for the vast majority of people. At present it still
functions in this way for a considerable number. But there are
many others who, for emotional or intellectual reasons, cannot
be nourished by this concept. They, believing that Man's destiny
is in his own hands, incline toward a different integrating concept: that of the Brotherhood of Man. This concept, though
closer to reality, is not free from wishful thinking. The inevitable
connotation is positive, and one thinks of the fraternal affection
existing between David and Jonathan or between Damon and
Pythias, who were *not* actual brothers, rather than of fraternal
rivalry existing between Cain and Abel and Esau and Jacob, who
were actual brothers.

The advantage of the Brotherhood of Man concept resides,
however, in the fact that the wishful thinking about what

brothers are like and how they feel toward each other can be remedied by actual investigation. The long inquiry here regarding first and later sons—or, to put it somewhat differently, elder and younger brothers—is, hopefully, a contribution in this direction. In any event, the ways and purposes of Man need not be as inscrutable as those of God. For those who cannot have unquestioning faith in Man's ability to endure or prevail as a species there is always, through the proper study of mankind, the opportunity to evaluate and to improve his chances.

References

CHAPTER I

1. Emile Durkheim, *Montesquieu and Rousseau: Forerunners of Sociology* (Ann Arbor: University of Michigan Press, 1960), p. 127.

2. Jean Piaget, *Judgment and Reasoning in the Child*, trans. Marjorie Warden (New York: Harcourt, Brace & World, 1928), p. 230.

3. *Ibid.*, p. 232.

4. *Ibid.*, p. 221.

5. Jean Piaget, *The Language and Thought of the Child*, trans. Majorie Gabian (New York: Meridian Books, 1955), p. 50. Originally published by Humanities Press, 3rd edition revised, 1959.

6. *Ibid.*, p. 52.

7. Irving D. Harris, *Emotional Blocks to Learning* (New York: The Free Press of Glencoe, 1961), pp. 178–81.

7a. Ernest Jones, *The Life and Work of Sigmund Freud*, Vol. I (New York: Basic Books, Inc., 1953), pp. 13–14.

8. Harris, *op. cit.*, p. 185.

9. Saxe Commins and Robert N. Linscott, eds., *Man and the Spirit: The Speculative Philosophers* (New York: The Modern Library, 1947), p. 209.

10. *Ibid.*

11. *Ibid.*, pp. 202–204.

12. E. T. Bell, *Men of Mathematics* (New York: Simon and Schuster, 1937), p. 13.

13. Saxe Commins and Robert N. Linscott, eds., *Man and the Universe: The Philosophers of Science* (New York: The Modern Library, 1947), p. 92.

14. Thomas Carlyle, *On Heroes and Hero-Worship*, and Ralph Waldo Emerson, *Representative Men* (New York: Doubleday & Company, Inc., n.d.), p. 313.

15. C. P. Snow, *The Search* (New York: New American Library, 1960), pp. 267–68. Originally published by Charles Scribner's Sons, 1959.

16. Edward Glover, *Freud or Jung?* (New York: Meridian Books, 1956), p. 97.

17. *Ibid.*

18. Fritz Stern, ed., *The Varieties of History: From Voltaire to the Present* (Cleveland and New York: Meridian Books, The World Publishing Company, 1956), pp. 362, 363, 364–65.

19. Carl Van Doren, "Benjamin Franklin," in *The Indispensable Carl Van Doren* (New York: The Book Society, 1951), p. 331.

CHAPTER II

1. C. E. M. Joad, *Guide to Philosophy* (New York: Dover Publications, 1936), p. 392.

2. "Shaftesbury, Anthony Ashley Cooper," *Encyclopaedia Britannica*, Vol. XX (14th ed.; Chicago: Encyclopaedia Britannica, Inc., 1951), p. 429.

3. Niccolo Machiavelli, *The Prince*, rev. trans. E. R. P. Vincent (New York: New American Library, 1935), p. 92.

4. *Ibid.*, p. 93.

5. Saxe Commins and Robert N. Linscott, eds., *Man and the State: The Political Philosophers* (New York: Modern Library, 1947), pp. 3–4.

6. *Ibid.*, p. 44.

7. *Ibid.*, p. 45.

8. Harold D. Lasswell, *Psychopathology and Politics* (New York: The Viking Press, 1960), p. 70.

9. William James, *The Varieties of Religious Experience* (New York: Random House, 1902), p. 34. Permission to reprint granted by Paul R. Reynolds & Son.

10. *Ibid.*, p. 36.

11. *Ibid.*

12. *Ibid.*, p. 38.

13. *Ibid.*, pp. 79–80.

14. *Ibid.*, p. 82.

15. *Ibid.*, p. 83.

16. *Ibid.*

17. *Ibid.*, p. 105.

18. *Ibid.*, pp. 131–32.

19. *Ibid.*, p. 142.

20. *Ibid.*, pp. 149–50, 151.

21. *Ibid.*, p. 151.

22. Albert Camus, *The Myth of Sisyphus and Other Essays*, trans. Justin O'Brien (New York: Alfred A. Knopf, Inc., 1955), pp. 10–11.

23. James, *op. cit.*, p. 154.

24. *Ibid.*, pp. 154, 155.

25. *Ibid.*, p. 157.

26. Carl Van Doren, ed., *The Indispensable Carl Van Doren* (New York: The Viking Press, 1945), pp. 91–92, 93.

27. *Ibid.*, pp. 94–95.

28. *Ibid.*, pp. 96–97.

29. *Ibid.*, p. vi.

30. *Ibid.*, p. vii.

31. Walter Lippmann, *A Preface to Morals* (New York: The Macmillan Co., 1929), p. 3.

32. *Ibid.*, p. 208.

33. *Ibid.*, p. 4.

CHAPTER III

1. Bertram D. Wolfe, *Three Who Made a Revolution* (Boston: Beacon Press, 1955), p. 56.

2. *Ibid.*, p. 57.

3. *Ibid.*

4. Saxe Commins and Robert N. Linscott, eds., *Man and the Universe: The Philosophers of Science* (New York: The Modern Library, 1947), p. 165.

5. *Ibid.*, p. 167.

6. *Ibid.*, p. 171.

7. *Ibid.*, p. 182.

8. *Ibid.*, p. 176.

9. *Ibid.*, pp. 176–77.

10. Col. Joseph I. Greene, *The Living Thoughts of Clausewitz* (New York: Longmans, Green and Co., 1943), p. 21.

11. *Ibid.*, p. 22.

12. *Ibid.*, p. 28.

13. Will Durant, *The Story of*

Philosophy (New York: Simon and Schuster, 1926), p. 126.

14. *Ibid.*, pp. 132–33.

15. Albert Einstein, *Out of My Later Years* (New York: Philosophical Library, 1950), p. 19. Reprinted with permission of the Estate of Albert Einstein.

16. *Ibid.*, pp. 16–17.

17. *Ibid.*, pp. 27, 63.

18. *The Philosophers of Science, op. cit.*, pp. 175–76.

19. *Ibid.*, pp. 74, 81, 87.

20. *Ibid.*, p. 74.

21. Einstein, *op. cit.*, pp. 60–61.

CHAPTER IV

1. Col. Joseph I. Greene, *The Living Thoughts of Clausewitz* (New York: Longmans, Green and Co., 1943), p. 20.

2. C. G. Jung, *Modern Man in Search of a Soul,* trans. W. S. Dell and Carl F. Baynes (New York: Harcourt, Brace & World, 1933), pp. 117, 118.

3. Newton Arvin, *Herman Melville* (New York: The Viking Press, 1957), p. 18.

4. Phyllis Bottome, *Alfred Adler: A Portrait from Life* (New York: The Vanguard Press, 1957), p. 27.

5. *Ibid.*, p. 27.

6. Ernest Jones, *The Life and Work of Sigmund Freud,* Vol. I (New York: Basic Books, Inc., 1953), p. 5.

7. Arthur M. Schlesinger, Jr., *The Age of Jackson* (New York: New American Library, 1945), pp. 19, 20. Originally published by Little, Brown and Company, Publishers.

8. *Ibid.*, pp. 21–22.

9. Will Durant, *The Story of Philosophy* (New York: Simon and Schuster, 1926), p. 137.

10. *Ibid.*

11. "Richelieu, A. J. du Plessis de," *Encyclopaedia Britannica,* Vol. XIX (14th ed.; Chicago: Encyclopaedia Britannica, Inc., 1951), p. 292.

12. Edmund Wilson, *To the Finland Station* (New York: Doubleday & Company, Inc., 1953), pp. 232, 233.

13. *Ibid.*, p. 245.

14. *Ibid.*, p. 246.

15. *Ibid.*, pp. 247–48.

16. *Ibid.*, pp. 248–49.

17. *Ibid.*, p. 250.

18. *Ibid.*, p. 266.

19. *Ibid.*, p. 267.

20. *Ibid.*, pp. 267, 268.

21. *Ibid.*, p. 268.

22. *Ibid.*, p. 274.

23. Eric Bentley, *A Century of Hero-Worship* (2nd ed. rev.; Boston: Beacon Press, 1957), p. 179.

24. Alan Bullock, *Hitler: A Study in Tyranny* (Completely Revised Edition, New York: Harper & Row Publishers, 1962), p. 191.

25. *Ibid.*, pp. 393, 394.

26. *Ibid.*, pp. 396–97.

27. Sir Edward S. Creasy, *Fifteen Decisive Battles of the World,* Robert Hammond Murray, ed. (Harrisburg: The Military Service Publishing Co., 1943), pp. 344–45.

28. *Ibid.*, p. 347.

29. Bullock, *op. cit.*, p. 587.

30. *Ibid.*, p. 594.

31. "Charles XII," *Encyclopaedia Britannica,* Vol. V (14th ed.: Chicago: Encyclopaedia Britannica, Inc., 1951), p. 285.

32. Bullock, *op. cit.*, p. 695.
33. *Ibid.*, p. 696.
34. *Ibid.*, p. 697.
35. *Ibid.*, p. 480.
36. *Ibid.*, p. 270.
37. *Ibid.*, pp. 327–28.
38. *Ibid.*, p. 326.
39. *Ibid.*, p. 327.
40. *Ibid.*, p. 331.
41. Harold D. Lasswell, *Psychopathology and Politics* (New York: The Viking Press, 1960), pp. 79–80.
42. *Ibid.*, p. 80.
43. *Ibid.*
44. *Ibid.*, pp. 96–97.
45. *Ibid.*, p. 106.
46. *Ibid.*, pp. 127–28.
47. *Ibid.*, p. 128.
48. *Ibid.*, p. 153.

49. *Ibid.*, p. 160.
50. *Ibid.*, p. 163.
51. *Ibid.*, p. 159.
52. Creasy, *op. cit.*, p. 58.
53. *Ibid.*, p. 59.
54. *Ibid.*, pp. 70–71.
55. *Ibid.*, p. 76.
56. *Ibid.*, pp. 5–6.
57. *Ibid.*, p. 6.
58. *Ibid.*, p. 7.
59. *Ibid.*, p. 8.
60. *Ibid.*, p. 29.
61. *Ibid.*, p. 30.
62. Fletcher Pratt, *A Short History of the Civil War* (New York: Pocket Books, Inc., 1952), pp. 156, 163.
63. *Ibid.*, pp. 244–45.

CHAPTER V

1. Thomas Carlyle, *On Heroes and Hero-Worship*, and Ralph Waldo Emerson, *Representative Men* (New York: Doubleday & Company, Inc., n.d.), back cover.
2. *Ibid.*, pp. 14–15.
3. *Ibid.*, p. 15.
4. *Ibid.*, p. 17.
5. *Ibid.*, p. 19.
6. *Ibid.*, p. 35.
7. *Ibid.*, p. 105.
8. *Ibid.*, pp. 179, 180.
9. *Ibid.*, p. 180.
10. *Ibid.*, p. 237.
11. *Ibid.*, p. 238.
12. *Ibid.*, p. 240.
13. *Ibid.*, p. 101.
14. *Ibid.*, p. 246.
15. *Ibid.*, p. 250.
16. Will Durant, *The Story of Philosophy* (New York: Simon and Schuster, 1926), p. 137.
17. Emerson, *op. cit.*, p. 251.

18. *Ibid.*, p. 254.
19. *Ibid.*, p. 255.
20. *Ibid.*, p. 256.
21. *Ibid.*, pp. 286, 289, 290.
22. *Ibid.*, p. 335.
23. *Ibid.*, p. 336.
24. *Ibid.*, p. 104.
25. *Ibid.*, pp. 227, 228.
26. *Ibid.*, p. 355.
27. *Ibid.*, pp. 357–58.
28. *Ibid.*, p. 367.
29. *Ibid.*, pp. 313–314, 315.
30. *Ibid.*, pp. 316, 320.
31. *Ibid.*, p. 320.
32. *Ibid.*, pp. 321, 323.
33. *The American Essays of Henry James*, Leon Edel, ed. (New York: Vintage Books, 1956), p. 34.
34. *Ibid.*, p. 39.
35. *Ibid.*, p. 36.
36. *Ibid.*, p. 37.
37. *Ibid.*, p. 47.

38. *Ibid.*, pp. 45–46.

39. Edmund Wilson, *Axel's Castle* (New York: Charles Scribner's Sons, 1950), p. 4.

40. Edel, *op. cit.*, pp. 64–65.

41. *Ibid.*, p. 69.

42. Walt Whitman, *Leaves of Grass*, Emory Holloway, ed. (New York: Blue Ribbon Books, 1942), p. 75.

43. C. E. M. Joad, *Guide to Philosophy* (New York: Dover Publications, 1936), pp. 229, 230.

44. *Ibid.*, p. 233.

CHAPTER VI

1. Bronislaw Malinowski, *Magic, Science and Religion and Other Essays* (New York: Doubleday & Company, Inc., 1954), pp. 64–65.

2. *Ibid.*, pp. 57–58.

3. Thomas Carlyle, *On Heroes and Hero-Worship*, and Ralph Waldo Emerson, *Representative Men* (New York: Doubleday & Company, Inc., n.d.), p. 332.

4. David Riesman, *Thorstein Veblen: A Critical Interpretation* (New York: Charles Scribner's Sons, 1953), p. 57.

5. Fyodor Dostoyevsky, *The Brothers Karamazov*, trans. Constance Garnett (New York: The Modern Library, n.d.), p. 262.

6. Riesman, *op. cit.*, p. 59.

7. Erich Heller, *The Disinherited Mind* (Cleveland and New York: Meridian Books, The World Publishing Company, 1959), p. x.

8. *Ibid.*

9. *Ibid.*, fly-leaf.

10. *Ibid.*

11. *Ibid.*, pp. xi, xii.

12. *Ibid.*, p. 96.

13. *Ibid.*, p. 115.

14. Saxe Commins and Robert N. Linscott, eds., *Man and the State: The Political Philosophers* (New York: The Modern Library, 1947), p. 523.

15. *Ibid.*, pp. 490–91, 500.

16. *Ibid.*, p. 495.

17. *Ibid.*, pp. 500–501.

18. Albert Camus, *The Rebel*, trans. Anthony Bower (New York: Vintage Books, 1960), pp. 208, 209.

19. *Ibid.*, pp. 226–27, 232.

20. Gilbert Murray, *Five Stages of Greek Religion* (New York: Doubleday & Company, Inc., 1955), pp. 76, 79. Originally published by Beacon Press.

21. *Ibid.*, p. 85.

22. *Ibid.*, pp. 89–90, 91.

23. *Ibid.*, pp. 92, 93, 94.

24. Bertrand Russell, *A History of Western Philosophy* (New York: Simon and Schuster, 1945), pp. 254–55.

25. *Ibid.*, pp. 255–56.

26. *Ibid.*, p. 269.

27. *Ibid.*, p. 267.

28. *Ibid.*, pp. 529–30.

29. Murray, *op. cit.*, pp. 96, 97–98.

30. *Ibid.*, p. 98.

31. *Ibid.*, p. 99.

32. *Ibid.*, pp. 100–101.

33. Russell, *op. cit.*, pp. 242–43.

34. *Ibid.*, pp. 243, 247–48.

35. *Ibid.*, p. 243.

36. Will Durant, *The Story of Philosophy* (New York: Simon and Schuster, 1926), p. 4.

37. *Ibid.*

CHAPTER VII

1. Bronislaw Malinowski, *Magic, Science and Religion and Other Essays* (New York: Doubleday & Company, Inc., 1954), pp. 64–65.

2. Peter Mark Roget, *Roget's International Thesaurus*, new ed., edited by Lester V. Berrey (New York: Thomas Y. Crowell Company, 1946), p. 443.

3. *Ibid.*, pp. 573–74.

4. Saxe Commins and Robert N. Linscott, eds., *Man and the State: The Political Philosophers* (New York: The Modern Library, 1947), pp. 332–33.

5. *Ibid.*, p. 334.

6. Bertrand Russell, *A History of Western Philosophy* (New York: Simon and Schuster, 1960), p. 616.

7. *The Political Philosophers, op. cit.*, pp. 72, 73.

8. *Ibid.*, p. 74.

9. *Ibid.*, p. 75.

10. *Ibid.*, p. 58.

11. *Ibid.*, p. 60.

12. *Ibid.*, pp. 60–61.

13. *Ibid.*, p. 66.

14. *Ibid.*, p. 106.

15. *Ibid.*, pp. 87–88, 89, 100, 101.

16. Russell, *op. cit.*, p. 625.

17. *Ibid.*, p. 630.

18. *Ibid.*, pp. 632, 636.

19. *The Political Philosophers, op. cit.*, p. 3.

20. *Ibid.*, p. 4.

21. *Ibid.*, p. 5.

22. *Ibid.*

23. *Ibid.*

24. *Ibid.*

25. *Ibid.*, p. 6.

26. *Ibid.*

27. *Ibid.*

28. *Ibid.*

29. *Ibid.*, p. 261.

30. *Ibid.*, p. 262.

31. *Ibid.*, p. 264.

32. *Ibid.*, p. 267.

33. *Ibid.*, p. 269.

34. *Ibid.*, p. 274.

35. *Ibid.*, p. 275.

36. Emile Durkheim, *Montesquieu and Rousseau: Forerunners of Sociology* (Ann Arbor: University of Michigan Press, 1960), p. 21.

37. *Ibid.*, p. 36.

38. *Ibid.*, p. 69.

39. *Ibid.*, p. 98.

40. *Ibid.*, p. 115.

41. Charles Maurice Wiltse, *The Jeffersonian Tradition in American Democracy* (New York: Hill and Wang, Inc., 1935), p. 22.

42. *Ibid.*, pp. 65, 69.

43. *Ibid.*, p. 99.

44. Arthur M. Schlesinger, Jr., *The Age of Jackson* (abridged; New York: New American Library, 1949), pp. 119, 120, 121, 122.

45. *The Political Philosophers, op. cit.*, pp. 304–305.

CHAPTER VIII

1. Susanne K. Langer, *Philosophy in a New Key* (New York: New American Library, 1948), p. 112. Originally published by Harvard University Press.

2. *Ibid.*, p. 111.

3. *Ibid.*, pp. 151–53, 155, 168, 169, 172–73.

4. *The Great Critics*, James H. Smith and Edd W. Parks, eds. (rev. ed.; New York: W. W. Norton & Company, Inc., 1939), p. 190.

5. *Ibid.*
6. *Ibid.*
7. *Ibid.*, pp. 200–201.
8. *Ibid.*, p. 382.
9. *Ibid.*, p. 383.
10. *Ibid.*, p. 694.
11. *Ibid.*, p. 443.
12. *Ibid.*, p. 558.
13. *Ibid.*, p. 179.
14. *Ibid.*, pp. 180, 183.
15. *Ibid.*, pp. 495–96.
16. *Ibid.*, p. 496.
17. *Ibid.*, p. 585.
18. *Ibid.*
19. *Ibid.*, p. 586.
20. *Ibid.*, pp. 586–87.
21. *Ibid.*, p. 588.
22. *Ibid.*, p. 589.
23. Eric Bentley, *The Playwright as Thinker* (New York: Meridian Books, 1955), pp. 140–41. Originally published by Harcourt, Brace & World.
24. Newton Arvin, *Herman Melville* (New York: The Viking Press, 1957), p. 77.
25. *Ibid.*, p. 80.
26. *Ibid.*, p. 262.
27. *Ibid.*, p. 263.
28. *Ibid.*, p. 85.
29. *Ibid.*, p. 108.
30. *Ibid.*, pp. 176–77, 179.
31. *Ibid.*, p. 174.
32. *Ibid.*, p. 18.
33. *Ibid.*, pp. 127, 131.
34. *A Kierkegaard Anthology*, Robert Bretall, ed. (New York:

Random House, 1946), p. 36. Originally published by Princeton University Press.
35. *Ibid.*, p. 43.
36. *Ibid.*, p. 45.
37. *Ibid.*
38. *Ibid.*, p. 48.
39. *Ibid.*, p. 49.
40. *Ibid.*, p. 57.
41. *Ibid.*, pp. 28, p. 29, 30.
42. *Ibid.*, p. 19.
43. Bentley, *op. cit.*, p. 105.
44. *Ibid.*, p. 106.
45. Lionel Trilling, *The Liberal Imagination* (New York: The Viking Press, 1951), p. 295.
46. *Ibid.*, p. 296.
47. *Ibid.*, p. 297.
48. *Ibid.*, pp. 298–99.
49. *Ibid.*, p. 299.
50. F. O. Mathiessen, *The Responsibilities of the Critic* (New York: Oxford University Press, 1952), pp. 36–37, 38.
51. T. S. Eliot, *Selected Essays* (new ed.; New York: Harcourt, Brace & World, 1950), p. 51.
52. *Ibid.*
53. *Ibid.*, p. 362, 363.
54. *Ibid.*, p. 110.
55. *Ibid.*, pp. 110, 111.
56. *Ibid.*, p. 112.
57. *Ibid.*, pp. 125, 126.
58. Edmund Wilson, *Axel's Castle* (New York: Charles Scribner's Sons, 1950), pp. 106–107.

CHAPTER IX

1. Johan Huizinga, *Men and Ideas*, trans. James S. Holmes and Hans van Marle (New York: Meridian Books, 1959), p. 23.
2. *Ibid.*, p. 43.
3. *Ibid.*, p. 48.

4. *Ibid.*, pp. 53–54.
5. *Ibid.*, pp. 54–55.
6. *Ibid.*, p. 59.
7. *Ibid.*, pp. 59–60.
8. *Ibid.*, p. 60.
9. *Ibid.*, p. 63.

10. *Ibid.*, pp. 77–78.

11. *Ibid.*, p. 80.

12. *Ibid.*, pp. 84, 85.

13. *Ibid.*, pp. 86, 87.

14. *Ibid.*, pp. 87–88.

15. *Ibid.*, p. 89.

16. Bronislaw Malinowski, *Magic, Science and Religion* (New York: Doubleday & Company, Inc., 1948), p. 101.

17. *Ibid.*, p. 117.

18. *Ibid.*, p. 112.

19. Isaiah Berlin, *The Hedgehog and the Fox* (New York: New American Library, 1957), pp. 7–8. Originally published by Simon and Schuster and Weidenfeld and Nicolson, Ltd.

20. *Ibid.*, pp. 11–12.

21. *Ibid.*, pp. 14–15.

22. *Ibid.*, pp. 19–20.

23. *Ibid.*, p. 20.

24. *Ibid.*, p. 22.

25. *Ibid.*, p. 29.

26. *Ibid.*, p. 31.

27. *Ibid.*, pp. 31–32.

28. *Ibid.*, pp. 58, 114.

29. *Ibid.*, pp. 64–65.

30. *Ibid.*, p. 67.

31. *Ibid.*, p. 115.

32. Edmund Wilson, *Eight Essays* (New York: Doubleday & Company, Inc., 1954), p. 219.

33. *Ibid.*, pp. 219–20.

34. *Ibid.*, pp. 224–25.

35. *Ibid.*, pp. 226–27, 228–29.

36. *Ibid.*, pp. 230–31.

37. *Ibid.*, p. 232.

38. *Ibid.*, p. 231.

39. *Ibid.*

40. *Ibid.*

41. *Ibid.*, p. 229.

42. *Ibid.*, p. 235.

43. *Ibid.*

44. *Ibid.*, pp. 231–32.

45. Alfred Kazin, *On Native Grounds* (New York: Harcourt, Brace & World, 1942), p. 447.

46. *Ibid.*, pp. 448–50, 451–52.

47. Edmund Wilson, *Axel's Castle* (New York: Charles Scribner's Sons, 1950), p. 115.

48. *Ibid.*, p. 119.

49. Stanley Edgar Hyman, *The Armed Vision* (rev. ed.; New York: Vintage Books, 1955), p. 54.

50. *Ibid.*

51. *Ibid.*, p. 55.

52. *Ibid.*

53. *Ibid.*

54. *Ibid.*, pp. 58, 56, 59.

55. *Ibid.*, p. 62.

56. *Ibid.*

57. *Ibid.*, p. 63.

58. *Ibid.*

59. *Ibid.*, p. 64.

60. *Ibid.*

61. *Ibid.*, p. 65.

CHAPTER X

1. "Darwin, Charles Robert, *The Encyclopaedia Britannica*, Vol. VII (14th ed.; Chicago: Encyclopaedia Britannica, Inc., 1951), p. 66.

2. *Ibid.*, p. 65.

3. *Lives in Science* (New York: Simon and Schuster, 1957), pp. 210–11. Originally published by *Scientific American*.

4. *Great Essays in Science*, Martin Gardner, ed. (New York: Pocket Books, Inc., 1957), p. 4.

5. *Ibid.*, p. 5.

6. *Ibid.*, p. 12.

7. *Ibid.*, p. 13.

8. *Ibid.*

9. Saxe Commins and Robert N. Linscott, eds. *Man and the State:*

The Political Philosophers (New York: The Modern Library, 1947), pp. 261–62.

10. *Great Essays, op. cit.*, pp. 16, 19.

11. *Ibid.*, pp. 21, 22, 24–25.

12. *Ibid.*, p. 146.

13. *Ibid.*, p. 155.

14. *Ibid.*

15. *Ibid.*, pp. 155, 160–61.

16. *Ibid.*, p. 36.

17. *Ibid.*, pp. 38, 41.

18. *Ibid.*, p. 43.

19. E. T. Bell, *Men of Mathematics* (New York: Simon and Schuster, 1937), p. 13.

20. *Ibid.*, p. 533.

21. *Ibid.*, p. 396.

22. *Ibid.*, p. 378.

23. *Ibid.*, p. 294.

24. *Ibid.*, p. 403.

25. *Lives in Science, op. cit.*, pp. xix–xx.

26. *Ibid.*, pp. 12, 14, 16, 17.

27. Arthur Koestler, *The Watershed: A Biography of Johannes Kepler* (New York: Doubleday & Company, Inc., 1960), p. 43. Originally published by The Macmillan Company.

28. *Lives in Science, op. cit.*, pp. 26–27.

29. *Ibid.*, p. 27.

30. *Ibid.*, pp. 29–30.

31. *Ibid.*, pp. 27–28.

32. *Ibid.*, p. 41.

33. *Ibid.*, p. 37.

34. *Ibid.*

35. *Ibid.*, p. 45.

36. *Ibid.*, p. 50.

37. *Ibid.*, p. 51.

38. *Ibid.*, pp. 54–55.

39. *Ibid.*, p. 55.

40. *Ibid.*, pp. xi–xii.

41. *Ibid.*, p. 61.

42. *Ibid.*, pp. 72–73.

43. *Ibid.*, p. 22.

44. *Ibid.*, p. 62.

45. *Ibid.*, pp. 61–62.

46. *Ibid.*, p. 65.

47. *Ibid.*, p. 22.

48. *Ibid.*, p. 67.

49. *Great Essays, op. cit.*, pp. 244–45.

50. *Ibid.*, p. 243.

51. Saxe Commins and Robert N. Linscott, eds., *Man and the Spirit: The Speculative Philosophers* (New York: The Modern Library, 1947), p. 342.

52. *Ibid.*, p. 346.

53. *Ibid.*, p. 436.

54. *Ibid.*, p. 349.

55. *Ibid.*, p. 428.

56. *Ibid.*, p. 437.

57. *Ibid.*, p. 387.

58. *Ibid.*, p. 433.

59. "Philosophy and Philosophic Studies," *The Encyclopaedia Britannica*, Vol. XVII (14th ed.; Chicago: Encyclopaedia Britannica, Inc., 1951), p. 759.

60. *Ibid.*

61. *Great Essays, op. cit.*, p. 205.

62. *Ibid.*

63. *Ibid.*, p. 203.

64. *Ibid.*

CHAPTER XI

1. Brewster Ghiselin, *The Creative Process* (New York: New American Library, 1955), p. 236.

2. *Ibid.*, pp. 236–37.

3. *Ibid.*, pp. 86–87.

4. Helen L. Koch, "The Relation of 'Primary Mental Abilities' in Five- and Six-Year-Olds to Sex of

Child and Characteristics of His Sibling," *Child Development*, Vol. XXV, No. 3 (September, 1954), p. 219.

5. *Ibid.*

6. *Ibid.*, p. 220.

7. *Ibid.*

8. Helen L. Koch, "Sibling Influence on Children's Speech," *Journal of Speech and Hearing Disorder*, Vol. XXI, No. 3 (September, 1956), p. 326.

9. Helen L. Koch, "Children's Work Attitudes and Sibling Characteristics," *Child Development*, Vol. XXVII, No. 3 (September, 1956), p. 293.

10. Peter Mark Roget, *Roget's International Thesaurus* (rev. ed.; New York: Thomas Y. Crowell Company, 1946), p. ix.

11. *The Portable Sherwood Anderson*, ed. Horace Gregory (New York: The Viking Press, 1949), pp. 552–53.

12. Ghiselin, *op. cit.*, p. 35.

13. John Malcolm Brinnin, *The Third Rose: Gertrude Stein and Her World* (New York: Grove Press, Inc., 1961), p. xiii. Originally published by Atlantic-Little, Brown and Company.

14. *Ibid.*, p. xvi.

15. Abraham S. Levine, " 'Perseveration' or 'The Central Factor,' " *Psychological Reports*, Monograph Supplement 5 (1955), p. 247.

16. *Ibid.*, p. 248.

17. *Ibid.*

18. *Ibid.*, p. 257.

19. David Rapaport, *Organization and Pathology of Thought* (New York: Columbia University Press, 1951), p. 697.

20. Helen L. Koch, "The Relation of Certain Family Constellation Characteristics and the Attitudes of Children Toward Adults," *Child Development*, Vol. XXVI, No. 1 (March, 1955), p. 32.

21. K. R. Eissler, "The Environment of a Genius," in *The Psychoanalytic Study of the Child* (New York: International Universities Press, 1959), Vol. XIV, p. 268.

22. *Ibid.*, p. 283.

23. Charles Kligerman, "The Character of Jean Jacques Rousseau," *Psychoanalytic Quarterly*, Vol. XX (1951) pp. 239–40.

24. *Ibid.*, p. 240.

25. *Ibid.*, p. 240.

26. *Ibid.*, p. 249.

27. Charles Kligerman, "The Psychology of Herman Melville," *Psychoanalytic Review*, Vol. XL, No. 2 (1953) pp. 129–30.

28. *Ibid.*, p. 130.

29. *Ibid.*, pp. 132–33.

30. Newton Arvin, *Herman Melville* (New York: The Viking Press, 1957), p. 144.

31. Edmund Wilson, *Axel's Castle* (New York: Charles Scribner's Sons, 1950), pp. 109–10, 111.

32. F. J. Ziegler, J. B. Imboden, and E. Meyer, "Contemporary Conversion Reactions," *American Journal of Psychiatry*, Vol. 116 (1960), p. 903.

33. *Ibid.*, p. 906.

34. *Ibid.*, p. 906.

35. *Ibid.*, p. 908.

36. Albert Camus, *The Myth of Sisyphus and Other Essays*, trans. Justin O'Brien (New York: Vintage Books, 1960), p. 28.

37. *Ibid.*, pp. 45, 46, 58, 59.

38. Lillian Ross, "Profiles: The Player—III," *The New Yorker*, November 4, 1961, pp. 115, 121–22. © 1961 The New Yorker Magazine,

Inc. Included in the book *The Player*, Simon and Schuster.

39. *Ibid.*, p. 125.

40. John H. Flavell, *The Developmental Psychology of Jean Piaget* (Princeton: D. Van Nostrand Company, Inc., 1963), pp. 65–66.

41. Sigmund Freud, *The Interpretation of Dreams*, trans. by A. A. Brill (New York: Macmillan, 1933), p. 249.

42. Irving D. Harris, "The Dream of the Object Endangered," *Psychiatry*, Vol. 20, No. 2 (1957).

43. Ernest Jones, *The Life and Work of Sigmund Freud*, Vol. I (New York: Basic Books, Inc., 1953), p. 5.

44. *Ibid.*, p. 8.

45. Irving D. Harris, "Typical Anxiety Dreams and Object Relationships," *International Journal of Psycho-Analysis*, Vol. 4 (1960).

46. Irving D. Harris, *Normal Children and Mothers* (New York: The Free Press, 1959), pp. 262–63.

47. Freud, *op. cit.*, p. 264.

48. Arvin, *op. cit.*, pp. 102–103.

49. *Ibid.*, p. 115.

50. *Ibid.*, p. 37.

CHAPTER XII

1. George Santayana, *Three Philosophical Poets* (New York: Doubleday & Company, Inc., 1953), p. 11.

2. *Ibid.*, pp. 11–12.

3. *Ibid.*, p. 181.

4. James Bryce, *Reflections on American Institutions*, Henry Steele Commager, ed. (Greenwich: Fawcett Publications, Inc., 1961), p. 9.

5. Alexis de Tocqueville, *Democracy in America*, ed. Phillips Bradley (New York: Vintage Books, 1954), Vol. I, p. ix.

6. Bryce, *op. cit.*, p. 22.

7. Tocqueville, *op. cit.*, Vol. II, pp. 420–21.

8. *Ibid.*, pp. 445–46.

9. Bryce, *op. cit.*, p. 10.

10. Tocqueville, *op. cit.*, Vol. I, p. 61.

11. *Ibid.*, p. 175.

12. *Ibid.*, pp. 432–33.

13. Bryce, *op. cit.*, p. 19.

14. Tocqueville, *op. cit.*, pp. 49–51.

15. *Ibid.*, p. 262.

16. Tocqueville, *op. cit.*, Vol. II, pp. 4–5.

17. *Ibid.*, pp. 42, 43, 45.

18. *Ibid.*, pp. 45–46.

19. *Ibid.*, pp. 76, 77.

20. Bryce, *op. cit.*, pp. 177–78.

21. Erich Heller, *The Disinherited Mind* (New York: Meridian Books, Inc., 1959).

22. *Mao Tse-tung: An Anthology of His Writings*, Anne Fremantle, ed. (New York: New American Library, 1962), p. xvii. Originally published by International Publishers.

23. *Ibid.*, p. xxv.

24. *Ibid.*, p. xxxiii.

25. *Ibid.*, p. xxxix, and Vol. I, pp. 161–62.

26. *Ibid.*, p. 77.

27. *Ibid.*, p. xix.

28. *Ibid.*

29. *Ibid.*, p. xliii.

30. Santayana, *op. cit.*, pp. 190–91.

Name and Subject Index

Name and Subject Index